Challenging Beliefs

memoirs of a career

TIM NOAKES

with michael vlismas

Published by Zebra Press
an imprint of Random House Struik (Pty) Ltd
Company Reg. No. 1966/003153/07
Wembley Square, First Floor, Solan Road, Gardens, Cape Town, 8001
PO Box 1144, Cape Town, 8000, South Africa

www.zebrapress.co.za

New edition published in 2012
Reprinted in 2012 (three times)

5 7 9 10 8 6 4

Publication © Zebra Press 2012
Text © Tim Noakes and Michael Vlismas 2012

Cover image © Russel Wasserfall
Back cover © Noakes family (courtesy of *You* magazine);
'Running man' © iStockphoto/Suzanne Tucker

'Blowin' In The Wind' (B. Dylan) © 1963. Renewed 1991, Special Rider Music.

PUBLISHER: Marlene Fryer
MANAGING EDITOR: Ronel Richter-Herbert
EDITOR: Jane Housdon and Bronwen Leak
PROOFREADER: Ronel Richter-Herbert
COVER DESIGN: Sean Robertson
TEXT DESIGN: Monique Oberholzer
TYPESETTER: Monique van den Berg and Jacques Kaiser
INDEXER: Sanet le Roux

Set in 10.5 pt on 14 pt Minion

Printed and bound by CTP Printers,
Duminy Street, Parow, 7500

ISBN 978 1 77022 459 9 (print)
ISBN 978 1 77022 460 5 (ePub)
ISBN 978 1 77022 461 2 (PDF)

Contents

Foreword

Few people have the ability to inspire and change the world around them. Tim Noakes is one of those people.

Tim has always been highly gifted and, after matriculating in 1966, was awarded an exchange scholarship to Los Angeles. It was during this time that he became aware of the achievement of Chris Barnard, who successfully conducted the first human heart transplant in 1967. This was a defining moment in Tim's life, as it informed his decision to study medicine and the workings of the human body.

In the same way that Tim was inspired by Barnard's legacy, I have been inspired by Tim. His approach, rigour and ability to unearth contradictions are, in and of themselves, inspiring. However, it is the application of his findings to all areas of life that has made his work truly profound for me.

One paradox explored by Tim is that running is not simple. I have been a casual roadrunner for many years. While I always enjoyed running, I, like many others, assumed the pastime to be fairly straightforward. It wasn't until I came across Tim's *Lore of Running* that I realised how limited my understanding of the sport was. What would become the seminal book on running for serious athletes, *Lore of Running* opened my eyes to the intellect, research and complexities in the field. Running is not a one-dimensional intuitive sport. Rather, it is multifaceted, spanning the scientific corridors of anatomy, physiology and psychology. Such is the nature of Tim's work: he uncovers the scientific substance of what looks uncomplicated to the untrained eye. Tim has taught me that what appears to be simple is not, and that competitive advantage is about embracing complexity where others see simplicity.

Another paradox examined by Tim is that running is not purely physical. I had always assumed running to be primarily physical in nature, and that a runner is constrained only by his or her body as a regulator of performance. Tim's work on the 'central governor theory' exposed a powerful truth: the mental side of competing is even more important than the physical. I recall Tim telling me that runners who come second and who do not die at the finish line do not try hard enough; they allow their governors to determine the outcome. Initially I thought that this sounded brutal. Over time, though, I have come to appreciate the intellectual robustness of Tim's assertion, and see its value in all of my pursuits. This insight – that performance is mental – underscores for me the importance of a positive attitude. It has also become clear to me that the ability to 'fool' the central governor is crucial in the pursuit of success.

Tim's legacy, however, is not defined only by the breadth of his academic accomplishments – albeit that he is extensively published and internationally renowned as possessing the 'source code' for all things sports science – but also by his style and approach. Good science is a necessary condition, but it is not sufficient on its own. Ask anyone who has worked with or been taught by Tim, and you will probably hear of his unique ability to communicate science in an exciting and engaging way. Tim's integrity, and his often quirky manner of bringing to life the 'inside track', has his audiences captivated. Underlying his distinctive style is a tenacious approach to critical thinking and the challenging of established norms. This combination has inspired many of Tim's students, colleagues and partners to further participate in, and add new chapters to, the field of sports science.

Later, Tim's passion for relating science to sport assisted me in shaping Discovery's vision – to make people healthier and to enhance and protect their lives. Discovery, and Discovery's wellness programme, Vitality, became the vehicle of change. From the start of Discovery and the inception of Vitality, the vision has been a societal one, playing a leadership role in health and healthcare in South Africa. In light of this purpose, collaborative partnerships have been and continue to be critical in achieving the goal of a healthier society. In this regard, Discovery has been truly fortunate for its long-standing relationship with Tim.

Discovery has also had the privilege of supporting Tim in his research as the Discovery Health Professor of Exercise and Sports Science at the University of Cape Town. This has, by virtue of Tim's excellence, enabled Discovery to be part of something powerful – the generation of exercise-science research that is meaningful, accessible and understandable. The partnership has resulted in cutting-edge scientific concepts that have defined global thinking in the field.

There is no doubt that Tim's work and leadership have evolved science.

More importantly, however, he continues to change people. He is a national asset, and future generations will benefit from his immense legacy. I am excited about this book and the opportunities it provides to learn from Tim's incredible knowledge of and his contagious enthusiasm for his field.

This work is the next sprint, by the ultimate insider, in what has been a lifetime's contribution to sport science.

ADRIAN GORE
CEO, DISCOVERY
JUNE 2011

Acknowledgements

This book would not have happened without the vision and literary skills of Michael Vlismas. The book was his idea. After perusing much of my writings, he identified those themes that he considered to be of the greatest general interest. He then interviewed me and wrote the first draft with a speed and insight that amazed me. Thereafter it became a much simpler task to complete the fuller story. The result is that the concept is Michael's but the words are mine, skilfully edited by Michael and Jane Housdon.

My life and my science have been influenced by a cast of remarkable people to whom I am especially indebted; the events and outcomes described in this book are a result of their inspiration. As a consequence of their example and guidance, each owns a part of the person that I have become. I am the most indebted to my wife Marilyn Anne. While still in her teens, she took an insecure youth, quieted the uncertainty and set him on his path.

I thank my parents Bindy and Wendy Noakes for raising me in Africa, for teaching me good values, for allowing me to choose my own destiny and for providing financial support at certain critical junctures in my career. Amanda Louise (Mandy) has provided considerate sisterly support and encouragement; I appreciate especially the kind interest she has always expressed in all aspects of my career.

Thomas Taravinga was my first African friend – his joyful smile flooded the first five years of my life, and therein originated my love for Africa and its peoples.

Four of my tutors – Lionel Opie, the late Ralph Paffenbarger, George Brooks and the late George Sheehan – are (or were) utterly extraordinary individuals: the best of the very best. It is said that a guru gives himself and then his system, whereas a teacher gives us his subject and then ourselves. From these gurus I learnt the methods of scientific inquiry, of scientific and popular writing, and of public speaking; through their personalities and their teachings, these icons gave me myself.

A most unlikely activity, running, became perhaps the defining feature of my life. I still find this difficult to comprehend. I can only conclude that it is the singular sport that captured my entire persona – body, mind and spirit. This, too, might not have happened without the input of those friends who, in 1971, taught me how to run with purpose – Tony Frost, and my medical classmates Manfred Teichler and Edward 'Tiffie' King – and those ultramarathon path-finders in the UCT Athletics Club who inspired me, especially Hugh Amoore, Mike Thackeray, John Greensmith, Joe Tyrrell and Dave Levick, the latter of whom won two of the iconic ultra-distance running events in the world: the 1971 85-kilometre London-to-Brighton race, and the 1973 88-kilometre Comrades Marathon. Interacting with one of the world's best taught me that greatness does not have to exist solely in Europeans and North Americans (or those else-where). This was a very powerful lesson.

Dave Levick also encouraged my first writings on running in 1972 and put me in touch with the North American magazine *Runner's World*, through which I met my personal running guru, the late Dr George Sheehan.

I came to running through rowing, which exposed me to the coaching of John Fielden, who worked without pay to fashion a group of ordinary and unskilled oarsmen into a competitive unit. He taught us that the speed at which we could row was a direct function of how hard we trained (especially in the depth of winter) – an obvious truth, but one that has to be learnt for it to have any enduring meaning.

John taught us that our success was determined by how much we wanted it … and how much of ourselves we were prepared to commit. From him we learnt the value of over-distance training and of peaking and of the extent to which our minds influence the outcome. A critical moment was the day he forced us to do four additional 500-metre rowing intervals at the end of a gruelling session that, in our opinion, had brought us to the brink of death. This simple experiment would help me better understand the role of the brain in the safe regulation of human exercise performance. And teach me that, however bad I might feel, I always have reserves.

To those with whom I rowed, especially in the UCT Eight in 1972, thanks for the effort and the memories. I can still feel the power, the precision and the endurance.

John Fielden's example added to my exposure to American football, and its coaching at Huntington Park High School, California, in the winter of 1967 inspired a lifelong interest in coaching, which, to my mind, is the most demanding human skill. George Sheehan once said that all humans are athletes, but that only some are in training. But all humans are also coaches, too. However, few of us ever understand this.

In later years I was supremely privileged to work with three of the greatest contemporary South African coaches – the late Bob Woolmer, Jake White and Paul Treu. I remain in awe of their intellectual and emotional abilities to manage the complex set of demands needed to produce world-class sporting teams.

More recently I have experienced the joy of working with John Dobson and Kevin Foote and their very special group of devoted wise men – Phil Kilroe, John le Roux, Greg Fury, Paul Day, Dugald and Neil MacDonald – and the unpaid coaches, managers, medical support staff and analysts that tutor my all-time favourite sporting team, the UCT Ikey Tigers rugby team. That generous community captures the very best of what sport at all levels should be about. In the incomparable words of American coaching legend Bill Curry, it is about driving players beyond their perceived limits 'to places they thought impossible, and make them continue'. It is about teaching these young men 'that virtually anything is possible when a determined group of people refuses to be divided or to quit'.

My former PhD student, Dr Sherylle Calder, winner of two Rugby World Cup winners' medals (2003 and 2007), has also played an integral part in the Ikeys' success, as has her work with many of the world's leading teams and sports stars. She is one of the most astute judges of sport and the human condition that I know. I thank her for the wisdom she has shared with me over the past two decades.

And for the players who enter those thrilling places, as they did in the final seven minutes of the 2011 Varsity Cup final in Pretoria, the vision of a new life beckons. There is the opportunity to become those better human beings that this nation so desperately needs; to go even beyond the extraordinary. I especially thank all those exceptional young men for allowing me to share their journey.

My career as a scientist was made possible by a collection of South Africans who themselves have gone beyond the extraordinary: Professors Wieland Gevers, J.P. van Niekerk and Johan Koeslag, without whom sports science would not have come to UCT; Morné du Plessis and the Rupert family of Stellenbosch, who made the Sports Science Institute of South Africa (SSISA) possible; the backing of Dr Mamphela Ramphele, former vice-chancellor of UCT, who was crucial in overcoming the curmudgeonly academic resistance to the founding of SSISA;

Adrian Gore and his incomparable team at Discovery Health, who provided the financial backing essential to further Morné's and my vision of using sport to help build our nation.

I am especially indebted to Adrian Gore for writing his very generous foreword to this book. I am truly humbled to think that my modest contributions might have impacted in some small way on the life of one of South Africa's modern entrepreneurial giants, a leader and creator for whom I have the very highest regard.

One of the great pleasures I experience in my daily life is the unrestrained bliss of working in our research unit at UCT. This is because of the vibrant team that has come together since 1981 and the bright, committed and original students that our collective efforts have attracted to our evolving discipline. Two individuals – Professors Mike and Vicki Lambert – are the crucial pillars around which this team has been built. They have now been integral to our success for more than a quarter of a century. Remove either and we could not have achieved half of what we have done. They are the glue that has kept our research and teaching flourishing; the bedrock on which our enterprise is founded.

The academic prowess and determination of Professors Martin Schwellnus and Wayne Derman, who were the next to join our team, have raised sports medicine in South Africa from an academic hobby to a fully recognised medical speciality – a rare achievement with great importance for the future of South African sport. Professors Andrew Bosch, Edward Ojuka and Malcolm Collins, and Dr Julia Goedecke have produced work – and continue to do so – that is world-leading in their specific fields.

We all teach and research because we want to change the world for the better. But our teaching would not be of much value if our students were not also committed, responsive, creative and inquisitive. So we are indebted to the quality students we have been privileged to teach over the past thirty years – each has made a personal contribution, not least in what they have taught us about ourselves and our discipline.

So it is that our next generation of academic researchers – Drs Yumna Albertus-Kajee, Cathi Draper, Juliet Evans, Dheshnie Keswell, Tertius Kohn, Tracy Kolbe-Alexander, Robert Lamberts, Lisa Micklesfield, Michael Posthumous, Dale Rae, Laurie Rauch, Alison September, Elske Schabort, Jeroen Swart, Ross Tucker and Mr David Karpul – many of them trained by us – will ensure that the momentum built over the past thirty years will be sustained and enhanced in the future.

We have also been blessed with an administrative support team of the kind that could only ever exist in heaven. Each member works with an unmatched intensity, focus and unselfish devotion without expectation of special material entitlement or recognition. So a massive thank you to Marisce Blackaller-Smal, Yvonne Blomkamp, Emile Diedrick, Ayesha Hendricks, Neezaam Kariem, Dr Jacolene Kroff, Lindi Matthee and Hendrina Victor for their individual and collective contributions to the efficient management of our unit, to our success, and hence to my personal peace of mind.

Lance Walburgh exudes a special warmth and professional concern in welcoming visitors to our unit, while Trevino Larry epitomises the permanent happiness and infectious 'can-do' attitude that characterises each member of our administrative team. Fiona Diedrich and Lesa Sivewright deserve special mention for ensuring that our financial affairs are run with a precision that would be the envy of the European Union (and some other global financial institutions)!

My professional life is expertly managed by Megan Lofthouse, the personal assistant who seemingly comes from a realm beyond even heaven. Her efficiency, fastidiousness, tireless appetite for work, respectfulness of others and unfailing good humour serve as a steadfast example of perfection for me and for all who interact with her.

The professional and support teams gathered by Morné du Plessis to manage all aspects of SSISA's operations are also exceptional. Their devotion to him and to SSISA ensures that an aura of selfless caring and committed service permeates our building. Justin Durandt, head of the SSISA Discovery Health High Performance Centre, deserves special mention for his tireless work in integrating our science into the care of the elite athletes for whom he is responsible. It should not be difficult to understand why, surrounded by such happy and considerate people, I consider my working life to have been so blessed.

But it is an expensive exercise to sustain the continuity of this committed group of South Africans and so to ensure that our work progresses expeditiously. In addition to the magnificent donation of the SSISA founding donors in 1995 and the extraordinary generosity of Discovery Health, funding for the research described in this book is provided principally by UCT, the Medical Research Council of South Africa and the National Research Foundation, especially through the THRIP initiative. There is never enough money for research – we always need more, especially in South Africa. But through their efforts, these organisations have developed South African science into one of the best value-for-money products in the world.

My travels across the length and breadth of South Africa over the past fifty years have taught me that our land is blessed with special people. To all who have treated me so well and who have inspired me in so many ways, thank you for what you have done for me, perhaps without ever realising it. There are so many South Africans in this category that it is impossible to acknowledge each individually. Please forgive me if your special contribution has not been recognised appropriately.

These special people have taught me that I would not have wished to live anywhere else in the world. By believing in an extraordinary shared future, our land will become that which former President Mandela imagined. All we need to understand is that the future really is what we believe it will be.

Finally, this book is dedicated to my wife Marilyn Anne, for all the reasons described in its contents, and to our children, Travis Miles and Candice Amelia. Thank you for the times we have shared, for your love and care, for always being yourselves, for making the right choices, and for adding to the lives of others, most particularly us. My love and blessings are with you every moment of your special lives.

TIM NOAKES
CAPE TOWN
JULY 2011

Author's Note

It was Eric Liddell who delivered what I believe to be one of the greatest lines in sport when, in the movie *Chariots of Fire*, he said, 'I believe God made me for a purpose, but he also made me fast. And when I run, I feel His pleasure.'

To my wife, Ursula, you bring similar meaning to everything I do and serve as my greatest inspiration. You are the most beautiful person that I know. To have your love and support is something I treasure every day of my life. You have been patient throughout my travels around the world writing about sport, and have shared my enthusiasm for all sport. And you never complain about watching *Chariots of Fire* for the umpteenth time.

To my parents, thank you for the most perfect childhood and for raising me to believe that I can achieve whatever I set my mind to. Of the good things in this world, Norman Maclean wrote, '[they all come by] grace and grace comes by art and art does not come easy'. You have taught me the art of living.

To Jack and Ethan, you are the greatest blessings in my life. You took turns sitting on my lap as I worked on this book, you offered your own words of encouragement, and sometimes you simply came in with a much-needed hug and a kiss. I hope that one day you can become independent thinkers who are never afraid to challenge beliefs in pursuit of the truth.

To Tim Noakes, thank you for the opportunity to work with you on such an important book. You inspire me with your dedication to truth, honesty and fairness, and the beauty that you see in the moving body. You have become a great friend ever since that first cappuccino, when we spoke about the idea for *Challenging Beliefs*.

To Megan at the Sports Science Institute of South Africa, thank you for always finding time in Prof. Noakes's busy schedule for us to meet.

To Marlene and Ronel at Zebra Press, and to Jane Housdon, my editor, thank you for your faith and patience.

And to Him, from Whom all blessings flow, thank you.

MICHAEL VLISMAS
PRETORIA
JUNE 2011

Abbreviations

ACSM	American College of Sports Medicine
ADH	anti-diuretic hormone
AFS	American Field Service
AIDS	acquired immune deficiency syndrome
AIS	Australian Institute of Sport
AKH	Allgemeines Krankenhaus
ATP	adenosine triphosphate
BCE	Before the Common Era
EAH	exercise-associated hyponatraemia
EAHE	exercise-associated hyponatraemic encephalopathy
EAPH	exercise-associated postural hypotension
EEG	electroencephalogram
EMG	electromyogram
EPO	erythroprotein
FIMS	International Federation of Sports Medicine
GPS	global positioning system
GSSI	Gatorade Sports Science Institute
HIV	human immunodeficiency virus
HSRC	Human Sciences Research Council
IMMDA	International Marathon Medical Directors Association

IOC	International Olympic Committee
IPL	Indian Premier League
IRB	International Rugby Board
IV	intravenous
LBW	leg before wicket
MCC	Marylebone Cricket Club
mmol/L	millimoles per litre
NFL	National Football League
ODI	One-Day International
RPE	ratings of perceived exertion
SA	South Africa
SADF	South African Defence Force
SARU	South African Rugby Union
SSISA	Sports Science Institute of South Africa
T20	Twenty20
TBW	total body water
UCB	United Cricket Board
UCT	University of Cape Town
USARIEM	United States Army Research Institute for Environmental Medicine
USATF	United States of America Track and Field
VO_2 max	maximal oxygen consumption

part one

LOOKING FOR THE MOUNTAINS

1 | The Sanctity of the Run

My personal life is largely defined by the years before and after 9 December 1966, when I met my future wife, Marilyn Anne. She gave me the love and support that instilled in me a confidence to look for the mountains in my field, and to attempt to climb them.

My academic life divides neatly into the period from 1949 to 1969, when I knew nothing about endurance sport, and the years thereafter. In 1973 I ran the Comrades Marathon for the first time. Three years later, as a qualified doctor who had survived a year's hospital internship, I competed in the race for a second time. But I still did not yet fully understand. Only after I had run the Comrades a third time, in 1978, was I able to do proper justice to the depth of the experience. Finally I understood enough to write that year:

> You may have suspected that the Comrades Marathon is different, but at the start all doubts vanish. The atmosphere is carnival. We are an eccentric family doing for one day what we like best. No matter how humble the results, for eleven hours we will be loved and applauded for it. From dawn until the sun sets in Durban, we are the children of the road, to be succoured, encouraged, praised, protected. Today there can only be one outcome, each runner a winner, each a hero.
>
> At the start, there is neither doubt nor fear. The outcome is pre-determined. The Comrades family will ensure our safe passage to Durban. Even when the last ounce of energy has been spent, there will be an arm for support, a shoulder to steady our shaking legs, someone to carry us over the finishing line.
>
> In faith, then, at 6 a.m. on 31 May each year, the Comrades Marathon

begins, each of us knowing that this is our year; that this year we are in peak condition. We are older, wiser, more experienced. This year, at the moment of truth, when once more the pain and discomfort become intolerable, the desire to quit almost irresistible, we will fight back with more courage, greater energy, supreme endurance. This year we will run the course on our own terms; we will become the heroes we were always meant to be.

For the first four hours of the 1978 down race to Durban, I know all these things. I know that this is finally to be my year. The approach march has been easy. The first forty-five kilometres have passed effortlessly, the pace has been a pleasure. The friendship, the scenery, the weather – all have been perfect. But then, as it always is on the down run, the steep climb past the Alverston Tower up to Botha's Hill Village makes the effort felt for the first time. Quite suddenly I no longer have breath to spare on conversation. I see only the few metres of road ahead and I shorten my stride, looking for maximum efficiency. These kilometres must be run in earnest.

Soon enough, however, the hill is crested and there is the human warmth of the crowded village. It is time to take stock. The distance has by now removed just enough energy for my legs to become concerned.

Sensing that today something extra is expected, my legs urge caution; they argue for energy conservation – a shorter, less flamboyant stride. But even now I know that their warning has come too late, that I have again been carried away by the occasion. For however easy the first four hours may have felt, the cost has been too high. Within one hour I must pay for my early excesses; I must enter the soul of the Comrades, that special confrontation between an exhausted body and mind, and an ailing but unbeaten will.

It is one of the strange ironies of this strange life that those who work the hardest, who subject themselves to the strictest discipline, who give up certain pleasurable things in order to achieve a goal are the happiest men. When you see twenty or thirty men line up for a distance race in some meet, don't pity them, don't feel sorry for them. Better envy them instead.
     – Brutus Hamilton, 1957 (quoted by J.K. Doherty, 1964)

Through Botha's Hill Village and Hillcrest, I must of necessity distract my mind from the oncoming holocaust. I wave, talk and smile to every spectator, interested or otherwise. My mind, as if preparing for the coming onslaught, is sharpened and extrovert. These are magic miles; on reflection, the best miles are always those immediately preceding the final collapse. Then too quickly I am past Hillcrest. Now, alone, unaided, I must pass into the void beyond. It is here, in the sudden solitude of the quiet lane that meanders gracefully through Emberton and Gillitts that, for me, the Comrades Marathon really begins. No longer do I progress on my own terms – the hopes and confidence stored in training now vanish before the reality. The course, which has been held at bay for fifty-seven kilometres, is now running me. I am approaching the line; isolated, uncertain, caring only for survival.

My legs, detecting the first signs of an ailing will, begin their own mutiny, and inform me that this is far enough. Why, they ask, must they continue to run, knowing that each step will become more painful, more difficult? After all, there is always next year. Through the blanket of developing fatigue, I begin to appreciate the logic behind these questions; begin to feel the attraction of that haven of rest at the side of the road, the bliss of not having to take even one more step towards Durban.

Around me, I know that each runner is engaged in this same battle. In common suffering, we are alone to find our individual solutions. A glance up the road shows a string of runners, each running alone, each separated by a constant distance from the runner in front and behind. A common thread holds us together, but only reluctantly do we defile the sanctity of the space that separates us – the space that is our universe – twenty metres of tarmac, our seconds, and just enough room left over for our thoughts.

My will power now comes from my second. Ever smiling, ever happy, he is pure encouragement, my sole precious link with a world that cares. In his hands he carries all our wealth: a bucket containing iced water, a sponge, and a choice of three different drinks. His presence confirms that it is all worthwhile, that to him and his world, I am the most important runner – that together, whatever the cost, we must endure, we must both survive.

Despite the mutiny of my exhausted legs, my mind is still in control as I approach Kloof Station. Yet whatever mental reserves I retain, I know that they will soon be challenged because, from Kloof Station, at the top of Fields Hill, the Comrades plays its most evil trick. Experience tells me not to look, that should I for one second divert my eyes from the road, I will most likely not finish. But I have no discipline and I see it laid before me: the final, infinite twenty-five kilometres that separate me from Durban and the finish at the Kingsmead cricket ground.

In each race, I have learnt of that powerful desire to quit. I know full well that it is a coward who, once beaten, does not return. But as I begin the descent of Fields Hill, even this knowledge is of no assistance as I constantly battle against the coward within. Now four kilometres from my second, who must wait anxiously in Pinetown, forbidden to help me on this major highway, my mind hovers in the balance. I progress only because it is automatic. And it is here, on this major descent, that I am joined by the final tormentor. The continual jarring brought on by the sharp descents from Inchanga, Botha's Hill and Hillcrest have taken their toll on my quadriceps muscles and every step now sends a painful shock down each thigh. The muscles are in rebellion; depleted of energy, their connective tissue is coming apart. The added pain is too much; my tenuous will power finally deserts. I become Maurice Hertzog descending from the epic first ascent of Annapurna when he says: 'It's all over, Lionel, I am finished. Leave me alone and let me die.' (Hertzog, 1952)

You may think that even now I could still walk. That a few minutes of rest would restore the desire to live, would defeat the coward within. But you would be wrong.

'After 18 miles,' wrote David Costill, the world's foremost running physiologist, 'the sensations of exhaustion were unlike anything I had ever experienced. I could not run, walk or stand, and even found sitting a bit strenuous.' Were the human brain able to recall the pain of Fields Hill, no one would ever run the down Comrades twice.

This, then, is the point that each runner must pass if he is to arrive in Durban on his own feet. It is here, stripped of any of society's false privileges, that he finds no hiding place, no shelter of convenience. Face to face with himself, he must look deep inside. 'These miles,' wrote George Sheehan, 'will challenge everything he holds dear, his value system, his lifestyle. They will ask nothing less than his views of the Universe.'

For me, in 1978, that desire to live did not come from within.

For coinciding with these darkest moments, twenty-three kilometres away Alan Robb was just completing his greatest Comrades. I learnt this from a lone spectator perched on the embankment that skirts Fields Hill. Alan Robb, everyone's complete runner – quiet, undemonstrative, humble in victory ('I owe everything to my seconds') – enshrines the Comrades ethic. He is a victory of purity, a victory for the human spirit, the affirmation of morality.

With renewed vigour, with renewed faith that if the test is severe enough goodness must always prevail, my gloom disappears and I enter Pinetown. Now I find sufficient energy to use the last trick of the ailing runner – a trick learned from Dave Levick. 'Run', he said, 'from face to face. Look into the eyes of each spectator. Look at their joy. Imagine who they are, what they do, how much they want you to do well. Let them pull you through.'

I enter the last dreadful sixteen kilometres.

I have survived Pinetown and climbed Cowies Hill. Through Westville, the endless downhill reactivates the ice pick that hammers ever more painfully with each downhill stride. At 45th Cutting, I have just forty-one minutes to cover the last eight kilometres to claim a silver medal. Down Black Hill I prepare for the last hill, the curving climb past the West Ridge tennis courts to Tollgate. My eyes see only the road at my feet. I no longer have the energy to lift them to the horizon.

Soon I reach the summit ridge, a cruel 100 metres from the top of the Tollgate ridge. My fatigue is extreme. There is no longer sufficient oxygen on the planet to keep me moving. My staggering gait and contorted face suggest imminent collapse. I wonder vaguely whether I will die; whether the psychiatrist, Coon, was right when he suggested that death may be the ultimate aim of marathoners. He likened us to the king's messengers – those who took pride in sacrificing themselves for their monarch. 'One always sees in these messengers a moment of exaltation, when they have finally won through and delivered the news; then it seems to be an almost inexorable destiny for them to drop dead – anything but death would be a dull, sodden anticlimax' (Coon, 1957).

But, like Maurice Hertzog, I am to be spared. Slowly the gradient eases, and I spill over Tollgate, encouraged by the spectators' assurance that from here it is all downhill.

Now, three minutes later, the fire in my chest has subsided, the ache in my legs begins to recede. Now I know for sure that I will finish, but can I meet the 7 hour 30 minute deadline?

The minutes speed by, but the road seems to stand still. I am straining to deliver full power. I wobble and groan monstrously. I begin to hope that something will burst.

Barely eight minutes remain as I turn into Old Dutch Road and see my marker, the trees lining the road outside Old Kingsmead. Like the Chinese who, it is said, could run great distances in the mountains by fixing on a distant peak and entering a trance-like state, I see only these trees. I run, oblivious to the surrounding noise and confusion.

Finally the entrance to Kingsmead beckons. From inside, the noise of 2 000 voices is deafening. 'Two-oo minutes, two-oo minutes.' I comprehend the meaning but can no longer calculate distances and times. When I am halfway around the field, the crowd, in unison, informs me that now only one minute remains.

Then I see the finish line. On the left, a haggard group of runners; on the right the elegant figure of Mick Winn, the race organiser. In his hand is the finishing pistol, the discharge of which will signal a silver death.

I am still ten metres short of the line when he turns his back, and the pistol arches agonisingly skywards. My last coherent thought is whether our happy friendship is about to end.

As Chris Chataway noted, it is in moments like these when a person forces himself to the limit and, in emerging from the challenge intact, 'will know more about himself, his character, his limitations, his emotions and his strengths, than any man who has never in some direction forced himself to his very limit'.

Later, from the comfort of the Kingsmead turf, when a measure of physiological normality has returned, secure in the knowledge that the last step has been taken, I know again why it is all necessary – what common bond unites all Comrades. Skill, you see, is not our require-ment, nor has our race anything to do with winning and losing. These are the spoils of other, lesser games, unable to transport you to the places we have been.

We who have accompanied Hertzog to the summit of our own Annapurna: 'For us the mountains had been a natural field of activity where, laying on the frontiers of life and death, we had found the freedom for which we were blindly groping … The mountains had bestowed on us their beauties and we adored them with a child's simplicity … Annapurna, to which we had gone empty-handed, was a treasure on which we should live the rest of our days. With this realization we turn the page: a new life begins. There are other Annapurnas in the lives of men' (Hertzog, 1952).

The only requirement, and the common bond that links all Comrades runners, is the need to look for the mountains in life: to take the paths least travelled, to go against the common stream, to search for the unattainable and, finally, as Menander said, to accept that we have no option: 'A man's nature and way of life are his fate, and that which he calls his fate is but his disposition.'

So, for several years, because I had no choice but to follow my fate, on 31 May, between 6 a.m. and 7 a.m., you would have found me in mind, if not in body, somewhere on the Old Main Road between Pietermaritzburg and Durban, secure in the knowledge each time that this was my year, that this year I would finally defeat the coward within, and so commence the hero's life.

I did not know it then, but by 1978, after I'd run my third Comrades Marathon, I had discovered my life's calling.

2 | Finding my Design

Sport has always been a compelling field of study for me, borne of a long-standing passion and fascination for the cut and thrust of sport and the unique demands it places on the human mind and body. Perhaps this explains why the only sports in which I ever achieved a modicum of success required great endurance and will power but little skill. And why, through the Comrades Marathon and my participation in it, I was able to experience everything I hold dear about sport and its study.

The best athletes are motivated to give 100 per cent every time they compete. For the scientist, this means that each competitive sporting event provides an opportunity to set up an experiment that cannot be recreated in a laboratory. Better are the results of the experiment that can be analysed immediately. That which works and that which fails are ruthlessly exposed in the heat of competition, and few other forms of human endeavour provide such immediate feedback so definitively. Rare, too, are those who subject themselves repeatedly to such ruthless and often very public interrogation of their strengths and weaknesses.

So it was perhaps only natural that, as I trained harder and raced more frequently over longer distances, ultimately experiencing the personal inquisition that is the Comrades Marathon, I began to ask what the physiological and psychological factors are that determine excellence in sport. But before I could attempt to answer those questions, I faced other obstacles; most notably, the fact that medicine in the 1970s was far removed from what it is today.

'MICKEY MOUSE' MEDICINE

During my medical training I began to realise that my profession was, at best, ambivalent towards sport and its value to the nation and its citizens. I became alarmed at the costs we doctors incurred in treating our patients. I could not always see the benefits that the patient derived from such expenditure, and sometimes wondered if the focus of our treatment did not have more to do with us than with the patients – in other words, that as doctors we were treating more our own psychological needs than the patient's physical complaints. Nor did I think that medicine was doing enough to promote health as opposed to simply treating diseases.

Then, when I suffered an injury while training for the Comrades Marathon, I discovered that no one could help me. Worse, some of my colleagues were not even vaguely interested. When I informed one rheumatologist that I developed knee pain after thirty kilometres of running, he told me, 'I have patients who are unable to walk thirty metres. So what is your problem?'

Years later, Jackie Mekler, who won the Comrades Marathon five times and who is a special hero of mine, told me that when he consulted a doctor in the fifties with the same complaint, he was told that when the pain began he could always 'run the rest of the race on [his] hands'. This to a world-record holder. I realised that athletes were not a medical priority. If change were to happen, someone needed to act. I decided then that, as conventional medicine was full of exceptional doctors and did not need my help, I would try to apply my knowledge elsewhere.

When I made that decision and chose to leave clinical medicine and the study of cardiovascular physiology for the exercise sciences, one of the professors under whom I had served my hospital internship stated that I was wasting my time, since sports medicine and the exercise sciences were 'Mickey Mouse'. In time I learnt that his disdain probably stemmed from his own failings. His attitude taught me a most valuable lesson: that if I were to make a success of a career in the exercise sciences, I shouldn't expect any support from my colleagues in the conventional medical and scientific disciplines, especially the narcissistic ones.

The singular event that stimulated my interest in the relationship between sport and medicine occurred several years earlier, in June 1969. As a medical student at the University of Cape Town (UCT), I had started to row and later to run. Our rowing club hosted a visit by a British Olympic rowing coach and, after coaching us on the water, we returned to the university, where he presented a classroom lecture on rowing training. Shortly after he had begun, he moved to the blackboard, where he plotted a graph with a vertical axis and a horizontal axis. The vertical axis, he explained, represented the concentration of lactic acid in the blood; the horizontal axis the distance rowed in a 2 000-metre race.

'Gentlemen,' he began, 'when you start a 2 000-metre rowing race, your blood

LOOKING FOR THE MOUNTAINS

lactic acid levels will be low – about 1 millimole (mmol) per litre. But, within seconds of starting the race, your blood lactic acid levels start to rise precipitously, reaching values of 5 to 10 mmol per litre by the time you have rowed 1 000 metres. The agony you feel at the 1 000-metre mark is caused by the excessive amounts of lactic acid that are beginning to accumulate in your muscles and in your heart – in fact, throughout your body.' He paused, pointing at the board, then resumed his talk: 'As you continue, the lactic acid concentration continues to rise, reaching its highest values the instant you cross the finishing line – exhausted. If the values were to go any higher, you would be dead.'

The Olympic rowing coach ended by saying that the reason we train is 'to ensure that we can outlast the lactic acid, and not die in its grasp. Lactic acid makes cowards of us all. But those who train the hardest can conquer the lactic acid. You must learn to embrace it. You must learn to make it your friend.'

I was utterly mesmerised by his simple graphic representation and the passion with which he spoke. I had only one thought: 'You mean it is possible to measure changes in the blood that can explain why we feel so bad when we row in competition?' As I left the lecture hall and walked down University Avenue onto the steps of Jameson Hall, I knew that all I wanted to do was to study the discipline – physiology and biochemistry – about which he had spoken with such ardour.

But when I began to study these subjects the following year, as a second-year medical student, I discovered that there was very little information available on exercise physiology and biochemistry, and even less on sports medicine, the three topics I really wished to explore.

The available information was either dated or impractical, written by scientists with little understanding of the real problems experienced by sportsmen and women. It seemed clear to me that these scientists were writing on topics they might have met in the laboratory, but which they had not experienced in athletic competition.

Only in the 1990s did the world's best medical journals, such as the *British Medical Journal*, the *Lancet* and the *New England Journal of Medicine*, begin to include regular articles on various aspects of sport and medicine, and so proffer their stamp of approval for our fledgling discipline.

My great good fortune was that the beginning of real change occurred in 1976, coinciding with my first year as a scientist in training. In late October of that year, the first New York City Marathon was held. I was fortunate to run the race and to participate in the conference on the marathon organised by the New York Academy of Sciences – one of the world's most auspicious scientific bodies – that was held at the same time, in New York's Astoria Hotel. Little did any of us know that this event was the beginning of a worldwide marathon boom when exercise and marathon running suddenly became a global phenomenon over the next decade.

Intrigued by this sporting boom of the late 1970s, I sensed a changing future. I realised that sport would grow to have important economic implications for private enterprise and that medicine would also be affected, but that medicine needed to act proactively to utilise the opportunity. Shortly afterwards, along came Nike, a company that sold running shoes. By the early 1980s, Nike was the fastest-growing company in the United States.

I also felt sure that the advent of the computer in our daily lives would create more free time for participation in sport, and that with this would come a demand for the growth of sports science and medicine. I did not then appreciate that the computer would impact on the exercise sciences in radical ways – in particular, that the amount of data that could be collected more accurately and analysed more quickly would revolutionise our ability to answer complex scientific questions. For example, when I began, it took many hours to determine the amount of oxygen used by an athlete when he or she was running on a treadmill. Today, the same analysis can be done in milliseconds. The use of the computer to study game film from various sporting events has also revolutionised coaching. My late friend Bob Woolmer once said that there are two eras of coaching – before and after the introduction of video analysis. I have observed that the more advanced the coaching of a particular sport, the more emphasis is placed on the use of computers and game analysis in that sport.

And, finally, I was certain in the late 1970s that, as professional sport grew, so too would the demands made by elite performers on medical innovation. Such performers would need medical advancements to help them remain at the cutting edge of their professions.

As I look back on what I said and wrote in those days, I am sometimes surprised at the certainty I expressed. I begin to understand why there were times when my wife was less than impressed with my directness. In an article published in 1983, I wrote that a recent defeat by the Western Province rugby team in the Lion Cup had cost their union a million rand in gate takings. I stated that the training and medical care of the players on whose performances such economic considerations hinged would become increasingly important. In retrospect, rugby at the time was a profoundly amateur affair. Players began training in late February after an extended five-month break from the game. As a result, many of them were often in pretty bad shape at the start of the season. On my office wall at work I have a billboard from that era. The headline reads: 'Boks told they are too fat'. The article, based on my statement to writer Dan Retief, effectively ensured that he was off-limits to the Springboks for the following five years. The point is, however, that training to play rugby was unheard of at the time – players believed that they prepared for rugby by playing rugby once the season started.

At a lecture I delivered to rugby coaches recently, I said that in 1987 the New Zealand All Blacks coach hired an athletics trainer to prepare the team for that year's Rugby World Cup. I stated that this marked the beginning of the professionalisation of rugby training. I had been led to believe that a new approach to rugby fitness began after that World Cup, which was won by the All Blacks. After my lecture, a member of that All Blacks World Cup–winning team who, unbeknown to me, had been in the audience, came up to me and said: 'Mate, it was really nice of you to say those things about our training, but actually it wasn't true – we did not prepare any differently for that competition than we had in the past. Looking back, it was a little embarrassing how little we trained.' It reminded me of how, until only recently, even English Premier League football followed the same methodology.

Coaches such as Arsene Wenger have been instrumental in revolutionising the training methods of English Premier League teams. When Wenger took over as manager of Arsenal in 1996, he completely changed the way his players trained. At first, he was derided for being more like an academic than a football manager. Yet the academic in him brought a new science to the training ground.

Training sessions were timed with a stopwatch and began and ended to the exact second. Wenger revolutionised the diet of the modern footballer, focusing on nutrition and discouraging the use of alcohol. He developed a fitness regime that produced players who were fitter than those in most other teams in the final fifteen minutes – the most important period in close matches. In short, he took a bunch of robust footballers and turned them into world-class athletes through attention to detail that was unparalleled in the sport at the time. Very soon the rest of the footballing world had to follow suit or be left behind.

Perhaps the time of real change in rugby occurred at the 1991 World Cup, when the two finalists, England and Australia, took rugby preparation to a new level. This heralded the beginning of the modern professional approach. The driving force in Australian rugby was coach Bob Dwyer, who wrote about his methods in his classic rugby book *The Winning Way*. Dwyer advocated a holistic approach to the preparation of the players – to the point where wives became part of the team. This was an unheard-of innovation in a sport characterised by its masculinity and chauvinistic disregard of the female sex.

I concluded my 1983 article on the importance of the training and medical care of rugby players whose performance had economic implications with the following: 'These forces are not going to diminish in the next few years or even decades. Indeed they will only intensify, regardless of the wishes of those who do not understand sport and who may be negatively disposed towards it.'

From early on in my career, therefore, I understood the economic significance of sport, and saw where it was headed in society. I also predicted that medical costs would spiral out of control, requiring cost containment and a growing emphasis on disease prevention and health promotion. Perhaps the foundation for this economic interest stems from my father's business acumen – something that allowed me to follow the profession I ultimately chose.

AN UPBRINGING IN COURAGE AND INDEPENDENCE

Both my maternal and my paternal grandfathers were businessmen in Liverpool, England, as was my father. My father's success in his line of business gave me a certain self-confidence, even though my natural inclination is to be shy. A big, robust, powerful, passionate kind of man, my father had a sense of humour that was legendary. He did not go to university, but spent his life educating himself. When not working or playing golf or making furniture – his abiding passions – he read, like my mother. His lifelong interests were history and geography, and his business interests took him all over the world, where he found everything to be of interest. Just as I loved my mother unconditionally, I adored my father. The fact that he was involved in an industry that I could never condone was irrelevant. He taught me that honesty is the first requirement in life. His great sense of humour, his love of a good story skilfully told, and his general disdain for both authority and pretence made him the perfect mentor for me in my career in science and education.

My father finished school the year after the Great Depression, which severely affected the family business in Liverpool. There was no work for him, so my grandfather told him, 'Here's five pounds and a return ship ticket. Go to Canada and look after yourself for a year. Learn about the tobacco industry from the ground up.' So straight out of school my father went to work as a labourer on a Canadian tobacco farm.

Then, in 1936, his mother – my paternal grandmother – was killed in a tragic car accident in Northern Rhodesia (today's Zambia). My grandfather was, I suspect, severely traumatised by the accident. As a result, at the age of twenty-three, my father took over the family tobacco business. Within three years, by the start of World War II, my father had turned the company around, reversing a severe business debt of £80 000, a frightening amount in the money of the day. He achieved this by building partnerships with tobacco companies around the globe. I presume that his success was not just because he was liked, but also because he was trusted, scrupulously honest and loyal.

At the end of the war, my father packed up the family and announced, 'We are going to Rhodesia.' Birkenhead, where they lived, had been bombed to the ground by the Germans. My father probably realised that England had been exhausted by the war and that it was entering a prolonged period of recovery.

So my parents moved to Southern Rhodesia (now Zimbabwe) in 1946 with my elder sister, Amanda, who had been born the year before. For the first year they lived in the Meikles Hotel. I was born three years later in our first home in Africa, in the suburb of Borrowdale in Salisbury (now Harare). The name of the house was Honeycut; a name, I suspect, that refers to a particular kind of tobacco.

As a young child, a special treat was to be left in the care of my father's personal driver, Thomas Taravinga. He became my first friend. I have tried all my life to emulate his Zimbabwean warmth and brilliant smile. My love of Africa and its people and the reason that I have never been tempted to leave the continent of my birth began, I believe, with that relationship. When Thomas died three decades later, his son wrote to thank me for what my father had done for him. 'Your father,' he wrote, 'paid my father well enough that I could go to university in Germany from where I graduated as an engineer. I am forever thankful for your father's kindness.' I responded that neither he nor I would ever know the extent to which his father had fashioned my life and made me the person I am.

I have always felt that it must have taken enormous courage for my father to say, 'We've survived the war, now let's move on.' But each day I thank him for having made that decision. It was not the only decision of his for which I am thankful. Years later, my mother, who did not adapt to the frontier mentality of the Rhodesians, told me that she had agreed in 1946 to leave England for eight years, after which time she wanted to return. When she raised the question in 1954, my father said that he would not go back to England; instead the family would settle in Cape Town and he would continue his business by commuting to Salisbury when he was needed. Once you have experienced it, it is difficult to give up the unmatched beauty, space and sense of adventure that Africa offers.

My father was a go-getter and an adventurer, and I have probably inherited those genes. There was always massive potential for conflict between us, as he had made his living selling tobacco and I became a medical doctor. Ironically, I have been one of the main beneficiaries of his work, which no doubt contributed substantially to the ill-health of those who smoked cigarettes containing the tobacco he exported from Zimbabwe. But such are the paradoxes with which we must live our lives. Many years later my father's excellent business relationship with the Rupert family of Stellenbosch helped in the development of the Sports Science Institute of South Africa (SSISA) – another unpredictable and unexpected consequence of my father's involvement in the tobacco industry.

In the late 1970s, after I had spoken on Zimbabwean television about the dangers of smoking, my father felt compelled to admonish me: 'Son, this is not exactly what a Noakes should be saying in Harare!' Near the end of his life, he said to me, 'Tim, I did not help enough people in my life – you had better do so.' But he was wrong. He helped so many people and I always had the greatest respect for him, which he knew. Yet we had a complex relationship in which I had to ignore both the nature of his work and the guilt I felt as a result of the benefits I had derived from his industry – perhaps the industry that has produced more harm to human health than any other. Through this experience with my father I learnt how to distinguish the person from the issue: you might disagree with someone, but that does not mean you have to demonise him or her.

My father did not understand my passion for running, just as I could not understand his apparent indifference to my rowing and running. He loved cricket and golf and could not comprehend that running or rowing could possibly be as enjoyable or as meaningful as those sports. So one of the opening sentences in my book, *Lore of Running*, was definitely for my father. It reads:

> At school I had been taught that sport was cricket and rugby, anything else was a trifle undignified for us South African 'English'. Of course, the pressure to conform to these sporting norms was extreme, and, eccentric as I may since have become, I was not then secure enough to question what was good for me. But doubts about the real attraction these games held for me first started, I suppose, at the age of fifteen when I discovered surfing. For the first time, I discovered a sport in which it was possible to be completely alone. I loved it. No rules, no guidelines, no teams, no coaches, no spectators, and in those distant days, few other participants. Just me, my surfboard, my thoughts and an almost empty ocean.

My father was quite upset by that paragraph. But he read each page of the book and grew to love it. The third edition, published shortly before his death in 1992, found a place on his bedside table.

I was first exposed to this traditional English view of sport when we relocated to Cape Town in 1954 and I began my schooling at a private primary school before starting at Diocesan College (Bishops) in 1963. The controlling premise at both institutions was that the sports for real boys were cricket and rugby. In this environment, soccer – considered in those circles to be the less intelligent sport of the working class – stood no chance. Surfers were considered to be drug-dependent dropouts – in truth, the problem with surfing was that it was independent of authority and thus perceived as a threat. Running was another sport developed by the English, at least, so it was acceptable. However, at the time I had yet to discover my running passion.

Only later would I realise that a prevalent mindset among some English-speaking families with whom I interacted in Cape Town in the 1960s was that we were all poor cousins of the real English – the ones who lived at 'home' in England. South Africa was a foreign country ruled by a government that we did not understand. That leadership was unrefined and 'not us'. I might add that this was not what my parents believed: both eventually gave up their British citizenship in protest of the British handling of Rhodesian independence and the fact that my father was targeted by the British government for continuing to trade in Rhodesia after that country declared its independence from Britain.

Sport again provided the best example of this truth. At the time, it was considered undignified to beat our colonial masters at cricket, but not at rugby. Australia, too, were considered invincible. So when, in my father's company, I watched Australia comfortably defeat South Africa in a cricket Test match played at Newlands, Cape Town, in December 1957, it was as if that was the way it should and always would be. The South Africans were honoured to be on the same field as the English and the Australians – that was pretty much all we could expect. Interestingly, the Australians had rid themselves of this inferiority complex in the 1920s, and the appearance of Donald Bradman – the undisputed greatest cricketer of all time – had hastened that change. In *Bradman: An Australian Hero*, C. Williams wrote: 'Sport in Australia thus became (after World War I) an integral part of politics … it both encouraged and disciplined the egalitarian individualism that was emerging as an identifiable Australian characteristic. It was to be Australia's way of showing the rest of the world that that continent was not just an appendage of the British Empire but a real and living nation.' I had yet to be convinced that the Cape Town I inhabited was ready to be part of a separate, living nation, but change was in the air.

Perhaps a hint of change had shown itself, albeit briefly, five years earlier, in 1952, when a South African cricket team under the captaincy of Jack Cheetham toured Australia. When the team left South Africa for the long boat trip to Australia, it was considered so poor that the Australians, full of the 'Invincibles' that under Sir Donald Bradman had completed an unbeaten tour of England in 1948, suggested that the tour be cancelled. They were certain that it would be a financial disaster. Only when South African cricket agreed to underwrite the tour did the Australians concede that it could continue. It was on the long boat trip to Australia that Cheetham set about changing the 'losing' mindset of South African cricket.

First he had to convince himself that Australia were beatable. Then he began to express his faith in two key players, Hugh Tayfield and Russell Endean, neither of whom had yet shown that they were especially competent. John Arlott wrote in 1972: 'On the sea voyage, Cheetham kept telling Tayfield what a fine bowler he was. Within a few days, Tayfield was telling Cheetham what a fine bowler Tayfield was.' By the end of the tour, Tayfield was South Africa's most successful bowler and Endean the most successful batsman.

Next, he emphasised fielding, so that the South Africans' practice transcended anything that had ever been attempted before.

Finally, he engendered an intense team spirit to make the players 'rise above themselves'. Arlott's conclusion was that 'the biggest single factor in the Springboks' rise to fame was the spirit of the side which, from the moment it assembled, began conscientiously, persistently and determinedly to apply itself to the formidable undertaking. It was a spirit that made its members play with their hearts when their technical talents were not equal to the task.' In the Test at Melbourne, Cheetham's Springboks became the first team in the history of Australian cricket to win a Test (by six wickets) when they batted second, after Australia had posted more than 500 in their first innings. The Springboks drew the series 1-1. At the time, Tayfield was the most successful bowler ever to tour Australia and the team was voted the best fielding side ever to visit Australia.

At Bishops I had grown close to Jack Cheetham's middle son, Robert, and I admired both his batting ability and that of his older brother, John, who was also at the school, but two years ahead of us. I remember vividly that John slept fitfully the Friday night before a big match, tossing and turning all night. When I asked him why, he explained that he was imagining his innings of the next day and playing it through his mind all night long. Only much later would I learn of this technique, now known as visualisation.

In the 1960s, Cheetham's mental approach was taken even further by the late Eddie Barlow, whose mind was his greatest weapon. Like another great South African sportsman, Gary Player, he did not ever consider a cause lost.

Barlow played his first Test for South Africa in 1961 and, on the next tour of Australia over the summer holidays of 1963/64, he began to weave his magic. In the opening Test in Brisbane, he became the first South African to score a hundred in his first Test against Australia. That tour had a remarkable impact on my understanding of what it meant to be a South African. In the fourth Test, in Adelaide, Barlow and the twenty-three-year-old prodigy Graeme Pollock slaughtered the Australian attack, Pollock scoring 175 runs off 283 deliveries and Barlow 201 off 395 deliveries. The Springboks won the Test by 10 wickets and went to the final Test, in Sydney, with the series squared 1-1. In this Test, the Springboks were again dominant, requiring just 100 runs to win with 10 wickets remaining when rain saved Australia. This team had changed the concept of what it meant to be a South African cricketer – the inferiority complex dumped by Australia in as early as the 1920s was finally being discarded by a remarkable group of young South African cricketers.

Australia toured South Africa in 1966/67, and the South Africans won the series 3-1 before they went one better during the 1969/70 tour, when they won all four Tests – the final ignominy for Australian cricket. The myth of South African inferiority had finally been debunked.

But the euphoria of that victory was followed by a new despondency, for the tour of England scheduled for the English summer of 1970 was cancelled as the sports boycott against South Africa began to take hold. South Africa would return to international cricket only in 1992. I had understood the national importance of our cricket success in the 1960s in addressing a national inferiority complex; I had also comprehended the importance of South Africans' willingness to accept that we are South Africans and not displaced Englishmen.

So, when in 1995 Bob Woolmer asked me to become involved with South African cricket to help make the team the best in the world, I absolutely could not refuse. I felt it was my public responsibility. In retrospect, it was perhaps the decision I most regret in my life. But more of that later.

The mindset of South African rugby was the polar opposite. There was no way that a South African rugby team was going to stand back for any team in the world, least of all the English. This admirable approach continues to explain why South African rugby has won two Rugby World Cups in twelve years, whereas our cricketers, playing in a less globally competitive sport, have yet to win their first World Cup.

'AH, BUT IT'S GOOD TO BE ALIVE'

My lack of mental ability as a cricketer influenced my life by forcing me to find the passions for which I was properly designed. When I discovered surfing, it transformed my understanding of sport. Surfing taught me many things, including independence.

It also brought me close to nature. When the water was cold and the off-shore wind so strong that each wave left an icy, stinging spray that bit into my wetsuit and scratched at my eyes, I felt the pleasure of knowing that it was good to be alive. I experienced the same pleasure that the great South African cricketer Jonty Rhodes felt. In those moments when his team's fate appeared to be beyond salvation, Rhodes said he always remembered the words of one of his coaches, who at such times would say, 'Ah, but it's good to be alive.' Even today, when the wind is blowing from the north and the tides are right, my thoughts turn to the beach – to those days of rare perfection when my life was uncluttered and my time was my own.

The pleasure of surfing is difficult to describe; it provides solitude, as does running, but the mental stimulation supplied by the contact with water and the wide vistas of sky and ocean is quite different. Like running, surfing allows one simply to be oneself. Skill is quite irrelevant – riding a wave, like the act of running, produces feelings of competence and enjoyment that are entirely independent of one's real abilities. One does not have to be any good to enjoy surfing, nor does one have to possess skill to enjoy running.

3 | Deciding on a Career

When I finished high school, I was unsure of my future career. Since my birthplace was Zimbabwe and my parents were British, I was still a British citizen. In my final year at school, however, I decided to take out South African citizenship specifically so that I would have to undergo military training after leaving school. I wanted to understand what it was like to be a South African, and I wanted to meet a wider group of people.

So I spent the first nine months of 1967 in the lowest ranks of the South African Defence Force (SADF) discovering myself. It was an experience that I remember with great affection, probably because I chose to do it for subconscious reasons that I still do not fully comprehend. I was also fortunate that I was never required to raise arms – I escaped active border duty in the 1970s and 1980s because by then I was a medical doctor. I had joined the SADF to learn about myself, not to harm others.

After completing my initial training in September, I went to America to study for one year in 1968 as an American Field Service (AFS) high school exchange student at Huntington Park High School in Los Angeles. Again, I was blessed to be in America during one of the most formative years in the history of the United States.

Time magazine called 1968 'The Year that Changed the World', the year that, in the words of L. Morrow, '[l]ike a knife blade, severed past from future'. It was the year of the assassinations of Dr Martin Luther King Jnr and Robert Kennedy, idealists who stood for something more than the world has since become. It was also the year in which the US Army, out-thought and out-manoeuvred by the more resilient and innovative North Vietnamese, made the mistakes it would repeat in Iraq and Afghanistan four decades later. The South African Boers had taught the British Empire in 1899 that a local force fighting for survival on its home turf is not easily overcome.

Yet for all its setbacks, which in retrospect signalled the beginning of the end of US global dominance, America in 1968 was an intoxicating environment. It was the land built by what has since been termed America's 'Greatest Generation' – the Americans who fought in World War II, who participated in the D-Day landing and the emancipation of Europe in 1945, and who returned to America to lead that nation into the most prosperous era of its history. Having survived and won a just war, the Greatest Generation embodied optimism, idealism and the sense that anything could be achieved. In Robert Kennedy and Martin Luther King Jnr they had men who could enact that destiny. Although we did not know it then, the assassination of these men within ninety days of one another signalled the end of the idealism.

In Los Angeles, the city where Robert Kennedy lost his life, I received the message that determined my destiny. It was a few words on the car radio that had a profound and lasting effect on my life, and provided the single greatest influence on my career choice.

On the Sunday afternoon of 3 December 1967, while travelling back to Huntington Park from a trip to San Juan Capistrano, the newsreader on the radio announced that a South African doctor, Dr Christiaan Barnard, had performed the world's first successful heart transplant at Groote Schuur Hospital in my home town of Cape Town. Suffering mildly from homesickness, the news made me immensely proud. Barnard, in time, became a special inspiration for me, even though I appreciated that his love of self made him less than he should have been. Born with a few different behavioural genes, he could have become, with Nelson Mandela, the greatest South African of all time.

Barnard also challenged the conservative mindset of Cape Town medicine in our parochial 1960s. As a result, many of his colleagues were reluctant to afford him the real recognition that he deserved. In a book edited by D. Cooper, titled *Chris Barnard by those who know him*, the following is written: 'Most of us think along straight lines, like a bus or a train or a tram. If the destination isn't up on the board, few of us would know where we are going – and that applies even to scientific researchers who should know better. We tend to let tradition lead us by the nose. It takes an effort of will to break out of the mould.' In order even to attempt the operation, Barnard needed to believe that a successful human heart transplant was possible. Then he had to have the courage and desire to be the person to achieve that medical milestone.

Barnard, too, had spent two years in America, and described it as 'the most fascinating time in my life'. His future career, and especially his ability to perform open-heart surgery in Cape Town, was utterly dependent on the generosity of the so-called Greatest Generation. For when he returned to South Africa after completing his training in Minneapolis, his former boss, Dr Owen Wangenstein, realised that Barnard would not be able to continue his work without a heart–lung machine. Neither Barnard nor Groote Schuur Hospital could afford such a machine at that time, so Wangenstein organised funding from the US government to buy the machine. Without it, Barnard could not have introduced open-heart surgery to Africa. The original machine can still be seen at Groote Schuur Hospital in the wonderful transplant museum that commemorates this most important event in the history of South African medicine.

Three months after that Sunday in December 1967, I awoke one morning in Huntington Park certain in the knowledge that, when I returned to Cape Town, I would study medicine at the faculty in which Professor Barnard worked. This event and many other incidents in my life have convinced me that much of our lives appears to be either preordained or dependent on chance.

Only much later did I learn of the other five minutes that had indirectly determined my future. On the afternoon of my seventeenth birthday on 2 July 1966, cardiac surgeon Dr Adrian Kantrowitz was preparing to perform the world's first human heart transplant at the Maimonides Hospital in Brooklyn, New York. But the heart of the donor ceased beating minutes before the operation could begin, ending Kantrowitz's brush with immortality. Instead, on the night of 3 December 1967, Dr Christiaan Barnard performed his historic operation. Had the New York donor lived another five minutes, allowing the heart transplant to occur, I would not be writing this story.

MY LIFE'S WORK BEGINS
In 1969, I began my medical training at the University of Cape Town, where I developed an interest in endurance sports. I joined the university's rowing team, and in rowing I found a team sport that demands total individual dedication and physical perfection, and an acceptance of physical pain and discomfort.

I suppose rowing introduced me to my need for self-inflicted pain – the special, nauseating, deep-seated pain that accompanies repetitive interval training and racing. Only later I realised that it is the continual exposure to and mastery of that discomfort that is an essential ingredient for personal growth, at least for those with a penchant for competitive sports.

At school I had not the slightest interest in running. Running was merely about suffering and working through the pain; but fate was to play a pivotal role once again. As part of our first-year medical training, we studied physics and zoology, botany and chemistry. At our first physics practical I met a tall, lean, angular, bilingual South African of Afrikaner descent, Edward 'Tiffie' King. Tiffie believed that university life was mainly about one thing – running. I had never before seen such intense sporting focus, and it captivated me – eccentricity always has attracted me. From 1971 on, Tiffie taught me how to run – at lunch times, as he ran the second of his three daily training sessions, I would accompany him – and, in time, I taught Tiffie all I knew about physics.

My next good fortune was that, at our first zoology practical, I was seated next to a student whose name was Manfred Teichler. Over time I learnt that Manfred was the last son of German medical missionaries who worked in Botswana. He had begun to run longer distances in his final year at high school, in part to express his independence and worth in a large family. As we passed the time dissecting all sorts of creatures, he told me that he was preparing to run a marathon a few weeks from then. When in that year I ran my first race as part of a rowing-club relay team, Manfred accompanied me over the final 500 metres. In September 1972 we ran my first marathon together, and in 1973 the Comrades Marathon. In my first year at university, however, all my running was done in training for rowing. We seldom ran further than three kilometres, and then it was always at maximum pace.

Then one day in December 1970, when the wind was too strong to row, I decided to run around the *vlei* at which we trained. The run was the longest I had yet attempted and much further than the distance to which I was accustomed. That run was decisive. After about forty-five minutes I experienced the 'runner's high' – that feeling of experiencing heaven on the road.

In that defining moment I discovered that my brain is genetically programmed to respond to the chemical changes that produce the 'runner's high'. Just as some people have brains that completely lack this response, I suspect that those of us who become runners have the brain variant that responds in this way. The result was that I had finally discovered the sport for which I had been searching.

I was fortunate in my choice, because, as briefly mentioned earlier, running experienced a tremendous boom in 1976 and, by 1978, we had the first scientific evidence that it was enormously beneficial for health. Only later, in the first decade of the twenty-first century, did we learn that humans had actually evolved to run.

I was also attracted to running because so many of the factors in the sport can be controlled. There is less of an element of chance than there is in other sports. You can train and work out pretty much what the result will be. Running taught me the importance of emotional control too. In all races, regardless of the distance, there is a point about two-thirds of the way through the race when the brain tells you that it is really not necessary to keep going. But to be a runner is to know that quitting is simply not an option. You just keep going until the race is done. Running has taught me a great deal about who I am, but even more about who I am not. In that perfect solitude on the road, at the point where fatigue drives each of us back into ourselves, into those secluded parts that we discover only under times of such duress, we emerge with a clearer perspective of who we really are.

EXERCISING THE MIND

So it was that I learnt through running how much I love privacy and solitude. I tend to mix best with people who are equally restrained and private. In fact, I have a tendency to become ill when forced to socialise too frequently. Only more recently have I learnt to don the mask of extroversion. Deep down I remain a reserved introvert who prefers privacy and my own company or that of my wife, Marilyn.

Running taught me that the quest for a perfect body places one on a similar path to mental or spiritual perfection. At medical school I was never taught that each human body has vast physical potential; I learnt later to take great pride in what I could train my body to achieve. Finishing races such as the Comrades Marathon gave me the self-confidence to know that, within my own limits, I could attain whatever physical or academic target I set myself. This is the gift that the Comrades Marathon bestows on all of its finishers.

The high points of my early university career did not provide anywhere near the same lasting pride and pleasure as silver medals in the Comrades and Two Oceans Marathons did. Only much later, as my work became increasingly accepted, did I begin to extract as much satisfaction from my intellectual pursuits as I had from the physical achievements of my youth. To some extent this is the nature of the human condition: we must begin by learning about our physical bodies. Then, as we age, there is the chance to use those lessons learnt from the physical struggle to advance the mind. Finally, in the stage of life in which I now find myself, we need to go back to our bodies to attempt to preserve our physical and mental functions for as long as possible.

Through running I discovered that the rewards, as in life, come only in direct proportion to the amount of effort I was prepared to exert. I also learnt that only I would ever know whether I was a success or not. Running showed me that life is self-competition. It made me appreciate that a potential weakness of some other sports is that the competitor does not learn to compete against himself and is therefore shielded from admitting personal imperfections. Rather, it is all too easy to blame another. Running educated me in humility, teaching me to realise and accept my limitations and to refrain from envying those who enjoy physical or intellectual gifts that I lack. I love the quote by Eric Segal, the author of *Love Story* and also a veteran marathoner, who was asked whether, despite his wealth and success, there was anything in life he regretted. 'Yes,' he replied, 'I never won the Boston Marathon.'

In my dealings with some of the world's greatest athletes, I have sensed a true humility that comes from the very real fear of failure; the fear that the day will come when no matter how hard they have trained and prepared, they will fail. The awareness that there will be times when I am wrong and could fail has existed in my own life as a physiologist and scientist. For this reason, I have always let the science guide me rather than try to force the science to fit my own desires.

Running epitomises what makes us uniquely human – namely, the need to discover and to perfect, to keep moving forward. And as we do so, we inspire others. As the Reverend J.D. Liddell says so memorably in the movie *Chariots of Fire*, 'Run ... and let the world stand back in wonder'.

I am privileged to have interacted with some of the greatest South African runners in our history as I researched their stories for inclusion in *Lore of Running*. I marvelled at the resolve of Arthur Newton; the amateur passion of Wally Hayward; the intensity, courage and aloneness of Jackie Mekler, who became a lifelong friend; the resolute determination of Dave Levick, who helped prepare me for my first Comrades Marathon; the shy introspection of Alan Robb; the articulate dreamer Bruce Fordyce; and Willie Mtolo, who 'ran' away from the bonds of apartheid and abject poverty to glory in the 1992 New York City Marathon. These runners have provided an example for life that goes far beyond running, and I have learnt a great deal from each of them. They have taught me a gentleness and a consideration for others.

While it has educated me in many things, running has also challenged me. I have always been bored by the mundane and stimulated by the unusual or unexplained. Marathon running brought me face to face with Kierkegaard's truth: 'I myself am my only obstacle to perfection.' I was perhaps fortunate to have many personal obstacles to perfection – I was not born with an exceptional ability that forced me in one particular life direction. Bruce Fordyce once famously said that 'Tim Noakes may have a gold-medal mind but he has a bronze-medal body'. So when I did win silver medals in the race that became Bruce's own, I did so because of the use I made of my mind to drive that bronze-medal body beyond its perceived limits. Although I have never considered myself to have any great talent or ability, sporting or otherwise – at school and at university I always came second, at best – I do have enthusiasm and passion.

I was attracted to running, therefore, because it is a sport that can be enjoyed regardless of one's talent. It has more to do with the mind and the passion. I enjoyed the fact that running involved a competition against myself: there was no interpersonal rivalry, and therefore there was none of the nastiness or emptiness if you lost.

American psychologist William Sheldon was the first to match a person's body type to his or her personality, and running crystallised in my mind that I had the emotional and personality traits of the typical ectomorph, whose eternal quest is to understand the riddles of life.

If I'm upset about anything, I run to find the answers. My most creative thoughts occur when I'm out there by myself, extending myself physically. I believe, like Nietzsche, that you must not give credence to any thoughts that come when you are sitting down, but only to those that occur, as he described, when the muscles are also active.

Interestingly, some of the world's greatest thinkers were prodigious exercisers.

The philosophers Emerson and Thoreau exercised daily. Thoreau observed that the length of his daily writing was equal to the length of his daily walk. Nietzsche also walked for inspiration, as did the American president Jefferson and the poet Wordsworth. Our own intellectual giant, General Jan Smuts, walked most days on the mountain that has been the source of my most lucid intellectual moments. Frequently I walk or run on the track on Table Mountain that bears the general's name – Smuts's Track. Some of my deepest moments of spiritual insight have come when I am pushing myself to the physical limit. It is in these moments that I realise that I have discovered the real values in life, beyond the obvious traits of skill and natural ability. It is at these times that we discover who we really are. We discover moments that cannot be read, but that must be lived. We uncover what is left when we have been pushed to the limit. That's what exercise can do. It gives us the spiritual courage to keep going back to face up to ourselves and to find out who we really are. And then to discover that we are not just body and brain, but something beyond all of that. As the great George Sheehan, running's most eloquent philosopher, with whom I shared a great friendship for fifteen too-short years, once said, 'We have yet to see the true marvels of mankind and the universe.'

I met Dr George Sheehan for the first time at the New York Academy of

Sciences Conference in 1976. At the time he was the only doctor who wrote a regular column in a lay-running publication, *Runner's World*. His writings so inspired me that I followed his example and within a year started writing a regular column in a local South African running magazine. Those columns ultimately led to *Lore of Running*. Sheehan, whose philosophical writings on running have not and will not ever be matched, wrote that through running we discover the five stages of man (and woman).

First, we have to become good animals. We have to recover that animal energy, that good tight body, that sense of occupying just the right amount of space. Next we become children again, discovering the play of our childhood and of doing something full of meaning, but without purpose or thought of reward. From this, meditation follows, and with it the chance to be our own artist and to uncover areas of our minds that we ordinarily fail to see, but which running can unlock. Then comes the chance to be a hero – to break the four-minute mile or run our own personal best in a marathon; to find out how much we can endure. Outside of war, Sheehan said, sport is the only way we can establish whether or not we are cowards.

And finally, through running we can become almost as the saints, because running teaches us our own limitations. It teaches us that effort, not performance, is what counts because, despite our greatest efforts, most of us will never be elite runners. When we see life and the race as an individual struggle, we will understand the need for cooperation and we will move beyond competition to enter the perfect society.

There are mental components to exercise that I still do not fully understand, but as a physiologist I know that each of us is a unique, never-to-be-repeated experiment. Our duty is to take what God has given us, accept it as our lot and extract the absolute best from it.

It is clear from all of the above that running has given me the clarity to understand who I am, and perhaps why. Had I never discovered running, I doubt that my life would have been as exciting and fulfilling as it has turned out to be.

TACKLING THE DOGMA

I suspect that I was not built to be content. I am fuelled by perpetual self-doubt. I begin each day wondering whether I am doing my best at something that is worthwhile and meaningful. I wonder whether today I will have anything of value to add as a writer, lecturer or researcher. Then I recall a passage by Ralph Waldo Emerson in which he wrote, 'There is a time in every man's education when he arrives at the conviction that envy is ignorance and that imitation is suicide; that he must take himself for better, for worse, as his portion; that though the universe is full of good, no kernel of nourishing corn can come to him but through his toil bestowed on that plot which is given to him to till.'

I have endeavoured to make a difference in my chosen field by seeking truth. There have been moments in my career when I have seen the truth with absolute certainty, even though that truth would be proven only many years later.

My first experience of this produced my first significant contribution to the field of sports science – the proof that marathon runners are not immune to heart disease, as had been proposed by Californian pathologist Dr Tom Bassler in the early 1970s. Tom popularised the incorrect theory that marathon running prevents heart disease. He drew this conclusion in part from a 1961 autopsy performed by two Boston doctors, Drs Currens and White, on Clarence deMar, a legendary American marathoner who won the Boston Marathon seven times and finished third in the 1924 Paris Olympic marathon. Upon his death, an autopsy revealed that the diameter of his coronary arteries was two to three times the normal size. Currens and White published their findings in the *New England Journal of Medicine*, the premier medical journal in the world.

Perhaps inspired by this finding, Dr Bassler surveyed the published literature on the subject. He was unable to find a single published report of a marathon runner who had died as a result of a documented heart attack due to coronary atherosclerosis – a disease of the heart's arteries. Tom took this as proof of the absence of such disease in marathon runners. But the absence of proof is not the proof of absence. His hypothesis was immensely attractive, as it was proposed at exactly the moment when marathon running was taking off globally.

Unfortunately, his hypothesis had the effect of promoting marathon running as the method by which anyone, regardless of their risk factors for coronary heart disease, could achieve total immunity to coronary atherosclerosis. Tom stated, 'Immunity to heart disease is synonymous with physical fitness.'

It was perhaps natural that when I began my research career in Professor Lionel Opie's laboratories at UCT in 1976, I was immediately interested in this topic. Lionel had already contested Tom's hypothesis in 1975 by claiming in a letter to the *New England Journal of Medicine* that a South African marathon runner had died of documented coronary artery disease. While the athlete's death certificate did indeed list the cause of death as coronary heart disease, no autopsy had been performed, so the case did not disprove Tom's claim that no marathon runner had been shown to die from autopsy-documented coronary athero-sclerosis.

After a few weeks in Lionel's laboratory, I flew around the country seeking permission to collect the hearts from autopsies on marathon runners who had died suddenly from what might have been coronary atherosclerosis. We learnt that marathon runners do not die only from heart attacks due to coronary atherosclerosis – in the first case we studied, we discovered that a form of heart disease other than coronary artery disease had been the cause of death.

Our first break occurred in the middle of 1976, when we tracked down two veteran marathon runners who had survived clinically proven heart attacks. Both runners agreed to undergo a procedure in which a dye injected into their coronary arteries would show whether or not they had coronary atherosclerosis. The results were unequivocal: both athletes had suffered heart damage due to the presence of coronary atherosclerosis, disproving the Bassler hypothesis. Neither Lionel nor I realised then that we still had some way to go before our proof would be accepted.

In about July 1976 I became aware that a conference on the topic of 'The Marathon' would be held in New York City in October of that year. As mentioned earlier, it had been planned to coincide with the first running of the New York City Marathon through the five boroughs of New York. The race was to be televised nationally and would be the spark that ignited the massive surge in marathon running around the globe, with copycat big-city marathon races springing up in many of the world's most famous cities over the next five years.

I was able to raise money from the Department of Sport to cover my travel expenses – about R900, as I recall – and was ready to go. Before I left, Lionel called me aside and said, 'Tim, I want you to take your slides about these heart attacks in marathon runners with you. As soon as you arrive, go to the conference organisers and tell them that you have evidence that disproves the Bassler hypothesis. Tell them that if Dr Bassler is going to speak, then you must be allowed time to present your contrary evidence in the interests of free speech. Tell them that I said this.'

So it was that in October 1976 I travelled to New York City to run the marathon and to participate in the New York Academy of Sciences conference, formally titled 'The Marathon: Physiological, Medical, Epidemiological and Psychological Studies'.

All of the top names in exercise physiology and sports medicine attended. My appeal to the conference organiser, Dr Paul Milvy, to be allowed to speak was, quite incredibly, accepted almost without discussion. I presume that this was because my boss, Professor Opie, is a globally recognised medical scientist.

So, as a naive twenty-seven-year-old, I stood up in this hall of giants and presented our evidence. Years later, my great friend George Sheehan said that I had 'charmed' the audience. My abiding memory is of being surrounded almost instantly after the talk by twenty or so delegates whose demeanour suggested that my life was in grave danger! This event, which occurred so early in my career, taught me that if you challenge someone's hallowed beliefs, you must expect an aggressive reaction.

But it is the search for the truth that has always kept me focused in the face of personal attacks. There has never been a point in my life where things have become so bad that I have considered throwing in the towel. Why? Because I believe that if I have done my homework and arrived at what I consider to be the clear truth, I should trust my judgement until new evidence becomes available to disprove that truth.

In the end we were right on the Bassler hypothesis. Our paper providing autopsy-proven evidence of coronary atherosclerosis in marathon runners was published on 7 December 1979 in the *New England Journal of Medicine*. An accompanying editorial by D. Rennie and N.K. Hollenberg, titled 'Cardiomythology and Marathon Running', included the following statements:

> Some of us certainly run because of a modern-day myth – that marathon running provides complete immunity from coronary heart disease. As pointed out as recently as October 1978, this notion is widely held; the evidence concerning this simplistic hypothesis has been debated most notably by Bassler (for) and Milvy (against) with more repetition than documentation being offered in support. The paper by Noakes and his colleagues on this issue, unequivocally destroys it.
>
> Now we know what most have suspected: coronary-artery disease does develop in at least some marathon runners … Does this mean that the *Journal* is taking an anti-exercise stance? Far from it. We merely point out that physicians who recommend ambitious exercise programs for their patients must remember that proof that this approach will prevent or even delay cardiovascular death is not yet available. We suspect that Paffenbarger is correct: everything else being equal, heart attack rates will decline with increasing activity.
>
> The fundamental question of whether running does good things to the coronary arteries will not be answered simply by studying self-selected runners. Until the data are in, the exercisers' enjoyment of the activity and the pleasure in the way they feel and look should be sufficient. In exercise, as in good deeds, the reward must lie in the act itself (p. 104).

The key to being a good scientist or a good doctor is never to believe that you are correct. I encourage all my medical students to understand that, when dealing with patients, they need to act as if they are absolutely certain of the diagnosis. At the same time they must presume that the diagnosis that they have arrived at is likely to be utterly incorrect. Unfortunately, many of the errors that we doctors make are the result of our absolute certainty that our diagnosis is the only one that can possibly be correct.

So, early in my career I understood the collective level of medical ignorance so brilliantly described by Dr Lewis Thomas: 'The greatest single achievement of science in this most scientifically productive of centuries is the discovery that we are profoundly ignorant; we know very little about nature and understand even less ... I wish there were some formal courses in medical school on medical ignorance; textbooks as well, although they would have to be very heavy volumes. We have a long way to go.'

I have always believed in challenging the truth when my gut feeling tells me that something is improbable. I believe that the role of medical research is to disprove, and thereby to improve, current practice. As Dr Sydney Burwell, former dean of Harvard, was quoted as saying in G. Pickering's 'The purpose of medical education', 'My students are dismayed when I say to them, "Half of what you are taught as medical students will in ten years have been shown to be wrong. And the trouble is, none of your teachers knows which half."'

The aim of science is to generate theories that can be refuted; only in this way can we move closer to the truth. Exercise scientists, like scientists in other disciplines, should spend their academic lives developing models of how they think the body works. These models do not necessarily reflect reality or absolute truth. Instead, we use them to make predictions that we can then test experimentally. If the experimental findings support the predictions of the model, then the model survives to make further predictions, which are again tested. But if the experimental findings do not fit the predictions of the model, then that model must be modified, or perhaps abandoned.

This is the concept of scientific refutability: science is never able to prove anything – rather we progress towards truth only by disproving that which is less true. Pioneered by Karl Popper, this philosophy is not one that is generally accepted in the exercise sciences. I have seen at first hand how a theory can be immunised from all attempts at refutation once it becomes the established mindset supported by influential scientists. I have witnessed how difficult it is for the scientific community to accept novel ideas. Personal attacks on me have revealed the darker side of this community. The great mathematician Stephen Hawking described this as 'refutation by denigration' – a process by which the scientific credibility of the person who questions the accepted model is brought into doubt and his or her professional standing is subtly undermined.

It is the classic case of shooting the messenger so that the message may be conveniently ignored. My career has provided some interesting examples of this response.

MY GREATEST INFLUENCES

If, through running, people like George Sheehan have had such a great impact on my life, their combined effect does not come close to the influence of my wife, Marilyn.

In my third year as a medical student I married Marilyn after a wonderful courtship of six years. We have two children, Travis Miles and Candice Amelia. Marilyn has been the single greatest influence on my life. We met on the evening that I left high school, and we have been inseparable ever since. Her love and support gave me the confidence to do what I have done and to be as outspoken as I have been. Marilyn is utterly her own person and my strongest critic. She is never scared to challenge anything I say or to chide me for behaviour that she considers inappropriate. An exceptional artist, she has an encyclopaedic knowledge of plant, insect and animal biology, all self-taught when she had time between raising our children. She has combined all of her skills to produce another of her masterpieces – a fynbos garden in which each plant, insect, reptile, bird and mammal has a special place.

Marilyn is also so perfectly pure that I can only describe her as an angel. It is impossible for her to harbour an unkind or impure thought.

In my opinion, we acknowledge too infrequently the women who shape our lives. I learnt the alphabet from my mother as she wrote each letter in the sands of Glencairn Beach. My mother's love of books and reading may have inspired my writing, which has become a great passion and helped me to find my place in the world. My interest in writing began when I ventured into the medical library of the University of Cape Town for the first time in 1970 and discovered an overpowering addiction to published scientific information on biology and medicine. But, in truth, my desire to write began in the popular media long before I became a competent scientist.

My first article on running, written in 1972, was a rather tentative effort on running injuries; my true writing breakthrough came the following year, when I was invited by the Germiston Callies Harriers to write an article for their Pieter

Korkie Marathon brochure. The article, titled 'Running in the Heat', subsequently found its way into a book published by the American running magazine *Runner's World*. I received a mammoth $30 for that article. Four decades later, I am still writing on the same topic.

In 1976, the editor of *Topsport* magazine in South Africa suggested that I write a regular column for the publication. I did this happily for two years before the demise of the magazine in the Information Scandal. It turned out that *Topsport* was funded by the then South African government as part of an attempt to control some of the media. Then, in late 1977, Peter Walsh, the editor of a new publication, the *SA Runner* magazine, approached me to write a monthly column, which I did for many years.

By 1982, I felt that I had accumulated sufficient material for a book. In the July holiday of that year, while on the Transkei coast, I began the first lines of what would become the first edition of *Lore of Running*. I felt that there was a need for a book that covered all aspects of running. In researching and writing the book, I read just about every relevant publication that I could find, so determined was I to produce the truly complete book on running. My inspiration came from Jim Fixx's phenomenally successful *The Complete Book of Running* – which I considered to be incomplete.

At that stage of my career I felt the need to convey the true and practical value of sports science to as wide an audience as possible. I also knew that the only way to progress sports science and sports medicine in South Africa would be to have the support of the general public. In the end it may have been *Lore of Running* that convinced the Rupert family to agree to support the development of the Sports Science Institute of South Africa. Without the research opportunities provided by SSISA, and especially the financial support of Discovery Health, my career as a scientist would not have advanced as it has done over the past two decades.

I have spent my academic life challenging those theories that Hawking describes as 'creaking and ugly edifices'. The English scientist Thomas Huxley wrote, 'The known is finite, the unknown is infinite; intellectually we stand on an island in the middle of an illimitable ocean of inexplicability. Our business in every generation is to reclaim a little more land.' Using this idea for the J.B. Wolffe Memorial Lecture I gave at the 1996 American College of Sports Medicine's annual conference in the United States, I said that my scientific life is the story of how a scientist from the city of Cape Town, which is situated on a small peninsula surrounded by two great oceans at the very base of Africa – far from the intellectual capitals of the world – has fashioned a challenge for exercise scientists to reclaim land in our young and still growing discipline. The core challenge is to question constantly the beliefs that we hold most dear.

This book, *Challenging Beliefs*, outlines how science works and how I came to believe what I do. It contains everything I have worked on during my years as a sports scientist and includes my work with some of the most talented athletes in the history of South African sport. All have helped me to learn more about the limitless potential of the human body.

Roger Bannister said, 'The human body is centuries ahead of the physiologist.' In this book, I am going to show you why.

4 | The History of Sports Science

While it is true that the news of Dr Christiaan Barnard's groundbreaking heart surgery inspired me to enter the medical profession, I was disheartened by Barnard's often disparaging comments about the value of physical activity. He is known to have said that jogging is more dangerous than extramarital sex; that he received enough exercise carrying the coffins of his recently deceased jogging friends; and that the most appropriate response to the desire to exercise is to lie down until the feeling passes.

But after watching the 1983 Comrades Marathon, the year that Bruce Fordyce ran what has been described as the perfect race, when he shattered his previous 'up' record by just over seven minutes, Barnard wrote that it had been a 'moving experience' and that he now realised that 'man was saddled with a Stone Age body that was not only designed for exercise but that demanded vigorous, sometimes painful, exercise to keep it functioning properly. Only the moving are alive.'

But not all of my medical colleagues had Barnard's ability to change his mind when the truth became obvious. While today medicine certainly seems to have embraced sports science and sports medicine, in my opinion the medical profession became involved in this process as a by-product of the global fitness boom of the 1970s, and cannot really take any direct responsibility for it.

OUR OLYMPIC ANCESTORS

The development of sport is very closely linked to the history of the Olympic Games. At the first Olympic Games in 776 BCE, there were boxing, wrestling, running, chariot-racing, and discus- and javelin-throwing competitions.

It is recorded that for ten months prior to an Olympic Games competition, the athletes underwent intensive training under *gymnastes* and *paidotribes*. The *gymnastes* were more than likely medical physicians with a broad knowledge of sport, while the *paidotribes* were essentially the forerunners of modern physiotherapists.

From what I have studied about the early training programmes of these athletes, it appears that they ate little and adhered to a strict diet of figs, cheese, bread and milk or diluted wine. They ate no meat and very little fish. They also slept outdoors on animal skins and bathed in mountain streams. Imagine such a regimen for today's highly paid athletes!

In the sixth century BCE there was a shift as the heavyweight boxers and wrestlers began to consume meat. The identification of such unique requirements of athletes drove the early evolution of sports medicine, which today has become truly multidisciplinary, involving teams of specialists within and outside of the field of medicine. Indeed, the most successful modern sporting nations are those that understand the crucial value of this team approach to athlete preparation.

In modern sport, medical interest reached a major landmark at the 1928 Winter Olympics in Switzerland, when the International Federation of Sports Medicine (FIMS) was formed.

At the turn of the century, exercise scientists studied athletes purely to understand more fully the workings of the human body. There is no evidence of a desire to study techniques that would enhance human athletic performance. The nature of sport at this time was also one of restraint. The idea of gaining an advantage by any method, even training, was contrary to the strict amateur ethos of sport.

This is why, when in May 1954 Roger Bannister became the first man to run the mile in less than four minutes, he was training for less than an hour a day. For Bannister, running was merely a diversion from the more serious pursuit of his medical studies. That he also employed the services of a coach, Franz Stampfl, was highly unusual, as it was considered beneath the dignity of an amateur – from the British upper classes – like Bannister, to be told what to do by a professional – viewed as from the working class – like Stampfl. Bannister's genius, like that of British Olympic 100-metre gold medallist Harold Abrahams in 1924, who employed a coach three decades earlier, was in part his understanding that he could not achieve his real potential without the input of a coach.

At this time the likes of Czech runner Emil Zatopek were also challenging the old perception as their superior training ushered in an era of unprecedented athletic performances based on very intensive training.

Once the amateur code fell away, there were no longer any restraints on the invasion and subversion of sport by those willing to use whatever means necessary to improve their chances of winning. This included, of course, the development of performance-enhancing drugs.

THE FIRST STEROIDS AND AMPHETAMINES

The development of performance-enhancing drugs can be traced back to 1935, when the male testicular hormone, testosterone, was isolated for the first time, and the first synthetic anabolic steroid, designed to act like testosterone, became commercially available in Europe.

Amphetamines were widely used during World War II, particularly by bomber crews flying missions of more than twelve hours. Over nine million doses of amphetamines were used by British troops during the war; the soldiers knew that amphetamines improved performance. Returning veterans soon introduced amphetamines to sport in the United States, and perhaps also in England. No one believed that this was cheating, as amphetamines were as much a part of normal society as caffeine is today. Only when it was understood that this class of drug is addictive and creates more harm than good did distribution become tightly controlled. Today the amphetamines that were so freely available in the 1950s can be used by South African doctors only with the written permission of the president. Hence they are essentially unattainable.

In 1954, the American team physician at the World Weightlifting Championship in Vienna, Dr John Ziegler, correctly concluded that the Soviet weightlifters were using steroids. He returned to the US convinced that without their own locally produced steroid, US athletes would be at a disadvantage.

In 1958, the first synthetic steroid created in North America, Dianabol, was released on the commercial market. It was produced to ensure that Russian athletes did not have the competitive edge over US athletes in the Olympic Games.

It was the development of high-performance sport in the former East Germany, however, that really took the prescription of performance-enhancing drugs to athletes to the next level. A clandestine programme of providing drugs to uninformed athletes earned the condemnation of the world when it was uncovered after the fall of the Berlin Wall.

The 1968 Olympic Games in Mexico City was an epochal event in this process. East Germany competed for the first time as a nation separate from West Germany, and their emergence was a serious sporting threat to the leading Western nations, especially the United States.

The East Germans initiated programmes to develop anabolic steroids that, at the time, were undetectable. Those who ran sport then naively believed that athletes were too 'pure' to wish to dope. Western scientists were equally naive – they tried to discourage the use of steroids by suggesting that they do not improve performance. But the practical example provided by the East German athletes suggested otherwise. In any case, athletes talk among themselves. It would not have taken long for an exceptional and unexpected performance by a competitor to be analysed. If drugs were involved, all the athletes would know within a short time.

And so sport began its journey along the road to professionalism and to the drug ills that plague it to this day.

SPORT AND WAR

Sport shares many characteristics with war. William James, Harvard's nineteenth-century professor of psychology, described sport as the 'moral equivalent of war'. Indeed, just as war exposes fragile man to environmental conditions, psychological stresses and injuries the magnitude of which are seldom found in civilian medical practice, so too does sport. My professor of surgery once remarked, 'Through the ages the greatest surgical advances have always occurred during war.' Initially I struggled with this statement; my difficulty stems from my personality, which resembles that of a physician.

Physicians are built for contemplation, intellectualism and endless discussion. The danger of this is that, by the time the physician reaches a final diagnosis, the patient could have been buried. When I decided to study medicine, the family with whom I had lived for a year in California on the American Field Service programme sent me home with a wooden plaque that proclaimed: 'God heals. The doctor collects the fee.' The plaque has a special place in my office at work.

Surgeons, on the other hand, do not have the patience to wait for God to cure (or not to cure) the patient. As the first sports doctors, surgeons attended to the wounds of the Saturday-afternoon gladiators. By the early 1970s, sports medicine had became synonymous with the treatment of sporting injuries, especially by orthopaedic surgeons.

Gradually, and more rapidly in the past decade, sports medicine has moved from the practice exclusively of orthopaedic surgery on athletes to the application of medicine and science to improve an athlete's performance. As more people have become active, medical schools and universities have become increasingly populated with sports-minded students, some of whom remain on the staff as faculty.

Whereas the 1960s were characterised by the belief that, given the money, medical science could provide all the answers and solve all the world's medical problems, by the late 1970s it was clear that something else would be required. Infectious diseases (HIV/AIDS had yet to appear) had largely been conquered in the developed world, yet two diseases – heart disease and cancer – were on the rise. Today, obesity is equally prevalent. The idea that these new killers were the result of lifestyle choices made by humans each day began to take hold. It also became increasingly apparent that regular exercise may just be the single most potent moderator of lifestyle known to medicine.

At the same time, a new 'disease'– the 'disease of excellence' – emerged, a result of the growing national and international prestige accorded to outstanding sporting performances. Athletes were under pressure to train even harder, and they expected the same level of excellence from their doctors.

I believe that, without these demands from athletes, the achievement of many medical advances would have been greatly delayed. During the course of my career I've seen many instances where the relentless drive of the athlete has helped to push science and medicine beyond its traditional boundaries into realms that we cannot fully explain but from which we must learn.

Jeff Farrell, America's Olympic swimming champion of the 1960s, resumed training one day after an appendix operation, and five days later he qualified to compete for the American team at the 1960 Rome Olympics, where he won two gold medals.

Consider also Abebe Bikila, a double Olympic marathon champion from Ethiopia and the first black African to win a gold medal in the Olympics. At the 1964 Olympics in Tokyo, Bikila made history by becoming the first athlete to win the marathon in successive Olympic Games. Five weeks prior to this monumental achievement, Bikila had had his appendix removed.

Similarly, the winner of the first Olympic marathon for women, Joan Benoit, had undergone arthroscopic knee surgery just weeks before her winning performance in the 1984 Olympic Games in Los Angeles. Without the surgery she would not even have made it to the start of the race.

My friend George Sheehan managed to complete a one-mile run three days after a gall-bladder operation. Four weeks later he was back to full training; another two weeks and he was racing again.

As a result of these cases and cases like them, surgeons began to ask whether the body really does need six weeks of inactivity to allow 'full' recovery after surgery.

Probably the most compelling example from my own experience relates to the change in the medical care of those who have suffered an acute heart attack. When I was a hospital intern in 1975, a patient with this condition was considered beyond help, so the emphasis in treatment was to admit the patient to an intensive-care unit where his heart rhythms could be monitored beat by beat. Forgotten at the time was the work done in Boston showing that, if the diseased heart required a period of rest during this time, then it was better to sit upright in a chair next to the bed. Those intrepid Boston doctors had broken tradition and allowed their patients to be out of bed for a few hours a day, sitting in a chair. Over time, the doctors had found that this approach provided enormous psychological, as well as physical, benefits.

The next significant advance occurred in the early 1970s, when a group of doctors in Toronto, Canada, under the leadership of Dr Terry Kavanaugh, began training some heart-attack patients to run a forty-two-kilometre marathon – an unheard-of precedent. Under Kavanaugh's direction, a group of these patients completed the 1974 Boston Marathon without incident.

This was the spark that inspired me to become involved in cardiac rehabilitation and to assist in establishing one of the first such programmes in South Africa, in Cape Town, in 1978. Today that programme continues at the Sports Science Institute of South Africa under the direction of two of my colleagues, Professors Martin Schwellnus and Wayne Derman.

Today a heart attack is regarded as a relatively minor medical incident, the proper treatment of which requires that the patient become an athlete if he or she is not already one. Astonishing is the longevity of some of the patients who enter these programmes – twenty or thirty years on, these patients, now athletes, are still going strong. I have learnt that those who are or were athletes adapt more quickly and with less psychological distress to a heart attack than those who have not previously been active. In my view, heart-attack patients provide the strongest evidence for the value of lifelong physical activity.

My experience has also shown me that elite athletes are impatient when it comes to science and medicine: they demand answers that science often cannot provide. But, again, their demands lead to new discoveries.

Who would have thought that a fourteen-year-old would bring about the demise of plaster of Paris as a means of immobilising an injured limb? It was indeed a young Canadian swimmer who needed a leg cast that would not interfere with her preparation for the 1970 Commonwealth Games who inspired the development of a lightweight, water-resistant polyethylene/fibreglass cast. The new cast allowed her to train for five hours a day for the six months during which her leg healed.

The rapid advancements in knee surgery can also be attributed to elite athletes, who constantly demand to become mobile and competitive as soon as possible. While previously an athlete was sidelined for about three months following knee-cartilage surgery, this can now be limited to only a few days. The same applies to arthroscopic surgery (minimally invasive) for repair of anterior cruciate – or knee – ligament ruptures. The recovery time is shortened and athletes are back in competition far sooner. As recently as the 1980s, a skier or rugby player who ruptured his or her anterior cruciate ligament could expect to be immobilised for up to six months. Today, some athletes with this injury are back to sport within that time (although I am not convinced that such a rapid return is always ideal; a slightly longer recovery period is, in my view, probably wiser in the long run).

Sport has therefore played a major role in pushing the boundaries of modern medicine, albeit in the face of an often unwilling medical fraternity.

5 | The Role of the Doctor

I believe that doctors are sometimes guilty of treating the disease and ignoring the patient.

I once met a runner who had undergone chemotherapy for cancer of the lymph glands, Hodgkin's disease. It was clear from his explanation of the treatment that few experiences can tax the human spirit so dreadfully. He told me that only when all his hair had fallen out, his teeth rattled as he spoke and he had reached the spiritual doldrums did he arrive at an important crossroads: he could either lie down, feel sorry for himself, waste away and die, or rebuild on what he had left.

He went on to run three marathons. His physician kept telling him to slow down, but he told his physician, 'If I cannot run, I will fold up. Running confirms that I am still alive; that the cancer has not yet won.'

Patients like this have inspired me to ask the questions: What if God's design for that individual was to be a great runner? As physicians, do we always have enough knowledge to be sure that we are not tinkering with that design unnecessarily, that we are not imprisoning that person in a state of frustration? It is an awesome responsibility to decide when an individual's talent is a danger to his life. Are we not too keen to keep our patients abnormal rather than letting them live the normal lives to which they aspire? And who are we to prescribe the limits, particularly when it comes to exercise?

So the heart patient must not jog, the asthmatic child must not play rugby, the patient with chronic obstructive airways disease must sit around indoors.

Early in my career I understood that patients are best served by doctors who have first cured themselves of the doctor's disease – the pathological compulsion to cure. As George Sheehan observes, it is time for doctors to feel guilty not because we cannot save lives, but because we prevent our ill patients from living.

The diseased who become athletes have had a great influence on medicine: they have taught us that there is a healthy way to be ill.

Sheehan also notes that our chief failing as doctors is that we are too educated, yet, conversely, too ignorant. We know too much about disease and too little about health. We know everything about the limitations of the human body and not enough about its potential.

I always advise my students to be intelligent enough not to use just their brains. Our bodies know things that our brains will never comprehend; our bodies have knowledge that will never be written in textbooks. I have learnt that only during exercise do we reach areas of the brain that normally remain undiscovered.

The area most affected by disability is the mind. I know from my experience with patients that mental disability caused by disease is best fought with movement. Exercise may never be able to cure disease, but, undoubtedly, it can mend broken minds and heal beaten spirits. When medicine understands this, we will understand that there is no such thing as disability.

When I began my medical training in the early 1970s, I was reliably informed by my teachers that exercise was dangerous for human health. Since I seemed to feel better after exercise, I concluded that my teachers could not be trusted. So I learnt to challenge accepted wisdom and understand that beliefs change as theories are tested. One of the basic tenets of my medical career has been that, to succeed and come out on top, we must accept that life changes. As a consequence, we must always be open-minded enough to the possibility in science for a different outcome from the one we expect.

This was a lesson first taught to me by the life of an early-nineteenth-century Hungarian physician.

THE COURAGE TO EXPOSE THE TRUTH

Hungarian doctor Ignaz Semmelweis killed hundreds of young women, and yet he remains someone I admire.

While Semmelweis was working at the Viennese Maternity Hospital, the Allgemeines Krankenhaus, between August 1844 and March 1849, he proved that doctors and obstetricians were responsible for the spread of puerperal sepsis, more commonly known as childbed fever.

His proof occurred ten years before Louis Pasteur established that bacteria cause contagious diseases like puerperal sepsis, so Semmelweis had to reach his conclusions without knowing that bacteria existed.

Puerperal sepsis at that time was a common condition of mothers who had recently given birth. Then, the disease was the second most common cause of death among women of child-bearing age, after tuberculosis.

It was Semmelweis who made the shocking discovery that the obstetricians were responsible for the death of these women. He concluded that the transfer of 'cadaveric corpuscles' on the hands of obstetricians who performed autopsies on the bodies of mothers who had recently died from puerperal sepsis caused the same disease in pregnant women whom they then examined while in labour.

On their soiled and unwashed hands, the obstetricians of the Allgemeines Krankenhaus unwittingly carried the virulent bacteria from the recently dead to those about to bring forth life. It was one of those unhappy ironies that often occur in the world of science – in their bid to save lives, these doctors were actually the agents of death.

Semmelweis's sense of guilt was enormous. 'Because of my convictions,' he wrote, 'I must here confess that God only knows the number of patients that have gone prematurely to their graves by my fault.' Yet it required the mind of a genius to come to this conclusion. For when Semmelweis began working at the Allgemeines Krankenhaus, it was well known that the mortality from puerperal sepsis was quite different in Clinics I and II, which rotated on a daily basis their intakes of pregnant mothers about to give birth. The popular explanation was that the disease was caused by a mysterious contagion that travelled in the polluted air, a miasma. Yet Semmelweis wondered how a miasma present in the air could explain this difference in mortality rates in two hospital wards that existed side by side, within metres of each other. And how could the effect of the miasma change so predictably every twenty-four hours?

Eventually, by a series of brilliant deductions, he concluded that the difference in mortality was because the mothers in labour in Clinic I were attended by doctors and medical students who performed autopsies on the mothers that had recently died from puerperal sepsis. He theorised that, as a result, on their unwashed hands and grubby clothing the doctors carried some disease agent, now known to be the bacterium *Streptococcus pyogenes*, from the autopsy halls to the delivery ward. By contrast, the mothers in Clinic II were treated only by nursing sisters, none of whom attended these autopsies.

In time Semmelweis conducted one of the greatest clinical trials in the history of medicine. He instructed the doctors and medical students in Clinic I to wash their hands in chlorine before they examined a mother in labour. The names of those who examined each mother were also recorded, and a large notice, prominently displayed, warned that those attending mothers who subsequently contracted the disease would be held accountable for those deaths. Most importantly, he fastidiously recorded the mortality rates in both Clinics I and II, and it was that data that allowed us to draw up an iconic figure proving his genius.

FIGURE 1

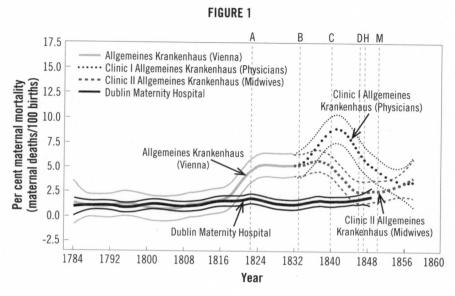

The bottom (dark) line records the average per cent maternal mortality (per 100 births) in the Dublin Maternity Hospital in the years from 1784 to 1849; the lines above and below the average line indicate the 95 per cent confidence band. The top lines are for the same measurements in the Allgemeines Krankenhaus (AKH) in Vienna between 1784 and 1848. The uppermost line (with 95 per cent confidence band) after 1832 is for Clinic I, the middle line thereafter (with 95 per cent confidence band) is for Clinic II. A: January 1823, appointment of Professor Johann Klein as professor of obstetrics in charge of the AKH. B: January 1833, obstetric services at the AKH split into Clinics I and II. C: 19 October 1840, staffing at the AKH split by gender, with males (physicians) in Clinic I and females (midwives) in Clinic II. D: 27 February 1846, Semmelweis is promoted to provisional assistant in Clinic I. H: Late May, Semmelweis introduces chlorine washings to Clinic I. M: 15 October, Semmelweis leaves Vienna for Budapest, where he is appointed honorary senior physician at St Rochus Hospital. Note that the rise in the mortality rate at the AKH begins after 1823, when Professor Klein introduced regular autopsies on deceased mothers for the first time. After the introduction of the two clinics, the mortality rate is less in Clinic II, staffed only my midwives, but the introduction of chlorine washings reduces the mortality rate in Clinic I. This reduction continued while Semmelweis was still working at the AKH (reproduced from Noakes, Borreson and Hew-Butler, 2008).

Semmelweis, however, is one of the tragic figures in medicine. Although he used scientific methods to prove his hypothesis, he failed to convince his colleagues of the truth of it, partly because he did not describe his findings as soon as he had made them. As a result, his proven idea was not accepted for decades – decades when young women continued to die needlessly. Frustrated, Semmelweis became increasingly antagonistic and dismissive of his colleagues. He regarded those who did not adopt his hygienic methods – in particular washing their hands in chlorine before they examined their patients in labour – as nothing better than common criminals. What he knew to be both true and lifesaving was not accepted nor immediately practised by his obstetrical colleagues, and hundreds of thousands of young women were condemned to death by a refusal to listen to a new idea. Sadly, Semmelweis slipped progressively into dementia.

His family had him incarcerated in a state-run asylum for the insane, where he died on 13 August 1865 at the age of forty-seven. His death was probably caused by a disseminated infection brought on by the very bacteria against which he had tried to warn the world's obstetricians. The infection occurred because of wounds he had sustained when assaulted in the asylum.

So why my admiration for a doctor who unwittingly led thousands of young women to their deaths and died alone and insane in a mental asylum?

It is because both his genius and his flaws are so apparent. For me, Semmelweis proved that failure, and not success, is the more honest tutor, and that without exposure we cannot move towards a solution. As Semmelweis put it, 'No matter how painful and oppressive such a recognition may be, the remedy does not lie in suppression. If the misfortune is not to persist forever, then this truth must be made known to everyone concerned.'

Too often science screams out an obvious answer or solution, only to be ignored. Semmelweis had the courage to expose his truth at whatever cost. But he failed, because those who needed to hear his message did not listen. The Semmelweis story teaches us that unless your message is heard, your work is of no consequence.

Semmelweis's experience is not unique, then or now. The Australian Dr Barry Marshall, who began his training in the same year as I did and whose initial medical interest was in heatstroke in runners, proved in 1984 that a specific bacterium, *Helicobacter pylori*, causes ulceration of the stomach and duodenum. Marshall would have been taught, as I was in Cape Town in the 1970s, that stomach ulcers are caused by stress and by excessive stomach acidity and are essentially incurable. Palliative treatment included surgery and a lifelong prescription of drugs that reduced the amount of acid secreted by the stomach. Since the condition was incurable, these palliative drugs provided the ultimate pharmaceutical dream, as they had to be used throughout a patient's lifetime. The drugs' manufacturers did not wish to see a guaranteed income stream slashed by the inconvenient finding of an Antipodean upstart who fell outside the North American–European axis of knowledge.

As a result, it was a decade before Dr Marshall's finding became the accepted medical practice, and only in 2005, twenty-one years after his original discovery, was he was awarded the Nobel Prize in Medicine.

There are, however, those scientists who choose to ignore the truth. In some cases it has to do with egos and lengthy intellectual battles. But I have also witnessed the nefarious side, when overriding commercial interests encourage scientists to ignore the facts or to ensure that an alternative message will not be heard. At best, this is unethical. At worst, it is dangerous and leads to unnecessary deaths.

part two

WATERLOGGED

'Man can sweat like a horse but cannot drink like one' — E.C. SCOTT

6 | A Global Obsession

We are obsessed with water. Just take a look around you: bottled water is the new craze. Our culture has seen hydration move from a biological necessity driven by internal biological signals to a fashion trend. Everyone is drinking. Why?

Well, quite simply, it is because we are told every day by the health and fitness industry that our bodies crave fluid, that we need to drink eight big glasses of water a day to be healthy, and that if we become thirsty during exercise we are already dehydrated and at risk because we have left drinking too late.

But where's the proof?

There isn't any. In fact, dehydration is a normal physical state. Drinking to excess is far more dangerous to your health than delaying drinking and waiting until your thirst tells you that you need to drink.

A short history lesson on how the human body evolved on the hot and arid African savannah will help in understanding this.

BORN TO RUN

Our species, *Homo sapiens*, split from the last common ancestor shared with the great African apes about seven million years ago. Indeed, Charles Darwin, unquestionably the most important biologist of all time, predicted that man must have evolved in Africa, since our closest mammalian relatives – the chimpanzees, bonobos and gorillas – are found only on the African continent. What he did not describe were the specific activities that made humans become human. Were it not for these activities, humans would have evolved along the branch that led to chimpanzees.

There are two crucial physiological differences that decided our differing evolutionary trajectories over the past seven million years:

1. Human's ability to run long distances at a moderate pace.
2. Human's ability to maintain a safe body temperature when exercising in extreme dry heat.

Over the past decade, evidence has accumulated that supports a theory that might perhaps have astonished even Darwin – that nature has equipped humans with all the tools they need to be the best hot-weather distance runners of all species on the planet.

To understand this process, we need to begin at the 'starting line' of the race that produced humans.

Evolutionary edge no. 1 – bipedalism

Roughly seven million years ago, the common ancestor of humans and chimpanzees stood upright. We know this thanks to the work of anthropologist Tim White and his team, who in 1994 uncovered the remarkable skeleton of *Ardipithecus ramidus* in the Awash region of Ethiopia.

Unexpectedly, more than four million years ago *Ardipithecus* walked on two legs, but was still an adept tree climber. This establishes that the most likely last common ancestor of chimpanzees and humans walked upright, which in turn means that chimpanzees moved from walking upright, or bipedalism, to what they do now – knuckle-walking – whereas humans became increasingly competent walkers and ultimately the world's most effective endurance runners.

As humans we differentiate ourselves by standing upright. At first it was thought that we had evolved to stand on two legs simply as a means to free our hands, which would then be used to fashion stone tools or weapons, or carry food or our offspring. This is an obvious benefit. But as the climate of eastern and southern Africa changed three to four million years ago, our ancestors moved from the security of the forests to the baking heat of the open savannah. This move produced two more reasons that favoured bipedalism.

First, bipedalism reduces the surface area exposed to the direct heat of the sun. It also raises the body into a cooler microclimate above the level of the surrounding vegetation, where there is an increased airflow. The cooler air drifting over our skin is heated up, thereby removing heat from our bodies in a process known as convection. So, to keep cooler in the hot sun of the African savannah, we needed to stand upright.

Second, bipedalism allowed us to become more effective runners, which, as Professor Raymond Dart noted in 1959, was of great evolutionary value in the environment of 'a more open veld country where competition was keener between swiftness and stealth, and where adroitness of thinking and movement played a preponderating role in the preservation of the species'. *Ardipithecus* walked upright, but would have been a poor runner because his lower limbs, pelvis and muscles were not yet adapted for walking and running. Four million years later, *Homo sapiens*, the direct descendant of *Ardipithecus*, is an extraordinarily graceful runner, as is visible whenever we watch the languid African distance runners.

Evolutionary edge no. 2 – sweat

The second important evolutionary development was that, of all the creatures on the earth, we became the animal with the most prodigious sweating capacity. Sweating is the most effective mechanism to remove heat from the body, especially the heat generated during exercise.

When you begin to exercise, the blood flow to your muscles increases. As the blood passes through your muscles, it is heated up. This heat is then distributed throughout your body, but especially to your skin. Your hotter skin then offloads its heat by convection, and by sweating, which is the process of evaporating water (as steam) secreted from the sweat glands. Relatively few mammals sweat. Baboons, horses, donkeys, camels and certain large antelope, such as the eland and oryx, do sweat, but none more so than humans.

This occurs because humans have a greater concentration of sweat glands in the skin than any other mammal. There has to be a reason for our large number of sweat glands. *Ardipithecus ramidus* would not have had as many sweat glands; chimpanzees, in fact, do not sweat, so they are unable to survive in climates in which the air temperature exceeds 38 °C. Some crucial event therefore occurred after the appearance of *Ardipithecus* that produced this extraordinary sweating capacity in *Homo sapiens*. Logic says that it had to be the need to lose great amounts of body heat. Simply living in hot conditions would not be sufficient to drive this development – if it were, chimpanzees would have the same capacity to sweat as modern humans have.

The key is that when mammals exercise, they generate heat in proportion to their body mass and the speed at which they are travelling.

Thus, the moment humans begin to exercise, they produce much more heat than they do when they are at rest. The faster they run, the more they need to sweat if they are to maintain safe body temperatures and not fall victim to heatstroke. Humans can survive in relatively hot environments without the need to sweat as much as they can, but once they start to exercise more vigorously, especially in the heat, they need to sweat more, in proportion to how fast they run.

The converse of this is that, because humans evolved this magnificent sweating capacity, they are able to survive in resting conditions at temperatures that appear to be impossible to survive.

Smaller mammals generate less heat and therefore need to lose less water by either panting or sweating to maintain a safe body temperature. Look at the elite distance runners of today, most of whom are physically small, weighing about fifty to fifty-five kilograms – not much bigger than *Ardipithecus*. Being smaller is definitely a major advantage during exercise in the heat.

The potential downside of sweating is that it promotes the loss of fluid and electrolytes, especially sodium chloride (salt). But the benefits of sweating in allowing humans to exercise safely, even in extreme dry heat, far outweigh any risks associated with these losses. In fact, we evolved an almost fail-safe mechanism to ensure that we do not endanger ourselves during exercise. We become thirsty and develop sensations of fatigue, including the feeling of unbearable hotness, when running in the heat and direct sunlight. These sensations cause us to slow down and ultimately to stop exercising, although our body temperatures are still within the safe range and all our other bodily systems are still functioning appropriately.

So although humans need both salt and water on a daily basis to survive, since both are lost in sweat, we do not need to replace those losses the instant they develop during exercise. Our complex battery of mechanisms allows us to replace them after exercise, when we have the opportunity to eat and drink without restraint.

Evolutionary edge no. 3 – no fur
The third advantage humans have over other mammals is an absence of fur. This allows an increased capacity to lose heat from the skin by either convection or sweating.

The disadvantage of having no fur is that it reduces our ability to reflect the sun's rays. As a result, humans absorb more radiant heat from the sun and the environment than, for example, antelope with light-coloured reflective fur, like the camel or oryx. As mentioned, however, standing upright reduces the area of our bodies exposed to this radiant heat load.

But the ability to sweat more efficiently and to lower the skin temperature more effectively during exercise in the heat outweighs any small disadvantage posed by the absence of the furry coating of our ancestors.

Evolutionary edge no. 4 – a brain that protects us from heat injury
The unmatched ability of humans to live in so many diverse environmental

conditions – from the heat of the desert to the cold of the Arctic – is due to many factors, the most important of which is that we can maintain an almost constant internal environment regardless of what is happening on the outside of our bodies. A large component of this ability is that we modify our behaviour when we are exposed to taxing environmental conditions – we are less active in the heat than in the cold, and we also wear less clothing. The modification of our behaviour to regulate our body temperatures is termed 'behavioural thermoregulation'. Naturally, it is the brain that ensures that these behaviours are appropriate for the environmental conditions, and it is the brain that protects us from damage.

During exercise in the heat, the brain ensures that we only ever exercise at an intensity and for a duration that won't allow our body temperature to rise to a dangerous level. It does this by calculating exactly the acceptable rate of heat production by the muscles. The brain then chooses the appropriate sweat rate that will keep the body cooled during the exercise.

If these systems should make an error and allow the body temperature to rise to 42 °C or higher, the condition of 'hyperthermic paralysis' develops. With this condition, the brain simply refuses to direct the legs to continue exercising; the athlete feels as if he or she is paralysed and is unable to continue.

The remarkable success of the sports-drink and bottled-water industries over the past twenty years has been based largely on their ability to market the opposite theory – specifically that humans are very poorly adapted for exercise in the heat and that they lack biological controls to ensure that they do not overtax themselves during exercise. Instead, unless they force themselves to drink 'as much as tolerable' (a phrase used in a 1996 volume of *Medicine & Science in Sports & Exercise*, the official journal of the American College of Sports Medicine), they will become 'dangerously dehydrated' and at risk of dying from heatstroke every time they exercise. Had this been the case, *Homo sapiens* would never have evolved from *Ardipithecus ramidus*.

HUMANS ARE HUMANS BECAUSE WE ARE DESIGNED TO RUN IN THE HEAT

It is necessary to understand that it is not alien for humans to run long distances in extreme heat. If we had not developed as hot-weather runners, we would not be human.

Part of the proof of this, as pointed out by D.M. Bramble and D.E. Lieberman, is an obvious indicator of our humanness – our legs. Relative to our body weight, humans have the longest legs of any species. Our legs are also relatively thin, reducing the energy cost of using them. In addition, we have 'springs' in our legs – long, spring-like tendons attached to short muscles – that allow energy to be alternatively stored and released with each stride as we run.

Running does indeed expose the joints to loading stresses when landing, but this is reduced by increased joint surfaces. Humans have substantially larger joint surface areas than chimpanzees, for instance.

We also have the ability to keep our centre of mass stable by rotating the upper body while stabilising the head and neck when both feet are off the ground. This occurs in running, but not in walking. Thus the fact that humans are able to rotate their upper bodies (to hit a golf, tennis or cricket ball, for example) while our nearest living relatives – chimpanzees and gorillas – cannot, surely indicates that the development of this ability became a crucial difference that drove our subsequent evolution. The only factor that could have compelled this was the need for evolving humans to become expert runners.

We are obviously less stable when running, so our body requires additional muscular stabilisation, including well-developed back muscles, the action of the uniquely human gluteus maximus muscle (the buttock muscle), and the necessary brain controls to maintain balance and prevent falling when running.

We also need to be able to maintain balance when one of our legs is off the ground while running. Again, evolutionary pressures ensured the optimum solution. When running, we instinctively swing the opposite arm independently of the pectoral girdle (the two shoulder blades and collarbones) while keeping the head still.

We have enlarged sensory organs in the ear to improve the sensitivity of the reflexes that control the rapid pitching movements that we encounter when we run. These forces do not develop when we walk, again confirming that it was the specific need to run, not to walk, that drove that change. Without these nervous controls, humans would be unable to perform acrobatic feats in gymnastics, surfing or other similar activities.

Another important part of our physiology is that we drink frequently in small amounts, and, as discussed earlier, can delay this need to drink until after the exercise bout ends. Indeed, humans are able to delay the onset of thirst. We drink the most fluid when we eat, especially at the evening meal.

A smaller stomach and intestine than most mammals means that humans cannot drink large volumes of fluid quickly. A camel can drink 100 litres of fluid in ten minutes and a donkey can consume ten to twelve litres in five minutes. Humans, by contrast, can usually drink about one litre in ten minutes.

So the evidence becomes increasingly clear: humans evolved to be extremely adept long-distance runners with an unmatched ability to regulate their body temperatures when exercising in the heat. And our brains developed the ability to delay the need to drink – a crucial adaptation if we were to chase after our potential meals in the midday heat when there was little water available and no time to stop the hunt to search for fluid. Any time spent searching for water would mean the difference between a successful and a failed hunt.

If you remain sceptical, let me take you on a typical hunt with a !Xo San hunter, drawn from the research of Dr Louis Liebenberg, who began studying the !Xo San hunters in 1985. What follows is based on two research papers by Dr Liebenberg, 'Persistence hunting by modern hunter-gatherers' (2006) and 'The relevance of persistence hunting to human evolution' (2008).

The hunters wait until mid-morning, when the temperature exceeds 40 °C and when a human's superior ability to maintain a safe body temperature while jogging for four or more hours in hot conditions gives our species the one unique biological advantage over the antelope.

The hunters follow an antelope, never allowing it to stop for sufficiently long to cool its body temperature by panting. Eventually, an animal suffering from hyperthermic paralysis becomes too hot to continue. Only when it is in that condition of complete paralysis are the small, unarmed humans able to throttle the exhausted animal to death without the risk of being impaled on its horns. (It was only about 400 000 years ago that humans first developed spears – until then, they killed large antelope with their bare hands.)

In his study of just under a dozen hunts, Dr Liebenberg found that most hunts lasted from two to almost seven hours in temperatures ranging from 32 °C to 42 °C, covering distances from seventeen to thirty-five kilometres at running speeds ranging from four to ten kilometres per hour.

In the film *The Great Dance*, produced by the Cape Town brothers Craig and Damon Foster, one of the last surviving !Xo San hunters, Karoha Langwane, ran in the Kalahari Desert for six hours in 40 °C to 46 °C heat with no cloud cover but in low humidity. He ran barefoot and covered approximately thirty kilometres. During the hunt, Langwane drank a total of about one litre of fluid.

Langwane did not die from either dehydration or heatstroke, nor did he describe any significant symptoms other than thirst.

Yet at least three female marathon runners in the United States, running in cool conditions with free access to all the fluid each would ever need, died from a disease – exercise-associated hyponatraemia (EAH), which I was the first to describe in 1981. Their deaths, we subsequently proved, were caused because they had drunk too much.

The lesson is a simple one: humans have the greatest capacity of all mammals to run in extreme dry heat without drinking much. Since evolution designed our bodies to function in this way, all we have to do is listen to our bodies rather than to those who wish to sell us a product on the premise that humans are fragile beings. We are not. If we were, we would not be here in the first place.

Considering all the evolutionary evidence indicating how perfectly designed the human body is to push itself to the limit of human endurance in hot-weather conditions, imagine the challenge faced by the manufacturers of sports drinks and bottled water, who must convince athletes that they need to drink regularly – even during exercise lasting only a few minutes – if they are to avoid severe injury, or possibly death. Once the evolutionary drives that made humans human are understood, it becomes more difficult to fall for the marketing deceptions that have been promoted by these industries for the past twenty years.

7 | The Science of Hydration

THE 'SCIENCE' BEHIND A DEADLY NEW DISEASE – THE NOVEL 'SCIENCE OF HYDRATION'

It is important to understand how scientists generate new knowledge and how we distinguish what is possibly true from what is false.

The key difference between science and marketing is that scientists try to discover the answer to an unsolved question, while marketers already know the answer; their function is to convince the consumer of the truth of that answer. Often pseudo-science is used to 'prove' that marketing claims are valid.

In the past thirty years I have frequently been asked to promote a new (legal) 'wonder product' that is allegedly about to revolutionise human exercise performance. You would think that by now I must have encountered thousands of such miracle products. The truth is that I have discovered only two that really work: training and a well-balanced diet, with added water and carbohydrate during prolonged exercise. Not much else comes close. However, this is not what we are conditioned to believe. So how do we decide whether or not claims for a miracle product are valid?

Many miracle products cite the opinions of one or more celebrities who enthusiastically describe the miraculous transformation they have experienced when using a product. The more important the celebrity, the more valuable the product is perceived to be. But this kind of advertising has no scientific validity. First, the celebrity appearance is nothing more than a paid commercial. Second, the placebo effect must be considered. Much of the effect of any intervention is determined by a person's subconscious belief in the outcome. Provided they believe in the powers of what they are using, between 30 and 50 per cent of patients will benefit equally from either an inactive powder or the supposed miracle product. Doctors and scientists cannot explain this fully, but it is an essential part of our human biology. Third, we are all unique. So, even if the miracle product really does work for David Beckham, Tiger Woods or Sachin Tendulkar, it does not mean that it will work for everyone.

The role of science is to determine whether a product will be more likely than chance to produce a measurable (and desirable) outcome without the development of side effects when tested on a cross-section of the normal population. To this end, a population of research subjects is recruited. Half of the group is randomly assigned to receive an inactive placebo, and the other identical half receives the miracle product. All are then studied for the duration of the trial. If the group receiving the miracle product experiences a significantly more favourable outcome than the placebo group without reporting significant side effects, the product is effective. The scientists then report their findings in an independent scientific journal of standing and the marketers of the product are free to make any claims supported by the scientific evidence.

The scientific message is often confused by the appearance of the 'scientific' celebrity. In his definitive book *Bad Science*, which describes the misuse of modern science, Dr Ben Goldacre takes issue with two such celebrities who ply their trade in South Africa: Matthias Rath, who claimed that the multivitamins produced by his company cure HIV/AIDS, and Patrick Holford, author of a series of bestselling books on 'nutritionism'. Goldacre finds that Holford does not have a formal degree in nutritional science nor any academic standing as a scientist. Nor does he undertake randomised, placebo-controlled clinical trials on all the topics about which he claims expertise. Holford's main thesis is that many human health problems result from nutritional deficiencies that can be cured by products, at least some of which are produced by companies with which he has a commercial link.

So whom to believe? The best advice is the following: be sceptical about any claim made for a miracle product. The only claims that are valid are those that have been published in reputable independent scientific journals.

That so many people still believe the marketers regardless of the science was again confirmed by the recent global success of 'power band' bracelets. Only in the face of overwhelming legal pressure did the manufacturers admit that there was no scientific evidence behind their claims that the product produced miraculous effects by improving the body's balance and power.

It seems as if, beginning in the 1980s, the sports-drink industry may have followed the defining dictum of the pharmaceutical industry, which is to develop a disease for which a company produces the only known cure. So the industry perpetuated the concept of a disease called 'dehydration', for which they provided the cure – a sports drink to be drunk 'as much as tolerable'. Their collective greed knew no bounds – at one point, Susan Wellington, a senior executive of Quaker Oats, then manufacturers of the most successful sports drink in the world, Gatorade, wrote: 'When we're done, tap water will be relegated to showers and washing dishes.' Perhaps she spoke too soon!

For a start, 'dehydration' is not a medical condition; it is not a disease that produces a whole spectrum of symptoms. Dehydration is simply a physiological term indicating a reduction in the amount of water in the body – the total body water (TBW) content.

When the reduction in body water causes the sodium concentration of the blood to rise, the brain detects this change and develops the symptom of thirst. Thus, the sole consequence of dehydration is to make you thirsty. Only if you live in an environment where there is insufficient water available – for example in the desert or at sea – can the body's water loss become so large that it is life-threatening.

What the US sports-drink industry seems to have achieved over the past twenty years is to convince the world that even in a place where there is enough fluid available to drown all the participants – such as in big marathons like the Boston, Chicago and Marine Corps Marathons – 'dehydration' is the single greatest danger to your health. So they developed what I have called the 'zero per cent dehydration rule', which encourages athletes to believe that if they lose even a gram of water during these marathon races, they are likely to die from heatstroke or develop overwhelming muscle cramps.

Instead, those who follow that advice put themselves at risk of developing exercise-associated hyponatraemia (EAH).

So, what does EAH really involve, and why is it so deadly?

THE ABC OF EAH

EAH occurs when the body retains too much water. There is no other cause. In all creatures the blood sodium concentration is controlled within a very narrow range. If this value is too high because the TBW is too low, the cells become parched. The body develops intolerable thirst and, if fluid is available, the affected individual will drink until his or her thirst is slaked. But if the blood sodium concentration falls too low in those who overdrink, the cells take up water and increase their volume, becoming 'waterlogged'.

Not everyone who drinks to excess develops EAH; fortunately, most people simply excrete the excess fluid. But in a small proportion – perhaps 30 per cent of those who overdrink – the fluid is retained. This occurs because the regulation of the TBW in these individuals is faulty – their brains continue to believe that they are becoming 'dehydrated', even as their cells become increasingly waterlogged. In these individuals, the hormone of water conservation, antidiuretic hormone (ADH), continues to be secreted when its production should be turned off. ADH is perhaps the most powerful hormone in the human body. At a concentration of three-trillionth of a gram per 100 millilitres of blood, it is able to suppress all water excretion by the human kidney.

This powerful hormone is also a relic of our recent evolution on the arid African savannah. Once we had developed the capacity to sweat profusely, and thus potentially to waste water at fast rates during exercise, we needed to keep the potential water losses from the kidney to a minimum. ADH was the solution. But for some humans, this solution is faulty. It is exposed when they have access to too much fluid and have been told to drink as much as possible during exercise, especially marathon running.

So in these unfortunate individuals, the excessive fluid they ingest in order to avoid 'dehydration' accumulates in the blood, in the fluid surrounding the cells and inside the cells. The increase in their TBW content causes the body's sodium content to fall. Once this happens, water moves into the body's cells, causing them to swell. It's quite obvious that ingesting even more fluid in this state will only worsen the problem.

The cells of the brain are much more resistant to shrinking than they are to swelling. As the blood sodium concentration falls and the brain cells swell, their function becomes progressively impaired. The increase in cell size causes an increase of pressure inside the skull, which gradually occludes (causes to become closed or obstructs) the veins that drain blood away from the brain, increasing the rate at which the brain swells. Then the pressure rises above the pressure present in some small arteries, preventing blood flow to critical brain areas, including the centres that control breathing and the heartbeat. This can cause the patient to stop breathing. If this does not occur, ultimately the soggy brain cannot be constrained within the skull and a small part bulges out, or herniates, through the opening at the base of the skull through which the spinal cord leaves the brain. Once this happens, the outcome is irreversible and death occurs quickly.

Faced with these uncomfortable facts, the sports-drink industry began to argue that EAH was not caused by overdrinking but rather by large sodium losses in 'salty sweaters', as E.R. Eichner put it. But sweating alone cannot cause

EAH due to significant salt loss, because the amount of salt lost during any bout of acute exercise is simply too little to make a difference. Why would the body allow an excessive sodium loss during exercise if such a loss had the potential to cause a catastrophic biological failure? We evolved the biological mechanisms to survive the stress of running prodigious distances in the heat without needing vast amounts of salt and water as we run. Instead, our evolution did not prepare us to cope with excessive fluid consumption during exercise. That is the real killer.

So, while EAH can cause you to lose consciousness during exercise, the only true 'symptom' of dehydration is thirst. If this thirst cannot be quenched, the body activates a series of emergency procedures that prolong life for as long as possible. Ultimately, though, if sufficient fluid is not ingested, death will occur as a result of a failure of the major bodily organs. This time frame is usually after two to three days without water in hot conditions. Death, therefore, results not from dehydration but from a failure of these major organs in their attempt to prolong life.

When you drink in response to thirst, receptors in the back of your mouth and gullet, and particularly in your stomach, detect how much fluid has been ingested. Once the stomach is filled, the brain's desire to drink is turned off temporarily but resumes as the stomach empties. Eventually, enough fluid has been ingested to return the blood sodium concentration to the normal range, at which time thirst is slaked and drinking terminates.

One wonders whether the US sports-drink industry funded the Gatorade Sports Science Institute (GSSI) and its associated scientists with the aim of developing the theory that dehydration is a disease. Their most remarkable achievement, and that of the entire sports-drink industry, has been to convince all the world's athletes that 'deadly dehydration' occurs not only if you are stranded in the desert for forty-eight hours or longer without water – the traditional understanding – but even if you exercise for only a few minutes in an air-conditioned gym surrounded by abundant water fonts – not to mention what might happen when you are running in a major city marathon with access to unlimited free fluid.

Notably, marathon athletes rarely complain of incapacitating thirst. Surely if they are as dehydrated as the sports-drink industry would have us believe, they must have an all-consuming desire to drink?

THE DEHYDRATION MYTH

After ten to fifteen years of astronomical growth, those in the sports-drink industry never imagined that it could end.

But it eventually had to, as science is always self-correcting. It may take ten or twenty years, or even a century, but eventually someone discovers the truth. The twin themes of 'dehydration' and 'heatstroke' were the two pillars upon which the US sports-drink industry based its commercial success. To succeed, they had to popularise false concepts of the causes of these conditions. Unfortunately, two South Africans contributed to this misunderstanding.

In 1969, a scientific paper by C.H. Wyndham and N.B. Strydom was published. It became a classic in the field and one on which the sports-drink industry based, in part, its advertising spin that dehydration is dangerous and can be avoided only by those who drink constantly during exercise.

Physiologists Cyril Wyndham and Nick Strydom, both working for the Chamber of Mines in Johannesburg, used their experience of miners working in hot conditions underground to advance a theory that marathon runners who fail to drink during exercise risk serious health consequences. Both were employed specifically to ensure that South African miners can work safely in hot underground mines without the risk of developing heatstroke. They achieved remarkable success, as, through their work, the incidence of heatstroke in South African mines reduced dramatically.

But they made a critical error when they tried to apply this research to runners.

They based their conclusions on a study of runners who had completed a thirty-two-kilometre race with different levels of weight loss, hence dehydration, because of differences in sweat losses and drinking rates. They found that those who had lost the most weight, and were therefore the most 'dehydrated', had the highest body temperatures.

So Wyndham and Strydom concluded that the two findings must be linked. In their long and illustrious academic careers, this was their biggest mistake. The problem was that the design of the experiment did not allow them to draw this conclusion. Sadly, their incorrect conclusion allowed the industry to promote a false model of physiology. As we shall see, if the model is wrong, so is the 'truth' it supports.

Wyndham and Strydom concluded that sweat losses during exercise led to dehydration, which, unless countered by adequate drinking, would ultimately cause the body temperature to rise until it was so high that the life-threatening condition of heatstroke would develop.

As they were among the world's most respected experts in the field of exercise in the heat, we all initially believed them. Only when we tried to reproduce their findings in studies completed between 1985 and 1988 did I begin to understand

FIGURE 2

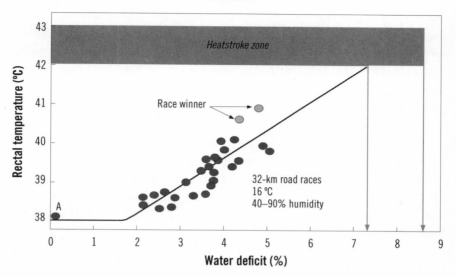

The iconic study of Wyndham and Strydom apparently found a causal relationship between increasing levels of weight loss and higher post-race rectal temperatures in runners completing two thirty-two-kilometre running races. But a study of this cross-sectional design cannot prove causation, since no variable other than the distance run was controlled in this study. There are therefore any number of explanations, other than dehydration, for the higher post-race rectal temperatures in those runners who also lost the most weight. Note also that the athlete who won both races had the highest post-race rectal temperature and was among the most dehydrated. This argues against the theory that dehydration and an elevated body temperature impairs running performance. In fact, the opposite might be true – losing weight might aid performance during weight-bearing activities like running, whereas the higher body temperature may simply be the result of running faster.

that their experimental design did not permit them to draw the conclusions that they did, and that the human physiology does not work in the way in which they described it.

But in the early 1970s, when I was an impressionable medical student, Wyndham and Strydom's message influenced my thinking, and I considered it my personal responsibility to safeguard all runners against the life-threatening disease that these experts had described.

I supported their theory in an article I wrote in my final year as a medical student, saying, 'The prime object of the marathon runner must be to avoid dehydration by drinking adequately during a run.' And the more my own running progressed, to the point where I competed in my first ninety-kilometre Comrades Marathon in 1973, the more convinced I became that runners must be encouraged – even forced – to drink more during exercise. Eight years later, in an article on how to 'improve the perfect peak', I wrote, 'The fourth performance aid is to drink everything in sight during the race.'

It was the last time I would ever be so certain of my opinion, for within months of the publication of that article, I had a life-changing experience that would ultimately define a good part of my future scientific career.

Why were Wyndham and Strydom so wrong? Well, for a start, they failed to notice that in the seventy-one years since the first official marathon at the 1896 Olympic Games in Athens, there had been very few cases of heatstroke in endurance athletes. Most of these cases occurred in athletes who were using performance-enhancing drugs, especially amphetamines. We now know that the controlling function of brain centres that regulates our performance during exercise and that specifically causes us to slow down when we are becoming too hot are inhibited by these drugs. So an athlete using amphetamines does not experience the usual symptoms that make us slow down should our body temperatures begin to rise excessively during exercise.

I have searched for documented cases of heatstroke in marathon runners prior to 1975, when marathoners were being advised not to drink during exercise, and I could trace only three cases. Since then there have been just three other cases reported, one by us.

But in 1988, in a single short-distance race – the eleven-kilometre Falmouth Road Race run in summer heat in Massachusetts, USA – there were nine reported cases of heatstroke. Earlier, in 1981, I personally treated four cases of heatstroke in the National Cross Country Championship in Cape Town. It is therefore not that heatstroke does *not* occur in runners – it does. But it typically occurs in runners running intensively for short distances, usually in the heat, for less than an hour. Because they have run for less than an hour, they cannot have developed 'dangerous dehydration' in such a short time, so something other than dehydration causes all cases of heatstroke in short-distance races. Conveniently, the sports-drink industry did not tell us that fact as they generated the myth that would bolster the commercial success of their product.

There is no – nor has there ever been – scientific evidence to support the claim that heatstroke is caused by dehydration, and that frequent drinking during exercise will ensure that heatstroke does not develop. Instead, the evidence has always been crystal clear – heatstroke, a complex and often fatal medical condition, almost never occurs during prolonged exercise. It is exercise performed at a high intensity for thirty to sixty minutes that produces almost all cases of heatstroke, whether in runners or in soldiers, the two groups of people in which most cases of heatstroke occur.

I was forced to consider this paradox when I served as the medical officer at the South African National Cross Country Championship held in September 1981 on an uncommonly hot Cape Town day. Three male athletes collapsed, unconscious, after the senior twelve-kilometre race. A female runner collapsed after she had run only four kilometres. All of them recovered, but I began to question how dehydration could be an important cause of heatstroke, as Wyndham and Strydom had proposed, since none of these runners could possibly have become 'dangerously dehydrated' after running for only twenty to forty minutes. The key, I concluded, was that they were running very fast. This, rather than the absence of drinking, was the real cause of their heatstroke.

WHAT SOME OF THE GREATEST ATHLETES HAVE TAUGHT ME ABOUT DRINKING

I have studied extensively the writings of some of the world's greatest distance runners on the subject of drinking during exercise. I have also been privileged to advise some elite runners on this subject.

The American Joseph Forshaw, who finished third in the 1908 London Olympic Marathon in a time of 2 hours, 57 minutes and 10 seconds, said, 'I know from actual experience that the full [marathon] race can be covered in credible time without so much as a single drop of water being taken or even sponging of the head.'

Another American runner, Matthew Maloney, who established a world record of 2 hours, 36 minutes and 26 seconds in the 1908 New York Evening Journal Christmas marathon, wrote: 'As to what I use when in a Marathon race: I only chew gum. I take no drink at all …'

South African resident Arthur Newton, who reinvigorated interest in ultramarathon running in the 1920s and who won the Comrades Marathon five times and set world records at distances of thirty to a hundred miles (the equivalent of 48 to 160 kilometres), as well as the world twenty-four-hour running record, stated, 'You can't lay down a hard and fast rule [about fluid ingestion during exercise]. Even in the warmest English weather, a 26-mile run ought to be manageable with no more than a single drink or, at most, two.'

The former world-record holder in the forty-two-kilometre marathon and arguably the greatest marathoner of all time, Jim Peters, wrote, 'In the marathon race ... every effort should also be made to do without liquid.'

South African Jackie Mekler finished second in the 1954 British Commonwealth and Empire Games marathon in Vancouver, won the Comrades Marathon five times and set world track-running records at distances of forty-eight to eighty kilometres. His advice on drinking was, 'To run a complete marathon without any fluid replacement was regarded as the ultimate aim of most runners, and a test of their fitness. In those days it was quite fashionable not to drink, until one absolutely had to. After a race, runners would recount with pride, "I only had a drink after thirty or forty kilometres."'

When I asked him about his drinking during those races, he wrote the following:

> To begin with my main drink was lemon squash [Oros or similar] diluted with water with added glucose powder and salt – a pleasing taste the only test. No scientific evaluation of the merits and demerits of this was available to me then.
>
> The other drinks were Coke and salt, or water or hot sugar-sweetened black tea. I recall that when Wally [Hayward] did his twenty-four-hour record in London [256.4 kilometres in twenty-four hours at Motspur Park, England, on 20 November 1953], he drank a lot of hot, sweet black tea. He kept telling [Arthur] Newton [who, like both Hayward and Mekler, also won the Comrades Marathon five times and set numerous world ultra-distance running records) the tea was not hot enough. He had lost his ability to differentiate the temperature.
>
> In addition, I would take about eight salt tablets during Comrades or a long run. The quantity was a guesstimate. It was a common belief among runners then that because salt tastes salty, one needed salt. I always believed that it was necessary to take salt to prevent cramps.
>
> Drinks were taken as and when one felt thirsty. In the Comrades 'up' run for instance I would never have a drink before Pinetown [twenty kilometres]. I always drank three-quarters up a hill, this helped me to look forward to this respite.
>
> In my time each runner had his own second – there were no feeding tables nor water points. Each runner had to organise his own drinks. Initially cars were allowed to follow the race but this became more difficult in the '60s as the number of entries increased. In my latter Comrades races [in the late 1960s] it was essential for the leaders to

have a motorcycle attendant as well as a car. None of us worked out that a thermos flask would be a great source of cold water! All the water we drank was tepid, accessed at various garages en route. Ditto other drinks.

My general philosophy always was to train in all temperatures, hot, cold and rain, only to try and become so much more able to withstand the negatives which might apply during the race. This applied to drinking too. I drank when I could, usually half a cup and obviously the longer the race or the hotter the more frequently the drinks. Among runners, drinking was seen as a 'sign of tiredness' – thus if any other was seen to be drinking frequently or excessively his opponents would interpret it as a sign of weakness. Thus many would boast about how long in a race they went without drinking!

Mekler also noted that he would speed up when he saw a competitor drinking, since he knew that the runner was drinking because he was tiring. In the sixty years between 1921 and 1981 that Comrades Marathon runners adopted this approach, there were no cases of EAH in these runners.

It was only after the introduction of regular (every 1.6 kilometres) drinking stations that it became necessary to provide elaborate medical care at the finish of this race, as well as other marathon and ultramarathon races, in order to treat the growing number of collapsed runners seeking medical care for 'dehydration and heat illness'. This paradox did not escape me. How could 'dehydration and heat illness' have become a significant problem in marathon and ultramarathon running *after* frequent drinking had become the accepted norm from the mid-1970s on?

Prior to 1976, our approach was the same as it had been for the very first marathon runners at the modern Olympics in Athens in 1896. Then, though, drinking during a marathon was considered a sign of cowardice! In the period from 1920 to 1970, when marathoners were not drinking much during races and were still fairly ignorant of the science around distance running, we saw the greatest improvement in performance. The encouragement of frequent drinking during marathons after 1976 didn't lead to better performances. In fact, the opposite happened – performances began to plateau.

In June 1981, while writing for *SA Runner*, I began crossing my own scientific Rubicon on this matter. In that month, I received two letters that radically challenged my thinking. The letters were from two female athletes who had run the 1981 Comrades Marathon and suffered greatly; one had almost died.

The letters described a similar phenomenon that had not been described previously. The first runner related how, on the way to the start of the race, she drank 500 millilitres of water. She also carried 750 milliltres of a mixture of Liquifruit and water, which she drank to avoid having to visit the first three refreshment tables, which were heavily congested. When this mixture was finished, she drank a weak mixture of Coke and water at virtually every refreshment table (there was one every 1.5 kilometres).

At the forty-kilometre mark, she began to feel nauseous. Thinking it had something to do with the Coke, she switched over to drinking plain water. By the seventy-kilometre mark, she was throwing up water. She made it to the finish line, sat down on the grass, and woke up five hours later in a bed in Grey's Hospital. Despite running well within herself, she had ended up in a coma. Fortunately she recovered fully and was soon released from hospital.

The second runner, Eleanor Sadler, was in hospital for almost a week. It was her experience that would change my life.

Eleanor related how she had run well psychologically, but at forty kilometres had begun to experience diarrhoea. She continued, but at seventy kilometres she passed her husband at the side of the road and did not recognise him. Alarmed, he argued with her, somehow convincing his wife that she should stop running and seek medical attention. She relented, and together they drove to the race finish, where she was treated with an intravenous (IV) drip for 'dehydration'. But the treatment did not help – if anything, she felt worse. So her husband decided to drive her back to their hotel in Durban, from where the race had started some hours earlier. En route, Eleanor had a grand mal epileptic seizure. Her husband drove her directly to Addington Hospital, where she was fortunate to come under the care of a physician trained at my alma mater. This was the late Dennis Pittaway, who, as a result of this case, subsequently became a friend of mine. Eleanor lapsed into a coma, from which she would emerge four frightening days later.

Fortunately Dr Pittaway had not been brainwashed to believe that dehydration is the only cause for collapse and coma in endurance athletes. Instead, he did what all physicians know they must do when faced with an unconscious patient – he measured her blood sodium concentration to ensure that an abnormality in blood electrolyte concentrations was not the cause. To his utter amazement, her blood sodium concentration was 114 millimoles per litre (mmol/L), substantially lower than the normal concentration of 140 mmol/L. He had just encountered the first case of exercise-associated hyponatraemia in the world. While Dr Pittaway did not at that time know what had caused the condition – no one did – he fortunately understood that she did not require too much fluid given intravenously. So he cautiously gave her an intravenous infusion of 0.9% (normal) sodium, and she recovered without any complications.

FIGURE 3

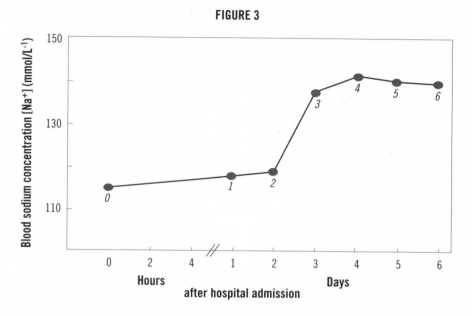

Daily changes in blood sodium concentrations in Eleanor Sadler during her recovery from exercise-associated hyponatraemic encephalopathy (EAHE), which developed during the 1981 Comrades Marathon. Note that it took four days for her blood sodium concentrations to return to normal. She remained unconscious during this time.

We now know that athletes with EAH must not be treated with 0.9 per cent sodium solutions. Rather, they recover more rapidly when given much higher concentrations of 3 to 5 per cent. Indeed, a few years later Dr Pittaway used exactly this form of treatment to save the life of another Comrades Marathon runner, whose condition was so serious that she was on the brink of death. Fortunately she responded appropriately when correctly treated with this more concentrated sodium solution.

In my subsequent dealings with Eleanor, I discovered that she had drunk everything in sight during the race, the first Comrades Marathon in which fluid was available every 1.5 kilometres for the entire ninety-kilometre race.

I was immediately challenged on what had happened to these two runners.

There seemed to be only two possible explanations – either they had lost excessive amounts of salt, or they had retained a large volume of fluid and diluted their blood sodium concentrations. Based on the collective belief that dehydration, and not overhydration, causes ill-health in long-distance running, I originally concluded that the first explanation had to be correct. I did not yet believe that it was possible for an athlete to drink so much during exercise that she could develop 'water intoxication', even though the story of the first runner was entirely compatible with that interpretation.

But it is difficult to see the obvious until your mind is ready to accept that which is so novel that it is completely unexpected. We had become so conditioned to believing that 'dehydration' was the real killer of athletes that I could not immediately let go of that 'truth'. In time, as more cases occurred and their stories began to fit a pattern of sustained and heroic overdrinking during exercise lasting four or more hours, I began to realise that my original conclusion was quite incorrect and that I would have to change my mindset. But I still did not have the definitive evidence.

Another epiphanous moment occurred eighteen months later, on the final day of the 1983 ocean surf-ski race between Port Elizabeth and East London. It became the singular event that inspired me to once and for all challenge the drinking dogma that had arisen from the study of Wyndham and Strydom. The race covers 244 kilometres and takes place over four days. At the start of the final fifty-kilometre stage, a young Oscar Chalupsky – arguably South Africa's most successful paddler – had lost the two large water bottles he carried on his ski as he paddled out through the shore break.

When I examined Oscar after the race, I found he had lost an astonishing 4.2 kilograms in body weight. It was the greatest weight loss I had ever observed in an athlete in competition. The dogma of the time dictated that any weight loss that develops during exercise represents a fluid loss that must be replaced to avoid heatstroke. So naturally I assumed that because Chalupsky was so 'dehydrated', his body temperature would be sky-high; according to the Wyndham and Strydom model (**see Figure 2 on page 67**), Oscar's body temperature would have to be in the heatstroke range. But it wasn't. It was 38 °C – only one degree higher than the normal value for a resting human.

I knew then that Wyndham and Strydom had to be wrong. But was I prepared to challenge my heroes, whose word was now gospel on this subject? It was a hard road for me to walk, but our research over the next few years would convince me that my conclusion was the correct one.

We had no research money at the time and the only equipment that we could afford was a single bathroom scale and a few rectal thermometers. The question we needed to address was the relationship between weight loss and body temperature during exercise. Since we did not have decent laboratory facilities, we had to study athletes in competition – a very cheap (and effective) way of doing research. The limited cost of this research allowed us to study many athletes in many races. And the more athletes we studied, the clearer it became that there was no relationship between the amount of weight that athletes lost during competition and their post-race body temperatures. We gradually accumulated the evidence that disproved the Wyndham and Strydom hypothesis.

If 'dangerous dehydration' and 'heatstroke' occurred so infrequently in marathon runners, as the evidence showed, and if there was no link between 'dehydration' and the rise in body temperature during exercise, why, I wondered, had the myth developed that marathon runners were at the greatest risk? The message should surely have been that those involved in very high-intensity exercise, such as running five to fifteen kilometres, were especially vulnerable, not because they were becoming 'dehydrated', but perhaps because they were running too fast in the prevailing environmental conditions. Only much later would I begin to wonder about the role of individual susceptibility and faulty brain controls.

So why was all this evidence ignored? Knowing what I know now, I suggest that there is a very small market for the sale of a sports drink to runners in five-to fifteen-kilometre races, purely because the distance is so short and runners in those races don't usually drink much. So it would be difficult to develop a frequent drinking philosophy if one were to focus exclusively on short-distance races.

In 1985 we published the iconic paper in which we became the first to describe four cases of the novel condition, EAH and EAHE. Published in *Medicine & Science in Sports & Exercise*, it was titled 'Water intoxication: a possible complication during endurance exercise'. Furthermore, by this time we were prepared to propose that EAH is caused by overdrinking and that 'advice [on sodium replacement during exercise] should be tempered with the proviso that the intake of hypotonic fluids in excess of that required to balance sweat and urine losses may be hazardous in some individuals'. Little did we then know that it would take more than twenty-five years for this simple statement to be accepted as the 'truth'.

In time, as I began to better understand human evolutionary biology, I realised that the flaw in the explanation developed by the US sports-drink industry and its scientists was that they were promoting what is known as a catastrophic model of human exercise physiology.

This model proposes that the exercising human continues without control or anticipation of future danger until the body suddenly collapses catastrophically, in this case as a result of heatstroke or the development of EAHE. This is quite literally a brainless model of human physiology, since it presumes that the brain, which determines how hard we run by ordering our muscles to work at the pace the brain chooses, will continue to drive the skeletal muscles to the point at which their actions cause our death, in this instance by generating too much heat, at too fast a rate, for too long, or by losing too much salt in our sweat.

But how would humans ever have survived for this long if this were indeed the case? Most certainly humans would have disappeared down some evolutionary dead end if we had been designed according to this model.

The model also doesn't explain how the marathoners and ultramarathoners of the early part of the twentieth century were able to survive, let alone run record times, when they drank very little during races. But the real tragedy is that this incorrect treatment (ingesting fluid at high rates) for a rare condition (heatstroke in marathon runners) that is not even caused by the condition (dehydration) for which this treatment has been prescribed, eventually spawned a whole new disease for a generation of runners who were never at risk in the first place.

Quite simply, a fatal error in science created a potentially fatal new disease in endurance sport – EAHE – that would ultimately cost the lives of exercisers who were simply following the advice they believed to be true.

Between 1981 and 1984, as more and more cases of EAH surfaced, I was witnessing first hand the factual evidence proving that it is possible for athletes to drink too much during exercise, to the point that this practice could ultimately be fatal. All of my studies after 1981 led me to the conclusion that athletes should drink according to thirst. And for those seeking specific drinking guidelines, it would be best to stick to 400 to 800 millilitres of fluid ingested every hour. As discussed earlier, Wyndham and Strydom advocated that marathon runners should be ingesting 250 millilitres of fluid every fifteen minutes to match their sweat rates. Few competitive runners in the history of the sport have ever achieved such a high rate of fluid ingestion. There is also no evidence to suggest that fluid ingestion at such high rates – that is, drinking 'ahead' of thirst – does anything other than impair performance. Instead, all the evidence now shows that it is never necessary to replace all the fluid or weight that is lost during exercise. The only proven effect of drinking more is the development of EAH due to water intoxication.

While running, most athletes, especially those running fast, have difficulty ingesting more than about 700 millilitres per hour. More than this and they begin to feel bloated. This is an obvious indication of the presence of unabsorbed fluid in the intestine. When they vomit clear fluid, they have drunk more than they can absorb and the body needs to rid itself of the excess.

The obvious question remains: Why was there a sudden increase in the number of athletes drinking far more than they would ever need? Our search for the answer began on the streets of New York in 1976.

8 | The Running Boom

In 1976, New York City found itself in the eye of a storm regarding marathon running and the science behind it. As I mentioned in Part I, the New York Academy of Sciences hosted a conference titled 'The Marathon: Physiological, Medical, Epidemiological and Psychological Studies' to coincide with the running of the first New York City Marathon. The deliberations at the conference were subsequently published, in 1977, and included our paper on heart disease in marathon runners.

The race was a tremendous success and it launched the concept of the big-city marathon. It also launched an unprecedented growth in marathon running. Before this, only about 2 000 runners would line up for any marathon. However, this soon grew to races with over 10 000 runners in 1980, to over 30 000 in the 1990s, and to more than 50 000 in 2010.

So, suddenly, a pursuit that had previously been limited to only the truly fit and elite athletes went global, generating a huge new market of runners – and wherever there is a potential market, there is always something new to be sold.

First in line to capitalise on this new market was the Nike company. Nike came into being in 1972 and built its reputation on being the cultish maverick in the industry, selling not only running shoes but also an emotion around running. In 1978, Nike ran an advertisement claiming that excessive pronation (inward rotation) of the ankle joint was the cause of running injuries. Of course, Nike also offered the only solution – specially designed 'anti-pronation' running shoes.

I must admit that most sports doctors, myself included, believed them. We were naive and failed to question whether Nike had, in fact, stumbled upon something revolutionary, or whether they were simply trying to gain a competitive market advantage to sell more running shoes to a gullible public.

I was also a 'Nike guy' and, as a friend of the runner who ran the Nike company in South Africa, I received free running shoes from Nike, South Africa, blunting my own desire to interrogate their global claims. It was only years later, when I no longer received free running shoes, that I started to see that excessive pronation is unlikely to be an exclusive cause of running injuries and may, in fact, at best play a very small role. In time, S.E. Robbins and G.J. Gouw asked whether expensive running shoes were as likely to produce injury as to prevent it. In part, this question stemmed from the realisation that our human ancestors successfully ran barefoot on the African savannah for two to three million years, chasing down antelope without the benefit of sophisticated running shoes.

The next to benefit from this global running explosion were the sports-drink and nutritional-supplement industries. It was in a laboratory at the University of Florida that the sports-drink industry was born.

DR CADE'S NEW WONDER DRINK

Before 1965 there were no sports drinks specifically designed and marketed for use during exercise. In fact, the world's first exercise drink was designed to prevent muscle cramps in US miners. The second was designed by South African ultramarathon legend Arthur Newton. He called it the Corpse Reviver. However, neither of these drinks was designed with a specifically commercial goal in mind.

In 1961, Dr Robert Cade, a renal physician from Florida, joined the renal division of the Department of Medicine at the University of Florida, and was later promoted to professor in that department. Of the stories of how Cade first developed Gatorade, the most likely is recorded in the book *First in Thirst* by Darren Rovell.

In 1965, former footballer and coach of the University of Florida's Gators football team, Dwayne Douglas, is said to have lunched with Dr Dana Shires, who worked as a fellow with Cade in the renal division at the university.

Douglas complained that twenty-five of his players had had to be admitted to hospital the previous weekend because of 'heat exhaustion and dehydration'. He also complained that those players who drank too much water suffered from stomach cramps, while those who ingested salt suffered from leg cramps. So he pleaded with Shires to come up with something that would protect his players from 'dehydration and heat exhaustion' without causing stomach or muscle cramps. Shires informed Cade of this conversation, and the two set about finding a solution.

Their 'research' led them to believe that a mixture of water, salt and glucose was the solution. The prototype drink is said to have tasted 'like toilet bowl cleaner', and on the advice of Mrs Cade, lemon was added for a more pleasing taste.

After a series of simple studies on the freshman football team had established that it was safe to drink this new solution during football matches, the first crucial field test was undertaken. The drink would be used by the Florida Gators in their game against the heavily favoured Louisiana State, who were ranked the fifth-best college team in the United States that year.

The drink was placed near the Gators players prior to the game, and some used it, while others didn't. The team came from behind to win 14-7, and the Gatorade legend was born. Here was the drink that would enhance performance by producing a surge of power in the final quarter of any match and so make winners of the underdogs.

But no conclusive evidence exists that it was, in fact, the sports drink that had produced this result. Yes, the Gators of 1966 – who fully embraced Gatorade that season – were considered to be the best football team ever to wear the Gators uniform, and were particularly adept at pulling off strong second-half come-backs. But this could also be attributed to the fact that the team had Steve O. Spurrier as their quarterback that season. Spurrier won the 1966 Heisman Trophy, awarded to the best collegiate football player in the United States. His strength? An ability to secure late victories for his team, hence his nickname, SOS. Also, the majority of the players in that team were remembered as being extraordinarily talented.

Spurrier himself was sceptical of the Gatorade effect. 'I don't have any answer for whether the Gatorade helped us be a better second-half team or not. We drank it, but whether it helped us in the second half, who knows,' he is quoted as saying in Rovell's book. The irony is that Spurrier did not drink much Gatorade, preferring instead to stick to Coca-Cola at half-time, since he recalls that Coke 'was what was provided'.

But perhaps the most burning question is why it was only in 1965 that a US football team found it necessary to take drastic steps to prevent 'dehydration and heat exhaustion'. American football has been played by US colleges since 1869, and professionally since the 1890s. So for almost a hundred years prior to Cade's 'discovery', not a single administrator, coach or player in US football had ever considered it prudent to drink fluids to prevent 'dehydration and heat exhaustion'. In contrast, some actually *exposed* their players to 'heat exhaustion and dehydration' in the belief that it was the way a coach developed the 'charac-ter' that his players needed to be successful.

Legendary football coach Bear Bryant was one of them. According to J. Dent's

The Junction Boys, he exposed 115 players trying out for his 1954 Texas A&M team to ten days of 'sandspurs, cactus, heat and practices without water'. Thirty-five players survived, including one who was treated for heatstroke. None died. Two years later, those players became the top-ranked college football team in the US.

But Cade believed he had enough evidence to prove that Gatorade was a success, and he was soon thinking about how he could commercialise his product. Cade and those who believed him, however, made a fatal error. Cade's presumption was that the success of a college football team could be narrowed down to a single simple factor, in this case the addition of sugar and a few electrolytes to water to make a sports drink. The reality is that professional team sports are so complex that they defy the analysis and control of all but a few coaching geniuses. If success in American college football could be reduced to one factor, the best coaches would not be paid more than $4 million for a five-month season.

But the marketing machine was in full swing. In 1967, Stokely-Van Camp, Inc. entered into a partnership with Cade, and they began to roll out the product on a national scale. This product was eventually marketed as 'the most thoroughly researched beverage in the world, and the only sports drink with more than 40 years of science to back up its claims that it works – hydrating athletes, replenishing electrolytes and providing fuel for working muscles'.

Soon the University of Notre Dame and Purdue University were using the product, and in 1967 the National Football League (NFL) made Gatorade its official sports drink – at a cost, mind you. (The current Gatorade contract with the NFL requires Gatorade to pay $100 million per annum to be the exclusive sports drink used by NFL teams and players.) So, in a remarkably short space of time, Gatorade was being used widely in all sports in the United States. As Cade himself said, 'Our stuff was on its way.'

The success of Gatorade in the United States, and the publication of the study done by Wyndham and Strydom in South Africa at around the same time in 1969, created the perfect vortex for Gatorade to blow its way straight onto the global market. It was helped by the fact that all the ingredients in Gatorade at the time were 'natural' – water, carbohydrate and electrolytes – so the product did not need to go through extensive development and testing as all new pharmaceutical products do.

Soon Cade's progeny was developing a novel 'Science of Hydration', based on a catastrophic model of how the body works during exercise and the need for revolutionary changes in drinking during exercise.

WHY CADE'S 'SCIENCE' WAS FLAWED

Yes, exercise causes a loss of salt and water from the body, and these can at times seem quite large. However, whether those losses are large enough to be dangerous to our health is a matter that can be solved only by proper scientific investigation.

The losses that Cade and his team measured in the Gators football players, for example, were not nearly as large as those measured in winning marathon runners or ultra-distance athletes, such as those competing in Ironman triathlons. Those water and sodium losses caused the blood sodium concentration to rise, which is always the case in those who do not drink at all or who drink little during prolonged exercise. If the losses were so dangerous, why did they not cause the blood sodium concentrations to fall, leading to EAH, as we had found in our two female Comrades runners?

Our finding in 1981 that EAH seemed to occur due to overdrinking came at an inconvenient time for the sports-drink industry, which wanted to increase its profits by encouraging athletes to drink more, not less, during exercise. The industry was not about to let an obscure South African researcher stand in its way. So, taking their cue from Cade, its scientists began to argue that, when athletes drank only water during exercise, they failed to replace their sodium losses. As a result of this sodium deficit, EAH must inevitably occur and can only be prevented by drinking a salt-containing sports drink like Gatorade at the high rates necessary to prevent dehydration.

But the truth is that the daily salt intake of the average runner in Westernised countries exceeds normal requirements by about eight grams. So the diet always contains more than enough to cover any sodium losses during exercise. If a diet is not generous in its salt content, the body has powerful salt-conserving mechanisms developed as a result of our genesis on the heat of the savannah. Even when exercising in daily heat, humans can survive on less than two grams of salt per day. Yet no modern human would choose to eat so little salt, as food would be unimaginably bland. Besides, as the growth of the salt trade in the fifteenth century shows us – for salt was the first globally traded commodity – humans have become addicted to a much higher salt intake.

Also, the concentration of sodium in most sports drinks is usually about 20 millimoles. If we had to follow the theory that sodium losses must be replaced according to the amount of salt lost in sweat, then the concentration of sodium in these drinks would have to be in the range of 40 to 80 mmol/L. That's two to four times higher than the concentration present in sports drinks claiming to do exactly this job. In fact, as we shall see, the amount of sodium present in these sports drinks has no biologically important effect on the blood sodium concentration and cannot prevent EAH.

Unsurprisingly, Cade and his team had not ever evaluated the effects of ingesting a sports drink on those variables in athletes encouraged to overdrink. So they couldn't rightly claim that they had developed 'the ideal replacement fluid for an exercising athlete who is vigorously perspiring'. This is a marketing statement, not a scientific one.

To address Cade's other contention, that a failure to drink can be life-threatening, I traced a large number of studies, including those in which athletes drank little or nothing during exercise. In not one of those studies could I find a single case of heatstroke or life-threatening dehydration. Some of these studies were even conducted in heat of up to 49 °C. The highest body temperature reached by any athlete who did not drink during these experiments was only 39.4 °C. There was simply no evidence to suggest any serious 'dangers' caused by 'dehydration'. Indeed, it has been known for more than a hundred years that there is no human model of heatstroke – it is simply not possible to generate heatstroke in a human during a laboratory experiment, regardless of what you might try to do.

Healthy humans are profoundly resistant to heatstroke. When heatstroke does occur, there must be extenuating circumstances to explain its rare occurrence. My current belief is that mild cases of heatstroke – those that are cured within minutes of placing the hot athlete in a tub of ice-water – are due to a transient brain abnormality in which the athlete's brain fails to calculate properly the rate of heat production (and loss) that it will allow for the duration of the exercise bout. When this happens, the body temperature reaches more than 42 °C before the end of exercise.

However, there is another group of heatstroke patients that is quite different. Even though they are properly cooled, these patients fail to regain consciousness when their temperatures return to normal. Instead, they develop progressive failure of all their major organs in a predictable sequence and usually die within twenty-four to forty-eight hours of their initial collapse. There is little that modern medicine can do to save the lives of these athletes, who, in my view, must have very severe but still unknown abnormalities that explain their individual susceptibility.

Cade's cardinal scientific error was believing his preconceived and simplistic hypothesis regardless of the facts. He had about him a scientific righteousness – perhaps he grew to believe in the truth of his theories. He helped to pioneer the erroneous belief that the 'dehydration' that develops during exercise will lead to death unless it is prevented by ingesting fluid at high rates, preferably to prevent any weight loss during exercise. So the Gatorade 'dehydration myth' was born.

For this dogma to become the international mantra of sport during the 1990s and beyond, however, Cade was assisted by the coordinated actions of many willing helpers.

THE MAFIA OF SCIENCE

It appears that Gatorade must have made a key strategic move when they decided that they would use science to establish the credibility of their product in order to increase their sales.

To do this, the company needed to develop a close relationship with at least some of the influential exercise scientists, particularly those with an established interest in fluids and exercise – or those who could be encouraged to develop that interest. Eventually, in my view, this approach was so successful that the industry was able to influence what was published in many of the world's important scientific journals. In my opinion, they were able to do this by exploiting one of the great weaknesses of the modern scientific method – the peer review system.

According to the peer review system, before one's work can be published in a credible scientific journal, it must first be reviewed by one's peers. The problem with this system is that it can easily be manipulated. For example, the editors of the journal know the scientific biases of the reviewers to whom they refer incoming manuscripts, so if they want the article to be rejected, they simply send it to those reviewers who they know have opinions that are the opposite to those argued in the submitted manuscript. So what is finally published is predetermined by whoever it is that selects the peer reviewers. In this way, the opinions of those who think otherwise can effectively be sidelined, while the theories of the group thinkers are richly rewarded.

But how do you discover which scientists are malleable and open to the suggestion that a novel science – the 'Science of Hydration' – needs to be promoted on a global scale? One solution might be to host a series of conferences that are attended only by invitation. Then you invite only those who will promote your message. In this way it becomes quite easy to determine who is keen to promote the party line and thus who can be trusted with repeated (expensive) invitations.

Interestingly, between 1987 and 1998, Quaker Oats, which then owned the Gatorade brand, held twelve annual conferences in exotic locations in the northern hemisphere, from Bermuda to Colorado. I was never invited to any of these conferences. Nor was EAH discussed to any great extent. This is surprising, given that the incidence of EAH rose dramatically during this time. There were fifteen scientists who attended at least eight of those twelve meetings. Some would become movers and shakers in our field, and a surprising number would be elected president of the American College of Sports Medicine (ACSM), which was funded by Gatorade. Gatorade was, in fact, ACSM's first platinum sponsor. This began in 1992 with the donation of a $250 000 'gift'. But gifts of this nature come with a price tag that is seldom disclosed. When Gatorade became the sole sports-drink provider to the Australian Institute of Sport (AIS), for example, their requirement was that all AIS-supported athletes would in future be required to promote the use of sports drinks and not water, with Gatorade as the sole sports drink. But this information became public only after a legal action was brought against Gatorade and the AIS under the Australian Freedom of Information Act. I suspect that this was not something Gatorade would have chosen to make public.

GATORADE FUNDING OF THE ACSM

The most apparent outcome of the gift to the ACSM was that the organisation produced drinking guidelines in 1987 and 1996 that were extremely advantageous to Gatorade. The annual Gatorade sales began to increase exponentially after the publication of these guidelines, as is apparent from the graph **on page 86**.

An important result was that Gatorade-approved scientists began to dominate the editorial boards of all but two of the leading publications in the exercise sciences. These two exceptions were the *British Journal of Sports Medicine* and the *Clinical Journal of Sports Medicine*, published in England and Canada respectively. It is my impression that the influence of these scientists, all of whom were of the same opinion, essentially made it impossible to publish any material that conflicted with the official Gatorade line. That certainly was my experience – most of the papers we submitted to those journals controlled by the Gatorade group thinkers were returned smartly, usually with antagonistic reviews informing us that we had no idea of how the body works during exercise in the heat, or how much athletes should drink during exercise in the heat.

As a result, the extensive work we did on fluid and exercise in South Africa was not properly acknowledged. In particular, the practical work we undertook on athletes in real competition was ignored until 2007, when the ACSM finally acknowledged that we had been correct all along. The group thinkers seldom studied athletes in actual competition, the benefits of which were discussed earlier. Instead, they studied subjects almost exclusively under laboratory conditions. They then argued that only laboratory studies are 'real', since only

FIGURE 4

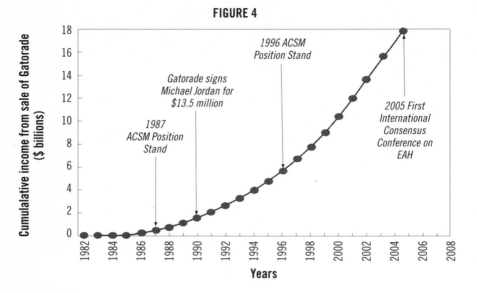

Cumulative income from the sale of Gatorade between 1982 and 2005. Note that the 1987 and 1996 ACSM Position Stands were followed by an increase in the annual income from Gatorade sales. Also shown is the effect of the 1990 signing of professional basketball player Michael Jordan for $13.5 million. The 2005 First International Consensus Conference on EAH concluded that overdrinking is the principal factor causing EAH.

in the laboratory is it possible to properly control sufficient variables to draw reasonable conclusions. The reality is that it is much easier in laboratory studies to control the variables to ensure a predetermined outcome – a process we call 'bent science'. So if you are determined to find what you want to find, the best way to do so is to undertake skilfully designed laboratory research. The problem with athletes in competition is that they may not do what you want them to do – and then you might have a real problem if the findings conflict with what the industry supporting your research wants as the outcome! When you study randomly selected runners competing in an actual race, you cannot influence what they will do. As a result, what you find will be the true biological response.

More importantly, it is simply not possible to exercise as vigorously or for as long in the laboratory as it is in athletic competitions. Athletes will simply not push themselves as hard in the laboratory as they do in regular competition. For example, the longest duration of exercise we have ever been able to impose on athletes in the laboratory is about eight hours. Yet athletes routinely complete the Ironman triathlon, which can last seventeen hours. So if you want to discover what happens to the human body after ten hours of exercise, it is unlikely that you will be able to do so in the laboratory. Nor can you predict with any accuracy what will happen after ten hours from an experiment lasting only two hours. As Roger Bannister – the medical student who became the first to run the mile in under four minutes – observed: 'Experiments in the laboratory are not of much practical value to athletes.'

As soon as we began to study Ironman triathletes, for instance, we found that those who finished near the front had often lost more than 6 per cent of their body weight, and some up to 12 per cent. Yet these athletes were performing better than those who lost very little, or sometimes even gained, weight during the race and finished hours behind them.

FIGURE 5

2000/2001 SOUTH AFRICAN IRONMAN TRIATHLON

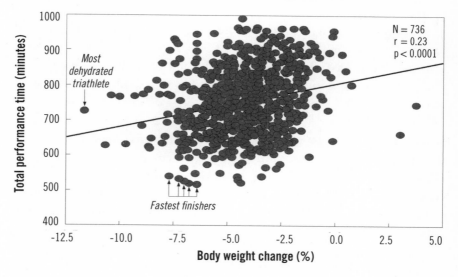

Data from the 2000 and 2001 South African Ironman triathlons, collected by K.A. Sharwood et al., found a significant relationship between the body–weight change and the total performance time in 736 competitors, so that the fastest finishers (arrowed) were among the triathletes who lost the most weight. These data conflict with the theory that any weight loss during exercise impairs exercise performance.

Since our findings were inconvenient, the group thinkers declared them invalid – on the grounds that they did not come from the laboratory. Our findings were therefore more likely to appear in journals that were independent of any outside influences.

My training has taught me that the most interesting phenomena to invite study are the paradoxes. When something does not make sense because it seems to disprove a widely held belief, *that* is a question worthy of study. At the very time that the group thinkers were saying that any level of dehydration would impair performance and perhaps lead to death, the evidence from our studies was that those who became the most dehydrated during competition ran the fastest. This was also compatible with the historical evidence that marathon runners set world records prior to 1969, even when racing without drinking.

Interestingly, during the past twenty-five years, the ACSM has produced four different position statements pertaining to fluid ingestion during exercise. These became increasingly forceful in promoting the belief that a high rate of fluid ingestion during exercise is necessary to prevent heatstroke and other heat illnesses. Not one refers to specific studies from which such definite conclusions can be drawn. This is understandable, since there *is* no scientific validation for their conclusion. But ultimately the ACSM had to acknowledge their error. In 2007 they introduced new guidelines, which, for the first time since their 1976 guidelines were implemented, encouraged athletes to drink to the dictates of thirst, but not to lose more than 2 per cent of their body weight during exercise. In private, members of the ACSM acknowledge that this change occurred because of the pressure I had brought to bear, especially through the publication of the drinking guidelines that I had developed for the International Medical Marathon Directors Association (IMMDA) in 2003, which in the same year had been accepted by USA Track & Field for use in all running races held under their jurisdiction in the United States. These guidelines promote the idea that athletes need only drink according to thirst at all times.

THE SPECIAL ROLE OF THE US MILITARY IN THE OVERDRINKING SAGA

With the growth in popularity of running among a far larger segment of the population, more and more cases of EAH were being reported in the medical literature. Interestingly, a large proportion of those cases were reported by the US Military.

In fact, a group that was crucial to the understanding of athletic overdrinking is from the US Military, in particular an organisation known as the United States Army Research Institute for Environmental Medicine (USARIEM). In 1982, a scientist from USARIEM recommended that US soldiers drink more in hot conditions in places like the Middle East and Asia. He coined a novel term – 'Water as a Tactical Weapon' – to explain his idea. He proposed that by drinking more, US soldiers would be able to fight more effectively in hot conditions. This despite the fact that the US Military had been fighting wars in hot conditions for at least a hundred years without following this advice.

He suggested that if each soldier were to drink 1.8 litres per hour when they exercised, they would eliminate the risk of developing an incapacitating heat illness when forced to fight in the heat. Remarkably, within five years his vision became official US Military policy.

New drinking guidelines forcing soldiers to drink more on an hourly basis, replacing the previous guidelines focused on daily drinking, were introduced. It wasn't long before the first few cases of EAH began to emerge in the US Military, and tragically the early fatalities began to materialise as well. All this we had predicted. Only much later did I learn that one of Gatorade's largest markets is the US Military. So large, in fact, that in 2005 there was a temporary shortage of Gatorade in the US since so much of the product was being used by their military.

Perhaps it was the adoption of these guidelines that helps explain why Gatorade sales rose exponentially after 1987, when the first ACSM drinking guidelines, proposing high rates of fluid ingestion during exercise, were promulgated.

By 1996, ACSM was proposing that athletes should drink 'as much as tolerable' in all forms of exercise to ensure that they optimise their performances and avoid catastrophic heat injuries. The commercial value of this proposal is obvious, since it requires that all exercisers must start drinking the moment they begin any exercise, regardless of its duration. Sadly, while the zero per cent dehydration rule might have had great economic value for Gatorade, it had negative consequences for those who adopted this advice without question and who developed fatal EAHE.

To their great credit, the US Military became aware that their new drinking guidelines were the cause of the problem, and in 1998 they completely revised those guidelines, reducing by 50 per cent the amount that soldiers were encouraged to drink. So as far as the US Military was concerned, according to J.W. Gardner, the adoption of the 'Science of Hydration', to which their scientists had made a significant contribution, produced only death and sadness. They would have been much better off without it.

Outside of this group of core thinkers was a tiny group of independents, most of whom were not from the US. I was interested in studying fluid balance during exercise because I began marathon running at the time we were advised not to drink during exercise. I thought that that might not be the best advice, so I started to advocate the opposite. But after I had been contacted by Eleanor Sadler, the world's first recognised case of EAHE, all of that changed. I did not know then that we were on the verge of a global pandemic fuelled by a novel 'Science of Hydration', skilfully manipulated by the US sports-drink industry. I could not have guessed then that we were about to witness a carefully orchestrated marketing scam.

9 | The Growth of EAH
as a Global Phenomenon

In the mid- to late 1980s, as the running boom continued, more and more cases of EAH were being reported in the United States, at exactly the same time as Gatorade was experiencing its boom in sales. The question that history has yet to answer is whether the two phenomena, related in time, are also causally linked.

FIGURE 6

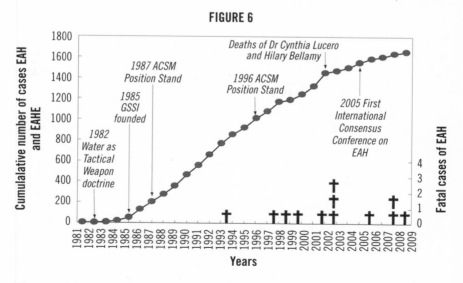

The cumulative number of cases of EAH and EAHE between 1981 and 2009. These cases were sourced from published medical literature and from cases occurring in the Hawaiian Ironman triathlon between 1981 and 1998. The crosses indicate the known fatal cases of EAHE and include the deaths of US marathon runners Dr Cynthia Lucero and Hilary Bellamy.

In 1983, Dr Tyler Frizzell, a twenty-four-year-old medical student, finished second in a 100-kilometre ultramarathon in Chicago, organised somewhat ironically by the American Medical Joggers Association. He had drunk about 300 millilitres at each fluid station, which were placed at 1.6-kilometre intervals. By the end of the race, he had drunk twenty litres. As Frizzel finished the race, he became disorientated and was rushed to hospital, where he suffered seizures and lapsed into a semi-coma for thirty-six hours before regaining consciousness.

In the same race, Dr Robert Lathan, a physician from Atlanta, Georgia, who later became a friend and came to South Africa to run both the Two Oceans and the Comrades Marathons, also drank about 240 to 360 millilitres of fluid at each fluid station. His total fluid intake by the end of the race was twenty-four litres. Half an hour after the race, he was admitted to hospital because he was disorientated and his speech was slurred.

The drinking guidelines for this specific race stipulated that runners should ingest 300 to 360 millilitres of fluid at each fluid station. The drinking philosophy of the race, as stated in a paper by R.T. Frizzell et al., was that runners should 'push fluids' and 'drink more than your thirst dictates, since thirst may be an unreliable index of fluid needs during exercise'. It is not clear where this advice originated, since official drinking guidelines that promoted this original component of the 'Science of Hydration' had yet to be published, appearing for the first time only in 1987.

The paper describing these two cases was published in 1986, a few months after the publication of our first paper, which described the world's original four cases of EAH. The 1986 paper was very important, since it supported our theory, unproven at the time, that EAH is caused by high rates of fluid ingestion. Only in retrospect did the paper contain one other gem: for whatever reasons, Drs Frizzell and Lathan had received quite different forms of treatment. Dr Frizzell had received the same treatment that Eleanor Sadler had – isotonic (0.9 per cent) or normal saline given intravenously. Like Eleanor, he had regained consciousness only after thirty-six hours and was in hospital for some days. In contrast, Bob Lathan had received a more concentrated (3 per cent) drip. The difference in his response was quite dramatic. Within hours Dr Lathan was fully conscious; he left the hospital in the early hours of the next morning and flew back to his home town of Atlanta by midday, sufficiently recovered to see patients in his medical practice that same afternoon!

We now know that a 3 per cent saline drip can be life-saving in this condition, whereas the infusion of 0.9 per cent saline can be fatal. Sadly, a number of deaths would have to occur before the importance of this early, random experiment was fully appreciated.

The next two South African events that fashioned my understanding of this condition occurred in the Comrades Marathon. In the 1985 race, the wife of an acquaintance, a minister in the South African government, collapsed during the marathon and was hospitalised in Durban. The press naturally presumed that she had not drunk sufficiently during the race. By then, I was convinced that the more likely explanation was that she had drunk *too much*.

Then, on the evening of the 1987 Comrades Marathon, I received a distressed call from a physician working at the hospital and admitting the seriously ill patients from that day's race. She told me that she had a ward full of Comrades runners with EAH and asked how she should best treat these sick athletes. I informed her that the runners must be treated with absolute fluid restriction, and if they did not respond, they should be given a diuretic to increase their urine production. Today I would have advised her simply to give all the patients 3 per cent saline – but that realisation had yet to come. Clearly, here was a problem requiring an urgent solution.

I realised that it was now very important to determine exactly what causes EAH, and to distinguish between our theory – that the condition is due solely to overdrinking – and the Gatorade-inspired hypothesis that the condition is due principally to large sodium losses in 'salty sweaters' who could have lost so much water that they were dehydrated. Accordingly, we decided to study those who were hospitalised with EAH and follow them during recovery. Simply by measuring how much water and sodium they took in and how much they lost during recovery until their blood sodium concentrations had again stabilised, we would be able to calculate precisely what had caused their EAH at the time they collapsed.

That is what my PhD student, the veterinarian Tony Irving, did after the 1988 Comrades Marathon with eight Comrades runners hospitalised for the treatment of EAH and EAHE. As they recovered, he collected all the urine that they passed and monitored any fluid or salt that they ingested. By the time they had recovered, he was able to calculate what had caused their illness. The answer was unequivocal.

Irving reached a definitive conclusion – their EAH and EAHE were caused by abnormal fluid retention. They had simply drunk too much during the race.

All had been overhydrated, as they had to lose between two and six litres of fluid before their blood sodium concentrations returned to the normal range during recovery. Importantly, the sodium deficits that the athletes developed were not greater than those that we measured in other ultramarathon runners who did *not* develop EAH or EAHE. So none of these critically ill athletes had developed a serious sodium deficit – even though their blood sodium concentrations were extremely low – so they could not have lost excessive amounts of sodium during the race. Thus we proved conclusively in 1988 that excessive sodium losses are not the cause of EAH or EAHE. It would take another twenty-three years for that finding to be accepted.

Instead we also found that there was a linear relationship with a negative slope between the fluid excess that the athletes developed during the race and their post-race blood sodium concentrations (**see the bottom panel in Figure 7 opposite**). In time, we and others would show that this is universally present in subjects with EAHE.

In one simple experiment that lasted just forty-eight hours, Tony had solved the problem – having athletes drink less and not ingest more sodium was all that would be required to prevent all future cases of EAH and EAHE. As far as I was concerned, this paper, finally published in 1991, was the final word on the condition. Since we had solved the problem, I presumed that it would simply disappear as everyone embraced the truth. How naive I was then!

In 1993 I strongly disagreed with the Gatorade-funded scientists charged with the care of athletes in the Hawaiian Ironman when I made the statement: 'Giving intravenous fluid at fast rates to a subject with hyponatraemia is definitely contraindicated and could be fatal.'

I take no pleasure in the fact that my comments were published a few months before the first case of fatal EAH in a thirty-two-year-old female competing in the 1993 Avenue of the Giants Marathon in California. Her full case was never reported in the medical literature, but I know from contact with her personal physician, who was not present when she died, that for seven hours the diagnosis of EAH was missed, since no one thought it necessary to measure the blood sodium concentration in an unconscious female athlete with no previous history of illness. By the time the diagnosis was made, she was brain-dead. I suspect she was treated with copious IV fluids for her 'dehydration'. However, acute 'dehydration' does not cause unconsciousness. Unconsciousness is a cardinal feature of EAHE.

The death of Dr Kelly Barrett in the 1998 Chicago Marathon was another seminal moment in the tragedy of this story. She was discovered in a confused state at the 38-kilometre mark. She complained of a headache, vomiting and nausea. Her family later reported that she had drunk 'gallons and gallons of water every day for about two weeks' in training for the race, following the dictum of

FIGURE 7

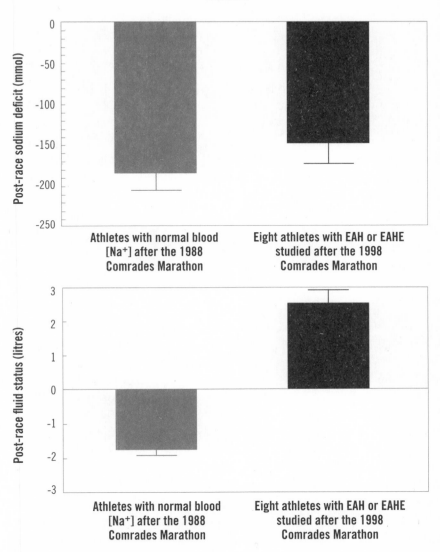

The study of Tony Irving and colleagues in 1991 established that runners who developed EAHE during the 1988 Comrades Marathon had not lost more sodium during the race than control runners who did not develop EAHE during the race did (top panel). But runners with EAHE were overhydrated by an average of two litres, compared to runners without EAHE, who finished the race with an average fluid deficit of two litres (bottom panel). [Na+] = sodium concentration

FIGURE 8

1988 COMRADES MARATHON

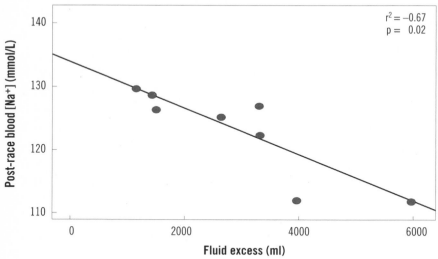

The study of Irving and his colleagues found a linear relationship with a negative slope between the amount of fluid excess present at the end of the race and the post-race blood sodium concentrations ([Na⁺]) in eight runners treated for EAHE after the 1988 Comrades Marathon. This established that the extent to which their blood sodium concentrations fell during the race was a function of the extent to which they had become 'waterlogged' during the race (as a result of overdrinking with fluid retention).

'drink until your eyeballs float'. Sadly, this is exactly what happened, as she was admitted to hospital and declared brain-dead three days later.

In the week before the 1999 Chicago Marathon, I received a phone call from Eric Zorn, a writer for the *Chicago Tribune*. He asked me to explain why Dr Barrett had died a year earlier. I explained that her death was probably caused by advice she was given to drink as much as possible, according to the 1996 ACSM drinking guidelines. He subsequently wrote two columns about this in the *Chicago Tribune*. To this day, whenever I reread these columns, I feel a mixture of bitter anger and sadness that such poor advice and ignorance has cost lives.

Zorn wrote, 'The simple, now pervasive message, "hydrate, hydrate, hydrate", is easier to remember than a formula for moderation and a better slogan than "water killed Kelly Barrett".' He concluded his column with a message from

Kelly's sister: 'Let other runners know the risks. If we can prevent someone else from making the same mistake, at least we can give this tragedy some purpose.'

Sadly, the marketing forces in opposition to this were too strong. It didn't take long before Eric Zorn received unsolicited emails from across the country accusing him of spreading dangerous information that could cause runners to die from 'dehydration'.

Dr Barrett's death prompted a very angry editorial on my part: 'When popular science fails: Avoidable athletic deaths from water intoxication (hyponatraemia)'. I submitted it to the American medical journal *Annals of Internal Medicine* in July 2000. I made the following point: 'This disease was caused by the adoption of a modern dogma, the "dehydration myth" and the advice that athletes should drink to excess during exercise ... By encouraging athletes to "consume the maximal amount that can be tolerated" without warning of the dangers of drinking too much during exercise, this popular advice to athletes continues to ignore a more fatal reality ... It is now time that runners were encouraged to drink enough but not too much during exercise. More importantly, especially female runners must be warned that they are at risk of a potentially fatal outcome if they consume excessive volumes of fluid during prolonged exercise. The advice provided by the manufacturers of sports drinks must acknowledge this reality.'

Not surprisingly, the article was rejected by one reviewer, who considered it to be 'a rant'. I suspect that the article's origin, 'darkest Africa', did not help. So I decided to submit the article to the *Journal of the American Medical Association*, where it suffered the same fate.

I rewrote it and submitted it to the *New England Journal of Medicine*. Again it was rejected. Finally, the *British Medical Journal* published it in July 2003, three years after it was first written. The editorial made the following points:

> From antiquity to the late 1960s, athletes were advised not to drink during exercise ... The publication in 1969 of an incorrectly titled article, 'The danger of an inadequate water intake during marathon running', provided the impetus for change, even though the study neither examined a 42-kilometre marathon race nor did it identify any dangers.
>
> This article's title provided the intellectual incentive for numerous studies, many funded by a fledgling sports-drink industry, culminating in specific guidelines for ingestion of fluids during exercise. These guidelines make four assumptions. Firstly, that all weight lost during exercise must be replaced if health is to be protected and performance

is to be optimised. Secondly, that the sensations of thirst underestimate the real fluid requirements during exercise. Thirdly, that the fluid requirements of all athletes are always similar so that a universal guideline is possible. Fourthly, that high rates of fluid intake can do no harm. Thus athletes are now advised to replace all the water lost through sweating or to consume the maximal amount that can be tolerated. But none of these ideas is evidence based ... Exercisers must be warned that the overconsumption of fluid (either water or sports drinks) before, during or after exercise is unnecessary and can have a potentially fatal outcome. Perhaps the best advice is that drinking according to the personal dictates of thirst seems to be safe and effective. Such fluid intake typically ranges between 400ml and 800ml per hour in most forms of recreational and competitive exercise ... The recent adoption of these guidelines by USA Track & Field provides the hope that this sad scientific abberation has finally run its tragic course.

While I wish that the publication of this editorial had been earlier, in that it might have prevented the deaths of many athletes, there is a time when new ideas are more likely to be accepted, and that time was 2003.

This editorial did not go unnoticed in the Chicago headquarters of Gatorade. Dr Robert Murray, then the director of the Gatorade Sports Science Institute, posted a response on the GSSI website the same day the editorial appeared in the print media.

The one-page editorial by Dr Timothy Noakes of South Africa that appeared in the July 19, 2003 issue of the British Medical Journal [sic] is best portrayed as one man's opinion on the topic of appropriate hydration during exercise. In brief, Dr Noake's [sic] editorial is not representative of the comprehensive research that is available on the topic of hydration during exercise. Nor does it factor in the very real dangers associated with the more common condition of dehydration ... In summary, there is no doubt that hyponatremia is a rare but dangerous condition that affects a very, very small subset of the population. However, dehydration and heat illness occur far more frequently and represent the greater threat to anyone who is physically active in a warm environment.

It wouldn't be the only time I clashed with Dr Murray and the GSSI. In 2005, the publication of the 2002 Boston Marathon EAH study by Dr Chris Almond and his colleagues showed that 13 per cent of the runners competing in the Gatorade-funded race had developed EAH.

In response, Dr Murray sent a letter to selected organisers of road races in the United States in which he stated: 'It's important that athletes don't allow this media coverage to create a fear of drinking – because it's essential that athletes drink appropriate amounts to replace their fluid and electrolyte losses.'

The ACSM continued to promote the concept of drinking 'beyond thirst'.

In South Africa, because we had been warning athletes of the dangers of overdrinking since 1985, and because we are less influenced by commercial drives than, perhaps, North Americans are, cases of EAH were rare, even in very long races such as the Comrades Marathon, in which the duration of the race and the free availability of fluid are key ingredients driving the condition. New Zealand was also following this trend, thanks to the hard work of my colleague, and now close friend, Dr Dale Speedy.

In 1996, Dr Speedy had been invited to be the medical director of the 233-kilometre one-day triathlon Coast to Coast Challenge across the breadth of the South Island of New Zealand. He chose to weigh the competitors before and after the race and to measure their blood sodium concentrations after the race. In results published in the *Clinical Journal of Sports Medicine* in 1997, he found that there was a relationship between the change in body weight during the race and the post-race blood sodium concentrations, such that the athletes who lost the least weight had the lowest post-race blood sodium concentrations, and vice versa. He was surprised by the number of competitors who lowered their blood sodium concentrations quite substantially during the race. He then read the literature and came across our description of the condition.

In order to determine whether the problem was more widespread than he thought, Dr Speedy studied a group of triathletes in the 1996 New Zealand Ironman triathlon. Again he found the same relationship – triathletes who did not lose much weight during the race were more likely to show a reduction in their blood sodium concentrations during the race (**see Figure 9 on page 100**). Indeed, the athlete who gained the most weight, 2.5 kilograms, during the race went unconscious and required hospitalisation for the treatment of EAHE. Dr Speedy did not now need much more convincing that EAH is indeed due to overdrinking.

FIGURE 9

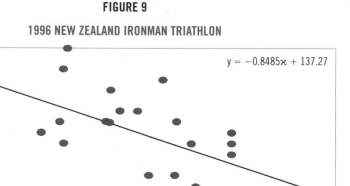

1996 NEW ZEALAND IRONMAN TRIATHLON

$$y = -0.8485x + 137.27$$

Athlete hospitalised in coma with EAHE

Post-race blood [Na$^+$] (mmol/L)

Body weight change (%)

The study of Speedy et al. at the 1996 New Zealand Ironman triathlon found a significant linear relationship with an inverse slope between body–weight changes during the race and the post-race blood sodium [Na$^+$] concentration. Hence athletes who did not lose any weight or who gained weight were at risk of developing EAH. The triathlete who gained the most weight (arrowed) was hospitalised in a coma with EAHE.

Accordingly, in the following year's New Zealand Ironman triathlon, Dr Speedy repeated the same experiment in a much larger group of 330 triathletes. Again, the findings were the same (**see Figure 10 opposite**). But, more importantly, fourteen triathletes were sufficiently ill with EAHE to require hospitalisation

Ahead of the 1998 New Zealand Ironman triathlon, Dr Speedy went against convention – he reduced the number of aid stations in the cycling and running legs. Then he told the triathletes that they would be expected to drink *less* during the race than they were usually advised to do. One professional triathlete at the time wrote of his reaction when he listened to Dr Speedy's pre-race medical instructions: 'I yawned and prepared myself for another lecture on maintaining sufficient hydration throughout the Ironman to avoid a decrease in performance and a trip to the IV tent. Here we go again, I thought.'

Then Dr Speedy began his briefing: 'The biggest problem we have expe-

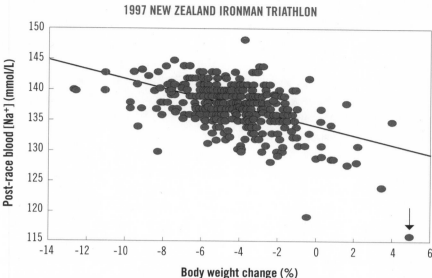

FIGURE 10

1997 NEW ZEALAND IRONMAN TRIATHLON

Dr Dale Speedy's study at the 1997 New Zealand Ironman triathlon again showed a significant relationship with a negative slope between changes in body weight and the post-race blood sodium [Na+] concentrations. The athlete who gained the most weight (arrowed) had the lowest post-race blood sodium concentration.

rienced in the New Zealand Ironman is athletes drinking too much. Last year fourteen athletes were hospitalised due to hyponatraemia (when the blood becomes diluted by drinking excessive amounts of water and too few salts). Three were critical, and one nearly died. So beware of over-hydrating. To this end, we have reduced the number of aid stations on the bike course.'

The triathlete recorded his response: 'You what? But it's all true. People have become so obsessed with the "more is better" philosophy. The fact is that over-drinking, if the weather is moderate, is as serious a problem as under-drinking. Having said that, the organisers' solution of reducing the number of aid stations to stop you succumbing to all that yummy fluid appeared to be a particularly drastic solution to me.'

Dr Speedy advised the triathletes to drink only between 500 and 1 000 millilitres per hour during the race. The frequency of drink stations was also decreased from every twelve to every twenty kilometres on the cycle leg of the race, and from every 1.8 to every 2.5 kilometres on the run.

The result? Only four triathletes were treated for EAH (0.6 per cent of race starters) and not one was admitted to ICU.

And in 2004, among 330 triathletes competing in the New Zealand Ironman triathlon, there were no cases of EAH, according to a study by Speedy and colleagues published in 2006. The 2002 42-kilometre City of Christchurch Marathon in New Zealand also found no cases of EAH in 155 participants. During the same time there were only occasional cases of EAH in the Comrades Marathon and in the South African Ironman triathlon. Not a single case of EAH has yet been reported in a standard marathon race in South Africa.

While the incidence of EAH was drastically reduced in the southern hemisphere at this time, this trend did not occur in the United States.

In fact, while EAH was successfully becoming a historical disease in the southern hemisphere, the opposite was the case in the US. In the 1998 and 1999 Suzuki Rock 'n' Roll San Diego Marathon, a total of twenty-six runners were admitted to hospital emergency departments for the treatment of EAH. Fifteen patients had severe EAHE; three with seizures required admission to the intensive-care unit. All confirmed that they had attempted to drink 'as much as possible' during and after the race.

The 2000 Houston Marathon reported a significant incidence of EAH, and the 2001, 2002, 2003 and 2004 races followed suit. Twenty-one athletes were admitted to the medical facility at the end of the 2000 race, all with EAH, and 53 per cent of those athletes had trained according to a beginner's marathon-training programme, which promoted aggressive drinking during exercise. They had all been told not to wait until they were thirsty to drink.

A study of 741 runners in the Boston Marathon that year found that 13 per cent developed EAH. C.S. Almond and the other authors of the study concluded: 'Excessive consumption of fluids is the single most important factor associated with hyponatraemia … efforts to monitor and regulate fluid intake may lead to a reduction in the frequency and severity of this condition'.

In 2002, twenty-eight-year-old Cynthia Lucero stepped up to the starting line in the Boston Marathon. The conditions were perfect, and Lucero, running her second marathon, was fit. She followed to the letter the drinking guidelines of the ACSM and drank to stay ahead of her thirst, ingesting Gatorade at a rate of 1.2 litres per hour, even though she was running at less than eight kilometres per hour in cool (10 °C), windy and overcast conditions.

After thirty-two kilometres, Lucero was lying on the ground, unconscious.

She was rushed to hospital, where she was diagnosed with EAHE. A brain scan showed evidence of swelling. She was declared brain-dead twenty-four hours later. She died from EAHE. Her autopsy report, according to S. Smith, concluded that she had died because she had drunk 'too much fluid', including a large volume of Gatorade. Lucero was another very public example of an athlete who had drunk herself to death.

But still we were faced with the question: How much should athletes drink during exercise to avoid EAH? In a series of studies that we began in 1985, we found that regardless of the duration of the exercise or the type of exercise – for example running, cycling or canoeing – athletes tended to drink the same amount, usually about 500 millilitres per hour. We could therefore conclude that when athletes drink according to the dictates of thirst, they typically ingest between about 400 and 800 millilitres per hour, as mentioned earlier.

In about March 2001, I was invited by the president of the International Marathon Medical Directors Association, Dr Lewis Maharam, to present a paper at the annual IMMDA conference that was to be held in association with the New York City Marathon that year. Unhappy with the ACSM drinking guidelines for US marathons, he wanted me to discuss appropriate drinking during marathon racing, and also the prevention of EAH and EAHE. About five years before this, at an ACSM annual conference, Dr Maharam had asked my advice on how the fluid requirements of marathon runners should be handled and how collapsed athletes should be treated. I gave the advice that we had developed in South Africa over the years.

I told him that athletes should drink according to thirst during a race and not more than 800 millilitres per hour. I advised that athletes who collapse during exercise have one or more serious medical conditions and must be treated by the appropriate medical experts. I also pointed out that the majority of athletes who collapse after exercise require no more specific treatment other than to recover while lying supine with the head below the level of the heart and pelvis.

I also told him that heatstroke should be treated by immersion in a bath of ice-cold water, while EAHE should be treated with fluid restriction and diuretics. (This was before we understood the great value of using concentrated [hypertonic] saline solutions for the treatment of EAH and EAHE.)

Dr Maharam told me that when he applied these guidelines to the marathon races at which he was the medical director, the incidence of EAH and EAHE was low and the management of collapsed runners significantly simplified. Based on this, he asked whether I would produce drinking guidelines that the IMMDA could implement at all the marathons at which their members were responsible for the medical care of the competitors.

I did so, and the article was published in 2002 and in a revised form in 2003. In 2003, one week before the Boston Marathon, United States of America Track & Field (USATF) announced that they would be adopting the IMMDA drinking guidelines that I had developed, with immediate effect.

Finally, in 2007, the ACSM modified their own drinking guidelines to include advice that athletes should drink according to thirst, and that this will usually mean that they drink between 400 and 800 millilitres per hour. This change meant that the ACSM had finally acceded to my suggestion, had given up the 'Science of Hydration' and had replaced the drinking guidelines with the IMMDA guidelines.

DISCOVERING MORE FAKE DISEASES

While we were undertaking this research, we also began to wonder why so many athletes collapse after exercise and require admission to medical tents at the end of races. Another of my students, Dr Lucy Holtzhausen, was crucial in providing the answers. Through a series of studies, Lucy established the following:

- That 85 per cent of athletes who collapse at the finish of marathon and ultra-marathon races and who are transferred for medical care do so only *after* they have completed the race. This allows for only one conclusion: that it is the action of stopping exercise, not the exercise itself, that causes these collapses. Since any 'dehydration' present in the collapsed athlete must also have been present when the athlete was running, 'dehydration' could not be a factor causing the collapse.
- That the body temperatures in the collapsed runners were not different from a control group of runners competing in the same races who did not collapse. Hence these athletes were not suffering from 'heat illness', and excessive body heat accumulation had nothing to do with their collapse. Thus the use of the term 'heat illness', or 'heat exhaustion', or even 'heat syncope' to describe this condition, was completely inappropriate.
- That the most effective way to treat collapsed athletes was to lift their legs and pelvis above the level of their hearts. This produced an immediate improvement in their condition and dramatically relieved their symptoms.

On the basis of these findings, we concluded that athletes who collapse after completing these races are suffering from the abrupt onset of low blood pressure, a condition we have called exercise-associated postural hypotension (EAPH).

EAPH is unrelated to 'dehydration' and is easily treated by lying with feet raised in what is called the Trendelenburg position. There is no need to give athletes with EAPH intravenous fluids, since they will recover just as quickly in this position whether or not they also receive IV fluids.

So we concluded that runners were not collapsing from any heat illness and certainly not from heatstroke, because their temperatures were too low and were no different from those measured in 'control' runners who completed the same races without collapsing. Rather, their problem was an inability to regulate their blood pressure immediately after they stopped exercising. By 1988 I was so certain that this was the case that, on invitation, I wrote an editorial about it for the *South African Medical Journal* in that year. My main point was that most athletes who collapse after the Comrades Marathon are not sick; they collapse because of a temporary inability to regulate their blood pressure. Since they are not sick, they do not need intensive medical care. Instead, the best treatment is 'masterful inactivity'.

The editorial produced a strong response at that year's Comrades Marathon, which took place a few days after it was published. I was working as a television commentator at the race when I was called out of the commentary box to take a phone call from the medical officer in charge of the Comrades medical tent. He wanted to know how I could possibly have suggested that the best treatment for runners who collapse is 'masterful inactivity'. To this day I'm not sure how else you should treat the vast majority of collapsed runners with EAPH, other than with 'masterful inactivity'. I was accused of harming the Comrades Marathon by discouraging doctors from working in the medical tent. Why would they want to work in the medical tent if all they were going to do was administer 'masterful inactivity'? If masterful inactivity is the best possible treatment, then that is what doctors should prescribe. I began to realise that my ideas were just as unwelcome in South Africa as they were elsewhere.

These arguments were, however, simply a sideshow. The real story of the 1970s and 1980s was that the running boom was continuing unabated. All the while, race organisers were being pressurised to ensure that ample fluid was available at multiple fluid stations along the race routes. The doctors working in the medical tents continued to be convinced that all the collapsed runners they were treating were suffering from 'dehydration' and were in desperate need of urgent rehydration, with copious amounts of fluid administered intravenously.

There was almost a wave of panic in pre-race publicity and in the media about the dangers of dehydration. No one had yet stumbled on the possibility that this was probably an orchestrated campaign to make drinking-water redundant and to increase the profits of the sports-drink industry.

So athletes were encouraged to drink even more. Those who required treatment in medical tents at races were treated with rapid intravenous infusions of fluid, which would have to be ineffective if the condition they were treating was not due to 'dehydration'. In the end there would have to be fatal consequences.

By this time we had established that 'dehydration' cannot be the cause of heatstroke, since body temperatures during exercise are related not to the levels of dehydration that the athletes develop but rather to how fast they run. So to prevent heatstroke you need to tell athletes to run slower and not to take drugs that are known to cause heatstroke in some susceptible individuals during exercise. Drinking more was never going to protect against heatstroke, the treatment for which is cooling and not the provision of large volumes of fluid either during or after exercise.

By then we also knew that the vomiting of clear fluids is not a sign of dehydration, but in fact of the opposite, overhydration, since it indicates the presence of unabsorbed fluid in the intestine that the body wishes to expel.

A LIGHT FROM DARKEST AFRICA

In March 1985, as mentioned earlier, the American scientific publication *Medicine & Science in Sports & Exercise* finally published our first full-length paper describing EAH for the first time. The paper went on to become a 'citation classic'. By 2007, it had been quoted more than a hundred times in published scientific literature.

It was also reprinted in full in 2005 in the publication *Wilderness Medicine*, with an accompanying editorial by Australian Emergency Medicine Physician Ian Rogers, who wrote, 'Tim Noakes was right in 1985, and the passage of two decades has done nothing to diminish the accuracy of his conclusions. In a recent editorial he summarized the situation as "exercisers must be warned that overconsumption of fluids (either water or sports drinks) before, during or after exercise is unnecessary and can have a potentially fatal outcome", and he expressed his hope that "this sad scientific aberration has finally run its tragic course".'

But when the article had been published twenty-five years earlier, we had very few supporters. One was the late Dr John Sutton MD, PhD, then president of the American College of Sports Medicine. He acknowledged the research in an interview with a journalist from the medical publication *Physician and Sports Medicine* in 1986, saying, 'Noakes documented a rather interesting situation of prolonged activity combined with overhydration ... the biggest problem remains the amount of fluid they've taken ... It could be a big problem during triathlons and ultramarathons.'

He also wrote: 'Funny how we solve one problem – dehydration – and people go overboard and create another problem. The pendulum swings from one direction to the other – dehydration to overhydration. Understanding and education is the key to it all.'

The erroneous ACSM guidelines that encouraged athletes to 'drink as much as tolerable during exercise' so that they did not lose any weight had to have been an important factor in promoting the epidemic of EAH cases that occured in the sporting world between 1981 and 2003.

If the information from Tony Irving's study had been correctly communicated to endurance athletes after we'd proved it in 1991, the world of endurance sport would not have suffered the ensuing pandemic of the condition, and lives would have been saved. Instead, it seems that the needs of the marketplace – the bottom line – required that an alternative message be promoted.

The sad reality is that only in 2002 was the work we had pioneered in 1985 beginning to be taken seriously. It still astounds me that this realisation took so long to dawn. The reason for this is probably because we had proven it in the marginalised parts of the scientific world – in South Africa and New Zealand. Only when the same findings were made in Boston, USA, was it no longer so easy to ignore what we had discovered a decade earlier.

So what we showed in the eighties and nineties had now been confirmed: it's how fast you run that determines how high your body temperature rises during exercise, and not, as Gatorade declared, whether you drink or not. How much you drink has a negligible effect on the extent to which body temperature rises during exercise. There is also no evidence to prove that increased liquid intake enhances performance.

Of course, if you choose to drink 'as much as tolerable', there will be only one outcome: if you do not collapse with EAHE, your performance will be negatively affected.

But Gatorade and their scientists were still not prepared to back down.

THE ZERO PER CENT DEHYDRATION RULE

It took me a long time to answer to my satisfaction the question: Why did the ACSM promote high rates of fluid ingestion after 1987?

To summarise, before the running boom of 1976, only those who were well trained considered entering a marathon or ultramarathon, but after the boom, the new generation of runners was not advised to train more to avoid harm during races; instead, they were told to drink more. Drinking a sports drink was marketed as the universal panacea – more important, apparently, than proper training.

When the ACSM eventually altered their guidelines in 2007, the crucial change was that they accepted my view that athletes should be encouraged to drink according to the dictates of thirst and not 'to stay ahead of thirst' by drinking 'as much as tolerable'. The only real difference from my guidelines was that the ACSM, unable to extract itself from the commercially favourable 'zero per cent dehydration rule' in one decisive move, continues to promote the incorrect belief that athletes should ensure that they do not lose more than 2 per cent of their body weight during exercise. It was perhaps too much to expect that an organisation funded by Gatorade and with a Gatorade presence on their board of directors would be able to take the final step to admit that the 'Science of Hydration' that it had supported for more than twenty years was no more than a skilfully directed scientific scam.

In contrast, the US Military, presented with exactly the same evidence, modified its drinking guidelines specifically to prevent EAH in as early as April 1998 – almost a decade before the ACSM took the same action.

So it seems clear that the GSSI and the ACSM, the 'Science of Hydration' and the 'zero per cent dehydration rule' are linked by both time and plausible physiological mechanisms to the subsequent pandemic of EAH and EAHE that swept the world after 1981. To suggest that either of these organisations is the saviour of distance runners and acts exclusively in the runners' interests is simply not supported by any of the above-mentioned facts.

When Quaker Oats purchased Gatorade and formed the GSSI in 1987, Quaker executive Phil Marineau – who was later appointed to the board of the ACSM – declared that, if the brand was to stay at the top, 'Quaker would have to constantly prove that it was the best thirst-quenching product in the world at all times.' Thus, one function of the GSSI was 'to make sure that the product did what it was supposed to do'. It seemed that Marineau was concerned that somebody would outdo Gatorade, which is another irony in this whole saga, as Gatorade is made from common kitchen ingredients and it would be difficult to arrange these ingredients any differently to produce a better product.

Marineau also described a second goal of the GSSI: 'to use our relationships with researchers to stay ahead of the curve on the latest in thirst research'. Yet no one has discovered anything other than those common kitchen ingredients to improve the current formula. So, is the GSSI there to develop the latest and greatest sports drink to truly benefit athletes, or to use science to best defend the status quo?

Another turning point came after the deaths of Cynthia Lucero and Hilary Bellamy from EAHE in 2002. The Boston Athletic Association responded by issuing 20 000 pamphlets advising runners to 'Drink to stay hydrated. Don't overdrink.' This was exactly the advice we had proposed eighteen years earlier.

By December 2010, I could trace twelve fatalities and over 1 660 cases of EAH. But it's possible that this is only the tip of the iceberg. EAH had become the single greatest health risk to endurance athletes, and not, as the sports-drink industry contended, 'dehydration' and heatstroke. In fact, during the same period I was unable to find a single case in which dehydration was established as the single cause of death or ill-health in any athletes.

Slowly but surely, the evidence that we had been correct all along became overwhelming. In 2004, *Runner's World* magazine included our work as one of the forty most important 'persons or events' in the sport of running over the past forty years. Now, even some of the most ardent Gatorade scientists are starting to say that I might be right.

As I mentioned earlier, I struggled for years to understand why that which seemed so logical to me was apparently completely incomprehensible to most of my colleagues and to the 'experts' of the sports-drink industry. The statement made by former US Vice-President Al Gore in the context of climate change finally helped me to understand this. He quoted Upton Sinclair, who famously said: 'It's extremely difficult to convince someone to understand something if his salary depends on his not understanding it.'

The final answers

When I decided to take on an industry with a R28-billion annual turnover, I knew I had only one certain ally – science. I believed that if I was correct, science would prove it, since proper science, honestly conducted, is always self-correcting. I also knew that however much Gatorade might wish to control the scientific process, they must ultimately fail, as they surely cannot control the editorial policies of all the world's scientific journals. Even if they could find a way to control 95 per cent of these, there would still be one, perhaps two, that would be sufficiently independent to publish information that disproved the mythical 'Science of Hydration'. Fortunately, we discovered two such journals – the *Clinical Journal of Sports Medicine,* edited by successively Drs Gordon Matheson and Winne Meeuwisse, and the *British Journal of Sports Medicine*, edited by Dr Karim Khan. Together, Mattheson, Meeuwisse and Khan provided the fierce intellectual independence that allowed us to publish the proof that attacked the foundations of the 'Science of Hydration'. But, ultimately, it was other scientists, including some employed by Gatorade, who provided the final evidence that confirmed we had been correct all along.

An independent researcher from the University of Quebec, Dr Eric Goulet, finally performed what is known as a meta-analysis of all the studies that have measured the effects of drinking fluids at different rates on exercise performance. What Dr Goulet's analysis reveals is that drinking to thirst always produces the best performance; drinking either more or less impairs exercise performance.

This 2010 study therefore closed the circle. It proves that there is no 'Science of Hydration'. Instead, there is only a normal human biology fashioned in the remorseless selection of the fittest by the ruthless Darwinian struggle for survival. Our prehistoric ancestors developed the mechanisms of thirst to optimise our survival as they exercised in the heat of the African savannah. Three million years of living to survive in arid conditions produced humans that have all the biological signals necessary to survive a six-hour marathon in the cold or a two-hour marathon in extreme heat.

So there it is, laid bare. The 'Science of Hydration' is propaganda conceived by marketers who wished to turn a collection of kitchen chemicals into a multibillion-dollar industry.

To their credit, they succeeded.

To their unending shame, they cost the lives of some of those they were pretending to protect.

part three

NUTRITION 101

'The cholesterol/lipid theory of heart disease is "the public health diversion of this century…the greatest scam in the history of medicine"'
— PROFESSOR GEORGE MANN MD (1993)

10 | The Facts They Don't Want You to Know

My mentor, George Sheehan, once wrote that to fully understand a disease the doctor needs to first develop that condition, and then learn how to live with it. I have a genetic predisposition to developing obesity, adult-onset (Type-2) diabetes mellitus and high blood pressure (hypertension), the triad of diseases from which both my father and uncle suffered. Since I was leaner, more active than both and a non-smoker, I thought that I would be spared. According to my conventional medical education, remaining active and avoiding excessive weight gain is all that is required to keep these diseases at bay. I was never told that the nature of the food I ate might be important in staving off all three conditions. But as I entered my seventh decade, I was beginning to wonder whether my conventional education might have missed a few important facts.

The first key moment was a night in December 2010 when I finished the final sentence in what would become my next book, *Waterlogged*, a project that has consumed much of my life since 1981 (see Part Two of this book). During that night I became aware that my mind had come up with a new directive. It said: 'In the morning you must get up and run. And you must not stop for the rest of your life.' Since I have learnt to trust my intuitions, I obeyed. Within a week of daily running I was physically re-addicted. And so began my new life as an ageing runner motivated to train regularly and vigorously.

However, to run properly I would need to lose some weight. But how to do that? There were times in my life when I had run more than 160 kilometres a week, even touching 220 kilometres in one week in 1978. But these gallant efforts had never produced the sustained loss of more than a few grams of body weight.

The only effect was to delay the onset of an inevitable weight gain the moment my training mileage returned to a more manageable volume.

So in forty-one years of running I have learnt that the numerous benefits of exercise do not include any sustained effects on weight loss. This has been confirmed by studies showing that otherwise healthy people who begin an exercise programme as the sole means of losing weight are likely to lose at most a few kilograms of body weight. Those few who lose more achieve this by making other changes besides just exercising more.

Clearly, I would need to find a novel way to lose weight. At the time I knew very little about this. But I would eventually discover that the only effective weight-loss method for myself is also the one that the professionals in this discipline are the least likely to prescribe. In fact, almost all the dieticians I know are vehemently opposed to it. It is another paradox that I knew would require a full investigation.

Even before I began this odyssey, I already knew that the conventional calorie-restricted diets that the professionals advise are, like the directive to exercise more, notoriously ineffective. Calorie-restricted diets may produce respectable weight losses for the first six months or so, but these losses are unsustainable because the only certain long-term effect of calorie restriction is to produce hunger, not weight loss. In time, even the most motivated dieter must succumb to his or her hunger, begin to eat more, and return rapidly to his or her former weight. Conventional diets prescribed for weight control produce a long-term weight loss of about one kilogram after a year of sustained effort.

Even though these diets are proven to be ineffective, they continue to be prescribed as the sole option. Those who persist with them seem to believe that repeating the same failed experiment enough times will somehow produce a dramatically different outcome. Instead of blaming the diet for the failure, they blame the patient for lacking the motivation to succeed.

So I concluded that if I was to avoid dying from the complications of diabetes and hypertension, I would not find my salvation by following the advice of my own profession. I would need to discover that which my conventional medical and scientific education had yet to grasp. In time, I would learn that this information is, in fact, well known. But the same immoral influences that were behind the false Science of Hydration described in Part Two of this book act to ensure that this information is hidden. And when it sometimes leaks into the public domain it is quickly demonised by a squad of compliant professionals, doctors, scientists and dieticians, most of whom have no idea of the part they play in a much larger scam. It is one of the greatest health cons yet perpetuated;

one that makes the scam described in Part Two seem utterly trivial by comparison.

While trying to find an unconventional answer to a common problem, I received an unsolicited email announcing a new dietary method to lose weight. I was on the verge of deleting the email when I noticed that this method claimed to be different in one crucial aspect: it promised weight loss without hunger. The diet suggested that you could lose weight while continuing to eat enough to satisfy your appetite. My natural response was that the claim was fraudulent. I had been conditioned to believe that the sole method to lose weight is through suffering, learning how to live with hunger, and convincing yourself that the denial and hardship will be worth it in the long run. Furthermore, I suddenly noticed that the book being advertised was not written by some diet guru without credible training, but rather by a trio of serious scientists, Drs Westman, Phinney and Volek, whose original scientific work I had admired in the past. I read further.

Within a few hours of receiving the email I had a copy of their book – *New Atkins for a New You* – in my hands. I was immediately impressed by the claim in the foreword: 'In more than 150 articles these three international experts on the use of low-carbohydrate diets to combat obesity, high cholesterol and Type-2 diabetes have led the way in repeatedly proving how a low-carbohydrate approach is superior to a low-fat one.'

By the end of the day I was sufficiently ready to begin the experiment of my life. I would adopt the high-protein/high-fat/low-carbohydrate diet that these authors were advocating. This would require that I immediately stop eating all the carbohydrates that had been key to my diet since beginning more serious running in 1972; the very carbohydrates that form the basis of the nutritional advice for athletes contained in my book *Lore of Running*. This change would clearly represent a major mind shift, including the possibility that I would have to apologise to all the readers of *Lore of Running* by having to admit that in this particular case, I was quite wrong. Sorry everyone.

A month later, after I had become certain that I had finally discovered the eating plan that would allow me to once again run decently, I was prepared to undergo the blood tests that would show my risk for developing diabetes. The results were unequivocal. Unless I learnt to live with my predisposition, I too would develop the full-blown disease that had killed my father and his brother. This fact alone was enough to grab my full attention.

A diagnosis of adult-onset (Type-2) diabetes is at least as bad as learning you have cancer. There are at least some cancers that are now curable, but diabetes is incurable and the illness leads to a progressive loss of bodily functions. It is a demeaning disease. I had to learn more. I needed to discover if a low-carbohydrate diet might be my sole hope for avoiding the fate that befell my father.

Since those defining moments I have learnt more about nutrition in one year than I did in the previous forty-two years of my medical and scientific training. More importantly, I have discovered why it is that this information is hidden. It is, it turns out, simply too dangerous to be more widely disseminated.

AGAINST THE GRAINS

I was so impressed by my response to this new eating plan that in May 2011 I decided it was time to share my discovery with the readers of the Discovery Health magazine, *Discovery* (Winter 2011). To say that the column produced some vigorous responses would be an understatement. But rereading the article makes me wonder why it caused so much unhappiness. All I had done was to report my personal experiences, which seemed to me to have been wholly positive. What could possibly be wrong with telling others how one simple change in my nutrition had produced such a dramatic change in my health? Clearly, I had exposed a very sensitive nerve. This, too, would need some investigating. This is what I wrote, corrected here very slightly for additional insights I have since gathered:

> I am not one to shy away from controversy. But I suspect that this column will attract more unfavourable comments than perhaps anything else I have recently written. Yet the message could be life-changing for some.
>
> It has taken me sixty-one years to suspect that bread and cereals – the biblical staff of life – as well as rice, pasta and refined carbohydrates may be as toxic for my body as are the calamitous saturated fats about which my tutors warned me in my third year at medical school.
>
> My attention to this possibility was piqued by the release of the most recent 2010 US Dietary Guidelines. These guidelines promote the concept of the Food Pyramid built on six to eleven daily servings of bread, cereals, rice and pasta. Although Americans now follow these guidelines more closely than ever, obesity has become the single greatest medical problem in the US. Thus the question: Is this epidemic linked in some way to this increased carbohydrate intake? I decided to investigate.

First, I learnt that cereals and grains have been a staple of the human diet for only the past 20 000 years, whereas we began to eat meat perhaps 2.5 million years ago. More interestingly, this change from a protein- to a cereal-based diet produced a reduction in average human height and the first appearance of nutritional-deficiency diseases, including beri-beri, pellagra and scurvy. These diseases led to the discovery of vitamins only in the early 1900s.

Second, there is a burgeoning literature written by those who experiment with low-carbohydrate diets. Some suggest that humans evolved our current size, and especially our large brains, over the past two million years only because we found sustainable novel sources of high-protein foods, especially meat and fish. Such high-energy sources are especially important during infancy and early childhood, when brain size increases rapidly. As a result the human intestine is especially well designed for digesting high-protein foods and bears more resemblance to that of the carnivorous lion than that of our nearest living relatives, fruit- and plant-eating chimpanzees. Perhaps humans are really closet carnivores.

Third, low-carbohydrate weight-loss diets produce results at least as good as those achieved with the traditional low-fat, high-carbohydrate diets. No published evidence shows that these unconventional diets will produce undesirable health consequences.

Fourth, I learnt that protein is a potent appetite suppressant, perhaps because a too-high protein diet is toxic to humans. As a result, low-carbohydrate diets with increased protein do not cause the frequent sensations of hunger that accompany calorie-restricted, high-carbohydrate diets. This absence of hunger is more likely to encourage the dieter, leading to sustained weight loss. In contrast, there may be an addiction, especially to rapidly assimilated carbohydrates like sugar and refined carbohydrates like white flour and pasta, which drives the overconsumption of all foodstuffs, fat included, and hence weight gain.

So my untested theory is that it is the unrestricted intake of especially refined, and hence addictive, carbohydrates that fuels an overconsumption of calories, and not a high-fat intake as is usually believed.

But why aren't we made more aware of this? There is a saying that to find the root cause, follow the money trail. If a low-carbohydrate intake is healthier than we might expect, then why is that fact hidden? The answer is that some very large industries, including the soft-drink, sugar and confectionery industries – all of which produce sugar-based products with no nutritional value – and those pharmaceutical companies that produce drugs to treat the medical consequences of this toxic foodstuff do not wish us to know this.

Finally, I submitted myself to the experiment of rigorously avoiding all sugar, bread, cereals, rice, pasta and other refined carbohydrates and replaced that nutritional deficit with healthy meats, fish, eggs, vegetables, nuts and dairy produce. Five months later I am at my lightest weight in twenty years, I am running faster than I have in twenty years, and I am getting faster. For the first time I have learnt exactly how to maintain an ideal body weight without any sense of hardship and fear of unsustainability. And with only as much exercise as I want to do.

Even my friends are impressed. They agree that not even the most expensive cosmetic surgery could have produced such a remarkable transformation.

I wasn't the first to uncover this truth. In fact, it's been known since the 1860s. And we have a forgotten English ear, nose and throat surgeon, Dr William Harvey, and his corpulent patient, William Banting, to thank for this.

THE IMPORTANCE OF WILLIAM BANTING AND GARY TAUBES

In pursuing the science of low-carbohydrate eating, it will not be long before you encounter the modern 'bible' describing the recent history of nutritional science – the book *Good Calories, Bad Calories* written by Gary Taubes. His book opens with the definitive but long-forgotten story of William Banting.

Banting was an undertaker who lived in London, where he constructed the Duke of Wellington's coffin in the nineteenth century. Banting's weight had become a problem already in his mid-forties. He was unable to do up his own laces and had to walk downstairs backwards to ensure that he did not fall over or strain his knees. He had also developed a range of other medical complaints. Being a man of social standing, he was able to consult the best medical sources in England. He wanted to lose weight.

The first doctor he consulted prescribed exercise. As Banting wrote in his *Letter on Corpulence* in 1869: 'I consulted an eminent surgeon, now long deceased … who recommended increased bodily exertion … and who thought rowing an excellent plan. I had the command of a good heavy, safe boat,

FIGURE 11

BREAKFAST: Four or five ounces of beef, mutton, kidneys, broiled fish, bacon or cold meat of any kind except pork. One small biscuit or one ounce of dry toast. A large cup of tea without milk or sugar.

LUNCH: Five or six ounces of any fish except salmon, any meat except pork, any vegetable except potato. Any kind of poultry or game. One ounce of dry toast. Fruit. Two or three glasses of good claret, sherry or Madeira. (Champagne, port and beer were specifically forbidden.)

TEA: Two or three ounces of fruit. A rusk or two. A cup of tea without milk or sugar.

SUPPER: Two or three ounces of meat or fish as for lunch. A glass of claret, or two.

NIGHTCAP (if required): A tumbler of gin, whisky or brandy with water but without sugar, or a glass or two of claret or sherry.

The 2 800-calorie diet prescribed by William Harvey that allowed William Banting to lose twenty-one kilograms between August 1862 and August 1863. Adapted from: Banting, 1869, p. 11; and Mackarness, 1956, p. 22.

lived near the river and adopted it for a couple of hours in the early morning. It is true I gained muscular vigour, but with it a prodigious appetite, which I was compelled to indulge and consequently increased in weight, until my kind friend advised me to forsake the exercise.'

Over the next twenty years Banting consulted at least twenty other doctors, 'but all in vain. ... I have tried sea air and bathing in various localities, with much walking exercise; taken gallons of physic and liquor potassae, advisedly and abundantly; adopted riding on horseback; the waters and climate of Leamington many times, as well as those of Cheltenham and Harrowgate frequently; have lived on sixpence a-day, so to speak, and earned it, if bodily labour may be so construed; and have spared no trouble nor expense in consultations with the best authorities in the land, giving each and all a fair time for experiment, without any permanent remedy, as the evil still gradually increased.' Regular Turkish baths and walking begun in his fifties also offered no respite from the 'evil'.

By age sixty-six, in August 1862, Banting's weight had ballooned to ninety-two kilograms. Since he was only 1.65 metres tall, his body mass index (BMI) was 34 kg/m^2, placing him in the upper range of what is now classified as Obese Class 1. Finally, with his hearing and sight failing, he consulted William Harvey, an ear, nose and throat surgeon. Harvey concluded that Banting's problems were caused by his obesity, for which he had a cure – a high-fat/high-protein/low-carbohydrate diet that could be eaten to the satisfaction of his appetite (**see Figure 11 on page 119**).

Finally, Banting had stumbled on an effective cure for his weight problem. By Christmas 1862 he had reduced his weight to eighty-two kilograms (BMI 31 kg/m^2), and by August the following year to seventy-one kilograms (BMI of 26 kg/m^2). Since an ideal BMI is 25 kg/m^2 or lower, the diet had almost cured Banting of his obesity.

To achieve this miracle, Banting had not suffered in the slightest; instead, he had eaten his fill each day. The key lay in the avoidance of carbohydrates: 'Bread, butter, milk, sugar, beer and potatoes, which had been the main (and, I thought, innocent) elements of my existence, or at all events they had for many years been adopted freely. These, said my excellent adviser, contain starch and saccharine, tending to create fat and should be avoided altogether.'

We now know that Banting should have continued to eat butter and drink milk, since the carbohydrate content of dairy produce is low and it is an excellent source of high-quality protein, fat and other nutrients.

Banting concluded: 'I can now confidently say that QUANTITY of diet may be safely left to the natural appetite; and that it is the QUALITY only which is essential to abate and cure corpulence.'

The question is: How did an ear, nose and throat surgeon know that the cure for obesity is a diet that restricts only its carbohydrate content, not its total calories?

The answer is that Harvey had travelled to Paris in 1856, where he had listened to the lectures of the iconic French physiologist, Dr Claude Bernard. There he heard Bernard express his new theory that besides bile, the liver also produces a substance related to starches and sugar, and which had been named glucose. Since Harvey knew that a diet rich in carbohydrates is used to fatten certain farm animals and, conversely, that 'a purely animal diet greatly assists in checking the secretion of diabetic urine', he came up with his own novel theory in 1858, as noted by Richard Mackarness in his book *Eat Fat and Grow Slim*: 'That excessive obesity might be allied to diabetes as to its cause, although widely diverse in its development; and that if a purely animal diet were useful in the latter disease, a combination of animal food with such vegetable diet as contained neither sugar nor starch, might serve to arrest the undue formation of fat.'

That his theory changed Banting's life for the better has been forgotten by those who do not know the full history of nutrition science so brilliantly described by Gary Taubes in his monumental works. Indeed, after adopting Harvey's diet, Banting lived another fifteen years, dying at age eighty-one.

Taubes's book and its successor, *Why We Get Fat and What To Do About It*, challenge much of what we believe in the nutrition sciences. When I had finished reading his books, I realised that he and others pose some serious challenges to nutritional 'truth' as it is currently believed. I also began to see that nutrition has been made too complex for a number of reasons – not least because if we really understood the truth, the employment of too many people around the world would be threatened. So instead, that which should be simple is made to appear unnecessarily complicated – a classic example of obfuscation to conceal a simpler truth. And the cost of this suppression is the modern epidemic of obesity, diabetes, hypertension and heart disease.

I decided that there must be some basic and simple rules of good nutrition. If we understand these basic rules, it should be much easier to decide what we should really be eating – to uncover the concealed truth in a universe of deception.

11 | The Key Rules of Nutrition

A question that has interested me can be simply stated: If the nutritional sciences have discovered the ultimate truth, why is it that obesity and diabetes are out of control in the developed world and becoming increasingly so in the developing world?

This is not a trivial question. Within the next decade, the exponential growth of diabetes and obesity will bankrupt the medical services of the developed world. Yet at the start of the twentieth century, adult-onset diabetes did not exist except in the very wealthiest families. Surely it should not be difficult to discover why a disease, formerly of privilege, has now invaded all sectors of modern society, regardless of their financial status?

The seriousness of this problem makes it the single greatest challenge that medical science has ever faced. If I were a nutritional scientist, I would be very wary of expressing dogmatic opinions about diseases that fall within my discipline but the growth of which are now out of control. This can only happen either because we do not understand what causes these diseases or because we know the facts but are powerless or unwilling to act.

It would be far better, in my opinion, to acknowledge our collective ignorance in this regard and invite any and all opinions, however contrary, in the hope that we might solve something that current beliefs deem insoluble. The words of Daniel Boorstin are especially apt: 'The greatest obstacle to discovery is not ignorance – it is the illusion of knowledge ... I have observed that the world has suffered far less from ignorance than from pretensions to knowledge. It is not skeptics or explorers but fanatics and ideologues who menace decency and progress. No agnostic ever burned anyone at the stake.'

My conclusion, one year into my personal experiment, is that William Harvey was correct. We know what causes both obesity and adult-onset diabetes. But this truth is, and has to be, successfully concealed by the carefully directed actions of immense global economic interests. This has to happen because the reversible factors causing diabetes and obesity generate too much wealth for too many people. Conquering these diseases would produce economic hardship for too many. So those at risk will continue to do whatever it takes to prevent this truth from being known. As a result, the obesity/diabetes epidemic will continue to accelerate until, finally, it bankrupts modern medicine. At which time it will in any case be too late to do anything, unless there is an unforeseen intervention.

It is with reluctance that I believe there will never be an effective, globally coordinated action to eliminate the preventable causes of obesity and diabetes, similar to those that were initiated to eliminate smoking when the toxic effects of cigarettes could no longer be hidden. The result is that populations will not be saved from obesity and diabetes by concerted government actions as part of a global initiative directed, for example, by the World Health Organization (WHO). Instead, the silence and compliance of those global organisations, like WHO, that have the potential to produce change will be purchased by those industries for which any change from the current status quo would prove the most damaging.

If civil society is not going to save us, our only hope is that we act as individuals to liberate ourselves. To do this, we need to understand just a few key rules of nutrition.

Rule 1: The most important rule. Industries determine what we believe about nutrition. This belief is engineered to increase food and beverage sales, not to protect or improve our health. In fact, most of what we have been taught is detrimental to our health.

Had I not done battle with the US sports-drink industry, I would never have considered it conceivable that many industries that claim to be acting in our best interests really could not care less about us. The dominant theme of modern business is the profit margin; all else, including the health of the users of their products, is relevant only if it can be manipulated to increase the company's profits. Unless you understand this, you place your personal health at great risk.

If you are sceptical of my claim, then I suggest you reread Part Two of this book. In fact, that example is tame compared to the numerous examples of fraud perpetuated especially by the US pharmaceutical industry. Perhaps you did not know, for example, that different US pharmaceutical companies have chosen to rather risk paying billions of dollars in retrospective compensation than to remove from the market drugs that are known to be causing ill health, often directly causing tens of thousands of deaths? There are far too many companies who put profit before their customers' well-being.

The only effective way to reverse the modern epidemic of obesity and diabetes, and probably a range of other conditions, including hypertension, heart disease, certain cancers and Alzheimer's disease, would be to limit the sale of products produced by a large number of established and highly influential food and beverage manufacturers whose reach is global. It is inconceivable that these industries do not know, as did the tobacco industry as early as the 1930s, that their products are a major cause of ill health in humans. So, behaving just as the tobacco industry did, these companies proactively protect their profits. They do this by ensuring that the public remains misinformed of the harmful effects of their products. A part of their scheme is to use science and compliant scientists to promote their incorrect messaging, just as the US sports-drink industry did. At the same time, any who might be foolish enough to expose the scam are demonised – the well-established tactic of 'refutation by denigration'.

Nutrition scientists and the organisations to which they belong are a favourite target for manipulation. If you wish to discover which companies are producing products that you should be avoiding, you can do no better than to trace the funding sources of the major dietetic and diabetes associations around the world. For example, the American Dietetic Association (ADA) lists Coca-Cola, Pepsico, Kellogg's, General Mills and Mars among its corporate sponsors. The British Nutrition Society (BNS) also accepts funding from Coca-Cola, Mars and Nestlé UK, while the British Dietetic Association (BDA) is funded by Kellogg's. The International Olympic Committee (IOC) and International Football Association (FIFA) also enjoy close relationships with their 'partner' Coca-Cola, while the International Cricket Council (ICC) draws its refreshment from Pepsico. Sugar-containing soft drinks and confectionery are without nutritional value, especially for athletes, and produce only negative health consequences. So why would the ADA, the BNS, the IOC, the ICC and FIFA wish to associate their organisations with the producers of these harmful products? The association of Coca-Cola and Pepsico to the Olympics and to world football and cricket sends the message that sugar is a desirable foodstuff for athletes.

Given that all these corporate sponsors produce products with high carbohydrate contents, it is perhaps predictable that the ADA advises those with diabetes to eat the same high-carbohydrate diet that is prescribed for healthy individuals. The American Diabetes Association, funded as it is by US pharmaceutical companies that produce drugs used by diabetics, is also reluctant to promote a change in the national dietary guidelines that would reverse the obesity/diabetes epidemic and so put their corporate sponsors out of business. As a result, they must continue to deny that the cause of obesity and diabetes is already established.

Similarly, in 2011 the BDA declared the low-carbohydrate Dukan Diet, allegedly followed by the Middleton sisters in preparation for the marriage of Prince William and Catherine Middleton, the 'worst celebrity diet of the year'. This despite the fact that Dr Dukan's book describing his diet has sold more than three million copies in France and that the French have the highest intake of saturated fat and, of any developed nation, one of the lowest incidences of heart disease. Perhaps the BDA would do better trying to understand why the French are doing so well despite eating so much saturated fat from a diet of the kind first promoted by William Harvey and now by the much-maligned Drs Atkins and Dukan, among many others.

They might also want to investigate whether the marked weight loss of Australian cricketer Shane Warne over the past year or so since he met English actress Elizabeth Hurley has anything to do with his adoption of a low-carbohydrate diet like that proposed by Dr Dukan.

The individual's search for leanness is indeed a global enterprise. But the world's leading dietetic associations seem to have given up that particular pursuit.

Rule 2: It is not only about the calories.

In Part Six of this book I describe how scientists use models like the Central Governor to understand how different complex bodies function, be they the Universe or the human brain during exercise. We develop these models that make predictions of what should happen. If the model is correct, we test what happens when we do something to perturb the system we are studying. If the outcomes that we measure were correctly predicted by the model, then the model survives until the next experiment. But if the model is unable to predict the outcome of any single experiment, then it is time to cast it aside and to develop a new and better model that is again consistent with all the known evidence and experiences.

The most popular modern model to describe how obesity develops and how it is sustained is the following: Obesity develops when the total daily intake of dietary calories exceeds the total daily calorie expenditure. When this happens, the excess calories are stored in the body's fat cells. This leads to a progressive increase in body weight that continues for as long as there is this positive energy balance. This model predicts that there is only one way to lose excess body weight – a negative energy balance must be created in which the energy intake must be reduced by eating less. At the same time, the energy expenditure must be augmented by an increase in physical activity. This negative energy balance must be maintained until the desired weight is achieved.

The model makes certain predictions that are universally accepted. The first is that the root cause of obesity is obvious – those who are obese are both lazy and greedy. If they were just more disciplined, if they ate less and exercised more, they, too, could be slim and athletic. This is a classic example of blaming the victim for his or her circumstances.

It also avoids asking the more obvious question: If the interventions that this model predicts will prevent and reverse obesity prove, in practice, to be useless, then perhaps the model is wrong? If a calorie-restricted diet is unable to produce sustained weight loss, then perhaps it is the diet and not the patient that is at fault. William Banting's successful weight loss did not occur because William Banting changed. It occurred because he changed his diet to restrict its carbohydrate content, not its calorie content (**see Figure 11 on page 119**).

The second prediction of the model is that the best way to lose weight is to remove all fat from the diet. This is because fat is the most energy-dense macronutrient. Thus it seems obvious that the easiest way to reduce the energy intake is to replace an equal number of grams of fat with the same number of grams of carbohydrate. This will surely produce an immediate weight loss. Simple.

This is the model that is promoted globally by virtually every nutritionist, dietician, scientist and medical doctor with any major influence in this discipline. It is also the model that is investigated by Mackarness and Taubes, among others.

The problem with this model is that it is just too simple to be true. Like the Hill model of exercise regulation (Part Six), it is 'brainless'. Do those who follow this model really believe that the brain plays no part in the regulation of body weight? This is like believing that the brain plays no part in exercise regulation.

In the first place, the brainless model cannot be true, since most fat people are in energy balance and are weight stable even if that weight is above a healthy norm. For most of their lives the obese are either in energy balance or very close to it. As in the lean, this occurs because humans, like all of earth's creatures, have an incredible ability homeostatically to regulate their weight. The brain does this with a degree of precision that defies our understanding. No machine will ever be built that can match this level of precision.

The key to this control is our appetite.

But the brainless model specifically ignores the role of appetite in the regulation of our weight. The moment we eat less and exercise more, our appetite is stimulated. And that is why the interventions that are supposed to cause weight loss, according to this conventional model, are utterly ineffective. All they produce is hunger and the desire to eat more. In this way, an energy deficit induced by exercise and calorie restriction produces just more hunger, not sustained weight loss.

It is time to develop a different model – one in which factors other than simply the calorie content of the diet need to be considered if sustained weight loss of the kind enjoyed by William Banting is to be achieved.

A key consideration is the influence of different nutrients on appetite. Thus whereas carbohydrate-rich foods stimulate appetite, leading to the ingestion of an excess of calories, protein- and fat-rich foods satisfy the appetite and produce sustained satiety at lower levels of calorie intake. This is the essential point that the conventional brainless model of weight regulation has unfortunately overlooked. It is a serious error.

Rule 3: There are two types of humans – those who can metabolise carbohydrates normally and who are therefore carbohydrate-tolerant (CT), and those who lack this capacity and who are therefore carbohydrate-resistant (CR).

The following is the currently accepted model of how eating too many calories and exercising too little eventually leads to obesity and diabetes mellitus: People who are prone to developing obesity and diabetes have a genetically diminished capacity to use fat as an energy source to fuel their bodily needs. As a result they are more likely to store any excess calories they ingest as fat in their fat cells. Over a sufficient number of years, a high-energy intake, especially from fat, eventually produces a state of carbohydrate-resistance (CR) in which the muscles and liver are no longer able to use carbohydrate normally.

It is further argued that the immediate cause of CR is the toxic effect of all this excess stored fat, which reduces the capacity of the muscles and liver to take up and utilise glucose from the bloodstream. As a result, the pancreas of anyone with CR must excrete excessive amounts of insulin to drive the glucose from the bloodstream into the increasingly reluctant muscles and liver whenever the blood glucose rises in response to the ingestion of highly refined carbohydrates especially. This insulin is crucial because glucose in high concentrations is toxic to most cells. But this excessive insulin secretion whenever carbohydrate is ingested cannot be sustained indefinitely. Ultimately, either pancreatic exhaustion occurs, with a failure of insulin secretion, or the liver and muscles become completely resistant to the action of insulin. When either happens, full-blown diabetes has developed.

According to this model, the villain is obvious – it is the fat in the diet. So the solution is equally simple: remove all fat from the diet and eat mainly carbohydrates. This will magically reverse the CR, leading, equally magically, to the immediate use of all the energy stored in the excess fat, which then simply melts away. But conveniently avoided is the question: What happens to the large quantities of carbohydrates eaten by those who remain CR (until the high-carbohydrate diet magically reverses this CR)? Also ignored is the evidence that William Banting's weight problem was cured when he substituted a high-fat and high-protein intake for his formerly high-carbohydrate diet (which prevented any weight loss, instead sustaining his obesity).

The contrasting explanation of what causes obesity is one that was popular in the first half of the twenty-first century, as noted by Mackarness in his book in 1958, but that was forgotten until resuscitated by the low-carbohydrate diet movement beginning with Dr Atkins's original book in 1972 and as fully exposed by Gary Taubes's detective work.

According to this earlier model, obesity is not a problem caused by the ingestion of a fat-rich diet. Rather obesity occurs in those with CR when they ingest a diet that is too *low* in fat. A diet with a low fat content must, by definition, have a high carbohydrate content. And a high-carbohydrate diet must lead inexorably, as night follows day, to obesity and diabetes in those with CR.

According to this model, people with a genetic disorder that predisposes them to obesity and diabetes have an inability to store and metabolise carbohydrate properly in the liver and muscles. Persons with CR have no difficulty using fat as a fuel. Their problem is that they must over-secrete insulin whenever they ingest any carbohydrate. As a result, they exist in a perpetual state of elevated blood insulin concentrations. And because that insulin works less effectively in those with CR, their blood glucose concentrations are also chronically elevated.

In addition, the principal effect of insulin in those with CR is to drive the glucose in the bloodstream not into their liver and muscle cells, but into their fat cells, where it is stored as fat. At the same time, the insulin prevents the release of stored fat from the fat cells. As a result, those with CR fail to metabolise fat, not because their tissues lack the capacity, but because their use of fat is prevented by their persistently high blood insulin concentrations caused by their high-carbohydrate diets (and their CR).

In this case, the prevention and treatment of obesity requires a diet that is the precise opposite of that suggested by the first model. It is the exclusion of carbohydrate and its replacement with fat especially, but also with an increased protein intake, that will produce weight loss and sustain the health of those with CR, just as it did for William Banting.

An interesting side question that is seldom asked: Why is CR such a common disorder in modern humans? The answer has to be that sometime in the course of human evolution, CR provided a biological advantage favouring the survival of those with that genetic trait. Clearly this is no longer the case. But if, as described in Part Two, humans evolved as persistence hunters living on a predominantly high-fat/high-protein/low-carbohydrate diet – the forerunner of the Harvey/Banting diet and as described by Dr Loren Cordain in his book *The Paleo Diet* in 2011 – then having CR would not have been a shortcoming, since there was never enough carbohydrate in the diet to expose any disadvantage in that genetic variant.

But what if humans with CR were favoured because when they did find carbohydrate-rich foods, for example honey or fruit, those with CR would be better able to store the excess carbohydrate energy as fat and so tide them over periods when food was scarce, for example in winter? Thus those with CR would be more likely to survive times of nutritional scarcity if they had been able to access a source of high-carbohydrate foods sometime before the onset of that nutritional hardship. Because those with carbohydrate-tolerance (CT) do not get fat when they eat carbohydrates, they would be at a disadvantage, according to this theory. But when exposed to high-carbohydrate diets on a daily basis, only those with CT would be able to stay lean and maintain reasonable health.

Alternatively, CR might be beneficial if it spares scarce carbohydrate for use by the brain rather than the muscles. This would be beneficial if the diet is low in carbohydrate, as was that of the original persistence hunters.

Importantly, any or all of these explanations may yet prove wrong in the long term, perhaps because they try to explain complex phenomena in simple, easy-to-understand terms. But according to my interpretation, this best explains all that we currently know. In contrast, the traditional 'calories in, calories out' model ignores a large body of evidence that it cannot explain. More importantly, interventions based on the alternative model described here are effective in reversing obesity (Rule 4), whereas those based on the first model have proven hopelessly inadequate.

Rule 4: It is the carbohydrate and not the fat in the diet that causes and maintains the obese state, leading to diabetes in those with CR.

For all the reasons described in Rule 3, it is the carbohydrate content of the diet that causes and maintains the obese state in those with CR. As a result, the more fat and the less carbohydrate eaten by those with CR, the lighter they will be.

A typical high-carbohydrate diet provides between 300 and 400 grams of carbohydrate each day, whereas those with CR need to eat less than 60 to 80 grams daily if they wish to be lean and at low risk for the development of adult-onset diabetes.

The high-fat/high-protein/low-carbohydrate diet produces weight loss in those with CR by reducing the glucose/insulin spikes whenever carbohydrate is ingested. This removes the brake imposed by insulin on the release of fat from the fat cells. As a result, the fat cells are restored to that function for which they are designed – to provide a continuous, uninterrupted supply of fat energy to fuel all the body's incidental needs, including those produced by vigorous exercise.

This uninterrupted supply of energy also signals to the appetite centres in the brain that there is more than enough fuel available at any time. The result is that hunger is suppressed and the energy intake falls naturally. That is why those eating the Harvey/Banting diet are able to eat less without feeling con-tinuously hungry. It also explains why the weight loss produced by this type of diet also results in feelings of increased energy (Rule 9).

Rule 5: There is no definitive evidence that a high fat intake is harmful to health.

In *Good Calories, Bad Calories*, Gary Taubes describes how the actions of one man, Dr Ancel Keys, initiated the false belief that it is the fat in the diet that is especially detrimental to health. Keys based his conclusion on a study in which he found a striking relationship between the amount of saturated fat in the diet and the incidence of heart disease in six, and later seven, countries. The problem was that either by error or evil intent, Keys ignored available data from a much larger group of countries. When those data were added to his original analysis, there was no longer any relationship between saturated-fat intake and the incidence of heart disease in that expanded sample of countries. Nor was there ever any relationship found between the total fat intake (from both saturated and unsaturated fat) and the heart-disease rate.

The same study repeated with currently available data would show the same result – Keys's hypothesis is mythical and is the result of 'cherry-picking' only the available data that supported his preconceived belief. It is a classic example of 'bent science' – using data to reach an outcome that was predetermined even before the investigation began.

The problem was that within months of his article's publication, Keys's contentious idea had become the new truth, an astonishing achievement given that new medical ideas usually take at least ten years to replace those which were previously believed. But Keys's idea achieved this transition within months, not years.

The result was that by 1977, the US Senate had produced its first Dietary Guidelines, the focus of which was to replace 'unhealthy' saturated fat in the diet with 'healthy' carbohydrates, according to Keys's doctrine. Instantly forgotten was the evidence, widely accepted until then, that a high-carbohydrate intake causes obesity and diabetes (in those with CR). The predictable outcome, as noted by A.H. Hite, R.D. Feinman and G.E. Gusman in their 2010 article 'In the face of contradictory evidence: Report of the Dietary Guidelines for Americans Committee', was the epidemic of obesity and diabetes that has engulfed the US since these guidelines demonising dietary fat have promoted a high-carbohydrate intake for all.

A key factor that those responsible for drawing up the US Dietary Guidelines continue to ignore, as we discussed in Figure 2 in Part Two of this book, is that association does not prove causation. Instead, the sole way to prove causation is to undertake long-term prospective studies in which the factor considered causative is changed only in the experimental group but remains unaltered in the control group. At present, studies to establish the effects of reducing especially saturated-fat intake on long-term heart-disease risk have not produced consistent, definitive results, perhaps because the studies have generally been too small.

So instead we must rely on associational studies. But they have the weakness that those who enter such studies and who eat more saturated fat might be different and less health conscious than those who eat more unsaturated fats.

They might, for example, smoke more, exercise less and eat more sugar. The latter relationship was first shown in 1964, when an English study by John Yudkin – 'Dietary fat and dietary sugar in relation to ischaemic heart disease and diabetes' – found a striking relationship between the amount of fat and sugar in the diet, so that those who ate the most fat also ingested the most sugar. Their poorer health may therfore not be because they eat too much saturated fat; rather it could be because of other aspects of their lifestyles.

However, when appropriate studies are analysed as a collective, as demonstrated by P.W. Siri-Tarino, F.B. Hu, Q. Sun and R.M. Krauss in their 2010 report 'Meta-analysis of prospective cohort studies evaluating the association of saturated fat with cardiovascular disease', it has been found that 'there is no significant evidence for concluding that dietary saturated fat is associated with an increased risk of coronary heart disease or cardiovascular disease'. These same authors make the point that replacing saturated-fat intake with an increased intake of polyunsaturated fats will produce a different result than replacing that fat with an increased carbohydrate intake. This is because an increased carbohydrate intake changes the blood fat (cholesterol and triglyceride) concentration to one that favours the development of heart disease (Rule 7). Thus they propose in another study, 'Saturated fat, carbohydrate and cardiovascular disease', that 'dietary efforts to improve the increasing burden of cardiovascular disease ... should primarily emphasise the limitation of refined-carbohydrate intakes and the reduction in excess adiposity'.

All of which sounds like an endorsement of the Harvey/Banting diet.

These studies should have caused the authors of the US Dietary Guidelines to modify their acquired bias against fat and to admit their error. But the opposite has happened, as also noted by Hite, Feinman and Gusman.

There is some evidence of progress. The most recent dietary guidelines for the prevention of heart disease appear to warn that the only dangerous fats to be avoided are the artificial trans-fatty acids – as noted by T.R. Frieden and D.M. Berwick in their 2011 paper 'The "Million Hearts" Initiative – Preventing heart attacks and strokes' – which were ironically developed by industry to replace the formerly 'dangerous' saturated fats found in red meat and dairy produce. This is in keeping with the view of Harvard's Dr Walter Willet, perhaps the most published nutritional scientist of all time, who wrote in his 2001 book with P.J. Skerrett – *Eat, Drink and Be Healthy. The Harvard Medical School Guide to Healthy Eating* – and his 2011 paper with D.S. Ludwig – 'The 2010 Dietary Guidelines – the best recipe for health?' – that there is no need to restrict the fat content of the diet, although his bias is still to limit saturated-fat

FIGURE 12

Increase in diabetes prevalance follows the increase in sugar consumption in the USA and UK

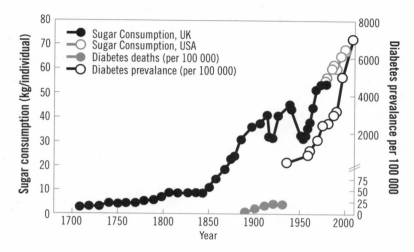

The rise in the incidence of diabetes in the USA and the UK exactly matches the rise in the sugar consumption of those countries. While this association does not prove causation, it should at least invite serious debate about the possible role of sugar in the cause of diabetes. But this has not happened. Rather, the global sugar industry, as observed by Jeff O'Connell in his book Sugar Nation, *and its principal commercial partners have effectively silenced any debate about the potentially harmful effects of our modern sugar addiction. Reproduced from Johnson et al., 2009.*

intake by increasing the intake of unsaturated fats, especially those found in fish and nuts.

Rule 6: Sugar, not fat, is the single most toxic ingredient of the modern diet. It is also the most ubiquitous foodstuff on the planet.

Before the beginning of the twentieth century, obesity, diabetes and heart disease were uncommon. The amount of sugar that humans ate was also much less – about four kilograms per person per year. Today that figure is closer to fifty kilograms per person per year. The single greatest change in dietary patterns over the past 150 years is not that humans are eating more calories or more fat calories – it is that we are eating ten times as much sugar as did our great-great-grandparents, few of whom suffered as we do from obesity, diabetes, hypertension and heart disease. Indeed, the exponential increase in the incidence of diabetes in the USA and the UK exactly matches the rise in the consumption of sugar in those two countries (see **Figure 12 on page 133**).

Surprisingly, when Dr Ancel Keys reported a (spurious) relationship between dietary fat intake and heart-attack rates in six countries (Rule 5), his idea that heart disease was caused by a high saturated-fat intake was immediately accepted as the final truth. Yet the association shown in Figure 12, first noted by English nutritional scientist Dr John Yudkin in 1957, has been met with a deathly silence. A flurry of books in the 1960s and 1970s briefly sparked interest in the possibility that sugar might indeed be the cause of ill health. But this soon disappeared as the theory took hold that dietary fat was the principal nutritional cause of ill health. Sugar instead gave all of us 'go'.

Interestingly, the best evidence linking a high sugar intake to disease, especially that of adult-onset diabetes, came from a South African researcher who has never received the recognition he deserves. His 'fault' was to discover information that was economically sensitive because it threatened one of the world's largest food industries.

Dr G.D. Campbell was the physician who, in the late 1950s, started the first Diabetic Clinic at the King Edward VIII Hospital in Durban, South Africa. This public hospital serves those inhabitants of Durban and its surrounds who cannot afford private health care.

It did not take long before Dr Campbell realised that he was seeing a novel condition – the appearance of adult-onset diabetes in increasing numbers of urban-living Zulu-speakers and in Indians who had come to South Africa, many to work on the sugar-growing plantations that surround Durban. His interest piqued, Dr Campbell decided to study the phenomenon. He came to a number of crucial conclusions.

First, the incidence of diabetes in the urban-living Zulu-speakers was much higher than was the incidence in Zulus who continued to live in their traditional rural areas. Similarly, the incidence of diabetes was at least ten times higher in Indians living in Durban than it was in the ancestral Indian populations from which the South African Indians had originated.

Second, the first signs of diabetes began in Zulu-speakers who had been living in urban Durban for about twenty years.

Third, as described in his 1963 work in the *South African Medical Journal* – 'Diabetes in Asians and Africans in and around Durban' – the key dietary change in both populations was a dramatic increase in the intake of sugar. Thus the daily sugar intake of the rural Zulu was about eight grams (three kilograms per year), whereas it was 106 grams (thirty-nine kilograms per year) in those Zulus who had become urbanised. Similarly, Indians living in Durban ate between thirty-five and fifty kilograms of sugar per year, compared to an annual intake of about five kilograms in Indians still resident in India.

Since there was no other dietary factor that differed so greatly between urban and rural Zulu-speakers, Dr Campbell concluded that it must have been a sudden increase in their sugar intakes alone that explained the dramatic appearance of diabetes in both Zulus and Indians living in Durban. He wrote widely on the topic and helped developed a novel term – the saccharine diseases – to explain what he had found. In time he concluded that the saccharine diseases, caused by the adoption of a high-sugar diet, were not confined solely to diabetes, but included also obesity, dental caries and gum diseases, varicose veins and haemorrhoids, peptic ulcers, coronary heart disease and a range of intra-abdominal infections, including appendicitis, diverticulitis, pyelonephritis and cholecystitis.

Support for Dr Campbell's hypothesis came from a study of Yemeni (Black) Jews who immigrated to Israel from Yemen, where they ate mainly fat and protein foods with very little sugar and did not suffer from diabetes. Their subsequent adoption of the native Israelis' high sugar intake was followed, now predictably, within twenty to thirty years by a sudden rise in their incidence of diabetes. Similarly, the introduction of sugar to the Cherokee Indians, Inuit (Eskimos), Australian Aborigines, Polynesian islanders and those living in Iceland and New Guinea was also followed within a predictable time by the appearance of adult-onset diabetes. Finally, it was calculated that the annual sugar intake of countries in which diabetes is common is at least three times the intake found in countries in which diabetes is uncommon (forty-one versus fourteen kilograms per year).

Another to take up the cudgels was English physician Dr John Yudkin. In his position as professor directing the Department of Nutrition at the Queen Elizabeth College at the University of London, he was a highly regarded scientist. Concerned by the possibility that sugar could be a cause of ill health, he initiated a series of laboratory studies of the effects of an increased sugar intake on the health of humans and rats. His extensive studies, reviewed in the expanded version of his first book, which he published later in his career, clearly documented the detrimental effects of diets high in sugar on the health of both humans and rats.

Given that diabetes would become the greatest health problem of the twenty-first century in developed and developing nations, one might have expected that the finding of Drs Campbell, Cleave and Yudkin – that the adoption of the Western diet with a high sugar intake is the direct cause of diabetes (in those with CR) – was so important that it must have led to the award of a Nobel Prize in Medicine and Physiology. But this did not happen. The opposite took place. Dr Yudkin, especially, was demonised. As he wrote with feeling in his book *Pure, White and Deadly* in 1986:

> Let me end this personal tale by repeating that I do not accuse those scientists who express disagreement with my views of doing so for improper motives. Nevertheless, I find it remarkable that there are still so many in this category, after several years of accumulating evidence that supports the conclusions that I and a few other research workers have reached. It is especially interesting that some of those who began by leaning towards accepting these views now reject them. It is difficult to avoid the conclusion that this is the result of the vigorous, continuous and expanding activities of the sugar interests … The result is such a compact nucleus of power that, like a magnet surrounded by a strong induction coil, it produces a field of influence that invisibly affects many of those not in direct contact with the centre.

He concluded with this compelling truth: Freedom of choice exists only if there is freedom of information, which naturally is not the case. The official position of the South African Sugar Association is clear, for on their website is the following:

> Unbalanced and scientifically inaccurate reporting on sugar consumption has led to excessive and negative speculation regarding the value of sugar as part of a balanced diet … Eminent bodies such as the World Health Organization and the Food and Agricultural Organization agree that sugar, like other carbohydrate-containing foods, has an indispensable role to play in balanced diets. These bodies concluded that there is no evidence of sugar being the direct cause of lifestyle diseases such as diabetes, heart disease, obesity or cancer.

They perhaps forgot to add that the US Dietary Guidelines also propose that sugar can provide up to 15 per cent of the daily calories in a 'healthy' diet. These utterances simply prove that money ultimately talks and that these three bodies have no real interest in reversing the global obesity/diabetes epidemic, or of giving us the tools to understand what really is a healthy diet.

Of course the profits of two of the most venerated global soft-drinks companies' products, as well as the entire confectionery industry, are entirely dependent on our not having freedom of access to all the evidence of the toxic effects of dietary sugar, or its most recent, equally toxic substitute, high-fructose corn syrup.

A key problem with sugar is that it is a highly addictive substance, with some like O'Connell placing it in the same league as nicotine and cocaine. So unless something extraordinary happens, the global use of sugar will simply continue to rise, as it has since the mid-1850s (see Figure 12). And so, too, will the global incidence of obesity and diabetes.

Rule 7: Cholesterol is not the unique cause of heart disease and may not even be an important factor (especially in women).

The idea that fat intake causes heart disease is based on the flimsiest of evidence. As told in detail by Taubes in *Good Calories, Bad Calories*, it was probably the determination of Dr Ancel Keys to become an international health celebrity that developed this falsehood. So once Keys had decided on inadequate grounds (Rule 5) that a high saturated-fat intake causes heart disease, he needed to come up with a mechanism by which this occurred. His solution was to propose that a high intake of saturated fat elevates the blood cholesterol concentration; the excess cholesterol in the blood is then deposited in the arteries supplying the heart. In time this accumulation obstructs these (coronary) arteries, leading, over a period of many years, to acute heart attacks, some of which are fatal.

This attractive explanation would in time launch a group of the most lucrative pharmaceutical drugs of all time – the statins, which lower the blood cholesterol concentrations and, at least theoretically, must therefore prevent the development of all heart attacks (if Keys's theory is correct). But there are a number of problems with his theory. Predictably, these uncertainties are hidden, most especially from those doctors who prescribe these drugs and the patients who use them – another example of the absence of freedom of information. Doubt cannot be sanctioned if it should threaten the profitability of large pharmaceutical companies.

First, there is no definitive evidence that reducing especially the saturated fat in the diet prevents heart disease, as it must if the theory is correct.

Second, the three most potent risk factors for heart disease are smoking, diabetes mellitus and hypertension, none of which, as far as we know, act by causing an increased intake of saturated fat. Rather, diabetes is a disease of abnormal carbohydrate metabolism caused by an excessive intake of carbohydrate (Rule 4), especially sugar (Rule 6) (**see Figure 12**), in those with CR. I would argue that hypertension is another consequence of a high-carbohydrate diet in those with CR.

Third, a 'healthy' high-carbohydrate diet causes unhealthy changes in blood fat concentrations that would predict increased, not reduced, heart-attack risk, according to the Ancel Keys model. Thus the blood concentrations of blood triglycerides, considered to raise the risk of heart attack, increase, whereas concentrations of the protective HDL-cholesterol fraction fall when a high-carbohydrate diet is eaten. Perversely, these adverse responses are reversed by the ingestion of an 'unhealthy' high-fat diet, suggesting that a high-fat diet should prevent, not cause, heart disease.

We also need to look at the effects of these different diets on the fraction that contains most of the blood cholesterol, the LDL-cholesterol fraction. It is argued, according to the Ancel Keys model, that a high intake of especially saturated fat increases the risk of heart disease by elevating blood LDL-cholesterol concentrations. But he was not to know that LDL-cholesterol is transported in the blood in particles of three different sizes – large, medium and small – and that it is only the LDL-cholesterol carried in the small particles that is considered to increase the risk of heart disease. A high-fat diet increases the concentration of healthy large LDL particles, whereas a high-carbohydrate diet increases the concentration of unhealthy small LDL particles, as observed by P.W. Siri-Tarino, F.B. Hu, Q. Sun and R.M. Krauss in their paper 'Saturated fat, carbohydrate and cardiovascular disease'. Thus the switch from a high-carbohydrate to a high-fat diet improves all the blood fat components that most believe are related to heart-attack risk.

But this information is hidden, since blood LDL-cholesterol particle-sizes are almost never measured, and especially not when an individual's need for statin therapy is considered. The reason is obvious. It is not known how many people with 'elevated' LDL-cholesterol concentrations currently being treated with statins do not need such treatment, since most of their 'elevated' blood LDL-cholesterol is carried in healthy large particles.

Fourth, a host of studies have established that if the blood total cholesterol concentration is indeed a risk factor for heart disease, it is only of marginal importance compared to many other, far more important factors that are improperly considered by those caring for persons who either have heart disease or who are at risk for its development.

Take, for example, the iconic Framingham Heart Study, which is considered one of the top ten medical advances in the past century because it developed the concept that a combination of correctable conditions, since termed 'risk factors', predispose individuals to the development of heart disease. One such factor identified in the very earliest reports from that study was an elevated blood cholesterol concentration. But while the importance of the other risk factors also identified by the Framingham Heart Study – such as hypertension, obesity and diabetes – have been confirmed in the 1985 work of W.B. Kannell – 'Lipids, diabetes, and coronary heart disease: Insights from the Framingham study' – the blood cholesterol concentration has not done quite as well.

Thus in 1987, a thirty-year review of the Framingham data by K.M. Anderson, W.P. Castelli and D. Levy – 'Cholesterol and mortality. 30 years of follow-up from the Framingham study' – found that 'after age fifty years there is no increased overall mortality with either high or low serum cholesterol levels'. Instead, *falling* blood cholesterol levels after age fifty-one were associated with an 11 per cent *increase* in overall mortality and a 14 per cent *increased* heart-attack death rate for each 1 mg/dL per year drop in blood cholesterol concentrations.

The authors concluded that although a very low blood cholesterol concentration improves longevity under age fifty years, after age fifty a low cholesterol concentration was associated with a reduced life expectancy. But this does not make any sense. How can the effect of a risk factor suddenly reverse simply because one turns fifty?

A subsequent report from the Framingham Heart Study by Castelli in 1992 –'Concerning the possibility of a nut...' – was even more damaging for the Keys theory, for it found that '... the more saturated fat one ate, the more cholesterol one ate, the more calories one ate, the lower the person's serum cholesterol ... the opposite of what the equations provided by Hegsted et al. (1965) and Keys et al. (1957) would predict ...' and that 'the people who ate the most cholesterol, ate the most saturated fat, and ate the most calories weighed the least and were the most physically active'.

Along these lines, a recent Norwegian study – 'Is the use of cholesterol in mortality risk algorithms in clinical guidelines valid? Ten years prospective data from the Norwegian HUNT 2 study' – by H. Petursson, J.A. Sigurdsson and C. Bengtsson has found that whereas smoking increased the risk of dying from coronary heart disease nearly threefold, there was essentially no effect from an elevated blood total cholesterol concentration even in those who smoked and had high blood pressure. Furthermore, in women, higher blood cholesterol concentrations were protective, so that women with blood total cholesterol concentrations of 7 mmol/L were at the lowest risk of dying from heart disease. The authors concluded that 'cholesterol emerged as an overestimated risk factor … indicating that guideline information might be misleading, particularly for women with "moderately elevated" cholesterol levels in the range 5–7 mmol/L'.

Importantly, this study is almost unique, since it was not funded by the pharmaceutical industry. So it is more likely to produce a finding that is truly independent.

My conclusion is that the theory that proposes that blood cholesterol causes heart disease is at best tenuous, and at worst wrong. It is sustained because a massive global industry requires that this truth should not be known. Dr George Mann, who first showed that the Masai tribesmen, whose diet comprises predominantly saturated fats but who have low blood cholesterol concentrations and a low incidence of heart disease (perhaps because they do not eat sugar and refined flour), is an outspoken critic of this theory and the factors that sustain it. As he wrote in 'Coronary heart disease: The doctor's dilemma' in the *American Heart Journal* in 1978:

> For twenty-five years the treatment dogma for coronary heart disease (CHD) has been a low-cholesterol, low-fat, polyunsaturated diet. This treatment grew out of a reasonable hypothesis raised in 1950 by Gofman and others, but soon a clot of aggressive industrialists, self-interested foundations, and selfish scientists turned this hypothesis into nutritional dogma which was widely impressed upon physicians and the general public. A nadir was reached when zealous doctors and salesmen arranged such 'prudent' meals for national meetings of cardiologists, rather like Tupperware teas. They grew up in the interface between science and the government funding agencies, a club of devoted supporters of the dogma which controlled the funding of research, a group known by the cynics among us as the 'heart mafia'. Critics or disbelievers of the diet/heart dogma were seen as pariahs and they went unfunded, whilst such extravagances as the Diet/Heart trial, the MRFIT trial and a dozen or more lavish Lipid Research Centers [*sic*] divided up the booty. For a generation, research on heart disease has been more political than scientific. All this resulted from the abuse of the scientific method. A valid hypothesis was raised, tested, and found untenable. But for selfish reasons, it has not been abandoned.

Dr Mann has also concluded that the Diet/Heart Theory is the 'greatest scientific deception of this century, perhaps any century'. Others have provided detailed reasons why they concur with Mann's maverick position (Uffe Ravnskov in *Ignore the Awkward*, Malcolm Kendrick in *The Great Cholesterol Con*, and Ernest N. Curtis in *The Cholesterol Delusion*), and the evidence they present is convincing.

On the basis of the epidemiological evidence showing (i) that heart disease was almost unknown before the growth of the global sugar industry (**see Figure 12**); (ii) that diabetes begins to appear in populations that increase their carbohydrate, especially sugar, intake without any significant change in their fat intake (Rule 6); (iii) that diabetes is one of the strong predictors of future heart-attack risk, as noted by Kannell in 1985; and (iv) that healthy blood fat concentrations improve on a high-fat but worsen on a high-carbohydrate diet, I conclude that heart disease is, in common with diabetes and obesity, a disease of abnormal carbohydrate metabolism in response to a high-carbohydrate intake (especially in the form of sugar) in those with CR. Thus the mechanism causing heart disease in those with CR must be related to repetitive spikes in blood glucose (and insulin) concentrations producing damaging effects to the lining of the blood vessels, especially those supplying the heart and brain, at the same time increasing the likelihood for blood clotting in those damaged blood vessels.

My advice is the following: If you have CR and wish to reduce your risk of developing heart disease, you need to avoid eating a high-carbohydrate diet. Instead, you need to eat a diet in which fat is the predominant energy source. This will reduce, and perhaps prevent, the risk that diabetes will develop, and as a consequence help protect also against heart disease.

In which case the key measurement to determine your risk for developing heart disease is not your blood fat concentration, especially cholesterol, but rather measures of your carbohydrate metabolism – your fasting blood glucose, insulin and haemoglobin A1c (HbA1c) concentrations. The latter gives a measure of your average blood glucose concentrations over the past three months so that the higher the HbA1c concentration, the worse your CR. What is more, HbA1c concentrations are among the very best predictors of future heart-attack risk. Thus, as written by K.T. Khaw, N. Wareham and S. Bingham et al. in 'Association of hemoglobin A1c with cardiovascular disease and mortality in adults: The European prospective investigation into cancer in Norfolk' in 2004: 'In men and women, the relationship between hemoglobin [*sic*] A1c and cardiovascular disease … and between hemoglobin [*sic*] A1c and all-cause mortality ... was continuous and significant throughout the whole distribution. The relationship was apparent in persons without known diabetes. Persons with hemoglobin [*sic*] A1c concentrations less than 5 per cent had the lowest rates of cardiovascular disease and mortality ... these relative risks were independent of age, body mass index, waist-to-hip ratio, systolic blood pressure, serum cholesterol concentration, cigarette smoking, and history of cardiovascular disease.'

To predict and manage your future risk of heart attack, you need to understand and better manage your CR. Knowing your blood cholesterol concentration is not really very helpful. In fact, I would argue that women should never have their blood total cholesterol concentrations measured, since there is no evidence in women that the blood cholesterol concentration can predict anything other than good health if it is in the range of 5–7 mmol/L, and the higher the value in that range, the better.

Similarly, if statins are to be used in men, which is not something I would easily advocate – I would prefer those with CR to be placed on a low-carbohydrate diet, since I suspect that this will be of much greater benefit in the long term – their use should be restricted to treating only those men with abnormally high concentrations of small-particle LDL-cholesterol. Treating all men regardless of their age with statins once their blood total cholesterol concentrations exceed 5 mmol/L without first knowing their small-particle LDL concentrations or appreciating that total cholesterol concentrations are of little predictive value in men my age, is irresponsible.

Even more irresponsible, indeed evil, is the recent proposal to measure blood cholesterol concentrations in all children, beginning between ages nine and eleven and repeating again between ages seventeen and twenty-one, as noted by B.M. Psaty and F.P. Rivara in their 2011 work 'Universal screening and drug treatment of dyslipidemia in children and adolescents'.

Since such screening must be done as part of an intervention, one must assume that there will soon be adolescents who begin their lifetime statin therapy at age nine, if not younger. None of these 'at-risk' adolescents will ever be informed by the pharmaceutical companies producing these drugs that the easiest way to prevent the future development of obesity, diabetes and heart disease is to remove all sugar and refined carbohydrates from their diet, while at the same time restricting the number of grams of carbohydrate eaten each day. That would be too simple a solution. And, ultimately, too damaging for the future health of the pharmaceutical industry and the wealth of its top executives.

Rule 8: All the exercise in the world will not make you thin or prevent the onset of diabetes and heart disease (if you are CR and continue to eat a high-carbohydrate diet).

Most exercise scientists have failed to make the diet–health connection. Rather, they seem to assume that, provided we all exercise enough, we will be both thin and healthy regardless of the nature of the foods we eat. While this may well apply to those who are CT, my experience has taught me that this is most definitely not the case for those with marked CR like myself. Instead, the main effect of exercise in those with CR who eat a high-carbohydrate diet is to stimulate their hunger (as Banting described), causing them to eat more of their habitual high-carbohydrate diet. This causes the secretion of yet more insulin, worsening their CR.

According to the theory of how obesity develops in those with CR, described in Rules 3 and 4, exercise does not cause thinness – that is, that athletes are not thin because they exercise. Rather thinness begets athleticism, whereas obesity begets sloth (Rule 9).

The sole way for those with CR to remain lean and disease-free is to eat a high-fat/high-protein/low-carbohydrate diet of the kind first described by Harvey and Banting.

Rule 9: Athletes are not thin because they exercise. Rather thinness begets exercise, whereas obesity causes sloth.

The forgotten theory of how obesity develops in those with CR if they eat a high-carbohydrate diet also makes two unexpected predictions. The first is that obesity is not caused by gluttony and sloth – as predicted by the conventional model (Rule 2); rather the obese state causes both greed and lethargy.

Thus the theory is that under the action of chronically elevated blood insulin concentrations, the fat cells of those with CR who continue to eat high-carbohydrate diets are unable to release their stored energy into the bloodstream. The cells then signal to the brain that the body is in a state of (internal) starvation. As a result, the brain does what it is designed to do in response to a perceived energy deficit; it increases the appetite, causing increased energy consumption. At the same time, it prevents the unnecessary wastage of energy. So it stimulates the illusory sensations of fatigue (see Part Six), promoting indolence.

The obese will thus only ever tame their excessive appetites and become more physically active if they first reverse this state of internal starvation by allowing their fat cells to release their stored-fat energy. All this requires is a sustained reduction in the blood insulin concentrations, which is achieved quite simply by following the Harvey/Banting eating pattern.

Rule 10: It is possible to exercise and train vigorously while eating a low-carbohydrate diet.

My experience has been that I am able to train daily at the highest intensity of which I am able at my age, even though my daily carbohydrate intake is less than about sixty grams. Since I train more intensively than the majority of persons with CR who wish simply to be healthy, my conclusion is that the Harvey/Banting diet is more than able to provide all the energy needed by recreational athletes who train less than an hour a day, regardless of their sport. Since I have raced up to twenty-one kilometres in competition without needing to ingest any additional carbohydrate either before or during exercise, I suspect that this low-carbohydrate diet is also more than adequate for competitive athletes competing in endurance events lasting up to at least two hours. So most people with CR who want also to be physically active will be able to exercise without restriction when ingesting a low-carbohydrate diet.

What remains unanswered is whether a low-carbohydrate diet is also optimal for those with CR who wish to train for more prolonged events, like the forty-two-kilometre marathon or for ultra-endurance events like the Comrades Marathon or the Ironman Triathlon. My suspicion is that most of those with CR will sustain relatively low exercise-intensities in these events, if only because of the extra fat weight they will be carrying if they are following the traditional high-carbohydrate diet prescribed for athletes. But the significant weight loss produced by a low-carbohydrate diet will substantially improve their endurance performance without the need for any increase in carbohydrate intake either before or during exercise.

Whether athletes who eat a low-carbohydrate diet can also sustain the higher exercise intensities required to achieve superior performances in ultra-endurance events without reverting to carbohydrate loading before and carbohydrate ingestion during exercise has yet to be properly researched.

My suggestion is that until our science gives us some answers, athletes will need to find their own solutions. But they should not be scared to experiment with their own bodies, as I have. Often this is the quickest way to discover the 'truth'.

12 | Welcome to the CR Family

Clearly, many of the most hallowed beliefs of nutritional science are simply wrong. Worse, they have produced very unfavourable long-term consequences in many whose health has been adversely affected, even though they ate as they had been advised. In the face of this uncertainty, how should we each proceed?

The first step is to decide whether or not you are CR and, if so, what the extent of your abnormality is. If you think you are overweight and have tried unsuccessfully to lose weight in the past when eating a calorie-restricted, high-carbohydrate diet, then you are also most likely CR. Welcome to the world's largest medical family. And consider this a blessing. You now have the opportunity of learning to live with, to understand and finally to overcome the most serious medical condition of modern times exclusively through your own actions and without requiring any input from either my profession or, probably, dieticians and nutritionists.

The higher your BMI, the more certain it is that you have CR. So if your BMI (weight in kilograms divided by your height in centimetres squared) is more than 25 kg/m^2, then the probability is that you are CR. You can determine the extent of your CR by having your fasting blood glucose, insulin and HbA1c concentrations measured. Your tolerance to the ingestion of a large glucose load – the glucose tolerance test – can also be tested. Recall that your blood HbA1c concentration is the strongest single predictor of your future risk for the development of heart disease.

Abnormalities in these markers of CR may develop progressively with increasing age and exposure to a high-carbohydrate diet, just as diabetes may take twenty years to appear. Thus it may be that they may not always be present in all younger persons with CR. In which case an inappropriately high BMI for that age is the best marker of the condition.

If you decide that you do not have CR, that is, that you are tolerant of carbohydrates (CT), then you can safely follow the conventional dietary advice. But limit your sugar intake, since sugar may produce toxic consequences, even in those who are CT. For those with CR, here are the most important steps you need to take.

Step 1: Reduce your total daily sugar intake to less than fifteen grams. This should be a universal goal but is essential if you already show advanced signs of CR with an elevated HbA1c concentration.

Historically, adult-onset diabetes did not occur in populations with sugar intakes of less than five kilograms per person per year, or about eighteen grams per day. Since sugar is an entirely unnecessary foodstuff, its removal from the diet can have only positive and no negative consequences.

Fifteen grams a day corresponds to three teaspoons of sugar. The problem is that sugar is ubiquitous in so many foodstuffs that it is almost impossible to ingest so little sugar without making some drastic dietary changes.

Confectionery and desserts, especially ice cream, have to be restricted, preferably eliminated, as do most beverages other than water and sugarless tea and coffee, for example. The ubiquitous soft drinks like Coca-Cola and Pepsi-Cola contain as much as thirty grams of sugar or high-fructose corn syrup in each 330-millilitre can and so exceed the total sugar intake allowed for two days. Fruit juices are also loaded with carbohydrate, much of which is sugar. A 250-millilitre serving of 'healthy' orange juice or similar fruit juices will likely provide up to twenty-five grams of sugar, again more than the daily allowance. Many low-fat, high-carbohydrate foods contain substantial amounts of sugar, for example many cereal products that claim to be 'healthy' contain ten or more grams of sugar per serving. There is a tendency for sugar to be added to otherwise supposedly 'healthy' products like yoghurt, from which the 'unhealthy' fat has been removed. The better advice is to stay with the full-fat, no-sugar alternatives.

Step 2: Adopt a low-carbohydrate eating plan for life.

CR is a condition that does not reverse itself. Perhaps in time the biological basis for this abnormality will be understood and it will be possible to reverse the condition using manipulations that alter our abnormal genes. But until that happens, it is possible to prevent the consequences of this abnormality by keeping the amount of carbohydrate that we habitually ingest to a minimum.

This is achieved by following a low-carbohydrate eating plan. There are a host of books and Internet websites that describe how this can be achieved. A good place to begin is to read Gary Taubes's exceptional books and perhaps Dr Pierre Dukan's bestseller, as well as the book that set me on this path, *The New Atkins for a New You.*

The key point is that if you have CR, it is for life. If you find that a low-carbohydrate eating plan produces the changes I have experienced, including effortless weight loss, then you need to remember that these changes can only be sustained for as long as you continue to follow this eating plan. Reverting once again to the (high-carbohydrate) eating pattern that produced your initially undesirable state will simply return you to where you came from.

The point is that no amount of weight loss induced by the Harvey/Banting eating plan will ever reverse your CR. Rather, CR presents a unique, once-in-a-lifetime opportunity. So you need to learn as soon as possible how to live with it.

Ultimately the key determinant of the body weight of those with CR is the number of grams of carbohydrate eaten each day. So the extent to which our weight falls when eating a low-carbohydrate diet will be determined principally by the number of grams of carbohydrate that we eat each day. This is largely a personal choice.

Crucially, if you have CR then it is highly likely that your offspring will be similarly affected. So it is important that you encourage your children also to adopt the same eating plan before they show any damage caused by eating a high-carbohydrate diet. Especially important is to ensure that their access to sugar is limited from birth so that they do not develop a sugar addiction from a very young age. Naturally there are a number of industries that do not wish your children to follow this advice and they will do all they can to maintain the status quo.

Step 3: Weigh yourself each day and record your daily weight.

Humans are excellent self-regulators, but we need accurate information on a regular basis to reinforce the conscious behaviours that assist that regulation, many of which are controlled subconsciously. It is very difficult to gain substantial weight if you are aware each day of how your weight is responding to the previous day's eating and exercising patterns.

Step 4: Check your CR status every six months or until your HbA1c concentration has normalised.

Provided your HbA1c concentration has returned to the safe range (below

5 per cent) and you remain weight-stable, indicating you are eating the correct diet, it is improbable that your HbA1c concentration will change for the worse.

Step 5: Exercise vigorously for thirty to sixty minutes at least five days a week, with one longer session at least every two weeks.

I suspect that the full benefits of a low-carbohydrate eating plan are achieved when it is combined with plenty of vigorous exercise. This may be my personal bias, but the benefits of regular exercise are well established.

Step 6: Monitor your blood pressure regularly if it has ever been elevated in the past or if you do not know what it is.

Aside from your HbA1c concentration, your blood pressure is probably the other key predictor of your overall health. But regular exercise and the low-carbohydrate diet will remove two key environmental causes of an elevated blood pressure. However, if your blood pressure remains above the ideal values even though you are lean, active and avoiding carbohydrates, then as much as I do not like to suggest it, it may be necessary to treat the condition with medication.

Step 7: Don't ever smoke.

This is obvious, but I had to add it in case you thought that I was somehow still influenced by the fact that my father worked in the tobacco industry.

Step 8: Do whatever else credible authorities suggest will improve your health.

Once you have learnt how to live with CR, you have solved your greatest health problem. As a result, it is likely that you will live a very long time. So you may as well find other ways to maximise the enjoyment of those added years.

Step 9: Spread the word.

This is the only way these truths will become more widely known. And practised.

part four

TACKLING THE RISK IN RUGBY

13 | A Battle to Make Rugby Safer

'First of all, find the cause'   —ARTHUR NEWTON, 1935

'I apologise if I have painted a rather gloomy picture of the hazards of rugby, which is a most enjoyable game. It is, however, a violent one and therefore the constituent bodies must always keep under review measures to reduce the incidence of injuries which necessarily interfere with the total enjoyment of this hazardous hobby' —DR LEON WALKDEN, 1975

One Saturday afternoon in August 1980, I sat in my kitchen listening to a Currie Cup match between Western Province and Free State being played in Bloemfontein.

Morné du Plessis, who in time would become a good friend of mine, was the captain of the Western Province team. I was keen to go for a run, but I wanted to catch the end of this game, which was a close-run affair. Suddenly, the commentary stopped as the game was held up. The news came through that one of the players had been seriously injured. There was a delay of about fifteen minutes before the game restarted, and I wondered what could have happened to cause such a long delay. Then it was confirmed: a player by the name of Chris Burger, the Western Province fullback, had been tackled after a long ruck and now lay motionless a few metres from the goal line that he had tried so desperately to defend.

A few hours later, Chris Burger died in a Bloemfontein hospital.

It was a shocking tragedy that had unexpected consequences in my life. The following morning, a *Sunday Times* journalist phoned me to ask a few questions about the incident. Why he chose to ask my opinion, I have absolutely no idea.

I was a running doctor with, at that time, little interest in the medical side of rugby. My first reaction to the journalist was that I had a couple of questions of my own. I wanted to know if Burger's injury had been preventable and if he had been insured in the event of a catastrophic injury that would either be fatal or leave him unable to work and care for his family. Most importantly, I wanted to know if he had received the optimum treatment on the field and thereafter.

In those questions I had formulated the three cardinal issues that were to guide me in my future dealings with these frightening injuries and their personal and national consequences.

As it turned out, Burger had not been insured. He had also not received even close to the best possible care, because no provision had been made to supply care for catastrophic injuries at the stadium. The reason for the delay in removing the injured Burger from the field was that there had not been an appropriate stretcher available; a changing-room door had had to be used as an emergency stretcher. Press photographs published subsequently showed that, when Burger was finally taken off the field, he was removed lying on his stomach instead of on his back. This is a critical error in the treatment of a serious neck injury.

That weekend of August 1980 made me realise that rugby – the national pastime and a powerful symbol in South African politics and society – was perhaps not as well managed as it could be.

But Chris Burger did not die in vain. His death exposed the weaknesses of sports medicine in South Africa at the time and was the catalyst for reform, over the next thirty years, of the attitude of the South African rugby authorities to rugby injuries. Controversy thrives on inadequate data, and this fatal event highlighted the fact that there was almost no information on South African rugby injuries in general, and catastrophic neck injuries in particular.

So Burger's tragic death, and the events that followed, transformed not only my own thinking about the game, but, ultimately, South Africa's entire approach to rugby injuries – from an attitude of indifference in the 1980s to one in which the South African Rugby Board would take full responsibility for the prevention of these injuries after about 2005. This change did not happen without a fight, however, and initially there were some ferocious enemies to confront.

That winter was a bleak one: political forces threatened not only the future of our country, but also the future of our rugby. South Africa at that stage was a dominant force in international rugby, but because of our support for the policy of apartheid, the British Lions tour of that year was the last sanctioned international rugby tour to our country for twelve years.

At the end of 1980, inspirational Springbok captain Morné du Plessis retired from the game with an unmatched record of leading South Africa to thirteen victories in fifteen Tests. There is a feeling that the death of his Western Province teammate, Burger, took a heavy toll on Morné and was perhaps one of the reasons that he retired when he was still at his peak. Morné said this about the incident:

> The passing of Chris was traumatic. It is not something I want to ever live through again. It came at the end of my career. It wasn't the sole reason that made me retire, but I think it contributed to my decision. It was a shock for all of us. We were young and had never experienced something like that. One second a teammate is with you on the field, and then the next he's fighting for his life and you're told he won't make it. It was a very traumatic week for all of us because we had the funeral of another player that week as well. Chris was completely coherent when we saw him in the hospital. His last words to me were, 'Sorry about losing the game.'

Wynand Claassen, another progressive rugby thinker, succeeded Morné as Springbok captain and led the Springbok tour to New Zealand the following year. It was a tour played under impossible conditions, and it mirrored more than anything the unhealthy state of our rugby. The Springboks played heroically, with Naas Botha at his best, and were denied a famous 2-1 series victory by outlandish home-town refereeing. If I had known about match fixing at the time, I would have concluded that the referee had been acting 'under the influence'.

But the Springboks' heroics could not hide the internal division, isolation from international trends, and general feeling of hopelessness, depression and moral uncertainty that gripped South African sport, a malaise that reflected the state of the country as a whole.

Amid all of this, however, Chris Burger's death provided the common ground for Morné and me to develop a partnership that blossomed over the following thirty years. Chris Burger's death inspired me to begin a national research programme focused on ascertaining the factors that cause critical rugby injuries, particularly those of the spinal cord. This put me in direct conflict with the rugby administrators of the day, but I found a fearless ally in Morné. He was one of the few who immediately understood the importance of our research to the future of the game in South Africa.

As I worked on the research and Morné on the initiation and management of what is now the Chris Burger/Petro Jackson Players Fund (**see page 180**), we had the inspiration to develop the Sports Science Institute of South Africa in Newlands, Cape Town.

The aim of the Institute, opened fifteen years later, in 1995, was to use science to help develop the future sporting heroes of South Africa. It sounds like an obvious concept now, but in those days it was quite revolutionary, at least in South Africa.

The Australians were already proving the success of such a venture as one of the first Western nations to embrace the idea of scientific athletic preparation. But Morné was a rare visionary. 'To build this nation, we need heroes. That's the philosophy which surrounds this facility,' he told the media when we first announced our intentions.

Our joint desire was that the Sports Science Institute should not become a national sports academy, but rather an environment in which we could undertake world-class research to produce new understandings of the factors that determine superior athletic ability. We could then pass along this information to athletes and coaches. Ultimately, through the knowledge we would acquire, we hoped to help make rugby a safer game.

With South Africa's return to international sport in 1992, following twelve years of isolation, rugby learnt a particularly hard truth: that its stubborn resistance to change and its inability to anticipate international sporting trends had made the national team uncompetitive and out of touch.

It was not easy for Morné and me to persuade the rugby powers that science could assist in bringing the South African game more in line with international standards, as well as reducing the incidence of injury in the sport. We spent years tackling some of the strongest forces in South African rugby before science was seen as an ally and not a foe to the game that had defined the Afrikaans culture and given hope to a young nation.

The rising incidence of rugby injuries over the past forty years is closely linked to the evolution of the game, particularly the rules, and the importance that we ascribe to the game of rugby. Professionalism has not reduced the risk of injury – it has probably had the opposite effect, as each crop of modern players is faster, fitter, heavier and stronger than the previous one. Today the rules and tactics ensure that the ball is in play for perhaps 100 per cent more time than it was even as recently as fifteen years ago. When faster, heavier players hit each other more frequently than ever before, inevitably there will be more injuries. However, this does not mean that the incidence of catastrophic neck injury has to increase, as this is one group of injuries that we should be able to reduce even further.

The truth is that there is more official concern about rugby safety today than there has ever been in the history of the game. That said, there is never enough work to be done to make rugby safer: if there is one catastrophic injury a year in rugby, it's one too many. There are still probably ten incidents a year in South Africa alone.

But we have certainly come a long way from where rugby began.

FROM VILLAGE GREENS TO PUBLIC SCHOOLS

It was to the organised playing fields of celebrated English public schools like Rugby, Westminster, Eton, Marlborough, Winchester, Charterhouse and Cheltenham that rugby moved, in the nineteenth century, from the local village greens. The modification of a wild, reckless pastime had begun.

The schools saw the game as a means of running off some of the energy of hormone-charged adolescents while at the same time helping to prepare a generation of 'muscular Christians' able to extend British values to the furthest reaches of their far-flung Empire.

Initially, each school played the game using its own set of rules: some kicked the ball along the ground, while others picked it up and ran with it.

In 1839, the first recorded rugby club was formed at the University of Cambridge. The differences in rules meant that when the public-school-educated boys came together in one rugby club, the old Etonians, who were used to kicking the ball, became incensed when a former Rugberian picked up the ball and ran with it.

Interestingly, there was one rule – hacking – on which these genteel Englishmen agreed. In those days it was entirely acceptable for one player to kick another on the shin. It was, in fact, so popular that time was often scheduled after games to allow players the opportunity for some uninterrupted hacking of their opponents.

The handling game grew in popularity, however, and eventually became the norm.

In 1871 the goal area on the field was designated by a line, and dotting the ball down behind the line resulted in a 'try at goal', namely an attempt at a conversion.

However, rugby faced a threat from football. While rugby was considered a game for the educated elite, football, regarded as a simple game for the masses, was growing in popularity, especially in the new manufacturing towns springing up in the north of England at the start of the Industrial Revolution.

So the need arose to make rugby more attractive and to turn it into a game based on skill and intelligence rather than on brute strength. On 26 January 1871, the top rugby clubs in London met at the Pall Mall Restaurant and formed the Rugby Football Union, with fifty-nine rules of the game.

The game continued to evolve to the point where, in 1949, South Africa introduced differentiation into loosehead and tighthead props, which saw the birth of the modern scrum. Hookers were now expected to win the ball on their put-in, and the backline players responded by adopting more of an attacking formation when they had the advantage of the scrum put-in. Their opponents would adopt a more defensive approach.

The emphasis in the scrum was placed on big, strong props and powerful locks. The evolution of backline players demanded that wings and centres be fast, strong runners; the game was being played with more power and more speed. Inevitably, when speed, mass and contact are combined – an irresistible force meeting an immovable object – the potential for injury increases.

In a classic study by Charles Roux in 1987 on the rugby injuries of South African schoolboys, he points out: 'The major factor in rugby injuries would appear to be the speed of the game. Evidence for this is: (i) the greater incidence of injury among the fast, mobile players playing in the best teams; and (ii) the high prevalence of injuries caused by tackling or being tackled, both of which occur at speed.' When these forces collide, it is damage to the neck vertebrae and the spinal cord that produces the most devastating injuries.

THE LANGUAGE OF INJURY

Injuries can be classified into two categories: extrinsic and intrinsic.

Extrinsic injuries occur when an external force is applied to the body, such as a tackle or a collision with another player, resulting in injury.

Intrinsic injuries result from repetitive overuse of the body, as typically occurs in repetitive non-contact sports like running, swimming, canoeing and tennis.

Injuries can be further differentiated into muscle injuries, ligament and tendon injuries, bone injuries, joint injuries, nerve injuries and injuries to specific organs, such as the brain.

Our early studies, which began in 1981 in response to Chris Burger's tragic death the previous year, identified a number of factors that heighten the risk of serious injury. Subsequent studies of larger numbers of players have served to confirm these findings. The factors related to injury risk in relative order of importance are the following:

The age of the player

Players in the older age groups are at increased risk of injury, while players below the age of twelve years are at very low risk of injury. Injury risk starts to rise at age fifteen and continues to increase with every subsequent age group so that injury occurs most commonly in senior players.

The level of play

The level of injury is greatest at the highest levels of play, therefore international rugby players are at the highest risk of injury. Early on in our campaign some claimed that unfit schoolboys are the players at greatest risk of injury. According to this theory, the injury problem would disappear as soon as schoolboys trained properly and became fitter. Of course, the opposite is true, as the evidence proved; while fitness may offer a measure of protection, the increased size, speed and strength of the fittest players place them at increased risk of injury because the impacts they cause and must absorb increase.

Match play

Most injuries occur during matches; injury is uncommon during practice. This is most apparent in the case of catastrophic spinal cord injuries, more than 90 per cent of which occur during matches. This indicates that matches introduce some factor into the injury equation that is not present during practices.

The playing position

Our original studies found that fullbacks, wings and eighthmen were at greatest risk of injury. More recently, as the modern game continues to evolve, it seems likely that flankers, centres and flyhalves will become increasingly at risk of injury, as these positions become more involved in contact, particularly in defence.

The phase of play

Tackling, being tackled, the ruck and the maul combined account for 75 per cent of all injuries, but tackling (21 per cent) and being tackled (30 per cent) account for more than half of all injuries.

The time of season

Most injuries occur in the early part of the season before players are 'match fit'.

When we focused our work specifically on spinal cord injuries, we found an almost identical pattern. Virtually all of these injuries occur during matches;

senior players are at the greatest risk of injury, and this risk presents itself at as early as under-19 level; players in the A and first teams are at the greatest risk; 72 per cent of these injuries occur at the point of tackling or being tackled; hookers, centres and flyhalves are at the greatest risk of such injuries; and most injuries occur at the start of the season.

Recently we have shown that socio-economic factors are also at play. Thus players from what are known in South Africa as previously disadvantaged communities are more likely to suffer long-term consequences, particularly permanent paralysis and early death, than those from better-resourced communities. This is probably a function of the standard of medical care available to these players, particularly within the first few hours of injury. The way in which these injuries are handled immediately after they occur has a crucial bearing on whether or not the injured player will recover fully or will end up completely paralysed.

Thus, the factors that explain the reasons for spinal cord injuries are not very different from those causing all rugby injuries. However, the mechanisms causing neck injuries are specific and usually involve excessive rotation and flexion of the neck. A blow to the top of the head when the neck is slightly flexed, which can occur, for example, to the tackler during a straight-ahead tackle, to the front row at scrum engagement or to the ball carrier who lowers his head to contact the body of a tackler, can also cause a catastrophic injury. This is known as 'spearing', a technique that is banned in American football, as it is known to be potentially dangerous.

THE PERMANENT PARALYSIS MYTH

In 1989 and 1990, one orthopaedic surgeon and two East London schoolboys challenged our entire understanding of catastrophic neck injuries and the probability that paralysis will be the final outcome of these devastating injuries.

As described in the book that Morné and I co-wrote in 1996, *Rugby without Risk*, Nigel Connellan and Stewart Mayberry were both initially paralysed as a result of cervical neck injuries that occured during their respective schoolboy rugby matches.

Connellan was a tighthead prop in the Selborne first team, which was playing against Queen's College. The scrum collapsed and Connellan was left lying motionless on the field. When the medics arrived to help him, they discovered that he was paralysed. But he was lucky. Watching the game was orthopaedic surgeon Dr Kerry Allerton. Allerton immediately sprang into action. Within an hour Nigel was in surgery, and Allerton realigned his dislocated neck vertebrae.

Twenty-four hours after surgery, Connellan had regained almost complete muscle power in both his upper and lower limbs. Three months later, he had fully recovered.

Almost a year later, Mayberry – also a tighthead prop – was playing in a first-team match between Dale College and Selborne College. Following a scrum, Mayberry was left kneeling with his chest on the ground and his head skewed off to one side. He, too, was paralysed.

Within twenty-four hours of surgery, he had regained some wrist and hand function, as well as sensation in his lower limbs. Three months later, he walked out of hospital on crutches, having avoided what could have been a catastrophic injury with permanent consequences.

These two cases highlight the simple, most effective prevention of permanent paralysis caused by rugby neck injury: correct treatment of the initial injury.

Both players received what Chris Burger had not when I posed that question to the *Sunday Times* reporter in 1980: optimum treatment.

The treatment administered on the field to a rugby player who has suffered a severe neck injury and is paralysed will therefore determine whether or not he ever walks again. Most importantly, thanks to the foresight of Dr Kerry Allerton and other surgeons around the world, these cases have shown us that a catastrophic neck injury on the rugby field does not have to lead to permanent paralysis.

CORRECT TREATMENT FOR SERIOUS NECK INJURIES

Both of the schoolboy players mentioned above – Nigel Connellan and Stewart Mayberry – were carefully removed from the field and transported to hospital for surgery as quickly as possible after their neck injuries occurred.

It is critical that, at the time of injury, the player is not moved by just anyone. Once qualified personnel arrive, they need to immobilise the neck before the player's body is moved.

The neck joints differ in one significant way from all the other joints in the back: they are designed to allow a considerable range of movement of the head and the neck. Whereas the back vertebrae are designed to resist movement and are protected by powerful muscles, the vertebrae in the neck are not. As a result, they are far less stable than the other joints in the back and are therefore more susceptible to injury.

Dislocation of the cervical joints (C1 to C7) usually leads to acute pressure on the spinal cord, which travels in the vertebral canal directly behind the body of the vertebral bones that are held in place by the cervical joints. This acute pressure can lead to permanent paralysis of all the muscles controlled by the nerves that exit the spinal cord below the site of the injury. But as the cases of Mayberry and Connellan show, this is not an inevitable consequence of all rugby-related spinal cord injuries.

Basically, the nervous system in the human body consists of the brain, the spinal cord – which runs in a protective, bony arch behind the vertebrae – and the nerves – which exit the vertebrae and run within the muscles to specific muscles and other body functions that they control.

One of the most common neck injuries in rugby is damage to the fifth cervical vertebrae (C5). In this case, the spinal cord is stretched and compressed opposite the site of the fracture or dislocation. This compression immediately prevents the transmission of any nerve impulses from the brain to the muscles or organs below the site of the dislocation or fracture, so that the player is unable to move his legs and arms and appears to be paralysed. Without proper treatment, permanent paralysis may develop, in which case a player with this type of injury will lose the use of his triceps, and his hand, chest, abdominal, leg and foot muscles, as well as his bowel, bladder and sexual functions. Other complications include psychological problems, an increased risk of obesity, heart and kidney disease, and high blood pressure.

It's a dreadful injury with awful consequences. But through the study of these injuries, and the example of the two East London schoolboys, we have discovered that the spinal cord is not necessarily irreversibly severed at the time of the dislocation or fracture. This is because the force that produces a cervical dislocation in rugby is not as great as in, for example, a motor-car accident. The higher forces involved in car accidents are likely to sever the spinal cord completely at the time of the injury. Fortunately, it seems that such total severing of the spinal cord is uncommon in rugby injuries. It is now evident that what happens in the first two hours after injury determines whether or not the paralysis will become permanent.

The priority in managing a rugby player with a neck injury is to immobilise the neck. This ensures that no further damage can occur to the spinal cord as a result of direct pressure from the dislocated vertebrae. But insidious damage to the spinal cord continues to occur for the duration of the dislocation and is reversed only once the dislocated vertebrae have been realigned. This is because the dislocated vertebrae interfere with the flow of blood to the spinal cord in the area of the injury, causing the death of more spinal cord cells. Ultimately, too many cells die and the spinal cord is irreversibly damaged, causing permanent paralysis, since spinal cord cells cannot regenerate themselves.

So if the dislocation remains untreated for more than two hours, or if it is incorrectly treated, the spinal cord may degenerate as a result of the impaired blood flow. Therefore, as stated above, it seems that there is a golden period of one to two hours before the spinal cord is irreversibly damaged in this type of injury.

This discovery has been a major breakthrough in our understanding of the optimum treatment of spinal cord injuries in rugby, because it means that careful realignment of the cervical vertebrae and spinal cord shortly after the initial injury may just allow the spinal cord to recover fully from the initial injury and, in so doing, prevent permanent paralysis.

Thus the correct treatment for any player suffering from such an injury is first to prevent the neck from moving and then to have the vertebrae realigned. Manual traction, either with straps or hands, needs to be applied to the head of the player, who must then be placed on a firm stretcher, face up if he is conscious. If he is unconscious and likely to vomit – in which case he could inhale the vomit into his lungs and so develop a very serious complication – he needs to be placed on his side with his face to one side and one of his legs slightly bent – the position most people assume when they sleep on their sides. This position reduces the risk of complication should the player vomit, but does not protect the unstable neck.

I cannot emphasise how important it is that this be done correctly to avoid further damage to the spinal cord. In the case of Chris Burger, being placed on his stomach in the incorrect position did not protect his neck from further damage. Once the player's neck has been correctly stabilised, he must then be transported to hospital as soon as possible so that his dislocation can be corrected either manually or surgically.

So not only have we discovered that paralysis on the field should not necessarily lead to permanent paralysis, but we also now know exactly what steps to take to prevent this from happening in the game.

If correcting the earlier belief that all neck injuries result in permanent paralysis was revolutionary, then so was the corollary: that the circumstances causing catastrophic neck injuries are entirely predictable, and therefore potentially preventable. My opinion has always been that most of these injuries can be prevented by paying attention to the six risk factors identified on **page 157**.

It took a monumental mindshift for rugby authorities to embrace without reservation the development of the BokSmart programme throughout South African rugby. It is a world-class programme that will ensure that the incidence of these injuries continues to fall at all levels of the game in this country and in all communities, including those most at risk.

There was a time, however, when I despaired that the South African Rugby Union (SARU), then led by Dr Danie Craven, would ever accept what I considered to be a crucial step in the evolution of the game.

THE FIGHT FOR RUGBY'S SOUL

In retrospect, rugby union, especially in South Africa, was slow in adopting measures to curb the rise in serious injuries that began in the mid-seventies. Perhaps the history of injury prevention in American gridiron football should have alerted us.

At the start of the twentieth century, American football was undergoing its own evolution from a violent sport with catastrophic injuries to one that has provided the most powerful example of the correct approach to injury concerns in a contact sport.

The Americans saw the need to develop a game in which the risk of serious injury was reduced. But not everyone agreed at first. A sector of the American population was concerned that any change to the rules would detract from the 'manliness' of the game. Even the American president, Theodore Roosevelt, subscribed to this view. In a speech at the time, he stated, 'If we lose the virile, manly qualities [promoted by football], America will reach a condition worse than that of the ancient civilisations in the years of decay.' Roosevelt continued by saying that he 'would a hundredfold rather keep the game as it is now, with the brutality, than give it up', and he expressed his 'utter disgust' at former president of Harvard University Charles Eliot's attempts to ban football at the university.

Similarly, brutality in rugby was very much aligned with the dominant Afrikaner nationalism of the middle of the twentieth century in South Africa. New Zealand shared this belief. In his book *All Blacks versus Springboks*, author Graeme Barrow sums up the role rugby played in the new nationalism of these two countries:

> Rugby became, for New Zealanders and South Africans alike, the national game, the course of its pride as well as pleasure, and the embodiment of national morale and virility … In both the southern hemisphere colonies the emergence of rugby as the national sporting obsession coincided with the emergence of the respective peoples as independent nations, fiercely proud and patriotic … Two pioneering nations, whose peoples led rugged and outdoor lives, took to a rugged and outdoor game. It was inevitable they would both be good at it.

It is stirring stuff, and as a result there was a reluctance to effect any change at all in this great, manly game. However, even some of its hardest players would later condemn this 'macho' approach to the sport.

In 1990, Uli Schmidt, the former Northern Transvaal and Springbok hooker and one of the true hard men of the sport, declared in his capacity as a physician, 'It is my firm opinion that in rugby there are two potentially dangerous attitudinal problems. These are the pressure to succeed at all costs, which often results in a player being poorly prepared, and the pressure to start playing again too soon after injury … rule manipulation will only achieve so much. The real challenge that faces administrators, coaches and the players themselves is in their whole approach to the sport … this macho approach to life is extremely dangerous.'

14 | An Unhealthy Obsession

Shortly after I began to research the issue of rugby injuries in South Africa, I developed the opinion that rugby was unnecessarily unsafe. People simply refused to see the negative side of the game because, in South Africa, it was, and remains, a national obsession.

As one who has always viewed sport as a vehicle to produce both physical and spiritual benefits, I was unsure of the value of an unhealthy obsession with any single sport, be it rugby, or even running, for that matter.

In an interview with *Fair Lady* magazine in September 1981, I declared: 'The physical education for boys in schools is bad because there is overemphasis on a handful of rugby players instead of letting pupils choose a sport for life. It's the sports dropouts, the ones who don't make the team, the ones who are regarded as losers who need to be given an alternative sport. Everyone is being short-changed in our driving need to make a few good rugby players.'

It was not a popular view at the time. I still often speak on this topic at schools and, while many are beginning to understand that sport at school must serve wider goals than simply producing a few good rugby teams, it remains a hard sell in some communities that believe that excellence in schoolboy rugby is the most important indicator both that a school is successful and that it continues to promote the 'correct values'.

In 1984, I was approached by an important South African sporting magazine to write an article on rugby. Given my strong feelings on the subject at the time, my article was considered too 'hot' to publish. This indicated to me that there must have been some truth in what I had written. The irony is that today I am quite involved in rugby at club and international level. I see no paradox – my focus was always to encourage the authorities to take rugby injuries seriously rather than simply to ignore them because they were 'inconvenient'. Now that that has happened, my argument is moot. What needed to be done has been done. I can now sit back and enjoy the spectacle.

My other point back then, as now, is that the position rugby holds in the social fabric of some South African communities has unfortunate consequences. My chief area of concern remains an overemphasis on competitive sport, rugby in particular, at schools, to the exclusion of other sports and physical activities, thereby denying less physically gifted children a rewarding involvement in sport. I have to stress that my argument was and is not against rugby itself, but rather against the cultural issues associated with the game.

In that same year, 1984, it was established that at least 85 per cent of all rugby players were whites under the age of twenty-five. This confirmed that rugby was then a sport for the young and did not cater to the needs of the majority of our population.

Two independent studies – one by the Human Sciences Research Council (HSRC) and the other a joint effort of the HSRC, the Medical Research Council and the Department of Health – also confirmed that, within a decade of leaving school, most white male South Africans stopped participating in any meaningful physical activity. This is undesirable, as it is possible to maintain optimum health only by keeping physically active for life.

Rugby at the time was also the major source of serious sporting injuries at school.

Finally, I could find no evidence to prove that rugby 'builds character' any more than other sports do. I now know that sport identifies character; it does not necessarily build character. Character is developed by those coaches who understand the true value of sport. Paul Brown, one of a handful of truly great American football coaches, held particular beliefs about the personal character-istics of players he was prepared to coach. B. Adler describes Brown's ideal player as follows:

Brown's ideal player was one of impeccable character and intellect. His conception of building a successful football team was based on his determination that the game was as much about people as it was about strategies, tactics, and motivational techniques. He contended that if you placed the best *individuals* (not necessarily the most talented football players) in the most advantageous positions, winning would almost come naturally. A Paul Brown 'individual' was one who was totally devoted to winning football games and was willing to sacrifice his entire lifestyle in order to achieve that ambition. He had to possess an unselfish attitude and never put personal considerations ahead of the organisation's goal of championship football. In addition, Brown greatly valued a player's learning capacity. 'Everywhere we did our testing, we found that players with low intelligence progressed only so far,' he said. 'Knowing a man's capacity to learn before we drafted him helped us calculate his potential.' In Brown's system, this intelligence-level measurement was even more important than it was with other teams.

Sport is about producing more competent and better human beings who are able to function well in all aspects of their lives, not just on the sports field.

I am not sure that all South African coaches share this philosophy, however. When I wrote the 1984 article that was rejected for publication, the coach of the Springbok rugby team at the time remarked that he was so proud of his team because '[t]hese are the men I would go to the Angolan border with'.

It was ridiculous and bordered on the fanatical.

Back in early twentieth-century America, public opinion was shifting in reaction to the fervour associated with their sport. Even Roosevelt began to feel the pressure to make American football safer, so in 1905 he made a dramatic about-turn and announced his support of radical rule changes that would make the game safer. Indeed, as early as 1910 the Americans were actively monitoring injuries in response to concerns about the future of their sport.

Two Americans, E.H. Nichols and F.L. Richardson, showed that the rule changes introduced after 1905 reduced the rate of injury in American football. These rule changes included the following: the players were encouraged to develop good physical condition before they reported for the start of the football season; practice scrimmages were also introduced early 'in order to harden the men up as much as possible before the violent work began'; and special pads and 'armour' were provided. These included headguards, shoulder pads, knee guards and thigh guards.

Because injury rates in American football were monitored from the early 1900s, it was a natural consequence that they were able to detect a sudden increase in spinal cord injuries in the game in the 1970s. Immediately, the relevant authorities could identify the cause (spear tackling) and provide effective preventative measures. Most importantly, they were willing to change the rules to make the game safer the instant that evidence was collected. Of course, it is not possible to identify a sudden increase in injury if there is no injury-surveillance system in place.

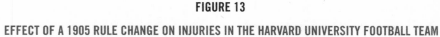

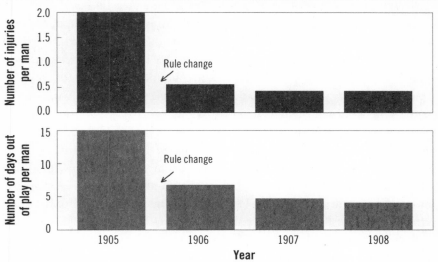

FIGURE 13

EFFECT OF A 1905 RULE CHANGE ON INJURIES IN THE HARVARD UNIVERSITY FOOTBALL TEAM

The number of injuries per man and the number of days out of play per man in the Harvard football team before and after rule changes introduced in the 1905 American football season. Note that the rule changes introduced after 1905 reduced the number of injuries per player by about 75 per cent and almost halved the time that the injured player needed to return to play.

It is astounding to note that, at the time that the US was acting to make their national pastime safer, not a single rugby-playing country seemed concerned about serious injuries. As a result, none was prepared for the international outcry that arose in the 1970s, when the growing prevalence of spinal cord injuries started to threaten the future of the game.

RUGBY'S GLOBAL INJURY CRISIS

In the late 1970s and 1980s, rugby was in trouble globally.

All the major rugby-playing countries – the United Kingdom, Australia, New Zealand and South Africa – began to express some level of concern about the long-term effects of rugby injuries.

In 1989, a major international conference on rugby injuries took place in the United States. It was not just a moral concern that these countries were seeking to address; they were also beginning to feel the financial costs of these injuries.

In New Zealand, for example, rugby injuries cost the country an estimated NZ$19 million in 1990, compared with NZ$6 million in 1983.

The rising incidence of rugby injuries also caused a reaction on the ground: on the one hand, concerned parents, especially mothers, began to discourage their sons from playing the game, while on the other, there were those who believed that the focus on rugby injuries was simply a means to detract from their great game. In the tumultuous South African environment, others took this even further by suggesting that any talk of rugby not being safe was a political attempt to undermine the game and its strong Afrikaner roots.

The general view was that those who were injured were 'soft' and simply not up to the physical demands of the game of rugby.

My approach has always been to seek the truth. At the time, I believed that rugby was essentially a safe game, but that elements of it were unnecessarily unsafe. It struck me as odd that so few studies of rugby injuries had been carried out. Probably one of the first was published in 1954, by Dr T.C.J. O'Connell, an orthopaedic surgeon from Dublin, Ireland, who reported a series of 600 rugby injuries that he had personally observed over a twenty-year period. But it was another twenty years before the next series of rugby injury studies emerged in the early 1970s. Clearly, few doctors foresaw the kind of global injury crisis that would engulf the game.

In 1975, Dr Leon Walkden was one of the first doctors to express publicly his concern about the issue. In a letter to the *Practitioner*, Walkden stated that 'tackle involvement and the collapsing of the set scrum' predisposed rugby players to spinal cord injuries. Stricter refereeing and the teaching of correct scrumming and tackling techniques were among his proposals to reduce the incidence of catastrophic injury. It took more than a decade for these concepts to make their way into the game.

Ironically, it was a South African study that first alerted the world to the rising incidence of spinal cord injury in rugby. In 1977, Professor Alan Scher, then of the Spinal Unit at Conradie Hospital in Cape Town, reported a series of twenty spinal cord injuries in rugby players. He identified two areas of major concern in the game – tackling injuries to either the tackler or the tackled player, and injuries in the scrum as a result of scrum collapse. He concluded that rule changes to the scrum could, at least, help to reduce the number of spinal cord injuries.

The *British Medical Journal* was among the first to focus on Scher's findings. In an editorial published in 1977, three improvements were proposed: the teaching of better tackling techniques to school players, more rigorous refereeing to prevent dangerous tackles and, importantly, the establishment of a central database for the recording of all serious neck injuries in the game. Worldwide, concern about the injury crisis was mounting.

In 1978, Dr Hugh Burry, a former All Black forward, and H. Gowland published a paper titled 'Cervical Injury in Rugby Football – A New Zealand Survey'. In it they declared: 'The 1978 rugby season in New Zealand was marred by an epidemic of fatal cervical cord injuries.' Their conclusions included the statement: 'The incidence of injury could be reduced by appropriate player selection, better coaching and amendment of the laws.' That same year, the New Zealand Rugby Football Union launched an inquiry into spinal cord injuries in rugby.

In South Africa, there was also concern, bordering on panic in some quarters. An orthopaedic surgeon from Durban, Dr G. Schweitzer, wrote in a sports magazine in 1978: 'As an orthopaedic surgeon ... and as a father of a schoolboy who plays rugby, I have been most disturbed by the recent spate of severe injuries to the cervical cord in rugby players ... I appeal to all members of the medical profession ... to exert pressure on the rugby administrators to put their house in order.'

It wasn't long before reports from all the major rugby-playing countries of the world revealed that there had been a definite increase in these serious injuries.

But in South Africa, sports scientists were faced with another problem. We were the only major rugby-playing country in the world that did not have a central register of all the catastrophic injuries that had occurred in the game. The only sources of reliable information were the records of patients admitted to Conradie Hospital in Cape Town, the database from which Professor Scher had collected the information for his report. Our attempts to access that data, however, were initially blocked.

From these records we were eventually able to ascertain that, between 1963 and 1989, 177 rugby players with spinal cord injuries were admitted to the hospital. As many as 83 per cent of these injuries occurred after 1977, culminating in a peak of twelve such injuries in the 1989 season alone.

Worldwide studies also began to show that senior players in the top teams were at the greatest risk of spinal cord injuries. For example, a Welsh study conducted by J.P. Williams and B. McKibbin, published in 1978, found that 79 per cent of injured players were seniors. The Welsh also discovered that the average age of the injured players was twenty-two years. In New Zealand, a 1981 study confirmed that 66 per cent of injured players were older than twenty-one, while in an Australian study in 1987, 60 per cent of injuries were to senior players; the average age of the injured players was twenty-four.

In none of these studies was there even a single case of a spinal cord injury to a player younger than fourteen years old. This proved that Danie Craven was incorrect when he said that any rising incidence of spinal cord injuries in South African rugby was the result of an increasing number of unfit schoolboys who had become 'television sissies' suffering from the 'couch potato syndrome'.

The resistance of the South African rugby authorities to take the problem seriously in the face of all this evidence was something I could not understand, and my frustration began to show. In the June 1988 issue of *SA Sports Illustrated* magazine, I wrote a strongly worded article aimed at what I perceived to be the reluctance of South African rugby administrators to address the problem of serious injuries:

> We have an epidemic of catastrophic neck injuries amongst rugby players in this country. How many more young men must be paralysed before the seriousness of the situation is recognised and admitted? How much longer will the parents of injured players or the players themselves continue to believe that a spinal cord injury that results from a collapsed scrum, 'popping' in the scrum or crashing the scrum is an act of God and is not grounds for legal action against the rugby administrators? How much longer will they continue to accept the hopelessly inadequate injury insurance cover carried by the vast majority of schools; insurance that comes nowhere near the estimated R500 000 [in those days] with which the family of a player paralysed from a spinal cord injury will eventually be saddled?

In the article I referred to an Australian case in which a paralysed player was awarded AUS$2 million on the grounds that he had not been warned that players with long necks are at increased risk of neck injuries in rugby if they play in the scrum. That year a similar case went before the British courts. At issue were two questions: firstly, whether a player who was paralysed in a tackle had been properly coached in the art of tackling, and, secondly, whether the school had been negligent in not having adequate insurance cover for such injuries. I corresponded with the lawyer of that particular case. He informed me that a further seven such cases were pending at the time.

I ended the article by saying, 'The message would seem to be clear. The issue of prevention of catastrophic spinal cord injuries must either be addressed by the rugby authorities as it has been in New Zealand, or it will be settled in the courts as it has been in Australia and Britain. Which road will South Africa travel?'

In August 1988, *Fair Lady* magazine produced a special report titled 'Killing Fields', which focused on the escalation in the number of serious neck injuries in South African rugby. The article echoed what I had written, stating, 'South Africa's annual rugby injury statistics are increasing at an alarming rate. More shocking is that hospitals throughout the country are admitting players with spinal injuries, but there is no national coordinating body that correlates data and keeps records of severe rugby injuries.'

The article highlighted the cases of two young South African rugby players who had died as a result of their injuries in March 1988. 'Tragedies like these,' it read, 'could be avoided if rugby administrators changed a few simple rules and enforced existing regulations.' The writer echoed my own frustrations in asking, 'Why is it that rugby authorities resist calls for a safer game? Why are changes in the rules considered an assault on players' masculinity? Why does the game have to be defended at the cost of human life?'

In September 1989, *SA Sports Illustrated* published another article of mine in which I highlighted the growing incidence of catastrophic neck injuries among schoolboy rugby players. I pointed a finger straight at the administration, and this time I didn't hold back. 'SA's rugby administrators are the culprits ... Apparently the South African attitude is that it really is too much effort to prevent catastrophic rugby injuries.'

I felt it was obvious that rugby was entering dangerous new territory in which injuries were becoming the scourge of the game, bearing not only serious consequences for the paralysed players, but also potential legal and financial implications for rugby administrators. When a sport has left the playing fields and entered the courts, I felt, surely something was amiss. I also felt that there was enough evidence and support worldwide to force South African rugby administrators to rethink their approach to the prevention of injuries caused by their game.

In 1980, the president of the Rugby Football Union, John Kendall-Carpenter, stated clearly, 'There is little doubt that rugby football at all levels, and in particular at young adult and schools level, has become a more dangerous pursuit in the last ten years.' As J.R. Silver reported, an English schoolboy who was transiently paralysed during a maul in a rugby match in 1984 also chillingly observed, 'These accidents are a high price to pay for some fun.' But, unfortunately, while the rest of the world's rugby-playing countries began to recognise this and take adequate steps, South African rugby remained unwilling to do so.

When the number of reported spinal cord injuries increased dramatically worldwide after 1975, most of the major rugby-playing countries began to introduce specific rule changes to the game.

The first reduction in serious spinal cord injuries that these countries witnessed came as a result of a change to the rules in 1978. The change reduced the risk of a tackled player breaking his neck when caught in a maul by ensuring a more controlled situation at the breakdown.

The second reduction came after 1984, as a result of the rule changes that prohibited the collapse of the scrum. These changes altered the binding methods of the players and prevented the scrum from wheeling.

When South African rugby administrators did finally start making changes in the middle of the 1990 season, it seems that the number of players who suffered spinal cord injuries did begin to fall, at least for a period.

A look at the reaction of the other major rugby-playing countries to the crisis indicates how slow South Africa was in following their lead.

New Zealand

Between 1973 and 1978, New Zealand rugby reported an average of nine spinal cord injuries a year. In 1980, local rule changes to the maul – identified as a particularly hazardous area of the game – brought about more controlled play after the tackle. Their average annual number of cervical spinal injuries decreased from three to one between 1980 and 1987.

In 1984, the New Zealand Rugby Football Union obtained permission from the International Rugby Football Union to change certain rules pertaining to scrumming. They reported a reduction of cervical spinal cord injuries caused by scrumming from an average of three per annum between 1973 and 1984 to one per annum after 1984 (**See Figure 14 opposite**). However, the total number of injuries rose again after 1987, and this led to the introduction of the Rugby-Smart programme in that country in 2001. (That programme, in turn, would form the basis for South Africa's BokSmart programme. **See page 180.**)

United Kingdom

Between 1973 and 1978, English rugby suffered twelve cases of catastrophic neck injuries. Two of these were fatal, while ten led to permanent paralysis.

In 1983, the Rugby Football Association brought about several law changes, including the ruling that a player in a scrum, ruck or maul should keep the level of his shoulder joints above his hip joints; players arriving at a breakdown and entering the ruck and maul should stay on their feet; and play should stop immediately when the scrum collapses.

FIGURE 14

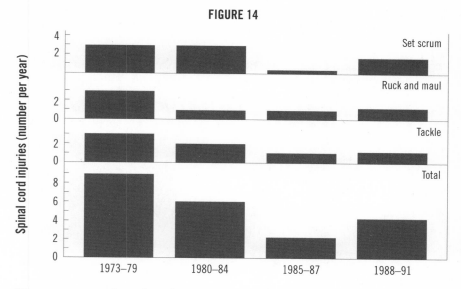

The average annual number of reported spinal cord injuries occurring in scrums, rucks, mauls and tackles in New Zealand rugby players between 1973 and 1991, showing the influence of rule changes introduced prior to the 1980 playing season. Note that the number of injuries occurring in the ruck and maul fell after 1979, whereas the number of scrum injuries fell after rule changes introduced prior to the 1985 season. Note also the rise in the total number of these injuries after 1987.

At the start of the 1985 and 1986 seasons, additional rules to reduce the forces experienced by front-row forwards at the moment of engagement in the scrum were also introduced.

From a peak in 1980, the incidence of spinal cord injuries began to decrease rapidly as a result of these new changes.

Australia

Studies in Australia revealed that of all players who suffered spinal cord injuries between 1960 and 1985, 42 per cent suffered the injury at the point of scrum engagement, while 19 per cent were injured when the scrum collapsed.

The Australian Rugby Football Union subsequently introduced the crouch-touch-pause-engage sequence in order to 'depower the scrum'. Deliberate collapsing, wheeling or popping of the scrum became illegal.

Again, from a peak in the eighties, the incidence of these injuries in Australian

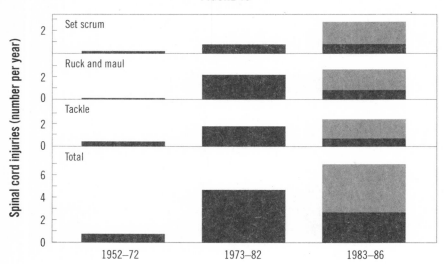

*Average annual number of spinal cord injuries occurring in scrums, rucks, mauls
and tackles in rugby union players admitted to the National Spinal Injuries Centre
in Stoke Mandeville (UK) (dark columns: 1952–72, 1973–82 and 1983–86) between
1951 and 1987. Also included are data (light columns: 1983–86) for admissions
to seven other spinal cord units in the United Kingdom between 1983 and 1986.
These additional data might suggest that the incidence of spinal cord injuries in rugby
players in the United Kingdom may have continued to increase further during the
1983 to 1986 seasons.*

rugby also began to decline following the introduction of these law changes. The
Australian Football Union was able to announce in 1993 that for the previous
eight rugby seasons (1985–1992) there had not been a single serious spinal cord
injury in under-19 Australian rugby played under these modified rules.

All of the above-mentioned countries also began to implement better coaching
and training methods, particularly in the case of tackling.

In 1988, the International Rugby Board (IRB) legislated many of these
rule changes for all rugby-playing countries. But what was happening in South
Africa?

I have always loved reading. The photo of me as a boy was taken on the stoep of our first home in Cape Town, The Anchorage, Glencairn, in 1955, and the other, on the right, in 2008

Prefects at Monterey Preparatory School, November 1962. I am sitting to the right of the headmaster, Mr Roger Vaughan-Williams

Surfing at the Inner Kom, Kommetjie, December 1965. The 11-foot board and torso-length wetsuit were 'state of the art' at the time

Rowing was a huge part of my life at university. Here I am, fifth from the front, rowing for the South African Universities crew in the Republic Festival Games at Zeekoevlei, 31 May 1971. From bow (back of the boat): Terry Marsh (UCT), Tom Clarke (Wits), Hugh Crail (UCT), Gordon Prestedge (Wits), Tim Noakes (UCT), Terry Munton (Wits), Robert Russell (Wits), Alan Marsh (stroke) (UCT), Peter Odell (cox) (UCT)

The South African Universities crew training at Zeekoevlei in July 1972. I am fourth from the back. From bow: Peter Odell (UCT), Dave Parkins (Natal), Robert Russell (Wits), Tim Noakes (UCT), Desmond Beard (Rhodes), John Leftwich (UCT), Ivor Hill (UCT), Tim Tasker (stroke) (UCT)

With my parents Wendy and Reginald on the day I received my MD in June 1981

Posbus 3101
COETZENBURG
Stellenbosch
7602

23 Julie 1987

The letter Doc Craven wrote to the head of the Conradie Hospital in Cape Town, requesting that he deny me access to data on rugby injuries treated at this hospital

Dr. P.J.M. Retief
Hoof: Rugmurgbeseringseenheid
Conradie Hospitaal
Privaatsak
HOWARD PLACE
7450

Geagte dr. Retief

Baie dankie vir u skrywe van 17 deser in verband met nekwerwel-beserings in rugby. Ek waardeer dit dat u direk met my onderhandel in hierdie verband, want dit is 'n aangeleentheid wat ons reeds probeer bestry. Ongelukkig slaag ons nie heeltemal in ons pogings nie, soos beklemtoon word deur die innames wat u in hierdie verband het. Graag sal ons wil help sover dit moontlik is, maar ek vra u 'n groot asseblief - moet nie dr. Noakes gebruik nie, want hy is klaar bevooroordeeld en die werke wat hy gedoen het vir die Onderwysadministrasie was, om die minste daarvan te sê, onwetenskaplik.

Ek wil derhalwe aan die hand doen dat die hoof van ons Mediese Komitee, Dr. (Brigadier) Etienne Hugo, u in hierdie verband nader. Hy het nie alleen hier ter plaatse baie goeie werk gedoen nie, maar het ook die aangeleentheid in Amerika bestudeer.

Hoogagtend die uwe

D.H. CRAVEN

The late Chris Burger, whose tragic death in August 1980 brought me together with Morné du Plessis and inspired my interest in the prevention of catastrophic rugby injuries

And the real deal … running in the 1980 Comrades Marathon with 20-year-old Isavel Roche-Kelly, the first woman runner to claim a silver medal in the race. She won the women's race again the following year, but was tragically killed in a cycling accident when she was only 24

A 1982 cartoon by Zapiro, depicting the 'running sports doctor'

Turning the sod with Morné du Plessis for the foundations of the Sports Science Institute of South Africa (SSISA) to be laid on the old Newlands B rugby field, May 1994

And in 2005, at the 10th anniversary of the founding of the SSISA

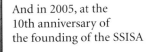

Looking after Paula Newby-Fraser, eight-times winner of the Hawaiian Ironman competition and Triathlete of the Millennium, at the Hawaiian Ironman Triathlon in October 1998. With us is her coach, Paul Huddle

The Proteas cricket team, under coach Bob Woolmer, visits the SSISA for medical and physical evaluations in July 1996. Gary Kirsten is next to me in the back row

With Shane Warne and Paul Adams at the Cricket World Cup in Asia, July 1996

Welcome to India! With the inspirational coach Bob Woolmer at the Cricket World Cup, July 1996

With my wife, Marilyn, on the island of Svalbard during Lewis
Gordon Pugh's attempt at the Furthest North Swim, August 2005

Helping Lewis out of the
water after he had swum
1.6 kilometres in 30 minutes
and 30 seconds off Deception
Island, Antarctica, on
14 December 2005

Inserting a probe into
Lewis's outer thigh
muscles a few minutes
after he had completed
the swim. His muscle
temperature at the
time was 31°C

Speaking at the 10th anniversary of the SSISA in 2005

Receiving the National Science and Technology Foundation Award for Lifetime Achievement in Science from Dr Phil Mjwara, director-general of the Department of Science and Technology (left) and the Minister of Science and Technology, Mosibudi Aaron Mangena in September 2007

I was honoured to be awarded the Order of Mapungubwe Silver in November 2008. Here I receive the order from Acting State President Kgalema Motlanthe and the Reverend Frank Chikane in November 2008

Enjoying a −15 °C run in Stockholm
during a lecture trip in January 2011

Celebrating the Ikey Tigers rugby team's victory in the
Varsity Cup final in April 2011. I am on the far right

I have been lucky that my work has taken me to many exotic locations.
Here I am en route to the North Pole. I wonder where it will take me next …

South Africa
My battles with Doc Craven

For years, Danie Craven – as president of the South African Rugby Board – and I were at loggerheads about serious neck injuries and whether his board should be doing something to prevent them.

I have the highest regard for Craven's status as one of the legends of South African rugby. He was an inspirational player and coach who pushed the boundaries of knowledge. Much of the current greatness of Springbok rugby is a direct result of his passion and dedication.

But I could not understand why Craven refused to acknowledge that rugby injuries were a serious problem. Instead, he resorted to personalised rhetoric: *'Noakes weet nie waarvan hy praat nie'* ('Noakes doesn't know what he's talking about').

Morné du Plessis has since tried to explain to me that Craven was of the old school. Craven's view was that you had to have a background in rugby to be involved in rugby, and he believed that the Springbok coach had to have been a Springbok himself. Morné is of the opinion that Craven was himself brilliant enough to acknowledge other brilliance.

According to Morné, Craven was the first to introduce match-specific training, and he showed innovation in many ways. The tight jerseys worn by today's players, for example, were instituted by Craven in Morné's day. Morné has also told me that in several respects, Craven was himself something of a scientist.

Of course, my English background and the fact that I had not played rugby at any level didn't really help matters, and Craven did not hide his antagonism. However, when it came to his wrath, I was not the sole target: he also baulked at the rule changes suggested by the IRB. 'We won't follow those recommendations because they make the game too complicated,' Craven said. 'It's impossible to control those rules. Referees and players would be arguing and bringing out rulers to check how far the scrum had moved. One of the changes is that the players in the scrum shouldn't be allowed to charge at each other while the scrum is being formed. They always charge at each other.' To his credit, Craven did concede, 'One of the main obstacles to safety in the game is that referees are not applying the existing rules.'

Craven tried his best to discredit my opinion so that my relationships were strained with many who valued the game. No one seemed to understand what I was trying to do. The opinion of some teachers at my old school was that I was trying to have rugby banned. What these people kept missing was that my argument was not about rugby; it was about injuries. I was caricatured as an anti-rugby figure but, as I emphasised earlier, I always liked rugby. I just wanted to help make it safer so that there did not have to be any more tragedies like the one that had struck Chris Burger. For me, it was about the simple fact that rugby was, and to a certain extent remains, a dangerous game. I wanted to see South African rugby authorities make the necessary changes to the game to stop these catastrophic injuries.

So there was a great deal of arguing in the press between me and South African rugby. Whenever there was a serious neck injury anywhere in the country, the media would contact me and I would repeat the same mantra: that the game was unnecessarily dangerous, the authorities were not protecting the players and nobody seemed to care.

From a scientific standpoint, Chris Burger's death had inspired me to initiate studies to determine the nature, prevalence and factors related to rugby injuries. Once again I believed that proper data, correctly collected, would allow us informed opinions. Ultimately, as in the case of the struggle with Gatorade, I was certain that the truth would eventually triumph.

We began in February 1982 with Mark Nathan, who would later become the team physiotherapist for the South African soccer team, Bafana Bafana. He joined the second intake of our BSc Honours Sports Science course that had started at the University of Cape Town in 1981.

For his research project, Mark studied all the rugby injuries that occurred at SACS High School in Newlands during the 1982 rugby season. The findings were remarkable in that, from a study of only one school, he was able to draw conclusions that were essentially identical to those from much larger studies of many more players. His study showed that injuries increased with increasing age and were most common in players in the under-19 A team; more injuries occurred in the first month of the season and again after the July vacation; and there were specific positions where the players were at increased risk of injury. In this case, hookers had an unexpectedly high incidence of injury, followed by fullbacks, eighthmen, scrumhalves and flyhalves. Tackling and being tackled, scrummaging and open play were the phases of play in which most injuries occurred. Finally, concussion was found to be the most common injury, followed by muscle and ligament injuries, and fractures.

The study was so successful that, beginning in 1984, Charles Roux used the same methods to research rugby injuries in twenty-six Cape high schools. His study was actively supported by the Cape Education Department. The major findings were no different from those of our first study and added another layer of certainty. Subsequent studies in many other countries have essentially come to the same conclusions.

But we were not yet addressing catastrophic neck injuries in rugby players. To do this, we needed access to the data at Conradie Hospital; the same data that Dr Alan Scher had used to warn the world of the rising incidence of these injuries a decade earlier. As mentioned before, for some reason we were unable to access the information, but in Craven's final years, we were suddenly granted access. I now know that Dr Craven actively prevented our seeing the data. Years later, an administrator at Conradie Hospital sent me a letter in which he apologised that I had not been granted earlier access. In the envelope he enclosed a letter Craven had written to him stating that under no circumstances was I to be granted access to the data. Before his death, Craven acknowledged to one of his biographers, Ted Partridge, that I had been correct all along.

Our student, Terry Kew, was then able to analyse all of the spinal cord injuries in rugby players that had been treated at Conradie Hospital in Cape Town from 1964 to 1988.

The data showed that the number of these injuries had increased from an average of one per year between 1964 and 1976 to five per year between 1977 and 1980, then to an average of eight per year between 1982 and 1986. In 1987, there were ten such admissions to the hospital. This meant that the incidence of such injuries had increased tenfold in a decade. At the time that I wrote the 1988 article for *SA Sports Illustrated*, I already had information that there had been as many as four admissions in the first month of that rugby season.

The conclusions we reached from this study were the following:

1. Thirty per cent of the cervical injuries would have been prevented by strict application of the rule restricting the high tackle, which was still considered legal in South African rugby at the time.
2. Twenty-one per cent of the injuries could have been prevented if the players had received better coaching in the art of tackling.
3. Ten to twenty per cent of injuries might have been prevented by strict application of the crouch-touch-pause-engage technique in the scrum.
4. Ten to twenty per cent of injuries would have been prevented by depowering the scrum and reducing the preoccupation with power scrumming that leads to collapsing of the scrum.
5. Eighteen per cent of injuries might have been prevented by players remaining upright in the ruck and maul.

We also recommended that improved pre-season fitness, early identification of serious spinal cord injury and correct early management, and continued monitoring of the incidence and cause of spinal cord injuries so that appropriate rule modifications could be introduced timeously, were of vital importance in the battle to reduce injuries in the game.

In 1999 we detected what we thought might be a reduction in the number of spinal cord injuries in schoolboys in the eight rugby seasons between 1990 and 1997. During that period we could trace fifty-four spinal cord injuries in adult players, but only thirteen in schoolboys. This represented a 46 per cent reduction in the number of injured schoolboys, but a 23 per cent increase in injured adults compared to the numbers we expected, based on our previous findings.

But our enthusiasm was premature, for at the end of the 2006 season we were informed by the management of the Chris Burger/Petro Jackson Players Fund that they knew of seventeen such injuries during that season. They encouraged us to reassess the data.

As a result, M.Sc. student Fiona Hermanus of the School of Public Health at the University of Cape Town was invited to collect all the possible information she could find relating to serious cervical neck injuries that had occurred in South African rugby players between 1980 and 2007.

Her analysis showed that a minimum of 264 cases had occurred during that time. The pattern showed that injuries were uncommon before 1975, with the first peak occurring in 1977, followed by three further peaks in 1989, 2000 and 2006.

Thus the methods that were introduced in an attempt to reduce injury rates have had less effect than might have been expected. The analysis further showed that hookers, flanks, props, wings and centres were the players at greatest risk while tackling (45 per cent), and that the scrum (37 per cent) accounted for more than 80 per cent of all injuries.

For the first time we also analysed the outcomes of these injuries and the factors that influence the outcomes. We established that 61 per cent of the cases for whom the complete data were available suffered a catastrophic outcome, and 53 per cent were in hospital for more than five months. Sixty-nine of the 264 cases died, and one-third died within the first eighteen months of suffering the injury.

The number of players who did not receive any financial compensation amounted to 66 per cent, and only 29 per cent of injured players had medical aid or health insurance. In only 50 per cent of cases were medical personnel present at the time of injury, and 49 per cent of injured players waited longer than six hours before receiving acute management for their injuries. Only in 5 per cent of cases did it seem that the injured player had received optimum medical care.

FIGURE 16

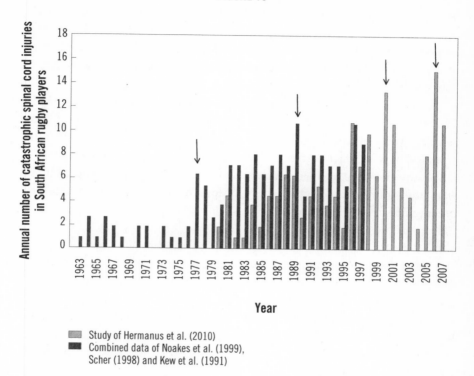

Study of Hermanus et al. (2010)
Combined data of Noakes et al. (1999),
Scher (1998) and Kew et al. (1991)

The most complete data for spinal cord injuries in South African rugby players between 1963 and 2007. The solid bars represent the data of Hermanus et al. (2010), whereas the light bars are the combined data of Noakes et al. (1999), Scher (1998) and Kew et al. (1991). The differences in the total reflect different methods of data collection in the three studies. The point is that these data reflect the absolute minimum number of all such cases; it is not clear how many cases were not detected by the different methods of data collection in the different studies. Note that the number of these injuries peaks in 1977, 1989, 2000 and 2006 (arrows).

We also showed for the first time that socio-economic factors have a major influence on the outcome of these injuries, since more white (56 per cent) and mixed-race (34 per cent) players recovered fully from a spinal cord injury than black players (10 per cent). Furthermore, only 50 per cent of black players were likely to survive the injury. We concluded that these data indicated an urgent need to prioritise preventive interventions and strategies to improve the acute management of spinal cord injuries among rugby players in disadvantaged communities.

It was after this study that South African rugby finally introduced the Bok-Smart programme, which, as stated earlier, seeks to reduce the number of these injuries to the absolute minimum. It is a world-class programme run under the direction of my former student Dr Wayne Viljoen. It is also a measure of how far South African rugby has come and the extent to which the attitudes of those who run South African rugby have changed in the past thirty-one years since the tragic death of Chris Burger.

Morné du Plessis and the Chris Burger/Petro Jackson Players Fund

The establishment of what is today called the Chris Burger/Petro Jackson Players Fund, inspired by Morné du Plessis in 1980, certainly helped to assist injured players financially. However, despite reported earnings of R4 million from the 1980 international rugby tours to South Africa, neither the South African Rugby Board nor its affiliated unions originally made any direct donations to the fund.

Du Plessis was a strong ally in our fight to make rugby safer. In 1988 he spoke out publicly on the matter:

> I've been involved with the Chris Burger Memorial Fund for eight years and it's forced me to look closely at the game. It worries me because my son has now started playing rugby – it's forced me to give the safety aspect of the game more thought. I feel there's a real need for more research and attention to the rules of the game and how safety can be improved.
>
> I think there needs to be a concerted effort from all rugby organisations and controlling bodies to come to grips with the problem of injuries in the game. If there are ways of cutting down on injuries, saving lives and years of misery for all concerned, then we must find a way to implement the necessary changes ... I do believe the game could be made safer.

In our many talks, Morné once told me, 'I never knew about any major injuries in rugby. The first I became aware of it was with Chris Burger. But after we started the fund, I realised that there were ten or twelve of these catastrophic injuries every year, mostly in the rural outlying areas where rugby was not controlled properly. But this was out of the public eye, and rugby at that stage found it convenient not to address the problem.'

In another interview, Morné was quoted as saying, 'Tim Noakes was the first to highlight this issue and speak openly about it. Tim was highlighting that it was a reality and it had to be addressed. He made the point that it's one thing for this to happen and another to do something about it. I shared his desire to make rugby a safer game. Tim is a master scientist and has a gift for making the science understandable. He simply asks the right questions. A good scientist, he says, asks the right question and finds the answer. That's what we had to do.'

The media was beginning to pick up on this shift in mindset towards the game. An article in the *Sunday Times*, under the headline 'Noakes and Du Plessis in the business of producing heroes', read as follows:

> An unlikely alliance between a man once regarded as anti-rugby, and another who was good enough to lead the Springboks, is poised to drag South African sport into a new era. That synergy was fostered by sports scientist Tim Noakes asking unpopular questions about the occurrence of rugby injuries and Morné du Plessis enthusiastically egging him on against an establishment which at first didn't want to listen.

Today, thanks to the work of Morné and his team, everything we called for then has finally been put in place. SARU now funds the Chris Burger/Petro Jackson Players Fund (Jackson died in 1989 as a result of a rugby injury he'd sustained in the league of the South African Rugby Union. SARU established its own fund in his honour. Unity in rugby saw the amalgamation of the two funds in 1992), which assists injured players financially. Rugby is far safer today than it's ever been. As Morné says, 'It's more dangerous for a youngster to go to a nightclub.'

At elite level, or even at a more privileged school level, our research has shown that it would have to be gross negligence for a player to be paralysed from a rugby neck injury. But, unfortunately, in the poorer South African communities, the situation is still unacceptable. There is still much to be done.

15 | The Recent Rise of South African Rugby

As slow as South African rugby was to adopt the new law changes to make the game safer, the authorities were even slower to promote better fitness conditioning among the players. Only relatively late in our rugby history was effective training and conditioning introduced at all levels of the senior game.

This despite the fact that the medical officers of the English Schools Association in the United Kingdom had recommended as early as 1979 that schoolboys be exposed to pre-season training to strengthen their neck muscles.

In 1980, the Rugby Football Union also issued a series of recommendations that included the need for greater attention to pre-season training. As they stated: 'Boys need to be fit to play rugby rather than hope to become fit by playing it.' They also recommended that their coaches attend sports-medicine seminars in order to better prepare their players physically for the challenges of the game.

Yet a rugby superpower like the Springboks seemed to subscribe to the philosophy that players became stronger and fitter by playing tough matches, and that was that. Morné du Plessis describes the training of the time as follows:

> We only trained twice a week, and it was relatively unscientific, if not completely so. In training we used to run through tyres or carry rocks around. It was very unsophisticated and based more on gut feel than science. I think we did too much stamina work and too little strength and explosive work. The players of today are much more explosive than we were. We didn't have the bulk muscle they have. We were much leaner. I was very focused on stamina and that's how I ended up

running long distances and even competing in a few races. But the reality is that it was completely counter to what I really needed for my game. I was actually losing weight and not building muscle. As for neck injuries, we knew nothing about them. I instinctively knew that if I was fitter, then the risk of injury would be less. But there was very little science in our training.

This despite the fact that by 1991, former England international Don Rutherford predicted that, '[t]he game of the future will demand rugby players who are athletically trained, and this will result in a far more free-flowing, running and handling game.'

I remember clearly the 1974 British Lions tour to South Africa in which the Springboks lost 0-3 in the four-Test series. The final Test was drawn, perhaps as a result of a home-town refereeing decision that was matched only by that of Clive Norling, who handed the All Blacks an unlikely victory in the final Test of the 1981 Springbok tour to New Zealand.

That British Lions tour was a devastating time for South African rugby. I recall being present at a wedding on the Saturday afternoon that the Boks were beaten 26-9 in the third Test, played in Port Elizabeth, to effectively lose the series. It was as if we were attending a funeral, not a wedding.

Some South Africans tried to put the success of the Lions down to the fact that they used a special salt tablet to offset playing in the heat and at altitude. As a medical student at the time, I couldn't believe such talk. That year I made my first rugby prediction and published it in a local newspaper, the *Cape Times*:

> There are many eminent physical educationists in this country who have been urging for some time that rugby training should be continued on a year-round basis with that part of the season traditionally looked upon as the 'off-season' being taken up by endurance training. Because of an increasing global interest in sport and a corresponding rise in the international prestige associated with winning, an increasing scientific interest in rugby can be expected ... Already there are scientifically proven ways in which performance in this game might be improved and the only hindrance to their acceptance in this country is the vast gap that exists between sporting science and sporting practice.

I continued by making the point that the British Lions won because they were the more skilled and better prepared team. Years later, Morné, who played his first rugby Test in that series, told the story of arriving at the match venue in the Springbok team bus at the same time as the Lions. The focus of the Springboks' preparation was that they were going to war. So they travelled in absolute silence, as do all condemned men, uncertain of who will still be alive at the end of the battle. In contrast, the Lions emerged from their bus singing lustily. Morné remembers wondering whether it was possible to win a rugby Test match if that was the way the team prepared. A few hours later, he had his answer.

In 1980, I sparked a great deal of controversy when I was quoted in the media as saying that certain players in the Springbok team were overweight and out of condition at the start of the season. This remark followed the publication of photographs of Springboks sporting beer paunches in a game in which they conceded a pushover try against the visiting Pumas. The reason why they were unfit was simple – none of them had begun training before the start of the season. Why should they have? They were Springboks and they would become fit by playing rugby during the season.

Despite my criticism, South African rugby players generally remained pretty unfit – certainly by today's standards – until at least around 1987.

It was Ian McIntosh who set about changing the status quo when, in the 1987 season, as coach of the Natal rugby team, he employed a local athletics coach, Victor Vass, to help get his players in shape.

This continued in 1989, when biokineticist Richard Turnbull, who had assisted South African long-distance runners Matthews Temane and Willie Mtolo to achieve success on the world stage, was called in to help prepare the Natal team for the coming season.

A year later, Natal won the Currie Cup – South African rugby's premier domestic competition – for the first time in 100 years. Suffused with the arrogance of victory, Natal immediately dropped Turnbull and lost the Currie Cup the following year. He was reinstated in 1992, and Natal again won the trophy. In scientific terms, we call this a crossover intervention trial. First you introduce the intervention that you think may have an effect (exercise training with Richard Turnbull) and then you measure the outcome (victory in the Currie Cup). Then you remove the intervention and see if the effect is lost. Then you reintroduce the intervention to see if it is able to recreate the effect that you first measured.

In scientific analysis the proof is convincing that Richard Turnbull and his work with the team was a very important factor in explaining why Natal won the Currie Cup in 1990 and 1992 but lost it in 1991.

In 1993, Natal again reached the Currie Cup final. They were beaten this time by Transvaal. However, Transvaal captain Jannie Breedt admitted that his team had adopted all the physical fitness innovations that Turnbull had introduced to Natal rugby.

Indeed, Morné himself was one of the first to experience the benefits of proper conditioning.

In November 1979, he began training for the forty-two-kilometre Cape Peninsula Marathon taking place in March 1980. He ran it in a time of 3 hours, 19 minutes and 20 seconds. Two months later, he captained the Springboks to victory over the touring British Lions. Many consider this to have been Du Plessis' finest season as a player. Slowly but surely the major South African rugby provinces began employing exercise specialists.

Former Springbok captain François Pienaar recalled in his autobiography *Rainbow Warrior* how the Transvaal coach, Harry Viljoen, had brought a 'fresh' approach to their training as recently as 1991:

> We prepared for the 1991 season not with a tough physical regime in Johannesburg, but with a carefully planned training camp at the coastal town of Hermanus. Suddenly, we were running on the beaches, training and having fun together. Chris van Loggerenberg, a respected fitness expert, was appointed to lead a new, scientific, enjoyable exercise programme … It was professional and it was fun. Each performance was monitored, and we pushed ourselves to new levels of physical fitness. The result was a memorable season. Transvaal played spectacular rugby during 1991, running the ball from our own line, dreaming and daring, hinting at a new game far removed from the attrition of the 1980s.

But there was still a way to go before this approach would be standard for all South African rugby, including the Springboks. For when the Springbok team returned to international competition in October 1992, they suffered a series of defeats foreseen by few acknowledged local rugby experts. What the experts failed to grasp was that years of isolation had taken their toll on the standard of South African rugby.

Pienaar made a very pointed observation when he wrote in his autobiography of the Springboks' re-entry into world rugby,

> Such was the pride, and perhaps arrogance, of Springbok rugby, it almost seemed unthinkable that a national coach [John Williams]

could lose Tests against the All Blacks, the Wallabies, France and England, against one win over the French, and survive. The reality, recognised by the players at the time, was that Williams should not have been held responsible for an overblown re-entry to Test match rugby. What other country would have had the nerve to stage their emergence after eight years in isolation by scheduling back-to-back Tests against Australia and New Zealand, and embarking upon an uncompromising tour to play Tests against France and England?

The local game had stagnated, and we had fallen behind international trends. Significantly, we had been left behind by the vision of one man, Bob Dwyer. As the coach of Australia, Dwyer revolutionised rugby during the period of South Africa's isolation.

I first read Bob Dwyer's *The Winning Way* when Morné and I were writing our book *Rugby without Risk*, shortly before the 1995 Rugby World Cup in South Africa. My interpretation was that there were at least five reasons for the success of the Australian rugby team under Dwyer in the 1991 Rugby World Cup.

First, he developed a new style of play. The irony, though, is that it wasn't entirely new. It had first been developed by the All Blacks in the 1920s and then been forgotten by all but one former player and coach at the club where Dwyer played his rugby.

It was a style based on forcing the opposition to react to your play in a predictable way, as if they were 'puppets on a string', and it focused on winning the game by your own team's excellent actions rather than as a result of the mistakes of the opponents.

Dwyer also eschewed the concept of a team built around a kicking flyhalf. His main objection to this was that it placed the destiny of the match in the other team's hands. In addition, he realised that, if the defending team's players are fully engaged and forced to commit themselves, that's when the attacking team can gain the overlap. Thus, the attacking team must run at the defenders and not away from them. So he had his backline lining up shallow on attack, close to the advantage line, and running straight at their opponents.

Another key to Dwyer's success was that he embraced the scientific approach. He had the following to say about the players' preparation:

It was not on the rugby field but in the sports laboratory that our secret lay. The secret to our success, if there was one, was the scientifically-based programme of physical preparation which we began implementing among Australia's elite players in late 1989. More than anything else, I believe this made the difference between ourselves and the rest of the world at the 1991 World Cup.

By the end of 1989 we had a well-researched scheme in operation which began to produce results from 1990 onwards. It was comprehensive, covering areas such as strength, fitness, diet and sports psychology. Implementing it was not an easy undertaking; apart from anything else, it required Australian rugby players to undergo a kind of cultural transformation.

The basis of the programme was that, every December, each player would be given a personalised three-month training programme, taking into account his size, physique, strength, stamina and metabolism. Players were also lectured and counselled by experts in fitness, nutrition and psychology. The playing strengths and weaknesses of each player were thoroughly evaluated by a team of experts.

Revolutionary? It seems quite obvious by today's standards, but in the early 1990s, it was ground-breaking. Dwyer was a committed advocate of this approach. 'Our experience with the Australian team has confirmed my belief that the more a player knows about his body, the better he trains; and the better he trains, the fitter and more powerful he becomes,' he wrote.

This led to another important principle in Dwyer's philosophy – confidence. Dwyer realised that because his players knew they had prepared themselves well, their mental approach changed and they played with more confidence. They had developed the winning mentality of the elite athlete.

In 1993, I contrasted this approach with the training practices of our then Springbok captain, Naas Botha. His wife Karen, an elite long-jump athlete, said in an interview, 'He only practises three times a week with his team. If I trained that little, I would be in serious trouble. An athlete has to train a lot harder than a rugby player.' The point perhaps is that Naas Botha is one of the greatest players ever to play for the Springboks – in my opinion. He did what he needed to do to become a great player in world rugby at the time. Were he playing today, he would train differently and be an even better player than he was in the 1980s.

A consequence of the limited training that rugby players undertook before the game turned professional after the 1995 World Cup was that the players of that era were never trained to their limits. They did not experience the consequences of pushing their minds and bodies beyond the limits to which both can reasonably go. So one of the reasons that I have clashed with coaches and former rugby players, like my medical colleague Dr Brendan Venter, about the consequences of playing too much rugby is that those players never personally experienced the excessively demanding conditions in which modern players are expected to perform. Rugby players only really started training to their limits in the first decade of this century. Many older rugby players do not understand that the human body can do only so much training, travelling and playing before the brain intervenes and forces a break. Runners, in contrast, have been stretching their limits since the 1880s, when the first six-day races were held on small indoor tracks in London and New York. In those races athletes would run and walk from midnight on Sunday until midnight the following Saturday. They soon learnt that there is a limit to which the human body can be pushed, and those limits are often somewhat less than most would expect.

In 1984 we published a classic study showing that changes in brain function occur in overtrained runners. This study proved that overtraining is a real phenomenon. Indeed, the chapter I wrote about overtraining in the first edition of *Lore of Running* was one of the first to detail the condition in a popular publication. In time the ideas presented in that chapter would help Bruce Fordyce and Paula Newby-Fraser to become two of the greatest ultra-endurance athletes of all time.

So when a coach, doctor and player of the calibre of Brendan Venter writes that the more a player plays, the better he plays, I become a little concerned. There is a biological limit to how much humans can train each day and how many rugby matches players can play each year. It is imposed by our evolutionary past. Perhaps if humans had not evolved as long-distance endurance athletes, we would have a greater capacity to train harder and to play rugby for eleven months of the year. Evolution, however, did not prepare us for that, and we need to understand this biological reality.

Strange as it may seem, when researching overtraining in runners I had come across a connection between the extreme physical demands of sport and the emotional demands of trench warfare. Lord Moran, later the personal physician to Winston Churchill, spent the last two years of World War I in the trenches in France with the Royal Fusiliers. He was present at some of the most vicious battles, including the Somme and Ypres, and he wrote about what he witnessed in his poignant treatise *The Anatomy of Courage*.

The generals of World War I simply assumed that all soldiers would last. They always had in all the previous wars. But Moran observed, 'In war, men wear out like clothes. All around me are the faces of men who do not seem to have slept for a week. Some who were tired before look ill; the very gait of the men has lost its spring. The sap has gone out of them. They are all dried up.' Moran concluded that in time all men in the trenches would feel fear, and it was the constant exposure to this fear that would eventually wear them out. It was how the men dealt with their fear that determined for how long they would survive.

At first, Moran thought it was the 'primitive' man without imagination that was best suited to war. Later he realised that the thinkers – those who could find meaning in the chaos around them – were the survivors.

Perhaps Moran had also read one of the greatest books on physical courage in the English literature, *The Worst Journey in the World,* by Apsley Cherry-Garrard. Cherry-Garrard was a member of Robert Falcon Scott's team that went to the Antarctic in 1911/12 in an attempt to become the first to reach the South Pole. In the end, the English were beaten to the South Pole by a far superior Norwegian team led by Roald Amundsen, as described by R. Huntford in another classic book about leadership and man-management.

In the perpetual darkness of the Antarctic mid-winter, Cherry-Garrard and two companions spent nineteen days walking more than 200 kilometres in temperatures below 50 °C in the dubious quest of bringing the egg of an emperor penguin (whose eggs are laid only in the Antarctic winter) back to England. It remains one of the epic journeys of that classic era of exploration. After his return, Cherry-Garrard wrote:

> I had come to the point of suffering at which I did not really care if only I could die without much pain. They talk of the heroism of dying – they little know – it would be so easy to die, a dose of morphia, a friendly crevasse, and blissful sleep. The trouble is to go on.
>
> What are the essential prerequisites for a polar traveler? A good blood-circulation, sound constitution, tough physique? – No, not necessarily at all. It is a matter of mind rather than body … It was the sensitive men with nerves, with a background of education – 'good blood' – who went furthest, pulled hardest, stayed longest.
>
> Other things being equal, the men with the greatest store of nervous energy came best through this expedition. Having more imagination, they had a worse time than their more phlegmatic companions; but they got things done. And when the worst came to the worst, their strength of mind triumphed over the weakness of body. If you want a good polar traveler get a man without too much muscle, with good physical tone, and let his mind be on wires – of steel. And if you can't get both, sacrifice physique and bank on will.

I have no doubt that both Moran and Cherry-Garrard would have appreciated that there are some similarities in the demands made on the modern rugby player, and the mentality of the players most likely to be able to cope with these extraordinary demands.

Back in 1993, most of today's rugby administrators played in perhaps ten major matches a year. This was the expectation of that era. The players they now oversee, however, play in as many as thirty major fixtures annually.

So, like the generals in World War I, these administrators fail to question the effect on their players. Will they wear out? Why should they? They never did in the past.

In 1993, I concluded that the defeat of the Springboks in the second and third Tests against Australia that year was not because they were beaten by a better team, but because they were beaten by a more rested team. This fatigue continued into the Currie Cup final that year, and into the Test against Argentina. I also observed that while the extroverts in the Springbok team provided the impetus in the series against Australia, it would be the introverts who would be better able to cope with the unprecedented demands of modern professional rugby.

I became certain that international rugby, so long the domain of men of action, would in future be dominated by superb athletes who also have creative minds. The superior mind would become dominant in South Africa's most phys-ically demanding game. I knew it would also become the critical factor in all of modern sport.

Fortunately, it now seems that the message is finally getting through. In an interview published in the *Cape Times* on 12 May 2011, inspirational World Cup–winning South African rugby captain John Smit said the following:

> The team that wins the 2011 Tri-Nations (between Australia, South Africa and New Zealand) will find it hard to peak again at the World Cup three weeks later. There's a fine line because obviously the Tri-Nations is valuable preparation for the World Cup but you need to be physically ready to add value in the World Cup.
>
> One perspective is that no team has won the Tri-Nations and then the World Cup in the same year. The peaking scenario is mostly mental, but you have to make sure your body can follow through on that.
>
> The team that wins the World Cup will be the one that understands the pressure and uses that to their [*sic*] advantage … The Tri-Nations will all depend on how the teams come out of Super Rugby. It's been a different level of physicality and intensity this year, plus the spice

added by the local derbies. It all depends on how your best thirty players come out of that competition.

You would like to field your best XV for the Tri-Nations, but it depends on how burnt-out they are after Super Rugby.

It is refreshing to hear a Springbok rugby captain acknowledge that burnout can indeed occur to professional rugby players. This is not a concept that the global rugby administrators, aiming to increase the amount of time rugby is shown on television (to counter the dominant position that soccer currently enjoys on that medium), will be too keen to hear. Perhaps it was the knowledge that his international rugby career was drawing to a close that allowed Smit to voice this politically incorrect opinion, which will not find favour with his local and global employers.

DEVELOPING HUMBLE RUGBY PLAYERS

Another aspect of Dwyer's philosophy was that he actively developed an attitude of humility in his players. He discouraged his players from regarding themselves as especially privileged members of society. This resonates with my own philosophy of sport: I have always seen sport as mental development – that's the key for me. It's not about winning; it's about the process of becoming a better and more productive citizen using the challenges provided by sport. I have always believed in the Greek credo that the mind and body exist in unison and cannot be separated. It was Plato who advised, 'Avoid exercising either mind or body without the other, and so preserve an equal and healthy balance between the two.'

That's what I focus on whenever I work with a team. It's a typically American approach. The American belief is that to win in sport, you have to go beyond winning on the field. Sport is about more than sport.

The Crusaders rugby team also employs this philosophy. Before the start of each season, before they put on their boots and hit the field, the players spend three days answering the question, 'Why do you play rugby?' Only when that question has been answered fully are the players allowed onto the field to start practising. Learning how to deal with people and stress, success and failure, and then learning how to succeed again – that's what makes a successful human being.

In my opinion, the greatest challenge is to produce the successful cohesion of a team of disparate individuals. Dwyer understood this. When addressing his players, he used words like 'love' and 'endearment' – words not often heard in the macho world of rugby, but which helped to develop a special bond between player and coach.

Dwyer also understood the need for analysis, particularly of the opposing team. In American football there is exhaustive analysis of the playing patterns of the competition. The success of a single match, and sometimes an entire season, may hinge on identifying and then exploiting a weakness in a single opposition player who is on the field for only a small percentage of the game.

My philosophy has always been that if you want to find out how to do something, go to the best in the world and learn. If you want to know how to produce fast bowlers, go to Australia and learn how the very systematic approach they have developed ensures that they are able to produce quality fast bowlers consistently.

In rugby, if you want to learn how to be a better coach, go to the National Football League in America. There are no better coaches of team sports on the planet than those who coach in the NFL. The competition is so tough and the athletes so skilled that being excellent is not good enough. There is only one measure – perfection. If a player is unable to perform a specific skill, perfectly, 100 per cent of the time, there is someone else who can. So either you lift your game or you will be moved out.

I read, for example, that at the end of each season NFL coaches decide whom they will continue to contract for the new year partly on the basis of how many 'mental errors' each individual player made during the previous season. This means that for each single play for the entire season, the performance of all eleven players on the team is analysed to determine when 'mental errors' are made. That is the level of detail required if one wishes to be sufficiently 'perfect' in American football. We still have a long way to go to reach that level of perfection in rugby.

Americans also invest heavily in their coaches. The best college football coaches in America can earn $4 million a year or more. That's just at college level. In the professional game it is probably even more. The competition among coaches is so great that in order to be something special, you have to really stand out.

Bill Walsh is considered to be one of the geniuses of American football coaching, because with the San Francisco 49ers he won five Super Bowl championships in the ten seasons he coached the team. His textbook on how to manage a team is the definitive work and his personal philosophies are utterly inspiring. Walsh's 50 per cent success record in the Super Bowl is unmatched. In terms of success over a career, only about ten coaches have ever won two-thirds of all the matches they have ever contested. So to win 66 per cent of all the games you play is the highest success rate that any NFL coach is likely ever to attain.

They set equally high standards for their players. Walsh worked with the great quarterback Joe Montana, and said that Montana came to him believing he was extraordinary. Walsh believed that his job was to convince Montana that he was beyond extraordinary – that's the level of coaching you are dealing with there.

A punt in American football needs to be in the air for 4.3 seconds before a player even makes the team. That's 4.3 seconds. Not 'about four seconds' or 'about five seconds' – 4.3. That's how precise they are. On each play, the quarterback knows exactly the length of time he has to execute a pass. One-hundredth of a second longer and the play will not work. In rugby, Jonny Wilkinson was lauded because he kicked for three hours every day. In American football, that would be nothing special, as that's what players are paid to do.

My impression is that many South African sportsmen and women don't yet understand what true excellence, let alone perfection, really is. As South Africans we just don't comprehend that we should learn from the best. This extends to our coaching as well.

South African rugby has, however, produced two coaches who understand. Both brought the Rugby World Cup back to South Africa.

WORLD CUP WONDER – LESSONS FROM 1995 AND 2007

I can say with some authority that none of the favoured teams came to the 1995 Rugby World Cup in South Africa with a more disrupted, less scientific build-up than the Springboks. It was clear that only a miracle could produce a World Cup–winning team from such disorganisation.

But in coach Kitch Christie, in team manager Morné du Plessis and in captain François Pienaar, that team had the leadership to produce that miracle.

The twenty-six players in the final squad were selected only one month before the start of the tournament. In that last month, the national team played two matches – one against Western Province and one against Natal. They managed to beat each team by just one point.

Springbok coach Christie had decided to train his players exceptionally hard, to the point where they would learn to play in an exhausted state with only their pride to combat the effects of fatigue and exhaustion. The result was that, two weeks before the tournament, there were four significant muscle-strain injuries among the top group of players.

The most significant was the hamstring injury suffered by Chester Williams, who had to be replaced by Pieter Hendriks for the opening games of the tournament. But Williams was back to play a crucial role in the knockout stages of the competition.

Certainly, Christie's approach flew in the face of conventional wisdom about tapering before a major event. Had he asked me, I would have told him that he was courting disaster. Fortunately, he did not ask me. The difference, of course, was that in 1995 players were not yet being chronically overplayed year in and year out as they are now. So the training that Christie gave the team was exactly what they needed. Training a modern team too hard too close to a major tournament is likely to produce exhaustion and poor performance, as happened to the fancied Irish team before the 2007 Rugby World Cup.

Christie believed that only a brutally harsh training programme would produce the mental fortitude and faith in their ability required to deliver a winning outcome in a month-long series of physically demanding matches. So he developed an extremely fit team, able, as the Springboks' motto of 1995 demanded, 'to do whatever it takes', especially in the last quarter of their matches.

There is no clearer evidence of the success of Christie's approach than the ultimate victory that the Springboks achieved. The proof that Christie's approach was correct can be found in the statistics of the final. Those data show that the physical conditioning of the players was such that during the extra time in the final against the All Blacks, sixteen of the twenty minutes were played in the New Zealand half of the field, and the last three minutes of the game were played close to or within the New Zealand 22-metre area.

Another key element of their success was that, despite starting the campaign with four injured players in the squad, at the time of the final all twenty-six players were fit. The team's superior defence was yet another crucial element in their 1995 triumph.

New Zealand brought with them to this World Cup a more expansive game played at a faster pace than any other team. Their players were young and fast and revelled in this new style of adventurous rugby, led by their giant wing, Jonah Lomu. But in the final, New Zealand's offensive strength was negated by South Africa's superior defence, and New Zealand's inability to change their game plan proved to be their downfall.

If offensive ability is a measure of a team's skill, then its defence is a measure of its character. It was through their impressive tackling throughout the 1995 Rugby World Cup that the Springboks expressed the special South African sporting will in the tradition of all the great South African teams and players of the past.

Another important factor that determined their success was that the South African team of 1995 was not made up of fifteen players each of whom was either the best or second-best in his position in the world. Instead, it was a team that achieved more than could have been expected from the sum of its individual players through the unique blending and cohesion of the team.

Christie and Morné also instilled a strict code of discipline in the team, on and off the field. This was evident in the low number of penalties given away in both the opening match against Australia (six against eight) and in the final against New Zealand (seven against fourteen). The outbreak of fighting in the match against Canada was the only blemish.

For South Africa, a greater victory than winning the Rugby World Cup was the rediscovery of this culture of discipline, and also of humility. The number of crushing defeats the Springboks had suffered since returning to international rugby in 1992 had produced players with a lack of confidence.

So Christie and Morné worked on improving the players' self-confidence using an honour code of conduct and instilling a culture of humility and discipline on and off the field, as well as exposing them to a physical training programme more demanding than anything they had previously experienced. Christie was also instrumental in introducing game analysis in 1995 in order to plot and analyse the playing patterns of the opposing teams. It was a bold stride into the scientific era of modern game analysis.

Other factors contributing to their success were home advantage and the mystical influence of the nation's support, the novelty of success and a renewed hunger to win after so many lean years.

So there was no *one* reason for the team's success. My conclusion is that the Springboks' 1995 triumph can be attributed to old-fashioned values of faith, discipline and teamwork, combined with supreme physical preparation and a clear understanding of the game plan, especially the defensive game plan. All of these factors allowed the team to seize its moment of greatness and to add one of the greatest chapters in the legend of Springbok rugby.

My own involvement in the 1995 triumph came about as a result of my friendship with Morné, the team's manager, and our joint venture in opening the Sports Science Institute of South Africa a few weeks before the first game.

Other commitments took me away from South Africa to Quebec City on the day of the opening match between South Africa and Australia at Newlands. Subconsciously, I must have been wondering whether there was something I could do to help Morné and the team. Quite by chance, the in-flight entertainment on the flight to London included a series of Winston Churchill's speeches, the most famous of which were those he delivered during the Second World War. I listened intently to his iconic tribute to The Few, the young airmen who had defended Britain against the German Luftwaffe in the Battle of Britain: 'Never in the history of human conflict has so much been owed by so many to so few.' It stirred me as much as one of the opening scenes in *Chariots of Fire* did, which also seemed appropriate for our Rugby World Cup players.

In that scene, actor John Gielgud takes the part of the Master of Caius College, Cambridge. He speaks to the entering class of 1919, welcoming them to the college and reminding them of the burden they must bear – the members of Caius College who had died, perhaps needlessly, in the bloody trenches of the First World War and whose place in history these young students would be required to fill. And so he spoke: 'And now by tragic necessity their dreams have become yours. Let me exhort you. Examine yourselves. Let each of you discover where your true chance of greatness lies … For their sakes, for the sake of your college and your country, seize your chance. Rejoice in it. And let no power or persuasion deter you in your task.'

When I awoke the next morning, the beginnings of a speech were already in my head. I started as I always do – with some scribbled notes; then a second draft on my computer. By the time we arrived in Quebec City, I had formulated my message. It flowed unashamedly from two men whose oratory I could never hope to match and from the images they projected – a few chosen men whose special abilities required that they carry the burden of an expectant nation. Should they succeed, their reward would be forever:

> There is a defining moment in each person's life when the true measure
> of who he is, is tested. Forever after he will be judged and, more impor-
> tantly, he will judge himself on the basis of how he answered in that
> moment of truth.
>
> That moment in your lives has arrived. In the eighty minutes
> against Australia, your moment of truth will come. You can no more
> escape your moment of destiny than you can recapture the moment
> that has just passed.
>
> Nor should you wish to escape that judgement. Everything you
> have done in your lives, perhaps by choice, perhaps by forces that you
> do not understand, leads to this conclusion. This has been your destiny:
> that you will play Australia at Newlands in the opening match of the
> Rugby World Cup 1995, in your home country. Whatever happens in
> the rest of this tournament will hinge on the outcome of this game.
> More importantly, whatever else may occur in your lives, you will be
> defined by what happens at Newlands on 25 May 1995. And that is
> your unique privilege. You have the opportunity once in your lives
> to define absolutely who you are.
>
> The Australian team has been through that moment. Whatever
> happens on the 25th, they have a position on which they can fall back.

They have already had their defining moment: victory in the 1991 Rugby World Cup. You do not have that escape, and so your desire must be greater. Their motivation can never be the same. Their hunger can never be as great as yours. Their past success is their greatest weakness and your decisive advantage. That is what you must exploit. You must want this success more than they. It has come down to something as complex as that.

Seize your moment for greatness so that future generations of South Africans may know that this was the finest hour in the long and distinguished annals of South African rugby. That when your moment of judgement came, you were not found wanting.

I faxed it to Du Plessis, who passed it on to coach Christie and the team; each player received a copy under his door before the match.

South Africa beat Australia 27-18 in that opening match. After Pieter Hendriks had rounded the world's greatest wing, David Campese, to score South Africa's opening try just before the half-time break, the team seemed to be on the road to success.

Afterwards, Mark Andrews, who had played such a crucial role in the team's triumph, said: 'I think our coach, Kitch Christie, in his heart of hearts, had his own fears about whether we would win. But what he did incredibly well was to make us believe that it was our destiny to win, that there were powers beyond our ability running matters. I believed it. To this day, fifteen years later, I still believe that we were destined to win that World Cup.'

AFTER THE 1995 RUGBY WORLD CUP

As much as rugby moved forward after this event, in both its thinking and playing of the game – helped considerably by the move to professionalism after the 1995 World Cup – I continued to wonder why South African rugby found it so difficult to learn from other sports and other countries, and from its own mistakes.

In July 1998 South African rugby was on a high: not only were the Springboks the world champions, but under the inspirational coaching of Nick Mallett the team was setting a world record for the number of consecutive matches without a defeat. Out of the blue, a newspaper journalist phoned and asked my opinion on what the Boks needed to do to become the first team in history to retain the William Webb Ellis Cup in 1999. My response was immediate – under no circumstances must the top players – those who would form the bulk of the team needed to defend the World Cup in Wales in 1999 – tour Europe at the end of the season.

Naturally, the opinion was not taken seriously. How could a team in the process of establishing a world record for consecutive Test-match victories be weakened before that record had been achieved? How could I be certain that the outcome of the World Cup would be critically dependent on whether or not these players played in Europe ten months before the competition?

So the team went to Europe intact and embraced a gruelling Grand Slam competition against the four home nations. All was going well until the final game, against England, which the Boks lost 7-13. Their attempt at breaking the world record of seventeen consecutive victories had come to an end. More importantly, their chance to defend the William Webb Ellis Cup had, in my opinion, also vanished.

Those who know better than me argue that there were two reasons for our losing the 1999 Rugby World Cup. The first was that the hard man of South African rugby, André Venter, from the Free State, was dropped in favour of the rising star of rugby in South Africa, Bobby Skinstad. It was said that players began to look around and think, 'If Venter can be dropped, then so can I,' so the cohesion of the team may have been affected.

The second was that the Springbok rugby captain, Gary Teichmann, was dropped from the squad by Mallett shortly before the 1999 World Cup, also in favour of Skinstad. It was a decision Mallett later described as the worst of his career. Skinstad tore his posterior cruciate ligament in a car accident in March 1999 and was never again the spectacular player he had been in the early part of his career.

My opinion is different: I still think that it was the European tour that was the major cause of our loss. There were two players, Teichmann and Henry Honiball, whose Bok careers essentially ended on that tour. At the end of the tour, Teichmann had played rugby for thirty of thirty-three consecutive months. Without a proper rest he returned to the Sharks and began playing Super 10 rugby again in February. It was too much to expect of even his superb body. Even if he had played in the 1999 World Cup, Teichmann's performance would have been affected by that 1998 European tour and the many years of rugby he had played without a proper rest.

More critical, in my view, was the fact that Henry Honiball had not been properly rested. According to Jake White in his book *In Black and White: The Jake White Story*, Honiball had played three matches on the 1997 European tour with injuries to his wrist, knee and neck. He was rested for the final game against Scotland only when he finally said that he was too sore to continue.

He desperately needed a prolonged period of recovery at the end of the following (1998) season to ensure that he was properly fit for the 1999 World Cup. Honiball is now recognised as one of the very best South African flyhalves of all time. It was suicidal to think that South Africa could win the 1999 World Cup without his presence. In his biography of Nick Mallett, Robert van der Valk is of the opinion that the fourth component of Mallett's recipe for success was that 'he had Henry Honiball in his first two seasons' and that it was the 'departure of that gifted flyhalf, Henry Honiball from South African rugby' that exposed Mallett to the actions of those who wished him no good.

Of course, his replacement, Jannie de Beer, played exceptionally in the World Cup quarter-final against England, scoring a world record of five drop goals, after which he could not reasonably be replaced by Honiball in the crucial semi-final against Australia. The point is that De Beer was a different player from Honiball and the team would have performed differently and perhaps more successfully had Honiball played in more games than just the final consolation play-off game against New Zealand, which South Africa won 22-18.

The approach of the Australians, coached by Rod Macqueen, to the 1999 Rugby World Cup was quite different. Their team, the best in the world and unbeaten in 1994, failed dismally in South Africa in the 1995 World Cup, proving for the first time that the team that is the best in the world one year seldom wins the World Cup the following year.

Macqueen had clearly decided that 1999 was going to be different. It was also the final tournament for three Australian stalwarts of the winning 1991 World Cup team: John Eales – nicknamed 'Nobody' by the Australians, since nobody is perfect – Jason Little and Tim Horan. The Australians did what they knew would be best for those players: they rested them for much of 1998 – in the case of Horan, for a full year before the tournament. They were rewarded, as Australia outlasted South Africa by six points in the semi-final, winning 27-21 thanks to a fifty-metre drop goal from Stephen Larkham in the dying moments of the game.

In the final, the Australians outplayed France, and Tim Horan, who had played almost no rugby for twelve months, was lauded as the player of the tournament. If ever there was an advert for the value of resting the key older players for prolonged periods to ensure one final magnificent performance before their careers end, this was it.

When Rudolf Straeuli was appointed in 2000 as the new Bok coach, he was encouraged to seek my counsel. We sat in my office at the Institute and I told him that to win the 2003 Rugby World Cup in Australia, it was essential that the twenty-two players he needed in the final two weeks of the tournament – to play the semi-finals and the finals – be identified as early as possible so that they could be managed appropriately for the next four years, especially in the final twelve months before the tournament. Only in this way would it be possible for them to peak and to ensure that they were injury-free for those two crucial games.

I asked him if he knew who those players were, and he replied that he did not. He knew the sixty best players in the country and he would select the best twenty-two of those players over the next four years.

Sadly, after two years, his campaign ran into trouble. Burdened by the inexorable pressures that engulf a failing Springbok coach, Straeuli abandoned science and I did not hear from him again. The 2003 Rugby World Cup was indeed a disaster, as South Africa was eliminated by New Zealand in the quarter-finals, having performed rather dismally in the earlier rounds. The problem was not purely as a result of tired, overplayed players. The reality is that Rudolf Straeuli is a more honourable person and a much more skilled coach than his record as Springbok coach suggests.

When Jake White was appointed coach of the Springboks, I became an official medical consultant to SARU. Jake was encouraged to consult me. When he did come to see me, in March 2004, shortly after his appointment as coach, he asked my advice on the medical issues he needed to understand in order to win the World Cup.

I told him that he needed to ensure that he had the twenty-two best players at his disposal in the final. Not the twenty or twenty-one best players, the twenty-two best players. I said to him, 'Jake, if you tell me who those twenty-two best players are, we'll make sure we get them onto the field in perfect condition for that final.'

So he immediately starting drawing up the list of his best twenty-two players.

This advice was neither new, nor was it rocket science. I was only following the Australian model that had been so effective in the 1999 World Cup. I was also strongly influenced by those elite endurance athletes with whom I had interacted over the years – Bruce Fordyce, Paula Newby-Fraser and, perhaps the greatest of all, American triathlete Mark Allen. All of them knew how to be right on the day that mattered. Bruce's statement was particularly pertinent: 'If you want to be right for the race that really matters, don't try also to be good in the races that are unimportant.'

The problem for most athletes is that they lack the self-knowledge of these three great athletes. To bolster their insecurity, they want also to be seen to be good on the days that don't matter. Coaches face the same problem. Their insecurity requires that they try to win everything, including the games that are less important and that interfere with achieving the bigger picture. The question was whether Jake had the personal security to buy into an approach that would cause him to lose some games that his team could otherwise have won. As a result, his overall international coaching record would not be as good as it might have been. In my view, this would be forgotten if his team won the World Cup.

At the end of our first meeting, Jake gave me his list in strictest confidence. It included most of the names of the team that would win the 2007 Rugby World Cup. Jake knew exactly whom he wanted on the field.

All the time Jake was encouraging me to speak to SARU about this plan. As he wrote in his book *In Black and White*, 'Professor Tim Noakes was constantly telling the South African Rugby Union bosses that players needed sufficient rest if we wanted to seriously contend for the world title. Ever since I'd been in charge, he'd been doing presentations and writing to SARU's top brass about player burnout and overuse injuries. Most of the time I think his observations fell on deaf ears.'

At Jake's insistence I made more than one presentation to the SARU CEO and members of his staff. I was greatly assisted by the excellent information provided by Jake's medical team, headed by Dr Yusuf Hassan, and which included physiotherapist Clint Readhead and fitness trainer Dr Derik Coetzee. Their carefully compiled data on injuries and playing time began to show some clear trends – players could play only so much before they required a decent break from the game. Without that break they would start to develop minor, niggling injuries. If these injuries were not properly managed, a major injury would be more likely to occur.

Of course, there are many factors that led to winning the Rugby World Cup. These three men did not win the Cup for Jake; but without the work they did over the four years leading up to the World Cup, and without the contribution of psychologist Henning Gericke and vision expert Sherylle Calder, I do not think Jake's team would have won. It is an important point that is too easily overlooked.

Then, in 2006, the Springboks had a bad year because a number of key players were injured. I was upbeat because I knew that to win the World Cup in 2007 it was vital to have as many key players as possible removed from competition for at least eight weeks at some stage during the year before the World Cup. Since injury is about the only control that will keep a professional South African rugby player off the field, it turns out that injury is the only ally that the Springbok coach has in his attempts to properly prepare a winning Rugby World Cup team.

I remember Jake sitting in front of me and saying, 'C.J. van der Linde is not playing this week. He's out for four weeks.' And I said, 'I know. If this goes on any longer, we are going to win the World Cup.'

At the end of 2006, on the tour to England, Jake held back the twenty-two best players. The team lost the first Test against England, in part because flyhalf Butch James had to be substituted near the end of the game as his knee was too sore to continue. Had he stayed on the field, the result might have been different, but such is the nature of the tiny margins in international sport.

That loss put Jake under tremendous pressure. He was called back to Cape Town to explain his actions to the SARU board. His agent phoned me and said, 'Tim, please write a letter to Oregan Hoskins [the president of SARU] and explain to him that they mustn't fire Jake.'

I subsequently wrote the letter, making the point that if we seriously wanted to win the Rugby World Cup, he had taken the honourable decision that was in the interests of the team and the nation but not in his own short-term interests. For in taking that decision, he was placing his own future employment as the Springbok coach at extreme risk.

In the end Jake was not fired. The Springboks won the final game against England the following week on that tour and Jake's position was safe – at least for another few months.

Jake followed this with the heavily criticised decision to hold back the twenty-six best players for the away leg of the Tri Nations in 2007. On 12 July, in a room in Christchurch, New Zealand, before the Test against the All Blacks, the coach was very clear about the reasons for this approach:

> I'm very happy about the overall plan and where we are at the moment. When I heard the criticism that the 'A Springbok team' wasn't in New Zealand, then I knew I'd done my job. Had I brought this team here in 2004, nobody would've said a word to me. They would've said it's an exciting and young team, and that's what we started with in 2004.
>
> Now that exciting young team we played against Ireland with in 2004 – the Juan Smiths, Schalk Burgers, Victor Matfields, John Smits and Bakkies Bothas – have forty Test caps behind them. When people said you've left all your main guys behind I realised we'd done the first part of our job well by showing succession and consistency. Basically, I've got a fully fit squad of forty players. It doesn't get any better than this. Now the second part is to make sure these guys are the back-up guys to the ones going to the World Cup.

Next week we pick our World Cup squad. Injuries happen between picking the squad and leaving for France, so the thirty you select are not necessarily the thirty that get on the plane and go to the World Cup.

So Jake had bought into a philosophy that placed his own career prospects at risk. In my opinion, it was the only choice he could have made. I was sure that we were on the right track.

But then he came to me with the idea of getting the group of players not going to the Antipodes in May 2007 to bond before they left for the World Cup. He wanted to send them to a special training camp in Poland. He was somewhat sold on this idea of training in specially designed cold chambers, also known as cryo-training, which was based on the belief that it would improve their strength by at least 10 per cent. Other rugby teams, he told me, had been to the centre and it had become a popular talking point in international rugby.

I told him that it was complete rubbish. It was insanity to take exhausted players who had just played the Super 14 and the first half of the Tri Nations and train them harder and expect them to improve. As Jake says in his book: 'I went to see Professor Tim Noakes for his opinion. "Listen Jake, with all due respect," he said, "there's no scientific proof that cryotherapy works. It's a thing that works on players psychologically, so they think they can recover." I'm a great admirer of Noakes and he's always supported me, so when I heard his views, I canned the idea immediately.'

My advice to Jake was simple: 'Just send them home. Os du Randt needs to be with his family. John Smit and Victor Matfield need to be with their wives and children. If they and the other key players can get two weeks off now, we will be in good shape for the World Cup.'

Fortunately the team never went to Poland. The Irish ended up taking the Boks' place: predictably, they performed dismally in the World Cup.

Just before the Boks left for Paris to take part in the 2007 World Cup, Jake invited me to speak to the team and to attend their final warm-up game against Namibia, played at Newlands. In my talk I spoke about what I had learnt about the importance of self-belief in determining the outcome of the challenge that they faced. I had been strongly influenced by the coach–athlete relationship I had developed with Lewis Gordon Pugh (see Chapter 20) and the importance we both placed on belief in each other and in the ultimate outcome of what we were trying to achieve. I began:

I want to speak to you tonight about the most important lesson I have learnt in thirty-eight years of studying the human body. For you would think that after studying the body for so long I would say that it is your perfectly trained bodies that will win the Rugby World Cup for you. I used to think that, but I do not any more.

What I now believe is this: What you really believe will happen is exactly what will happen. In other words, for something to happen, you really have to believe it is going to happen. Now I am not sure how you achieve this – if we knew, none of our teams would ever lose.

But what I am certain about is that to win the World Cup, even before you play the first game, all thirty of you have to believe absolutely that it is your destiny to win the 2007 Rugby World Cup.

I have a premonition that this is going to be a great tournament for you and for South African rugby and that you have the opportunity to be remembered as one of the greatest Springbok rugby teams of all time.

The rest, of course, is history. At the World Cup the Boks played as if it were their destiny to return the World Cup to South Africa for the first time since 1995.

What of these lessons? Has South Africa learnt anything?

If the Springboks do not succeed at Rugby World Cup tournaments in the future, it is not, in my opinion, because we lack the players. Rather, it might just be because we have yet to learn the key lessons from their previous two World Cup triumphs.

'BENT' SCIENCE AND THE 2011 RUGBY WORLD CUP

In December 2007, I received a phone call from the agent of Coach Peter de Villiers. He asked if I could meet Peter at an upmarket hotel at Cape Town's Victoria & Alfred Waterfront. There, Peter told me that he was applying for the post of Springbok coach, the position that Jake White had recently vacated. He asked if I would be able to provide him with the same sort of medical assistance that I had given Jake. I naturally agreed. I was impressed by his enthusiasm and his expressed certainty that he would be the next Springbok coach. He agreed to contact me in the New Year after the appointment had been made.

Over the next four years, in the run-up to the 2011 Rugby World Cup, Peter, his fitness trainer, Neels Liebel, and team physician, Dr Craig Roberts, did contact me on five or six occasions to ask advice about the workloads of the top Springboks. Neels and Craig were always steadfast in their conviction that the Boks were playing too much rugby and needed more rest. But both were resigned to the reality that a majority of the team were already overplayed and tired by mid-season, when each new season's Test matches began. Neels, in particular, indicated that when he took charge of the Springboks' training either in mid-season or at its end, it was not possible for him to prepare the players physically, as they were already too exhausted. The best he could do was to ensure that they were allowed to recover physically without making them even more tired.

These contacts confirmed what I had learnt with Jake White; Peter was perhaps more direct in his opinions. He suggested that South African rugby comprises seven franchises – the five Super 14 (now 15) franchises (including the top provincial teams), the Springbok Sevens and, finally, the Springboks. In practice, he said, the five provincial franchises always come first. Since they pay the major portion of the players' salaries, not unexpectedly, these franchises believe it their fiscal duty to capitalise on their investments. And so the problem is that between January and June each season, these franchises have the first call on the players' time in the Super 15. Their financial focus is determined by how their teams fare in that competition. The result is that they cannot worry about how the Springboks will perform in the Test matches that come later in the season and again at the end of the year after the Currie Cup competition.

So I learnt that the battle for the health of Springbok rugby is played not on the rugby field, but in the boardrooms of our provincial rugby unions.

For the first two years of Peter's reign, the Springboks did extraordinarily well, climaxing with their series victory over the visiting British & Irish Lions. At the end of 2009, still with two years to go to the 2011 Rugby World Cup, the team was ranked number one in the world. With the Springbok Sevens under Paul Treu and captained by Kyle Brown – a player who had been with our original 2008 Ikey Tigers University of Cape Town team before being 'stolen' by Treu – winning the IRB Sevens Trophy that year, it was a golden moment for South African rugby. Never before had one country been world champion in both these rugby disciplines.

While I shared in the national joy at this unique achievement, I was less certain that it was in the long-term interest of the team, or of South African rugby. It seemed to me that the Springboks were peaking far too soon to be a force in the 2011 Rugby World Cup. Very few teams that are the best in the world the year before the World Cup actually win that competition. Australia in 1994, South Africa in 1998 and New Zealand in 2006 had each been the best in the world the year before a World Cup competition but were no longer the best when it mattered – in the tournament the following year.

And now the Springboks were the best in the world twenty-four months before the 2011 World Cup. I began to worry that the seeds of future failure were being sown in these moments of great triumph. Iconic American football coach, Bill Walsh, has described how success most often leads to subsequent failure: 'Mastery requires endless re-mastery. In fact, I don't believe there is ever true mastery. It is a process, not a destination. That's what few winners realise and explains to some degree why repeating is so difficult. Having triumphed, winners come to believe that the process of mastery is concluded and that they are its proud new owners.'

To win the World Cup, I was certain that our players had to retain the hunger and the humility that had brought them these successes; they had to continue learning the process of mastery. And they had to understand that there would be short-term financial implications, since they would need to play less and thus earn less in 2010.

But then came the first nail in the coffin, the dreaded end-of-year (EOY) tour to Europe. My antipathy to that tour is well known because, in my opinion, it is the tour that cost us the 1999 Rugby World Cup and is one of the key reasons why the Springboks are never able to stamp their authority on world rugby in the way that New Zealand has. I do not recall if Peter consulted me before that tour, but if he had, I would have said what I always say: The EOY tour is one bridge too far for those players who have played more than about 1 600 minutes of competitive rugby during the year. Those who have played the most in a year need this time to be at home with their families, to recover and build their emotional strength for all the challenges that lie ahead in the coming season.

Sadly, a bunch of tired players went once again to Europe and played tired rugby. The results were as I had expected – for the best team in the world, the Springboks played poorly.

At the end of the tour, rugby writer Peter Bills phoned me to ask what I thought. He said that he had been at the games and it was obvious to him that the players performed poorly because they were tired. I naturally concurred. His newspaper article describing his conclusions was published a few days later. It included my off-hand comment that I thought the team leadership had 'lost the plot'. My point was that our best players either went on the EOY tour or they won the Rugby World Cup. They could not do both.

The Springbok performance on that tour was clearly a cause for concern, for the new year had hardly begun when Peter de Villiers's secretary phoned to ask if I would please talk to the contracted Boks before the 2010 Super 14 competition began.

So it was that on Sunday 13 January 2010, the contracted players assembled at the Sports Science Institute in Newlands so that I could explain what I thought they needed to do that year to give the Springboks the best chance of winning the 2011 Rugby World Cup. The special importance of the year before the World Cup is that it is also the third year in the four-year cycle between World Cups. Our data suggests that players who have not been rested properly during that cycle are more likely to break down in the third year. This is best shown by the experiences of players like Schalk Burger Jnr (**Figure 17**), who play progressively more rugby each season until they become injured, and contrasts with those of others like Danie Rossouw (**Figure 18**), who play almost the same amount of rugby each year without the highs that seem to foretell injury the following year.

FIGURE 17

Schalk Burger Jnr

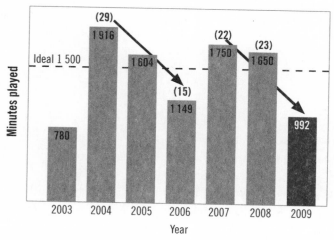

The annual number of minutes of top-class rugby (Currie Cup or higher) played by Schalk Burger Jnr each season between 2003 and 2009. Note that the playing time of exceptional players like Burger typically rises from a low number in their first season to much higher values in the following two years, to be followed by a slump due to injury in the third season of heavy competition. The pattern then repeats itself over the next three years. This pattern suggests that Burger would be better off limiting his game time to about 1 500 minutes per season if he wished to avoid a serious injury every third season.

FIGURE 18

Danie Rossouw

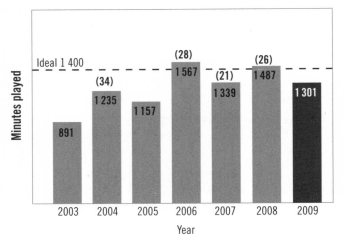

By contrast, the annual playing time per season of Danie Rossouw has remained remarkably constant for the seven seasons between 2003 and 2009, indicating the absence of serious injury, perhaps because the amount he plays is within his body's tolerance levels.

Under Jake White's coaching, a number of key players had played little in 2006, largely because of injury, and had then peaked perfectly in the 2007 World Cup. I thought that this should be the focus for 2010 – an easy year for all the senior players, followed by a gradual build-up in intensity leading into the 2011 tournament.

I began my talk by asking the players why they played rugby. It cannot, I said, be because of the money, because no rugby player ever earns enough that he need never work another day in his life. 'Your rugby careers,' I suggested, 'must give you the opportunity to spend the rest of your lives working at something you really enjoy doing. That should be the parallel focus of your active playing careers. Nothing will influence so profoundly what you do after your playing careers are over as winning the 2011 Rugby World Cup.'

Next I said that it cannot be about the fame, since their fame resides not in themselves but in the Springbok jersey they wear; they are known for now by the number on the back of that green-and-gold jersey. 'Fame,' I warned, 'is ephemeral. There may indeed be one or two of you who will yet become iconic

Springboks. But for most, that instant fame will pass as soon as your number is worn by somebody else. The jersey will transfer its fame to its new owner.'

'No,' I concluded, 'it is about each of you, the team and the nation. By winning consecutive Rugby World Cup titles, you have the chance to become immortal in the annals of world rugby. You have the chance to move beyond the fame just of the Springbok rugby jersey into a space in the national conscience never before occupied.

'But it will not be easy to get there, for most of you will have to do something that conflicts with your instincts. You will have to play less in 2010. You will have to lose money in 2010, confident in the belief that your financial and other rewards for the rest of your lives will be much greater once you have won the 2011 Rugby World Cup.' And I warned that if they did not play less in 2010, there was a strong possibility that they would be beaten in the quarter-finals by a more physical and better rested team, perhaps one from the Pacific Islands.

I then presented the data we had for the number of minutes each of the twenty-nine contracted players had played between 2003 and 2009, and proposed the number of minutes of top-class rugby I thought each player should play in 2010 (**Figure 19**).

I finished the talk by saying: 'Fourteen Springboks played too much rugby in 2009. There is always a cost.'

FIGURE 19

Player ranking by number of minutes played in 2009	Player (franchise)	Minutes of rugby played in 2009 before the end-of-year tour	Minutes of rugby prescribed for 2010	Actual minutes of rugby played in 2010
1	Bismarck du Plessis (Sharks)	2 422 (2 001)	1 400	1 466
2	John Smit (Sharks)	2 081 (1 906)	1 600	1 730
3	Pierre Spies (Bulls)	2 068 (2 436)	1 600	1 964
4	Morné Steyn (Bulls)	2 018 (2 564)	1 700	2 108

Player ranking by number of minutes played in 2009	Player (franchise)	Minutes of rugby played in 2009 before the end-of-year tour	Minutes of rugby prescribed for 2010	Actual minutes of rugby played in 2010
5	Zane Kirchner (Bulls)	1 961 (2 493)	1 700	2 503
6	Tendai Mtawarira (Sharks)	1 913 (1 729)	1 600	1 309
7	Odwa Ndungane (Sharks)	1 906 (2 315)	1 700	1 837
8	Gurthrö Steenkamp (Bulls)	1 844 (2 096)	1 200	2 042
9	Fourie du Preez (Bulls)	1 835 (2 373)	1 500	1 172
10	Heinrich Brussow (Cheetahs)	1 718 (2 544)	1 600	371
11	Victor Matfield (Bulls)	1 695 (2 162)	1 500	2 149
12	Bryan Habana (Stormers)	1 637 (2 262)	1 600	2 139
13	Wynand Olivier (Bulls)	1 611 (2 092)	1 600	1 938
14	J.P. Pietersen (Sharks)	1 529 (1 934)	1 600	1 415
15	Ryan Kankowski (Sharks)	1 526 (1 935)	1 500	1 602
16	Ruan Pienaar (Sharks)	1 525 (1 609)	1 600	1 381
17	(Dr) Jannie du Plessis (Sharks)	1 487 (1 298)	1 500	1 583
18	Bakkies Botha (Bulls)	1 454 (1 740)	1 320	436

Player ranking by number of minutes played in 2009	Player (franchise)	Minutes of rugby played in 2009 before the end-of-year tour	Minutes of rugby prescribed for 2010	Actual minutes of rugby played in 2010
19	Adi Jacobs (Sharks)	1 414 (1 655)	Incomplete data	472
20	François Steyn (Sharks)	1 381	Incomplete data	
21	Jongi Nokwe (Cheetahs)	1 359	Incomplete data	
22	Juan Smith (Cheetahs)	1 301 (1 433)	1 500	1 530
23	Johann Muller (Sharks)	1 278	Incomplete data	
24	Danie Rossouw (Bulls)	1 301 (1 719)	1 400	1 373
25	Jaque Fourie (Stormers)	1 267 (1 687)	1 600	2 114
26	Jean de Villiers (Stormers)	1 171	Incomplete data	
27	Schalk Burger Jnr (Stormers)	942 (1 270)	1 500	2 011
28	Earl Rose (Lions)	845	Incomplete data	
29	Andries Bekker (Stormers)	667 (1 205)	1 700	1 473

Data provided by Justin Durandt of the Discovery Health High Performance Centre of the Sports Science Institute of South Africa. The numbers in brackets for 2009 and all the data for 2010 were provided by Neels Liebel, fitness consultant to the 2011 Springbok Rugby World Cup team.

Captain John Smit was the first to express himself. He stated as directly as he could that my talk was wasted on the players, since they were merely the employees of a large industry. The people who really needed to hear the talk were those who paid the players' salaries. It was clear from his body language that he had not taken kindly to my words. Later, when I asked him why he was clearly upset with me, he said it was because of the Bills article and my statement criticising him for 'losing the plot'. He asked that in future if I wished to criticise him publicly, I should please speak to him first. I was overcome with instant remorse at my insensitivity and apologised profusely. That night I wrote a contrite email confirming that I was genuinely sorry for having caused him this unnecessary and undeserved discomfort. Later, I followed this with a public apology.

But what I really wanted to know at that meeting was why none of the senior players had been honest enough to admit that, as a group, they were overplayed and overtired on the EOY tour. So, in response to John's comment, I asked why no one was prepared to admit that they were tired. Two of the senior players answered that it was bad form for a Springbok to offer excuses for poor play, as this demeaned the efforts of the opposition, especially if the Springboks lost. While I understood this noble sentiment, I suggested that it was not very helpful. All it did was perpetuate the belief in the public's mind and the minds of their employers that Springbok rugby players could handle any number of matches each season without consequence. There was, however, one player who broke ranks by saying that he was very, very tired and he wanted everyone to know.

My next contact with team management occurred ten months later, in October 2010, when Peter and his management team sought my opinion on which of the senior players could be taken on the 2010 EOY tour. I was adamant that none who had already played more than 1 500 minutes of competitive rugby should be taken. To some extent this advice was followed, but I do think that a few players who were taken might have been better off left at home. But at least some key players were spared the discomfort of another pointless EOY tour.

Peter next contacted me in the final stages of the 2011 Super 15 tournament. By this time, Dr Derick Coetzee, who had been so instrumental in preparing the Springboks perfectly for the 2007 Rugby World Cup, had joined his management team as a fitness consultant. I had complete faith in Derick's ability to do what was best for the team depending on the state in which he found them. My advice was simple: Rest the players as much as you can at the end of the Super 15 competition and only start your World Cup conditioning programme at the last possible moment. I knew that Derick's unmatched experience with the team would allow him and Neels Liebel to choose that moment perfectly. Fortunately, no South African team made the final of the Super 15 competition, which added a critical additional two weeks of rest for the senior players. In addition, Peter followed the advice that had been so successful in 2007 and withdrew the senior players from the away leg of the Tri Nations competition. I began to hope that perhaps a miracle could still happen at the World Cup.

I had little further contact with the team until the week before the Springboks were to leave for the 2011 Rugby World Cup. It was a Sunday morning when I received a phone call from Lewis Pugh. As always, Lewis was animated. He said that he had been invited to speak to the Springboks the following Thursday, just before they left by plane for Sydney. He wondered what I thought he should say to them. After we had exchanged some ideas, he said to me, 'Coach, you know what you must do. You must write down what you have told me in a letter to all the Boks. If you can do that within the next twenty-four hours, I will then have it translated into Afrikaans for the Afrikaans-speakers.'

By chance I had to go to Johannesburg on the Thursday morning. So I carried with me a parcel of forty-six individually signed letters to all the members of the team and management and handed them to Lewis just minutes before he began his talk.

By midday Lewis had phoned to say that the lecture had been a great success, and that he had shared my letter with the team coaches. They had decided to store the letter and give it to the players during the flight to Sydney.

Two days later, I received a phone call from Dick Muir, Springbok assistant coach. He had just landed in Sydney with the team. He thanked me for writing the letter and said it had had the desired impact.

By then I 'knew' that our Boks were going to win the 2011 Rugby World Cup.

My letter to the 2011 Rugby World Cup Springboks

Dear

When Lewis Pugh wanted to swim for 1 km at the North Pole in water of minus 1.8 degrees Centigrade, he was told by all the 'experts' that it was impossible. Worse, he was informed that if he tried, he would die in the process. The fact that Lewis is here with you today should warn you not to believe those who say that something is impossible. It is only impossible in their (small) minds. Lewis's example shows that *to achieve the impossible you must first believe that it is possible.* Gary Kirsten became the most capped Proteas cricketer also because he did not believe it impossible for a number 9 batsman in club cricket to one day play 100 Tests for South Africa as an opening batsman.

When I had the great privilege of speaking to you on August 13th 2007 in Cape Town prior to the start of the 2007 Rugby World Cup in Europe, I began with the following: '*I want to speak to you tonight about the most important lesson I have learnt in 38 years of studying the human body. For you would think that after studying the body for so long I would say that it is your perfectly trained bodies that will win the Rugby World Cup for you. I used to think that but I do not any more.*

'*What I now believe is this: What you really believe will happen is exactly what will happen. In other words, for something to happen, you really have to believe it is going to happen.*

'*I am not sure how you achieve this. But I am certain that to win the World Cup, even before you play the first game, all 30 of you have to believe absolutely that it is your destiny to win the 2007 Rugby World Cup.*'

After being with you for that evening and for the warm-up game against Namibia a few nights later, I 'knew' that you would win the 2007 Rugby World Cup. This was obvious to me from the strength of character, the discipline and the purposefulness with which you went about your business. I had concluded this even as I spoke. I ended the talk with: '*I have a premonition that this is going to be a great tournament for you and for South African rugby and that you have the opportunity to be remembered as one of the greatest Springbok rugby teams of all time.*'

Nothing that has happened in the intervening four years leads me to conclude that you are not the best group of rugby players ever to represent South Africa at the same time. Your record, especially against Australia and New Zealand over the past two years, is not the result of you suddenly becoming less-than-good rugby players. Those performances have nothing to do with your true ability as individual rugby players and as a team. It is very important that you understand this or else you could begin to believe otherwise. Your less-than-good recent form is because you played too much rugby and rested too little over the past two years. But that is now history. It is time to move beyond the past and to face the task at hand.

The challenge is now to achieve that which is 'impossible' because it has never been done before – to win successive World Cups. To achieve this, the experts predict that you will have to beat the All Blacks at Eden Park in the semi-final. I am aware that the All Blacks have not been beaten there since 1996. (In statistical terms, this only means that the probability that the All Blacks will lose there becomes increasingly more likely with each successive game that they win. Clearly it is impossible that the All Blacks will never ever lose another game at Eden Park. So the only reality is that the probability that they will lose their next game at Eden Park **increases** with each new game. Not the opposite, as some would want you to believe.)

To beat the All Blacks and to win the 2011 Rugby World Cup requires that, as a team, you must take the collective decision and accept the responsibility that it is your destiny to be the next team to beat the All Blacks at Eden Park. You are so privileged to be in this position. By accepting the greatest modern challenge in rugby, you have the chance to define yourselves absolutely as who you really are. In the words from the scene in the film *Chariots of Fire* that I also showed you in August 2007: '*Let me exhort you. Examine yourselves. Let each of you discover where your true chance of greatness lies. For their sakes; **for the sake of** your college and **your country**, seize this chance. Rejoice in it. **And let no power or persuasion deter you in your task.**'*

This is no different from the challenges that the 1995 World Cup team faced and which you faced and also overcame in 2007. There is no reason why you should allow it to be any different in 2011.

Understanding the 'why'

The team comprising the individuals who best understand 'why' they are playing in the 2011 Rugby World Cup will win it. The 'how' of rugby is the tactics, the skills and the fitness; the 'why' is what gets you out of bed in the morning ready to face another arduous day of training and competition. The greater the importance of the team's collective 'why', the better that team will perform. The 'why' is what ultimately determines the outcome, not the 'how'.

The 1995 Springboks won because they had a more important 'why' than the All Blacks. The nation had recently staged its first democratic election; the contribution of former President Mandela was perhaps the deciding factor. So important was the event for the

future of South Africa that a book and film have since been produced
to explain those extraordinary events and remarkable individuals to
the world. The unique circumstances of the time dictated that the
Springboks could not lose that final. Your hope must be that your
performances are so important that a book and film will also be
produced about the social importance of your joint contributions.

My favourite quote to explain what you are trying to achieve comes
from Tony Dungy, coach of the Indianapolis Colts American football
team: *'But winning the Super Bowl is not the ultimate victory. And once
again, just to make certain we're on the same page, it's not all about
football. **It's about the journey** – mine and yours – and the **lives we can
touch**, the **legacy we can leave**, and the world we can change for the
better.'* Your unique privilege is that simply by playing rugby you are
influencing the future of your nation.

But to win the World Cup you have to find a bigger 'why' than the
New Zealand or Australian teams. You have to understand that the
World Cup is about your contribution to the future of your nation.

If you get the 'why' right, your reward will be that you will be
remembered as the greatest team of players ever to represent South
Africa. But if your focus is exclusively to be known as the greatest, you
will fail. For you will not have understood the greater 'why'.

You must not give yourself permission to believe that the New Zealanders are invincible at Eden Park

When I spoke to you in August 2007, I presented the story of Roger
Bannister and the first sub-four-minute mile and how Bannister
succeeded because his coach, Franz Stampfl, believed in him. Stampfl
later said, *'the great hurdle is the mental barrier'*. My point then, as now, is
that you have first to overcome the **mental barrier** before you can win
on the field.

Many would think that to win you have to convince yourselves that
you are better than the All Blacks. I think the key is NOT to allow
yourselves to believe that the All Blacks are better than you. The reality
is that the crucial games in the 2011 World Cup will be won by a single
kick or perhaps a single try. And this will include the game at Eden Park.

My belief is that the outcome of all sporting contests is decided
when one team accepts as a collective unit that the other is better. The
team that wins is the one that refuses to accept that notion at any time
before or during the match.

To win the big games, you do not have to believe that you are better than the opposition. But you can never afford to believe that they are better. Once you do that, the game is over.

Life is short. You have seven more games and then most of you will never again play this game at this level
You have seven more games at this level. After those seven games, most of you will never again play the game at international level. At most you have 560 minutes of international rugby left in your entire life. Then it is all over. The Australian team certainly, and to a lesser extent the New Zealanders, do not have this time urgency to finish the job off.

When Lewis speaks, he will tell you about what happens if you quit before the finish. It means that everything you have done up to that moment is wasted.

There is no reason, other than what you believe, stopping you from completing the task you began when you won the Junior Rugby World Cup in 2003. This is the final leg of an extraordinary set of achievements – a set that will be matched with great difficulty in the future annals of South African rugby.

I wish you every success as you successfully complete this most remarkable journey.

Yours Sincerely,
Professor Tim Noakes

All that remained was for the team to do the job on the field.

At the end of the league phase of the competition, it was clear that the Springbok coaches and fitness consultants had indeed achieved the impossible. They had turned a tired team into one that, as had happened in 2007, was peaking perfectly for the knockout phase of the competition. By then I was certain that the Springboks had become the team to beat, an opinion I was later informed was shared by many experts following the tournament, not least those supporting the All Blacks.

But none of us had considered the one factor over which the Springboks had no control – the performance of the World Cup referees, and especially that of Bryce Lawrence in the quarter-final match played between the Springboks and Australia on Sunday 9 October 2011. It was, in my opinion, one of the most notorious games in the history of Rugby Football.

THE 2011 RUGBY WORLD CUP QUARTER-FINAL MATCH BETWEEN THE SPRINGBOKS AND AUSTRALIA

Like many South Africans, I watched the quarter-final match against Australia with growing incredulity. By chance I was participating in a SuperSport television broadcast that required I be interviewed within a few minutes of the completion of the game. My opening comment was to express my concern that rugby is in trouble if the referee can have such a major influence on the outcome of the game, as was rather obvious in that one. I contrasted this with a sport like American football in which there are many more officials on the field during the matches, in which the final decisions of the referee are always precise, as dictated by the unambiguous nature of the laws of the game, and in which there is a recourse to television replays if either team believes that the referees have made an incorrect call. My point was that if any of these factors had applied to that game, South Africa and not Australia would have advanced to the 2011 Rugby World Cup semi-finals.

Over the next few days my certainty that the Springboks had suffered a grave injustice was strengthened by two events. The first was the statement by one of South Africa's most revered rugby referees, André Watson, to the effect that Bryce Lawrence's refereeing had been 'a mess'. Then there was a letter from an Australian supporter, Chris Davis, published in *The Australian*, which best summarised what most South Africans were feeling at the time. He wrote:

> There are no doubt a lot of Australian rugby supporters celebrating our victory over the Springboks yesterday. There are also a number of us that are wondering how on earth we managed to pull it off against a side that dominated possession and territory and lineouts. Now, I don't want to take anything away from the Australian victory… our boys did perform superbly, but on the day the Springboks were, we have to admit, the better side. The Boks, as always, were magnanimous in defeat with a somewhat pragmatic approach to the result. I wonder what our boys would have said faced with the same situation of blatant incompetency by Mr Bryce Lawrence. I support Australia and always will but for those of us who believe in fair play this was a hollow victory. This was very much like fighting an opponent with one arm strapped behind his back – it leaves a bad taste. There were rumours

about Mr Lawrence's impartiality before kick-off from a lot of ex-pat South Africans now living in Australia, but we tend to dismiss these conspiracy theories with a grin. Certainly, Mr Lawrence's performance on the field did nothing to dispel those theories. His performance was nothing short of abysmal. He did not award the Bok try because of a dubious forward pass. I have looked and looked and to me, anyway, it did not look forward. Minutes later when the Boks once again breached our defences and were well on the way to scoring another try, he called them back for a forward pass. If the first call was contentious, there certainly was nothing wrong with the second one. Here, I must ask – why not use the 'eye in the sky' – an impressive and expensive piece of equipment that should be used for such decisions? He failed to penalise (David) Pocock for slowing the ball down. If we had played like that against the All Blacks, they would not have been so quiet about it – and rightly so. In the dying minutes of the game he (Lawrence) was in full view of at least two high tackles by our boys that went unpunished. Any of these transgressions, if properly acted on, would have surely given the game to the Boks with their advantage over territory. To rub salt in the South African wounds, he awarded a high tackle to the Wallabies for a chest high tackle. We won, but did we really? Our sport has always been regarded as a 'hooligan's game played by gentlemen'. If we do not want the rugby union to degenerate into a farce that soccer can become we need to make sure that our refs are of suitable calibre. They need to be trustworthy gentlemen. Mr Lawrence, I would advise against any planned holidays to South Africa for a couple of years.

The end result was that early the following week I knew it was time for me to write something to my local newspaper expressing my personal disquiet at the possible implications of Mr Lawrence's performance, while complimenting the Springboks for the manner in which they had accepted the unfair way in which their quest for immortality had been stymied.

I began the article by saying that the distinguishing feature of science is that the outcome of any novel experiment cannot be known for certain before the experiment has been completed and the new data analysed. In contrast, science that is directed to produce a predetermined outcome is dishonest. We call this 'bent' science. Such science is usually funded by industry and serves a commercial purpose. Part Two of this book presents some examples of such 'bent science'.

Similarly, the joy of sport is that the outcome of any event cannot be known before its completion. But if the outcome is predetermined, we call this dishonest variant 'match fixing'.

I then suggested that anyone watching the game between South Africa and Australia the previous Sunday might have considered that the outcome had been predetermined, perhaps 'fixed'. In which case my suggestion was that the IRB needed to act expeditiously to prove that any such interpretation was false. For without decisive action, this single game would tarnish the good name of world rugby in a way that none has ever done before.

The outcome of the letter was somewhat more than I had expected. Within hours of its submission, a reporter from the newspaper was in my office wishing to write a front-page story relating to the letter. I acceded to her request on one condition – that she indicate that I was not accusing anyone of 'fixing' the game. My point was that to me, and to many others, including Chris Davis, it seemed as if the outcome of that particular game had been decided before the kick-off; in effect, that the game had been 'bent'. My point was that the function of science is to disprove hypotheses. Thus, in my opinion, it was the IRB's responsibility to investigate that game to prove to everyone's satisfaction that my hypothesis was false; that the outcome of that game was fair and had not been influenced by nefarious actions.

When the article appeared that afternoon it dutifully carried my statement that I was not accusing anyone of fixing the game. Yet the banner headline suggested the opposite – a logical disconnect that I find difficult to understand.

By the next morning the story had gone global and I began to receive comments and emails, some of which were less than appreciative, particularly one from an Australian referee who is a close friend of Bryce Lawrence. When I argued that my interest was purely to see justice done on the rugby field, he responded by admitting that his friend had made a hash of that particular game.

Which was essentially what I had said. I simply wanted answers to the bigger question: Why?

LESSONS FROM THE 2011 RUGBY WORLD CUP

Global sports suffer when damaging perceptions of dishonesty are not addressed. When it failed to address the widespread state of match fixing that had become endemic in the sport by the 1990s, the game of cricket lost the credibility it had earned over the previous three centuries. The result of the limp-wristed response of its international administrators is that the game will never again enjoy its former status. Sadly, the statement 'it's just not cricket' has lost its ring of authority.

Similarly, the strongest lesson from the 2011 Rugby World Cup was that refereeing decisions play too large a role in determining the outcome of closely contested games. Since referees are human, they are, at the very least, prone to subconscious bias; at worst, that bias can be influenced, and perhaps even controlled.

The lasting legacy of the 2011 Rugby World Cup is the possibility that the best team did not win the tournament, but that refereeing decisions in five crucial games aided an ultimate All Black victory. In as much as those decisions influenced the outcome, one might entertain the thought that there was some evidence for a possible conspiracy. But the only people who know whether or not this is so are also those who will never tell.

Australia's unexpected loss in their pool game against Ireland set up a bruising quarter-final match-up between two of the best teams in the tournament. It meant that New Zealand would face a more tired southern-hemisphere team a week later in the semi-final. Thus it was in New Zealand's interest that Ireland should win that pool game.

By the time of the quarter-final between South Africa and Australia, it was clear that South Africa was the better team, that, as in 2007, they had timed their progress to peak to perfection and that they would pose a real threat to the All Blacks. Thus it was in New Zealand's interest that Australia, and not South Africa, progress to the semi-final. The improbable refereeing performance of Bryce Lawrence ensured that outcome.

In the semi-final game between Australia and New Zealand, South African referee Craig Joubert essentially blew Australian fetcher David Pocock, Man of the Match the previous week against South Africa, out of the game. With the same dominance over Australia that South Africa had enjoyed the week before, New Zealand won by fourteen points, the same difference that South Africa should have enjoyed the week before had Joubert also refereed that game. Again, the refereeing performance had favoured an All Black victory.

In the other semi-final between France and Wales, Alain Rolland's controversial decision to red-card Welsh captain Sam Warburton after only nineteen minutes ensured that France would be the more likely team to make the finals. It is alleged that France has never lost a Test match in which Alain Rolland has been the referee. Despite playing against fourteen men for sixty-one minutes, France ultimately won by a single point. This suggests that Wales were the better team. If so, it was again in New Zealand's interest that France, and not Wales, advance to the final.

In the final, the All Blacks played poorly in the second half in which they were dominated by the French, who came within one point of victory. The French, too, believed that refereeing decisions, in particular the reluctance of referee Joubert to award some penalties in the second half, contributed to the All Blacks' victory. Had Wales been in the final, would they have done even better than France?

In order to better understand what I had seen, I consulted widely. One leading referee told me: 'The rugby rules may be in black and white, but the referee's decisions are entirely nebulous.'

That, he indicated, is rugby's Achilles heel, since it allows the possibility for individual bias to enter. Indeed, the question that the rugby world needs to ponder is simple: If the rugby rules are indeed so nebulous, is it reasonable to expect that the subconscious bias of any human referee will not influence the outcome of a Rugby World Cup final in which one of the competing teams is from the host nation? If the answer is in the affirmative, then the same applies equally to all other rugby matches that are closely contested and considered important.

COULD THE SPRINGBOKS HAVE WON THE 2011 RUGBY WORLD CUP?

If there was a third force acting to ensure that New Zealand won the 2011 Rugby World Cup, then no matter what the Springboks did, they would not have won the William Webb Ellis Cup in consecutive competitions. If there was no such conspiracy, then the team and its coaches came up short. What might they have done differently?

It remains my opinion that we continually overplay the top echelon of our best rugby players. Once Peter de Villiers had decided to play the bulk of the players who had won the 2007 Rugby World Cup also in the 2011 World Cup, his main aim should have been to limit their playing time in the intervening years. The team knew how to play winning World Cup rugby; they did not have to re-learn how to do that. Nor did they need to remain at peak fitness during that time. What they desperately needed was a minimum of eight weeks' rest each year in 2008, 2009 and 2010, and a soft 2010 season, leading into a tougher 2011 season. This could have been achieved if the decision had been taken already in 2008 that no senior players would be allowed to go on the EOY tour or to play in the Currie Cup unless they were completely free of injuries and had played less than a certain amount of rugby – say about 1 500 minutes – during that year.

The result of this decision would have been to force the development of a second tier of players able to represent South Africa with distinction on the EOY tour. That South Africa has such players was clearly proven by the performance of the 2011 Currie Cup–winning team, the Lions, under the coaching of John Mitchell. Mitchell proved that there is a sufficiently large population of South African players who have the ability to play rugby at international level if they are properly managed and coached, and correctly motivated. We do not need to continually play only a select twenty players, year in and year out. The pool is large enough for the international rugby load to be shared more widely among South African players.

The result of trying to play the same pool of players in all the Test matches from 2008 to 2011 was that some, like Bryan Habana, Pierre Spies and John Smit, were unable to recreate the form they had shown earlier in their careers, while others, like Bakkies Botha and Juan Smith, developed chronic injuries that prevented them from playing the role that was needed for South Africa to retain the 2011 Rugby World Cup. The outcome of the World Cup often hinges on the availability and form of a single player. A 2011 Springbok team with those five players playing at the height of their powers might have been impossible to beat regardless of who was refereeing their games.

So why do we overplay our players? I have already mentioned the first, and perhaps most important, reason – the franchises that pay most of their salaries expect the players to honour their employment commitments. But there are also two other reasons.

First, the coaches want to play their best players all the time to ensure that they do not lose their jobs. They also have an eye on their win/loss ratios, since these are ultimately how they will be judged by history. Second, the players want to play because they earn more money that way. And they know their careers are short.

The cost of all this was that the 2011 Springboks did not achieve the immortality to which they had come so close. They have the rest of their lives to ponder whether, given their time over again, they could have done it differently.

part five

THINKING CRICKET

'In my opinion, cricket at the professional level is played 90 per cent in the brain and 10 per cent with raw ability. Yet 100 per cent of players spend 100 per cent of their time practising the 10 per cent. Why?'

— TONY FRANCIS, 1992

16 | Challenging Conventional Theories

MY GOOD FRIEND BOB

When Bob Woolmer was found dead in a hotel room in Jamaica on 18 March 2007 during the Cricket World Cup in the West Indies, the cricketing world immediately presumed that his death had something to do with the book he had just completed.

People believed that Bob was about to reveal all sorts of revolutionary information, including some about the sordid world of match fixing in cricket.

They were right about one thing: the book that Bob was producing *was* revolutionary and would indeed astound the cricket world, but for different reasons altogether.

Six weeks before his death, Bob wrote the following: 'In 1996, Professor Tim Noakes said to me, "You should write down all the knowledge you have gleaned over the years so that people might better understand the game and the passion it invokes."'

In the book that would become his legacy, *Bob Woolmer's Art and Science of Cricket*, Bob assembled the thoughts of a man whose innovation in the game was never truly appreciated, especially by those who employed him in South Africa.

I first met Bob when he was appointed coach of the South African cricket team, the Proteas, in 1994. It was not long before I realised that he thought about the game of cricket differently from others. Richie Benaud remembers watching Bob when he was playing English county cricket for Kent in the 1970s. He recalls, 'He impressed me as being a good thinker on the game.'

As a player, Bob represented Kent and England, but it was as a coach that he truly made his mark on the game. He first coached Warwickshire to an unprecedented level of success in English county cricket. Then he coached Canada, the Netherlands, Ireland, Namibia, Kenya, Pakistan and, of course, South Africa.

Bob's method as a coach was not simply to tell a player how to do something. He wanted the player to understand the 'why' behind what he was doing. In fact, if Bob was satisfied that a player understood the *reason* for something, he was often happy to allow the player to decide for himself how to go about achieving his objective.

Bob's example taught me that if we want South Africa to dominate world cricket, then we need to produce more thinking cricketers and, more importantly, more thinking coaches.

Many players, coaches and administrators know the 'how to' of cricket but don't understand the 'why', nor do they see any value in understanding the reason for what they do. They believe that what has worked in the past will always work in the future. This view is at variance with that in other sports, like American football. The difference is the level of competition: in cricket there are so few nations producing competitive teams that there is no real pressure to do anything innovative to gain an advantage. Instead, it seems as if a global cricketing truce has been declared: let's continue to do only what we have always done; that way we can maintain a comfortable status quo. Bob understood this and once wrote, 'Cricket has always resisted change. If the game is to survive, we must ensure that it moves with the times.'

Bob was a great coach because he was a phenomenal teacher. There is no better example of his ability to teach than the effect he had on the career of Jonty Rhodes. It was Bob who helped Rhodes redefine the fielding game by teaching him to be a good enough middle-order batsman to play international cricket.

It was also Bob who began using technology in his coaching and strategic planning, from filming specific players to enable them to understand their games better to collecting valuable data about teams and their performances.

In me, Bob found a kindred spirit – someone who was prepared to challenge conventional thinking and who wished to use sports science as a powerful weapon in developing cricket. He invited me to work with him for a simple reason: 'Tim,' he said, 'I will teach you about cricket if you teach me about science.' I suspect it was an unequal task, since I definitely learnt more about cricket from Bob than I taught Bob about science. Long before we met, he had gleaned a working knowledge of how science is conducted. He had a lifelong interest in the sports sciences and told me that, had he not become a professional cricketer, he would have studied sports science at Loughborough University in

England. I found it interesting that England's most successful rugby coach, Clive Woodward, whose team won the 2003 Rugby World Cup, holds a bachelor's degree in the sports sciences from Loughborough.

The partnership Bob and I developed between 1995 and 1997 occurred at the time when South Africa became, with Australia, the best one- and five-day Test team in the world.

It was a great tragedy that Bob was denied the opportunity to work as a coach in South Africa after the 1999 World Cup or to see out the days of his life as a coach raising the standard of cricket coaching in his adopted country, which he loved so passionately.

But he left an indelible legacy to cricket. It is a legacy that began when his father placed a bat and a ball in his cot two days after his birth in a hospital in Kanpur, India. Bob told me that his father reportedly said at the time, 'Son, I hope this will be your life.'

A NEW APPROACH

As a schoolboy I always wanted to be a star cricketer. However, I lacked most of the ingredients essential for cricketing success, including an understanding of myself and the mental side of the game. While at school, I was a successful second-team opening batsman, but whenever I played in the first team, I froze. I just couldn't hit the ball. Only in my final game in the first team, when it was too late, did I learn to bat as if I were playing for the second team. I realise now that, at the time, there was nobody willing to teach me how to overcome this problem, which, it turns out, is more common than I imagined then.

A remarkable coincidence is that, at a different level, Bob Woolmer experienced exactly the same problem: on the Marylebone Cricket Club (MCC) tour of India in 1976, Bob discovered that he could not hit the ball beyond the inner ring of fielders. When he sought the advice of the touring coach, Ken Barrington, an exceptional batsman who averaged more than fifty runs per innings in his international career, Bob was told: 'Just go out there and hit the ball.' That was exactly the advice that I had been given and that had been utterly unhelpful, since it made no sense to me. Bob and I were both choking. The way to cure choking is to learn to stop thinking and simply react, especially when batting, and to practise under game pressures, which we never did. Bob realised that if he wished to continue as a professional cricketer, he would need to discover for himself the solution to his problem.

In the end, he did so very successfully. In his official international career, in which he played nineteen Tests, he scored three centuries, all against Australia, and finished with a Test-match batting average of thirty-three.

He told me that by the end of his career he was able to enter the 'zone' the moment he crossed the boundary rope on his way to the wicket. Then, when batting, all he saw was a red ball coming out of a white background – everything else was blocked out. So Bob solved his problem, whereas, fortunately, I did not. I became a runner – a sport in which it is not possible to 'freeze', as far as I know – and a scientist, and Bob became one of the greatest cricket coaches of all time.

Many years later, my doctoral student Tim Harkness showed me how he taught a similar technique to Abhinav Bindra, who as a result won an Olympic gold medal – India's first in an individual sport – in the ten-metre shooting event at the 2008 Beijing Olympic Games. But more of that later.

Although I stopped playing cricket, I never stopped caring about the game and remained an avid follower, despite the fact that South Africa was excluded from international competition after 1970. My interest was intense when we returned to international competition in 1992, at the Cricket World Cup in New Zealand and Australia. Then, in 1994, Bob Woolmer was appointed to coach the Proteas. That year he attended the opening of the Sports Science Institute building in Cape Town, introduced himself to me and suggested that we consider working together in the future.

In fact, my first involvement with South African cricket preceded my involvement with Bob. In 1993, I was invited by the United Cricket Board (UCB) of South Africa to attend an indaba on the future of the game in the country. There I met some of the heroes of my childhood – Jackie McGlew, Mike Procter and Eddie Barlow, among others. My belief then, as now, was that South Africa had the potential to become an international cricketing power once again.

The challenge was to identify the active steps needed to achieve this.

My contribution to the indaba was to argue the importance of a quality research and development programme in the science and medicine of cricket. The great attraction of cricket – indeed of any sport at the elite level – is the narrow margin between victory and defeat. This means that small adaptations in many areas can produce a large advantage to the team prepared to innovate. I made a number of suggestions and argued that perhaps we needed to start selecting and developing different players able to perform best on different surfaces.

The areas of weakness that I saw in the game included the design of cricket pads and gloves, which seemed medieval, as they were not completely effective in preventing injury. I suggested that an investigation be undertaken into new materials that would not be so bulky but would be able to absorb more shock. That way the pads would not hinder the running of the batsmen. Later, Bob made the point that different pads were required for one- and five-day games. He argued that pads in one-day cricket needed to be more rigid so that they would deflect the ball as far as possible. By contrast, especially when playing on turning wickets, pads for five-day cricket needed to absorb as much energy as possible to reduce the risk of being caught off the bat and pad.

In 1993 I also suggested a greater focus on nutrition and training, as young players need to be conditioned from an early age to adopt the attitude of elite athletes. This approach is practised in most other sports. Another prediction I made was that modern cricket would demand the evolution of the cricketer as an elite athlete for whom excellent physical condition would be a prerequisite for success.

I thought, too, that there could be a more focused approach to skills training, ensuring that training is relevant and specific. In particular, I could not understand why so much training is done in the nets in conditions that hardly apply to what really happens in the middle during cricket matches.

In addition, since I was an ardent follower of American football, I had seen the success of a more scientific and less subjective analysis of the playing patterns of opponents. At the time, Australia led the world, as they do today, in the application of the scientific approach to cricket, and I predicted that it would be only a matter of time before that scientific effort would be evident in the performance of their cricketers.

Unfortunately, after a promising start, by 1997 – only four years after the indaba – innovation in South African cricket came to a standstill. Australia, by contrast, invested heavily in science and moved ahead. In my opinion, the inability of South African cricket to be competitive in four consecutive Cricket World Cups after 1996 can be traced to a particular mindset that took over at the top of South African cricket after 1997.

My scientific interest in cricket began in the early 1990s, when we completed some rudimentary studies of the visual clues that batsmen need to hit the cricket ball. In one study, we showed that an international cricketer like Peter Kirsten was able to predict the ball's trajectory and where it would pitch with 70 per cent accuracy, even if he saw the ball's initial trajectory for only about 100 milliseconds.

We did this by turning off the indoor lighting as soon as the ball left the bowling machine. The results were perhaps not unexpected and favoured my belief that genetic factors play a key role in the development of the very best batsmen and bowlers. For in the same experiments, some leading fast bowlers were unable to hit the ball when batting in the dark. In fact, as soon as the lights went out, one bowler chose to run away rather than risk being hit by a delivery he could not see.

This suggested to me that all the world's truly exceptional batsmen, like Donald Bradman, Graeme Pollock, Barry Richards, Brian Lara and Sachin Tendulkar, must have a superior ability to predict the ball's trajectory early in its flight. They then must have spent tens of thousands of hours developing this genetic gift to an exceptional level. Only later would I discover how all of these great players honed their skills during thousands of hours of early childhood play.

As a result of this rudimentary study, in June 1993 I wrote in the *Financial Mail*: 'The country that first identifies the clues the batsman uses to calculate the trajectory of the ball will have a significant advantage over other cricket-playing countries. It will allow the more effective identification of batting talent; it will improve training techniques; and it will allow bowlers to develop techniques to deceive the opposing batsmen.'

My belief then was that South Africa had the scientific sophistication necessary to undertake such research. All it required was administrators able to share our vision and enthusiasm. I knew Australia had such administrators in abundance at all levels of the game. But what of South Africa?

The professionalism of rugby preparation in 1989, especially through the work of another Australian, Bob Dwyer, and the English coach Geoff Cooke, produced the first two well-matured and equally physically prepared teams that contested the final of the 1991 Rugby World Cup. Again, it did not surprise me that an Australian was at the forefront of this change. In the early 1980s, Australia had changed the balance of sporting power in the southern hemisphere and become a global sporting superpower through the development of a holistic, nationwide sports-development programme founded on sports science and coaching at the Australian Institute of Sport (AIS). By the 2000 Olympic Games, Australian Olympic sport had achieved its ultimate goal – fifty-eight Olympic medals. As Wilma Shakespear, an inaugural member of the AIS in the early 1980s, told me at a 2004 dinner in Oxford to commemorate the fiftieth anniversary of the running of the first four-minute mile, 'Australia's success is based on a simple idea – we no longer have any dumb coaches.'

To my mind, no other coach, player or administrator in South African cricket understood this approach or embraced it better than Bob Woolmer in the early 1990s. Indeed, he was perhaps even ahead of the Australians at that time. 'You can be involved with this game for fifteen minutes or thirty-five years and you will still learn,' Bob once wrote. 'Those of you who are convinced that you are doing it the right way may find suddenly that "your way" is challenged ...'

But for the rest of the game, there was – and remains – a tremendous reluctance to see what is obvious to those who look on with the objectivity of a scientist and ask just one question: 'How can we do it better?' Not enough of our cricketers are trained to question. We focus too much on the past – what has always been done – and fail to ask whether there are possibly not better techniques to develop batting, bowling and fielding skills right from the moment cricketers begin the game. Then we fail to analyse in sufficient depth the most appropriate tactics to use against various oppositions.

As I will point out later, batting is the one area in which the way we teach children from a young age will have a critical bearing on whether or not they can be successful in the future at the international level of the game.

When Bob and I began to work on the book that would become his legacy, I was charged with the responsibility of uncovering all that had been written about the science of cricket. So I accessed all that I could about the game and purchased at least fifty books about cricket and its great players to add to my collection of the scientific studies undertaken on cricket.

However, on a trip to London I discovered the one gem that I really needed – a book written by Tony Shillinglaw in 2003, titled *Bradman Revisited*. Perhaps predictably, there was another wrinkle to the story. Tony Shillinglaw is not just from Liverpool, the home town of both of my parents, but from the suburb of Birkenhead, in which both of my parents grew up. Then, interestingly, Shillinglaw played cricket at Birkenhead Park Cricket Club, the very club for which my father played cricket after he left school in 1931. It was in these indoor nets that, in 2008, Tony demonstrated to me what he had discovered about Sir Donald Bradman and the lessons Bradman had unwittingly learnt about the best way to acquire the art of batting from a very young age. Here was an opportunity to find out how best to prepare our youngsters to be as good as Bradman. There has not been another Bradman in nearly 100 years, but this does not mean that there could not be one in the future. It will not happen, however, if we fail to learn the lesson that Bradman's experience teaches.

17 | The Bradman Project

The traditional method of teaching batting – elbow up and bat lifted straight back towards the middle stump – is, quite frankly, a complete and utter disaster. Players taught to play this way will simply never reach the highest levels of the game. Watch for yourself. When you see a world-class batsman who lifts his bat directly backwards in the direction of the wicketkeeper, a batsman who places his foot next to the ball and plays 'straight' so that the struck ball returns exactly in the direction from where it came (as it must if the batsman hits with a 'straight' bat), that player will be unique in the modern annals of cricket.

Yet this method continues to be drummed into the minds of young cricketers, despite the fact that no great batsman in the history of cricket has ever batted this way. (Had they, they could not have been successful.) Many generations of cricket coaches have failed to notice this, and so they have continued to teach an ineffective technique.

There remains a belief about what exactly the perfect batting style is, but to quote Sir Vivian Richards, the great West Indian cricketer who was voted one of the five Cricketers of the Century in 2000, 'No one will ever persuade me that there is one method of batting which can be imposed on young cricketers by the book. Let the mind of the youngster fly … show him a big field with no fielders, no barriers, no batting rules, and let him whack the ball in all directions.'

Bob Woolmer was also very specific when talking about this subject. 'There is no right or wrong way to play or teach this game,' he said. 'Inevitably, it is the player who will shape his own destiny … There is no cloning in cricket. Yes, youngsters will have role models, but they will still have their own style.'

Bob outlined what he believed to be the five basics of batting:

1. Watch the ball.
2. Keep your head still at the release of the ball.
3. Judge length accurately: line will change with swing and spin.
4. Allow your hands to lead your body and feet into the correct position.
5. Select the correct shot.

Bob does not make any specific reference to the direction of the backlift at the start of the stroke. This is because it is assumed by many coaches that this does not require debate – the bat must be lifted directly backwards towards the stumps. Only in this way will the bat come through in a straight line and so strike the ball with a 'straight bat'. Legions of young batsmen have been told that if their bat is coming down from somewhere near second slip, they'll never be successful batsmen. So they are told to straighten their backlifts.

Sir Donald Bradman, the most consistent run-scorer in the history of the game, did not lift his bat straight back towards the stumps. Graeme Pollock did not either, nor does Sachin Tendulkar, and Pollock and Tendulkar are the two modern players considered the next best after Bradman.

Instead, Bradman lifted his bat towards the second-slip position, as did Brian Lara. On the wall in Bob's study was a photograph of Lara, generally considered to be one of the greatest batsmen in the game and whom Bob coached at Warwickshire. It shows Lara executing his fantastic pull shot in which there is no evidence of a straight bat. Above his autograph on the photo, Lara had written cheekily, 'Teach this one, Coach.'

BATTING LIKE BRADMAN

Finding Tony Shillinglaw's book *Bradman Revisited* provided the 'missing link' that in my view discloses the secret to successful batting. Bob was fond of saying that there are two eras of cricket coaching – the era before and the era after the video camera. The same can be said about batting: our understanding of the most effective batting technique can be defined similarly – the era before and the era after Shillinglaw's book. However, without the video camera we would not be able to explain properly what Shillinglaw uncovered.

Shillinglaw revealed the key characteristics of Bradman's technique. First, in Bradman's stance, his bat rested between his feet with the face 'closed', touching his left big toe and pointing towards about mid-wicket. Second, with his bat facing towards mid-wicket, Bradman's grip was also rotated further around towards the back of the bat. One of the consequences of this batting grip was that Bradman tended to hit his leg-side shots – especially the hook and pull shots

– downwards into the ground, thereby eliminating a common cause of dismissal. Third, his backlift was always the same. It travelled in a single rotary action – a circle – with the initial movement towards point/second slip. Fourth, his backlift always began only the instant before the ball left the bowler's hand. Until that moment, he was absolutely immobile. Fifth, he hit the ball as if he were striking a golf ball.

As I watched historical footage of Bradman batting, I wondered why he lifted the bat towards second slip rather than straight back towards the wicketkeeper. A few seconds of practising this technique with a cricket bat in my hands soon revealed the answer.

I immediately realised that, as soon as the bat is lifted straight back towards the wicketkeeper, weight is transferred onto the back foot. Importantly, this weight transfer happens very quickly. But if the bat is taken out to second slip,

Sir Donald Bradman did not strike the ball with his 'elbow up' and his bat 'straight'. Instead, he struck it as if he were driving a golf ball. This technique, now used by all batsmen of international standard, involves a rotation of the upper body, which generates the bat speed necessary to produce the prodigious hitting power now required to succeed in international cricket, especially in the abbreviated forms of the game.

the weight transfers initially onto the balls of both feet and only thereafter onto the back foot.

The key, I realised, was that Bradman delayed the initiation of his backlift *until he had detected the length of the delivery*. Thus, his backlift began only after his subconscious brain had calculated the length of the delivery, or, alternatively, until after he knew what shot he was going to play. Of course, the length of the delivery can be determined the moment the bowler releases the ball. The later the ball is released, the shorter the delivery and the longer the time it will take the ball to reach the batsman, since the ball slows down after it pitches. So the longer the bowler holds on to the delivery, the longer the batsman has to play the delivery, since it will pitch further away from him. I know that Bradman did not arrive at this technique by thinking about it. He was entirely self-coached – he learnt a novel technique that was simply the most efficient method yet discovered.

So this initial simple analysis showed that a large part of Bradman's unique secret was that he delayed by a few hundredths of a second the transfer of his weight onto his back foot. It took another few months of watching Bradman videos and thinking about his technique for me to observe what I think explains why he could score runs so quickly without needing to hit the ball in the air, and why he was able to average 99.94 in his Test career. The question I asked myself was how this method translated into Bradman's average, which is 50 per cent better than any other batsman in the history of cricket.

The key, I believe, is that Bradman also timed the movement of his feet to the length of the delivery. So when the delivery was too short to play off the front foot (because it had been released from the bowler's hand slightly later than a fuller delivery), he moved his back foot and his bat backwards *in unison*. As a result, he was able to transfer his weight backwards in one single movement that began shortly after the bowler released the ball. This allowed him to be in the best possible position (well back in the batting crease, near to his wicket) with extra time to play the bowler's worst deliveries (because they were 'short'). Bradman's superior technique also ensured that those bad deliveries were even shorter. From this position it would have been easier for him to direct off his back foot any delivery that was a few inches short of a good length to any part of the field. This explains why bowlers said it was a waste of time moving the fielders when bowling to Bradman: he would simply direct the next delivery to the part of the field from where the fielder had just been moved.

In contrast, when the bowler released the delivery earlier, Bradman would begin his backlift but would not move his feet. Only when the bat had reached the apex of its backlift so that most of Bradman's weight had been transferred onto his right (back) foot, would he begin to move his left (front) foot in the direction of the delivery.

But, as mentioned at the beginning of this chapter, for the past 100 years the MCC coaching manual has taught that the bat must be lifted directly backwards towards the wicketkeeper. Alternatively, batsmen are taught to be in a ready position with the bat already off the ground *before* the bowler releases the ball.

But, as evident from the discussion above, that's not how Bradman or other stand-out batsmen of the past, such as Graeme Pollock, Sir Garfield Sobers or Sir Vivian Richards, batted. They all lifted the bat out to second or third slip, and they all delayed the initiation of their backlifts until the bowler had already released the delivery. Modern giants like Adam Gilchrist and Sanath Jayasuriya, both very fast scorers, bat in the same way. As a result they are both able to play short-pitched deliveries deep in their batting creases.

Many of the world's current best batsmen, by contrast, all move into the set position before the bowler releases the ball (**see Figure 21 opposite**). As a result, their weight is distributed onto the back foot even before the bowler releases the ball. Batsmen who use this technique, including Jacques Kallis, Kevin Pietersen and Michael Clarke, must prefer to play off the front foot and will be less effective off the back foot, at least against faster bowlers, for when playing off the back foot, they do so with the back foot planted on the batting crease, not a metre behind it as Bradman did.

Of course, this does not make batsmen who use the set-position technique 'bad' – they are, after all, each extremely talented, quite exceptional performers. My argument is, however, that none will ever match Bradman's average, as none has a technique as ideal as Bradman's. By preferring to play forward, they allow the bowler a larger margin of error – in other words, the ball has to be much shorter before they will play backwards than was the case for Bradman. Furthermore, because they play shorter-pitched bowling from the batting crease rather than from a metre further back, as Bradman did, they have less time to play the short delivery. As a result, they require more skill to direct the short delivery between the fielders.

Bradman could not understand why anyone ever went out when they were set. I believe that the longer he batted, the easier it became for him, since his flawless technique allowed his brain to respond even more spontaneously the longer he was at the crease. I suggest that the less perfect technique of all the other great batsmen in the world requires that their (subconscious) brain must work just a little bit harder with each delivery. As a consequence, they tire more quickly and so do not produce the very big innings as frequently as Bradman did.

FIGURE 21

© Carl Fourie

© QUINTIC

Modern batsmen are usually taught to adopt the set position immediately before the bowler releases the ball (top). Instead, Sir Donald Bradman, the greatest batsman of all time, delayed his initial movements (above) until he had detected the length of the delivery. This allowed him to play shots off his back foot from deep inside his batting crease. This is very difficult for a batsman who has transferred his weight onto his back foot by standing in the set position at the instant the bowler releases the delivery.

The beauty of all of this is that Bradman was self-taught – the greatest batsman the game has ever seen was never coached in batting. He taught himself to bat in his backyard, using a golf ball and a cricket stump. His secret was that he did not teach himself how to play cricket, but rather how to control a fast-moving ball with nothing wider than a cricket stump. What is more, at school he played only five matches; until the age of seventeen, he had played almost no formal cricket.

Because Bradman's technique was so unorthodox, it was easy to explain his prowess as that of a one-off genius. However, Tony Shillinglaw believes that Bradman possessed the ideal batting technique, which is hard to argue against considering the cricketer's prolific run-scoring ability.

As Bradman himself said, 'Coaching should deal with what to do with the ball, not so much as how to do it. The coach must have sufficient intelligence not to be dogmatic but to discern what method is best for the pupil.'

I would like to add that visualising the desired outcome rather than thinking about how to hit is the key. This is best understood in terms of the evolution of the human brain.

JUST HIT IT

Our brains evolved the pathways necessary to control complex movements – the 'what to do with the ball' components – long before we developed the pathways to analyse *how* to do it.

Monkeys, for example, do not analyse how to swing through the trees at great speed. They simply leave the complex calculations that direct their movements to their brains and get on with swinging through the trees. Similarly, a peregrine falcon does not 'know' how it catches a pigeon when it descends at more than 200 kilometres per hour. It simply does what nature selected it to do over tens of millions of years.

My other favourite example is Mrs Ples, our 2.1-million-year-old ancestor discovered by Dr Robert Broom in the Sterkfontein Caves in Gauteng in 1947. Mrs Ples was only three foot (one metre) tall and she weighed only thirty kilograms. But because she was a rudimentary runner, she would have been able to rotate her upper body (one of the key skeletal-muscular adaptations necessary for running), which means that she would have been able to strike a golf or cricket ball. Even though her brain was only about one-third of the size of our (modern) brains, it very probably contained the hardware to make all the necessary calculations to hit a cricket ball. This is so because the control of these actions resides in the primitive parts of the human brain. These parts developed millions of years before the thinking part of the brain, which evolved only in the past 500 000 to one million years. Some, including L. Liebenberg, argue that it was the need to track antelope that produced our larger brains and that early persistence hunters were the first 'scientists'.

For early humans, it was far more important to know *what* to do in a particular situation rather than *how* to do it; that is, to act instinctively rather than thoughtfully, because this often meant the difference between life and death.

So evolution has equipped us with all the brain pathways that we need to bowl, catch and hit a cricket ball without ever having to engage the higher brain centres that control thinking about or analysing these actions. The same, of course, applies to other skilled sports, like golf. It is simply not possible to 'think' how to play a golf shot – the control of the proper execution of a golf shot lies deep in the subconscious brain. As described in Beilock's book devoted to the topic, consciously 'thinking' about how to hit a golf or cricket ball simply impedes the functioning of those subconscious controls, producing a less favourable outcome. In this sense, one of the great frauds of modern sport is the coach who tries to teach that hitting a golf or cricket ball must be done by conscious thinking. In accordance with this, Greg Chappell once observed, 'The brain is a better cricketer than you'll ever be.' The (subconscious) brain is also a better golfer than you will ever be.

The key to Bradman's success was, as I remarked on earlier, the game he developed in the backyard of his parents' home in Bowral, Australia. There he amused himself after school by using a cricket stump to hit a golf ball thrown onto the circular, brick-and-cement base of a water reservoir. The ball would bounce back at speed and in an unpredictable direction off the cement floor. As Bradman noted, 'The golf ball came back at great speed and to hit it at all with the round stump was no easy task.' In his mind, there was no style or technique to adhere to. He was simply focused on the single task of hitting that golf ball. Wherever it bounced and however it came to him, he just hit it. As his skill improved, he began to play 'Test matches', featuring all the great players of the day. Hitting the ball to certain areas produced different numbers of runs. A missed delivery that struck the kitchen door behind him signalled that he had been bowled out.

Interestingly, South Africa's great batsman, Barry Richards, read of Bradman's technique and also trained with a ball thrown against the garage door. But the Richards' home was perched on top of a steep hill. So every time Barry missed the ball, he would have to go down to the bottom of the hill to collect it. Presumably he learnt how not to miss the ball too often.

No one, perhaps other than Tony Shillinglaw, knows how Bradman's practice technique produced his revolutionary 'rotary action'. For how does hitting a golf ball off a cement floor with a cricket stump translate into facing deliveries bowled at 100 miles an hour (160 kilometres an hour) by Harold Larwood, especially when some of those deliveries were aimed at the heart or head? This was the case in the famous 1932/33 Ashes series between England and Australia, which became known as the 'Bodyline' series.

I suspect that, by doing this repetitive practice on a daily basis from an early age, Bradman maximised the training of the subconscious and primitive parts of his brain at the precise time when these pathways are most easily trainable. Bradman's example teaches, I think, that there may be a crucial period in the brain's development – perhaps between four and twelve years of age, more or less – when it is most receptive to eye-hand coordination training. Today, the concept of 10 000 hours of practice has become popular since the publication of Malcolm Gladwell's book *Outliers*, and others. Bradman earned his 10 000 hours in his parents' backyard in a way that he could never have done had he been playing in the nets against schoolboy bowlers. Perhaps his greatest blessing was that he was not exposed to traditional methods of cricket coaching at a young age.

Most great batsmen of the modern era to whom I have spoken also did not earn their 10 000 hours playing cricket in the conventional way. As I mentioned earlier, Barry Richards, one of Bradman's best eleven players of all time, developed his technique in much the same way as Bradman. Rahul Dravid, who, like Bradman, is perfectly still at the moment of ball release, told me that he learnt his cricket on the streets of Indore in central India. I asked him if he learnt 'defensive cricket'. 'No,' he responded, 'we only had about an hour to play each day. We had to hit the ball as hard and as far as we could with each delivery. There was not time to block.'

Commentators who watched a young Bradman described him as an 'ugly, half-cock player'. Another observed, 'He will always be in that category of the brilliant but unsound ones ... He does not correct mistakes or look as if he were trying to do so.'

But Bradman was unmoved by these comments and wrote: 'I refuse to be dogmatic about one's grip, because I believe various holds can be satisfactory. So much depends on the batsman's methods ... I refuse to condemn an unorthodox grip just because it is different. The use of wrist and arms and the method of stroke production cannot be stereotyped.'

Then he adds the clincher in the entire debate around batting technique: 'I am more inclined to teach boys what to do [rather] than how to do it – so long as there is no fundamental or glaring error. Better to hit the ball with an apparently unorthodox style than to miss it with a correct one.' But, in fact, Bradman's key was that he could score runs off almost any delivery because of his ability to play off the back foot to all but the most perfect deliveries.

Bradman's penchant for lifting the bat towards second slip and not directly towards the wicket was considered equally astounding by the purists. His answer to this criticism was typically direct:

Reams of matter have been written about the necessity of taking one's bat back perfectly straight ... I am all in favour of a straight bat at the right time and place, but *technique must be the servant, not the master* [emphasis added]. Too many players fail because their thoughts are concentrated on where their left elbow is or where something else is, instead of on hitting the ball. I was never conscious of my backlift and I did not take any particular notice where the bat went until I saw movie shots of me in action. Then it was clear that my initial bat movement almost invariably was towards the slips ... For defensive shots the bat should naturally be as straight as possible, but for a pull shot, for instance, a perfectly straight backlift would make it far harder to execute the stroke ... there should be all possible emphasis on attack, on the aggressive outlook. Think of some of the great batsmen and you will find very few who did not depart in some degree from orthodoxy.

In a letter to Shillinglaw before his death, Bradman reaffirmed his view by stating, 'The perpendicular bat theory virtually eliminates pull shots (which can only be played with a cross bat) and square cuts (except by angling the blade), which, in turn, is a recipe for giving catches in the slips.'

Yet anything unorthodox continues to be damned in cricketing circles.

Bob Woolmer provided his own example of this debilitating attitude in the game. Many coaches have berated players for supposedly using 'too much bottom hand' in their batting. Bob himself was accused of this during his playing career, but he believed that too many coaches neglect the importance of the use of the bottom hand. He had a very effective way of challenging this belief. He said, 'I asked a group of fifty coaches to raise their hands if they thought batting was controlled by the top hand: almost all raised a hand. I then asked them to think about the drill of hitting high catches for fielding practice: Which hand did they use? Top or bottom? All answered that they used the bottom hand. So I asked them again: Which hand controls the shot? The debate started afresh.'

Bob believed that batting is most definitely a two-handed technique. But everybody has a dominant hand, and it is this hand that provides the power and timing in batting.

As someone who knew absolutely nothing about batting until I discovered Tony Shillinglaw's book on Bradman, I offer a different solution: it is not the hands that determine the power of the stroke, but rather the rotation of the upper body on a fixed base. Golfers and tennis players do not speak of a 'bottom' or 'top' hand. Yet they strike the ball powerfully with the identical technique used by those modern batsmen who are the best strikers of the ball.

FIGURE 22

© Gallo/AFP

*One of the great modern batsmen, Matthew Hayden, demonstrates how, like
Bradman, he strikes the ball as if he were playing a golf shot. He does not hit
the ball with a straight bat and a high elbow, as is usually taught.*

The power in any hitting shot begins with the rotation of the upper body. The
hands simply transfer and direct that rotational force through the bat onto the
ball.

One of the fundamental advantages of Bradman's 'unorthodoxy' was that,
by moving the bat and therefore his mass towards point, his weight was also
transferred onto the balls of his feet. The orthodox technique, in which the bat
moves backwards, initially transfers the weight onto the back foot, from which
it is extremely difficult to perform any shot other than one off the front foot.
So to play backwards requires a secondary movement that returns the weight
to the balls of the feet. This is why there is a dominance of front-foot play in the

game. Yet clearly Bradman's technique allowed him to play any shot he liked equally well off the back and front feet. As the great cricketer noted, 'I allowed my bat to rest on the ground between my feet simply because it was a comfortable and natural position. It is regarded as more orthodox to teach a pupil to rest his bat behind his right toe. This position encourages a straighter backlift, is perhaps sounder for defensive play, but I feel it has greater limitations in versatile stroke making.' Quite simply, the pendulum motion of the bat in orthodox batting is designed primarily for defence of the wicket, while Bradman's focus was on attacking the bowler.

Again, it has been easy for cricket to dismiss Bradman as somehow biologically superior to any other batsman. As a scientist, however, I know the dangers of presuming a cause unless it has been proven. We have no evidence to suggest that Bradman was in any way biologically superior, so we have to entertain the possibility that perhaps his brilliance was the result of a superior, if unorthodox, batting technique.

My analysis of his technique has also revealed that, without exception, the game's great batsmen – including W.G. Grace, Graeme Pollock, Garfield Sobers, Viv Richards and Brian Lara – all adopted elements of Bradman's technique. None lifted their bats directly backwards; nor did they hit the ball with a straight bat – if they had, all they would have achieved would be to have hit the ball straight back to the bowler. Neither did they adhere to the conventional cricketing wisdom never to play 'across the line', nor did they usually strike the ball with the foot next to the ball. More often their most powerful front-foot shots were struck when the front foot was nowhere near the pitch of the ball.

In fact, a scientific study of eight of the top batsmen in world cricket in 2006 – Ricky Ponting, Jacques Kallis, Mohammad Yousuf, Inzamam-ul-Haq, Kevin Pietersen, Damien Martyn, Herschelle Gibbs and Andrew Symonds – undertaken by my sports science student, Jason Douglas, revealed that not one of them lifts his bat directly backwards at the start of his backswing. Nor do any of these great players play 'straight'. Instead, in our analysis of their batting performances in Test matches, all were shown to drive across the line so that they drove balls pitched up to fifty centimetres *outside* the off-stump towards the mid-wicket area. Even the most cursory viewing of Twenty20 (T20) cricket will show that there is not a single batsman who plays according to the traditional MCC batting model.

So if they all do this, and the success of Bradman's technique is proven, how should coaches be coaching young cricketers in the art of batting? Using my scientific training and analysis and what Bob Woolmer taught me about cricket, I would suggest the two guidelines that follow.

1. A player must first learn to control a fast-moving ball

In South Africa, we need to start getting bats and balls to children in the townships, because good, old-fashioned street cricket is the only way that we will ever yield the next Bradman. Just as conventional Australian cricket coaching in the 1920s could not have produced Bradman, so conventional coaching in South Africa will not produce the next great South African batsman. The only method to generate such unique talent is to introduce hundreds of thousands of young children to a bat and ball at a young age. From among that group, hundreds will develop superior skills because they have a natural aptitude, they learn quickly and, as a result, will practise more than all the other children. From those hundreds will come a few – perhaps one or two – who can match the ability of Graeme Pollock and Barry Richards. With luck, we will be able to go one better than even those two extraordinary players and produce the next Bradman.

So it's perfectly simple: street cricket, hitting a ball in unstructured games and hitting a ball against a wall for hours each day from a young age is the only way to develop the next generation of great batsmen. Indeed, I believe that the reason for the decline in the standard of batting in world cricket is because the number of children playing in the street or in the backyard has decreased, at least in England, South Africa, New Zealand and Australia, while the number being coached according to the traditional methods has perhaps increased in those countries. I suspect that this is not the case in the Asian countries – there street cricket may be as popular as ever.

Children should also be learning to bat with an implement that is fashioned more like a squash racket with a large 'sweet spot', so that they can learn to hit the ball as if they were playing tennis or golf; that is, they must learn to hit the ball by rotating their upper bodies, and not with the traditional 'left elbow up' nonsense.

2. Future generations of cricket coaches must think differently about batting

Coaches must seriously consider Bradman's observations and, perhaps more importantly, those of Shillinglaw, who believes that 'the very minute a young player is told to stand with his bat open-faced behind his rear foot, the battle is lost. From this position the only natural movement is straight back. Bradman's style of batting cannot be adopted from this stance.'

The recent evolution of the game, especially the introduction of T20 cricket and a greater emphasis on the one-day game, means that unless the player can play 'across the line', hit the ball far by rotating his upper body, play the hook and pull shots and more deliveries off the back foot, he will not go far. None of this can be achieved by those who are taught to bat according to the conventional MCC technique.

Most young children interested in ball sports simply want to hit or kick the ball as hard and as far as they can, with scant regard for technique or direction. Insisting that a very young child holds the bat or shifts his weight correctly usually leads to irritation and then tears, and can turn him against a game like cricket for good.

When looking for talent in young children, Bob recommended the following: 'Watching under-ten batsmen, for instance, I'm not looking for high hands or a straight bat: at this age, the prospective stars simply need to show good eye-hand coordination, good balance and athleticism.'

So technique should not be formalised until a child has developed the ability to strike the ball with the same technique that a golfer or a tennis player uses to hit the ball. Indeed, I believe that Rafael Nadal would have been an astonishing batsman had he chosen cricket over tennis. Why? Because he can strike, at arm's length, more than a metre away from his eyes and with exquisite precision a ball travelling at very high speed. Any short delivery outside the off stump would be dispatched to the boundary. He would not need much time to learn the other strokes.

Once the player has learnt this technique, he probably needs to progress to the fast-moving golf-ball-and-cricket-stump technique. Only once these methods have been mastered would I consider exposing the player to conventional cricket training. The goal would be to learn the timing of the backlift to the length of the delivery – that is, to the instant of ball release. The key skills to develop would be:

1. no movement of the bat before ball release;
2. continuous rotary backlift that is identical for all deliveries, whether short or full length; and
3. moving the bat and the back foot backwards at the same time when playing a short delivery.

Somehow I doubt that these ideas will find much favour with cricket coaches around the world. However, what I do know is that the next superstar-batsman – the one who averages more than seventy to eighty runs per innings in Test cricket – will bat this way and will be closer to Bradman's technique than any other batsman in the past 100 years.

18 | The Science of Batting

Great batsmen do not need great vision. Sir Donald Bradman's eyesight, for example, was relatively poor. What they do need, however, is the mental ability to anticipate on the basis of specific visual clues observed in the bowlers' run-up and delivery what the trajectory of the delivery will be once it has been released.

The accuracy required to make this prediction is remarkable. For a delivery that is bowled at 150 kilometres per hour and which takes only 450 milliseconds (0.45 seconds) to reach him, the batsman must hit the delivery in a time window of about 440 milliseconds in order to play an effective shot. He must also calculate the position of the ball to an accuracy of less than one centimetre in three-dimensional space. Remarkably, the great batsmen are able to do this with astonishing accuracy on the basis of information received before the ball is bowled, and then in the first 350 milliseconds of the flight of a fast delivery. Any change in the ball's trajectory in the last 120 milliseconds occurs too late for the batsman's brain and body to produce a compensatory movement that was not anticipated by the brain's earlier calculations.

Had Bradman not possessed a superior ability to predict the trajectory of the delivery and to execute his shots with perfect precision, his perfect technique would not have been as successful. The point is that players with an equal ability to predict the trajectory of the delivery will not match Bradman's performance if their technique is less effective than his was, particularly if they get into the set position before the ball is delivered.

Conversely, when Bradman played a fuller-length delivery off the front foot, he would delay the movement of his front foot until his bat had reached the apex of the backlift. This would naturally transfer his weight onto his back foot, releasing his front foot and allowing him to begin to move his front foot forward.

It would also allow him additional time to refine his prediction of the ball's trajectory and where it would pitch.

Sadly, I could access very little footage of Bradman batting in Test matches. However, I believe that he played mostly off his back foot – this explains why he could score so rapidly, since a short delivery allows a wider range of placement options. Indeed, Bradman was puzzled by the dominance in modern batting of strokes off the front foot, for example by players like Kallis, Pietersen and Clarke. In the classic video he first recorded in 1934, which was updated in the 1980s, Bradman commented that he was uncertain of the reason for batters playing more off the front foot today than in his day. He implied that perhaps they might do better if they played off the back foot more frequently. But to do that, they would need to change their technique so that they are not in the set position before the ball is delivered.

To sum up, the skill of batting requires the batsman to predict the path of each delivery with exquisite accuracy on the basis of information that begins to be collected during the bowler's run-up and delivery stride. The greatest batsmen can predict the path of the delivery with great accuracy by the time the ball is released. This explains, for example, why Sir Donald Bradman was able to choose between two different playing methods at the moment the ball left the bowler's hand. By then Bradman's subconscious brain had made the decision whether to play back or forward. If his brain decided he needed to play backwards, he would begin moving his back foot backwards immediately he began his back-lift. If his brain wished to play off the front foot, it would delay any movement of his front foot until his weight had already transferred to his back foot, freeing his front foot to play forward. Since these calculations were made with greater automaticity than perhaps any other player has ever achieved, Bradman was able to play a very long innings before making an error through fatigue. This is why he found it difficult to understand why a batsman goes out once he is 'set'.

Once the batsman has calculated the path of the delivery, he must hit the ball with the perfectly executed and correctly chosen shot that will produce the greatest return from that particular delivery.

These skills are the same as those required by all players of fast-moving ball sports, like tennis and baseball. Each sport has slightly different requirements, but the general visual and movement skills required are essentially the same.

The final irony is that ultimately the batsman must hit the ball without knowing precisely where it is at the moment he hits it. Successful batting is, at the moment of impact, based upon blind assumption. Most of the top players are able to make this predictive leap with an accuracy of movement and timing that cannot be equalled by any human-made system.

Then they also have to deal with a bowler determined to upset this whole process by changing his action slightly to disguise exactly what he is doing. As an American baseball pitcher once said, 'Hitting is timing; pitching is upsetting timing.'

In essence, cricket becomes a battle between the visual motor skills of the batsman and the strength and skills of the bowler. And it is in the strength versus the limitations of either one from where some of the greatest cricketing contests in history have emerged. The reality is that, by chance, the fastest speed at which the world's fastest bowlers are able to deliver the ball over eighteen metres, and the fastest speed at which the brain is able to compute the trajectory of the delivery and then move into position to strike the ball, are closely matched. If fast bowlers were able to bowl a little faster and the batsman's brain took slightly longer to make its calculations, the contest would be unfair and batsmen would be unwilling to take on the world's best fast bowlers.

If I go back to the experiment we did in the 1980s with Peter Kirsten, where we established the superior ability of better batsmen to predict the ball's trajectory early in its flight, then we can better understand why a player such as Bill Ponsford, who batted with Bradman in the 1930s, said, 'Don sees the ball two yards earlier than the rest of us.' By turning off the lights as the ball was delivered from the bowling machine in the indoor net, we were able to show that Peter Kirsten was able to detect the path of the delivery with about 70 per cent accuracy, even though he could see only the first 100 milliseconds (0.1 seconds) of its trajectory before the lights went out. By contrast, lesser batsmen, specifically club-level bowlers, simply had no idea where the ball was and rapidly moved out of the way of the delivery they could not see.

Interestingly, Test-match fast bowlers must have some ability to bat – that is, to predict the trajectory of the delivery with reasonable accuracy – or else it would simply be too dangerous for them to play Test cricket. They may not always look like very accomplished batsmen, but this hides the reality that very few humans have the ability to bat against fast bowling. However unskilled a tail-end batsman may appear to be when facing fast bowling, be assured that just being able to avoid being hit by a fast delivery is a skill that exists in only a small, select group of humans. It is not something that one should consider attempting!

So we are able to conclude that the makings of great batsmen lie in their brain software and their ability to process the information they receive from the bowler during his run-up and delivery stride. But in the case of spin bowling, the bowler has the chance to exploit certain weaknesses in the human visual apparatus – particularly when the ball is above the batsman's eyeline – and cause him to misjudge the exact length of the delivery.

In 2005 my PhD student, Sharhidd Taliep, with UCT lecturer Lester John, measured the electrical activity of the brain in expert and novice batsmen while they watched video footage of inswing, outswing and slower deliveries. They found that the brains of expert batsmen needed about 10 per cent less time (405 versus 445 milliseconds) to detect outswinging deliveries and about 12 per cent less time (438 versus 495 milliseconds) to detect the inswinging deliveries that they watched on a video projection.

The expert batsmen also had much greater alpha-wave activity in the brain at the moment the ball left the bowler's hand, indicating that they were able to calm the brain at the instant they needed to collect the most information; that is, at the moment the bowler released the ball.

BRAIN RESEARCH HELPS TO WIN AN OLYMPIC GOLD MEDAL

Some time after we started the brain research to determine how athletes perform complex activities like hitting a fast-moving cricket ball, I was approached by Tim Harkness, a sports psychologist working in Durban. Tim had completed his master's degree by studying baboon behaviours in the wild. Like the great Eugène Marais, Tim had learnt to live with the baboons and had observed how they use complex body language to express dominance and submission and so avoid risky physical contact.

The two key methods used by baboons to indicate submission, thereby showing that they do not wish to have a physical confrontation, are to avoid eye contact and to relax the muscles that stabilise the core of the body – the abdominal and trunk muscles – the moment a dominant male baboon wishes to show supremacy. So Tim realised that to survive with the baboons, he had to learn to divert his eyes and to relax his core muscles whenever an aggressive male approached. That he survived is testament to his ability to understand the body language of baboons and to respond appropriately.

In time, it came to Tim that the control of this primitive behavioural signal might be subconscious, like the muscles of the face, which express our subconscious emotions and which cannot be consciously controlled. Imagine, thought Tim, if the control of the core muscles of the trunk and abdomen are under subconscious control and reflect the emotions that an athlete is experiencing at the moment he performs a complex action like kicking a rugby ball or striking a golf ball?

If, Tim reasoned, the golfer was experiencing submissive emotions at the time he addressed the ball, perhaps his core muscles would collapse at the moment of impact, just like when a subordinate baboon is suddenly approached by an aggressive and dominant male. This would surely produce an abnormal swing, resulting in either a hooked or sliced stroke. Similarly, a rugby player kicking at goal might suffer the same outcome if his emotional state were not controlled immediately prior to kicking.

So Tim developed the following hypothesis: The player's emotional state at the moment he begins a skilled movement may determine how the muscle-activation sequence for the core abdominal and trunk muscles occurs. If the activation of the core muscles occurs inappropriately because the golfer or goal-kicker is either in an aggressive or submissive emotional state at the time, then an inappropriate sequence of action may occur, producing a false shot.

To answer this question, he purchased the equipment necessary to evaluate his hypothesis – an electroencephalogram (EEG) to measure electrical activity in the brain, and an electromyogram (EMG) to measure electrical activity in the limb and abdominal muscles. Then he began his research.

The next I knew of the direction Tim's work had suddenly taken occurred one day in 2007, when he arrived at the Sports Science Institute in Newlands in the company of a man whom he introduced as Abhinav Bindra, India's most successful ten-metre shot specialist. Of all the scientists in the world, Abhinav had chosen Tim Harkness to help him prepare for the ten-metre shooting competition in the Olympic Games to be held in Beijing the following year.

Over the next twelve months, Tim and other members of our team, including Dr Laurie Rauch, studied Abhinav as he trained for his competition. By the time of the Olympics, Tim had spent more than 200 hours on experimentation as he studied Abhinav's brain and muscle function and the effect of different brain activities on his shooting accuracy. Remarkably, Tim discovered that Abhinav performed best when his brain showed the same quiescence as the brains of the best batsmen at the instant the bowler released a delivery. So Abhinav shot most accurately when his brain showed the least activity. It seems as if Abhinav does not shoot with his eyes, but with his body.

The results in the Olympics were unexpected. Ranked seventeenth in the world when the Olympics began, Abhinav secured a position in the final. Then, after sixty-nine of the seventy shots had been completed in the final, there were four shottists still in contention. It all came down to that final shot. There, the

200 hours of brain study paid off, as Abhinav's final shot was millimetres closer to the bull, securing the gold medal – as mentioned, the first by an Indian in an individual sport in the history of the Olympic Games. In the days after his success, Abhinav was unrestrained in his praise for the importance of Tim Harkness's contribution to his gold-medal success.

WATCH THE BALL?

Every child who has ever picked up a cricket bat has been told to watch the ball. The truth is that batsmen do not, in fact, watch the ball onto the bat.

Two English researchers, Michael Land and Peter McLeod, used sophisticated video technology that recorded the direction of the batsman's gaze, as well as his head movements, while facing a bowling machine. They found that the batsmen kept their heads and eyes still for the first 140 milliseconds after the ball was released. Then they shifted their gaze downwards by 7.5 degrees in a rapid non-tracking movement known as 'saccade', so that their eyes were looking at the spot on the pitch where they expected the ball to pitch.

The eyes then rotated upwards for 300 milliseconds while the head moved downwards through the same angle, the eyes remaining fixed on the pitch where the ball was expected to bounce. Once the ball had bounced, the head and eyes quickly moved down in order to track the latter part of its flight. This took place from about 350 to 550 milliseconds after the ball's release, after which the ball was no longer accurately tracked as it travelled further ahead of the batsmen's gaze. The eyes, therefore, did not follow the ball for the last 100 milliseconds of its flight.

So, for a delivery that took 650 milliseconds to reach him, the batsman had his eye on the ball for a total of 340 milliseconds – 140 milliseconds after release, and another 200 milliseconds after the ball had bounced – a total of 52 per cent of its flight.

We described this process in full in Bob's book, *Bob Woolmer's Art and Science of Cricket*. The lesson is obvious – the earlier a batsman can perform the saccade, the more swiftly and accurately he can respond to the delivery.

So should all young cricketers be taught *not* to watch the ball? Of course not. What this experiment reveals is that the saccade is an automatic reflex that involves no conscious attempt to track the moving ball. No amount of coaching will ever alter this, since it is a fixed biological response determined by our evolutionary history.

THE EYE OF THE BATSMAN

We are physically unable to follow an object that requires our eyes to alter their angle of observation at a rate of more than seventy degrees per second. If anything moves across our field of vision at a faster speed, our brain takes over and predicts a point at which an object will appear in the immediate future. It then performs a saccade that takes the eyes to focus on that point.

But all batsmen have a point of no return, a point beyond which they are simply unable to respond to any late deviations. The human nervous and muscular systems just cannot respond quickly enough.

This frontier of reaction time, beyond which the batsman is more or less paralysed by our species' lumbering reflexes, was first found to be around 170 milliseconds before the ball reaches the batsman's hitting zone. This was discovered by a series of experiments conducted by Peter McLeod in Oxford in 1987. Further study revealed this figure to be closer to 200 milliseconds. This explains why a fast bowler's delivery that pitches about 200 milliseconds before it reaches the batsman is considered such a valuable one. Since the spin bowler's delivery travels a shorter distance in 200 milliseconds, the area for a good length-delivery from which a spin bowler must pitch is closer to the batsman. This, too, we described in full in Bob's book.

Under no circumstances, therefore, is any batsman able to adjust his stroke in less than 200 milliseconds after the bounce of the ball. In other words, any delivery that makes an unpredictable movement less than 200 milliseconds from the batsman is physically unplayable. One of the interesting developments of the past ten to fifteen years is that pitches have become more predictable and therefore there is less probability of the ball deviating in the final 200 milliseconds after it has pitched. Also, there appears to be less effective swing bowling today than there was in the past, for reasons that are unclear. An absence of swing and movement off the pitch allows batsmen to play more aggressively (and speculatively) off the front foot than was possible twenty years ago.

So how does a top batsman counter any late movement when receiving perhaps a hundred or more such deliveries in the course of a long innings? He gets as close to the pitch of the ball as possible, so that even if it deviates after pitching, it will not have moved far enough to beat the edge of the bat. He also plays with 'soft hands' so that if the ball does deviate and take the edge of the bat, it will not have the momentum to reach the waiting grasp of the close-catching fielders.

The control of all of these events – the bowler's ability to pitch the ball in a particular spot while trying to deceive the batsman about his intent, the batsman's ability to execute a shot and the fielder's ability to catch the ball – occurs in the primitive parts of the brain, known as the subconscious.

We all have this ability, but the success of the best batsmen and the best fielders is due to the ability of their subconscious brain to process this vital information more accurately and more rapidly than most others. To do their job effectively, top batsmen must avoid the temptation to think about what they are doing. They must not allow the conscious brain to become involved in this process until after the shot has been played. Their success in this area results from their ability to control what will take them into 'the zone' – a state where the subconscious brain can best deal with the great visual and motor challenges posed by sport in general and cricket in particular – or keep them out of it.

As a scientist, I can only marvel at a game that seems to have been perfectly designed to test the limits to which humans can develop these ancient brain systems.

19 | The Physiology of Cricket

Cricket appears at first glance to be a relatively genteel sport in which physical fitness is less of a requirement than skill and technique. The reality is that today's fast bowlers need to be among the most athletic of humans.

In the early nineties, I foresaw that modern cricket would demand the evolution of the cricketer as an elite athlete for whom excellent physical condition is a prerequisite for success. When Bob and I started working together, we agreed that the modern cricketer would have to be as fit as world-class triathletes in order to play at his best for a sustained period and to avoid serious injury. The game has simply become too demanding to allow otherwise.

Consider this. In the 1998/99 cricket season, the South African team played eight five-day Tests, seventeen one-day internationals (ODIs), and were eligible to play in eight four-day and ten one-day provincial (county) matches. They could therefore be required to play for a total of ninety-nine days.

In 1970, the South African team played four five-day Tests, and were eligible to play four three-day and three one-day provincial matches in one season. This adds up to thirty-five days of cricket.

So, within three decades the demands on the elite South African cricketer increased by 280 per cent. Today, the addition of the Indian Premier League (IPL) has further increased the amount of cricket that has to be played by the leading exponents.

A look at the workload of fast bowlers reveals a similar increase. Pakistan's Imran Khan, in the period from 1970 to 1992 – a career spanning twenty-two years – bowled an average of 806 overs per year. Australia's Glenn McGrath, in a period from 1993 to 2007, spanning fourteen years, bowled an average of 1 108 overs annually.

Fortunately, cricket has finally realised – years after Bob pioneered the idea – that modern players require considerable expert input from biokineticists, nutritionists, physiotherapists and a host of others in the sports-science and sports-medicine disciplines.

Those who remain traditionalist in their approach and do not employ the sports sciences will undoubtedly see cricket in their countries fade into obscurity in an increasingly competitive and technologically advanced world.

Yet besides Australia and, to a lesser extent, England, and with the influence Gary Kirsten and Paddy Upton had in India, cricket has been notoriously unwilling to accept a more scientific approach.

In investigating cricket, I was not able to find many studies on the physiological demands of cricket, or the specific physiological, biochemical or anthropometric (body size and shape) attributes of exceptional cricketers.

I presume that this is a case of cricket devotees being more interested in the 'how' than the 'why' and perhaps being a little wary of science and scientists. I recall the iconic commentator and former Australian cricket captain Richie Benaud once saying that whenever he heard a scientist speak about cricket, he ran for cover – figuratively, of course. Clearly, Benaud does not have much time for science.

So how demanding is cricket and how fit do modern cricketers need to be?

In 1953, J.G. Fletcher embarked on the first such study when he collected data during the Ashes series in England that year. He wanted to calculate the average energy expenditure of the cricketers involved. He found that if all the activity during the five Tests of that series were divided equally among the twenty-two players, the mean daily physical activity for each player would have been as follows:

- The average player would bat for 38.5 minutes per day, scoring fourteen runs.
- He would bowl a total of 4.2 overs in fourteen minutes.
- He would field for 116 minutes, during which he would retrieve sixteen deliveries.
- The remaining 191.5 minutes each day would be spent resting in the pavilion.

For an average cricketer with a body surface area of $1.8m^2$, this would translate into an energy expenditure of approximately 650 kilojoules per hour. This is slightly more than that required simply to stand, and less than that required to walk at a leisurely pace of six kilometres per hour!

The reality is that Fletcher's calculations underestimate the true effort involved in playing cricket. However, they did a spectacular job of contributing to the perception that cricket is a physically undemanding sport.

It was forty-seven years before another such study was done, this time by Candice Christie and her colleagues at Rhodes University in Grahamstown, South Africa. Christie's findings revealed that the estimated physical activity in batting during one-day cricket in a player who batted for one hundred runs showed that he would run about 3.2 kilometres in about eight minutes, spread over his innings. The average running speed would be twenty-four kilometres per hour. Put into perspective, the world speed record for the half-marathon is 21.6 kilometres per hour.

More recently, confirming my theory that the Australian cricket research now leads the world by some way, the University of Western Australia published a series of studies in which they used the Global Positioning System (GPS) and other sophisticated techniques to track the movement patterns and, hence, physical demands on cricketers in different playing positions in the different formats of the game.

In the first study, Petersen and colleagues tracked the movements of a single Australian Test-match fast bowler during twelve ODI matches. The study found that the bowler completed an average of eight overs in each of those games during which he covered an average of sixteen kilometres, of which eleven were spent walking, two running, two striding and one sprinting. On average the bowler was involved in a fast repetition – running, striding, sprinting – every sixty-eight seconds for an average duration of three seconds. He completed sixty-six sprints per game, covering an average distance of eighteen metres and reaching sprinting speeds of thirty kilometres per hour. The authors noted that a fast bowler's workload was about twice that of a cover-point fielder in first-class cricket or of a batsman scoring a century in an ODI.

In the next study, Petersen and Pyne compared the physical demands of five different playing positions in Twenty20 players. Batsmen covered 2.5 kilometres in about thirty minutes, sprinting twelve times for a mean distance of fourteen metres and a total sprinting distance of 160 metres. In contrast, fast bowlers covered an average of nine kilometres, sprinting forty-two times each with an average distance of seventeen metres for a total sprinting distance of about 700 metres. Fielders covered an average distance of five to nine kilometres during the eighty-minute innings, sprinting for between 100 and 700 metres. Even wicketkeepers were surprisingly active, covering six kilometres, but they sprinted only for a total of about sixty metres.

When the demands of T20, one-day and multi-day matches were compared by these researchers, it was confirmed that fast bowlers worked the hardest of all players, especially in multi-day games, during which they covered an average of twenty-three kilometres per day, of which they sprinted for 1.4 kilometres. Wicketkeepers covered a daily distance of about seventeen kilometres, but rarely sprinted. The intensity of one-day and T20 cricket was much greater, requiring about 50 to 100 per cent more sprinting per hour, but the much longer duration of multi-day games meant that players sprinted 16 to 130 per cent more times in those games. The authors concluded that the shorter formats of the game are more intensive per unit time, but that multi-day games cause a greater overall physical load. Not unsurprisingly, Petersen and Pyne found that multi-day Test matches involved more high-intensity running than county (state or provincial) games.

Finally, the authors found that the typical conditioning drills used by Australian cricketers matched or exceeded the demands of actually playing cricket matches, whereas most skill and stimulation training drills did not, as they were of too low an intensity. They concluded that the physical demands of skill and stimulation training drills need to be modified so that they match more closely the actual physical demands of match play.

These findings show that cricket is now a far more demanding activity than it was in earlier times. Clearly, the physical demands on a cricketer need to be taken very seriously. My advice for a suitable exercise programme for cricketers is one that is based on the following eight principles:

1. Progressive overload

The human body adapts to the level of physical stress to which it is exposed, but it needs time for this adaptation to occur. If the stress is excessive, the body fails to adapt and breaks down.

The stresses of training must therefore be increased gradually, beginning with fairly gentle training and reaching a maximum only when the cricketer's body is physically mature, in his middle to late twenties.

2. Specificity

The more closely the stresses imposed during training mimic those that will be encountered in competition, the better prepared the cricketer will be for that competition.

Traditional methods of cricket training ignore this law. For example, most cricket training consists of nets practice, which is far removed from everything a real cricket match is all about.

Consider the following. Few net pitches have the same characteristics as a match pitch. Also, the balls used are often in a worse state than they would be in a match, so this rules out the possibility of variable movement off the pitch caused by new balls.

Fast bowlers seldom bowl at their top pace in a nets session, and even medium pacers tend to bowl off a shortened run-up and without the usual swing experienced in a match.

Few coaches insist on their bowlers obeying no-ball rules in net sessions.

Net sessions have no fielders. During a net session, batsmen face too many different bowlers in too short a space of time, whereas in a match a batsman will face one particular bowler for up to six consecutive deliveries.

In a nets session, batsmen don't practise running between the wickets.

Lastly, batsmen seldom bat for longer than twenty minutes in the nets, but are expected to bat for many hours in matches. This is like training a marathon runner by only having him sprint and never having him run more than a few kilometres in training.

These constraints rob the cricketer of optimum physical preparation.

Indeed, the key problem in cricket preparation is that in order to improve, the batsmen need to hit more deliveries than the bowlers need to bowl for their training. The result is usually a compromise in which the batsmen bat too little and the bowlers bowl too much.

3. Quantity first, quality later

This is also known as base training versus peaking training.

While low-intensity base training can be continued throughout a cricketer's athletic life, peaking training can only be maintained for relatively short periods – six to ten weeks, depending on the individual. One of the key components of proper training is to discover for exactly how long an individual athlete is able to train at a very high level before requiring a break from such heavy training.

4. Training regularity

Daily training, with maybe one day of rest a week, is the minimum amount required to achieve optimum fitness levels at national and international level.

However, cricketers must focus on skills training as well, leaving less time for specific fitness training.

The fitness coaches of some of the leading international teams advise their players to follow a fitness programme specifically tailored for their individual cricketing needs, for two-and-a-half hours a day, six days a week, all year round.

My opinion is that this kind of programme is likely to lead to burnout and injury. I suggest that, at elite level, players should train this hard for three to five months before and during the season, followed by eight weeks of rest, and then three months of gentler base training leading up to competition again.

I also believe that the competitive sporting season should not last longer than seven months. This approach will maximise the cricketer's playing career.

5. Variety

Practices should be stimulating, otherwise there is the risk that players will become bored and training therefore less effective.

6. Individualism

The greatest mistake a coach can make is to assume that one training method is optimal for all.

Every cricketer is unique. Some adapt very quickly to physical training, while others take much longer. The same applies to the mastering of certain skills. The key to coaching is to identify the best training programme for each player and to avoid a 'one-size-fits-all' approach.

7. Stretching and strengthening programmes

One negative consequence of increased international competition is that there are too many players with too many injuries, caused simply by playing too much.

The incidence of injury can be reduced by using proper warming-up and warming-down procedures. This can be as simple as a fifteen-minute jog and essential stretching.

All players also require strengthening programmes to prevent injury, especially in one-sided activities like bowling and batting.

8. Evaluation

Measuring and evaluating progress is essential to ensure that players remain motivated. All players should be encouraged to keep logbooks, as this enables them to monitor their own progress and to set milestones: without goals and measurement, it is impossible to move forward.

20 | The Introduction of Science into South African Cricket

My introduction to international cricket came about in October 1995, when Bob Woolmer, the coach of the Proteas, came to my office at SSISA to invite me to join the team in Pakistan for the 1996 Cricket World Cup, which was also being played in India and Sri Lanka. He was accompanied by his support staff, physiotherapist Craig Smith and fitness trainer Paddy Upton.

At the time, like the majority of (white) South Africans, I was captivated by the success of our national team, the Proteas, on their return to international cricket. In 1992, I had been absorbed by their near success at the Cricket World Cup in Australia and New Zealand, by the batting of Peter Kirsten, the bowling of the handsomely enigmatic Richard Snell, and, of course, Jonty Rhodes's fielding and his sensational run-out of Inzamam-ul-Haq. Then there was the dramatic rain-ruined semi-final against England.

These events had transported me back to my childhood love of cricket.

As a schoolboy I had followed the remarkable South African team of the 1960s, first under Ali Bacher and then UCT alumnus Peter van der Merwe. These teams were, in my opinion, better than any I have since watched – the array of skills the players possessed was, to me, unbelievable. The joy of watching Barry Richards, Graeme Pollock, Lee Irvine, Eddie Barlow, Colin Bland and Mike Procter batting for the same team, Bland fielding, and Peter Pollock and Procter bowling, was a feast matched by few other teams in the history of the game. That they were South African (with the exception of Bland) was all I needed to know, as a teenager, that I lived in one of the great sporting nations of the world.

Bob's request was even more compelling because of his accompaniment by Paddy Upton and Craig Smith – both of whom were former students of mine. Based on what they said, I decided to start working with the team. We all wanted to apply the scientific method to take the Proteas to the next level of performance. In essence, that meant becoming a better team than the Australians.

After comprehensively beating the touring English team during the 1995/96 summer, the team was off to Rawalpindi in Pakistan, our base for the next six weeks. The Proteas played brilliant cricket for five games and were the favourites to win the tournament. But in the sixth game, the quarter-final against the West Indies, the wheels came off and a winning position was inexplicably lost. A single spell of bowling by the part-time West Indian spinner, Jimmy Adams, stopped the team's momentum and took away our dream of winning the World Cup for South Africa. I couldn't understand what had happened. In the end, I assumed that the stress of being away from home for six weeks and the incessant travelling, including a long and exhausting journey to Calcutta and back for the opening ceremony, had left its indelible but undetected mark.

When we returned to South Africa, I tried to explain how demanding it is to live on the Asian subcontinent for any length of time and how this can lead to poor performance. I wrote an article along those lines, and it was published in *Sports Illustrated* some time after we returned to South Africa.

I suspect that the article was not well received in South African cricketing circles, and it is probable that it sparked what happened over the next two years. After it was published, I gained the distinct impression that the management of South African cricket did not welcome the presence in its ranks of someone not in their employ who wielded a laptop and who had access to the media. That may explain why my request to write a book about the South African team's experiences at the World Cup was vigorously vetoed.

To keep my mind active during the long down-time on a cricket tour, I had aimed to interview all the players and to write a log of what happened during the six weeks of the tour. Within a few days I was told that this was not going to happen. Of course, today, players have their own blogs and tweets and can, it seems, write whatever they like. But fifteen years ago there was tight control of what could and could not be written.

Naturally, I was stunned by this decision. Would I have written something to embarrass the players and South African cricket? Of course not. I could not understand why anyone would be suspicious of my motives.

In a book he wrote in 2001, the team manager, Peter Pollock, who was utterly supportive of Bob and to whom Bob was totally committed, incorrectly wrote that, while on the bus travelling to the ground, I had told him that I thought the team was in good shape for that quarter-final match against the West Indies. He continued: 'Imagine thus my surprise when months later I was to read an article by Tim suggesting that South Africa's loss to the West Indies should have been anticipated because of some syndrome or other that had to do with being away from home for an extended period!' Elsewhere in the book Pollock also wrote that, in his opinion, professional cricketers must be able to play for this length of time away from home.

I like Peter because he is direct and lacks pretence. But he showed no interest in advancing a scientific understanding of cricket, and as a result our relationship could not progress. His son Shaun, however, does understand. He has many appealing qualities that transcend his abilities as one of the world's great cricketers of all time. He is one of the best cricket commentators on the current circuit, specifically because he speaks like a scientist. He develops hypotheses of how the pitch is likely to play and how this will affect the batsmen and the bowlers. Then he analyses the data as the game progresses and modifies his hypothesis on the basis of what he has observed. That is why he was such a successful bowler – he based his entire success on hypotheses of how to dismiss certain batsmen under specific conditions. Then he conducted the experiment by bowling a sequence of different deliveries to each batsman to see whether his hypothesis had merit. If not, he would replace the hypothesis with a modified theory and he would keep doing this until he was successful. That is exactly how a scientist is expected to work.

After I had read Peter's book I wrote to him and followed it up with a phone call. I challenged his memory and said that I did not remember passing an opinion on the team's psychological health on the bus trip to the quarter-final in Karachi. He was clearly upset that he had hurt my feelings and was genuinely apologetic, saying something to the effect that he had written this in good faith and had meant no harm, and that only a few thousand people would ever read his book.

In fact, significant damage would have been done, not so much by the book, which was published after Bob and I had exited the scene, but by the attitude it revealed. For what Peter wrote must reflect his belief that scientists like me are unreliable witnesses, since we are forever changing our minds to suit the moment. The implication seemed to be that we don't really know what we are talking about and so we should not be taken seriously.

This was exactly the sort of opinion that those who feared the influence of scientific analysis of South African cricket and who wanted me and, more import-antly, Bob out, were only too keen to hear. The ramifications also went beyond cricket, since there is a cartel of well-paid, high-level sports administrators in South Africa who do not wish to have scientists around asking difficult questions that they are unwilling or unable to answer. Better to undermine the scientists' reputations so that they can be conveniently sidelined.

Of course, the point is that if I had thought that the team was in great shape before the quarter-final and they had subsequently performed poorly, then my job was to try to understand why – not to ignore it. My conclusion at the time was that there had to be an obvious explanation for the team's poor performance. Being away from home for six weeks and suffering from 'hotel syndrome' – so named by Springbok rugby coach Ian McIntosh – seemed to me to be the most probable explanation. That I was clearly suffering from that syndrome at the time no doubt influenced my interpretation.

Anybody who has played this game at an elite level will tell you just how difficult it is to keep focused and stay motivated for such an extended period away from home.

The Australian coach Bob Simpson said it took the Australians thirty years to learn how to play in India and Pakistan because conditions are just so different. The lifestyle is also different for middle-class South Africans. We live in privi-leged circumstances, and sometimes it takes a trip to India and Pakistan for us to appreciate this.

Peter Pollock included the following in his autobiography: 'Visiting India is a massive challenge and all the positive talk in the world can't hide the awesome task that revolves in the main around unfamiliar playing and living conditions. It's a whole new ball game. A few one-dayers is one thing, a fully-fledged three-Test series, plus a whole lot of limited overs games, is another!' Indeed, the Proteas team that played in the 2011 Cricket World Cup, again on the Asian subcontinent, took specific precautions to limit the amount of time they were away from home. Apparently South African cricket had finally learnt that its players are not automatons who can be sent away from home for any length of time with the expectation that they will continue to perform at their highest level regardless of the circumstances.

Despite the setback of the 1996 Cricket World Cup and the challenges we faced from the science sceptics, Bob and I were still determined to make science count in South African cricket. So I gave an inordinate amount of time to cricket. I watched five-day Test matches at Newlands, which is not in my character, as I am simply not a person who can sit and watch cricket for such an extended period, but I thought that what I was doing would ultimately be in the interests of South African cricket.

At one Test match I was interviewed on television, at the request of the then managing director of the United Cricket Board of South Africa, Ali Bacher. I explained all the plans that Bob and I envisioned – how we were going to track the cricket ball to work out the best bowling plans to opposition batsmen; how we were going to study the biomechanics of batting and bowling in order to better prepare our players; how we were going to film Shane Warne's deliveries so that we could use virtual reality to help our batsmen detect his different deliveries, and especially his famed 'flipper', among many other exciting ideas.

Indeed, during one series in Pakistan, Bob arranged television footage of ultra-slow-motion pictures of Saqlain Mohammed bowling his standard off-break and his difficult-to-detect topspinner. The video footage clearly showed how the two deliveries could be distinguished – specifically, if the batsman could see Saqlain's thumb at the instant of delivery, it was the off-break; if the thumb was hidden, it was the topspinner. As a result of this simple discovery, after the first innings of the first Test in which he mesmerised the Proteas batsmen, the threat of Saqlain was removed from the series.

I was appointed the first chairman of the UCB medical committee, and we were fastidious about what we did. Everything was designed to give our players the best possible medical and scientific support to make them the best in the world. There was no other consideration.

Bob and I even put in a proposal for the setting up of a biomechanics laboratory to study the factors that determine superior cricketing ability. At the same time, members of our research team formulated and tested in our laboratories at UCT the concept that would become the HawkEye ball-tracking system. The story describing our idea was carried in the London *Sunday Times*, and *Carte Blanche* featured our footage that showed how the system could be used to determine whether or not a batsman was out LBW.

But to advance these ideas, we needed the wholehearted support of South African cricket. Instead, both ideas were dismissed rather contemptuously by the UCB, who began to wonder whether Noakes was attempting to use South African cricket for his own interests. As a result, the HawkEye system was developed by an English cricketer who had connections with South Africa and who had read about my idea. As he had copied the idea, he was never able to patent it; nor was I, since in my naivety I had spoken about it in public before submitting a patent proposal.

The irony is that even without the UCB's support – in fact, in the face of their anti-science position – we did eventually raise the one million rand we required to equip a state-of-the-art biomechanics laboratory. For a time, before they restructured, we were certified as an International Cricket Council (ICC) Centre for the testing of suspect bowling actions. As a result, we worked with a number of international and South African bowlers, notably Johan Botha. We soon discovered an entirely novel explanation of why Botha and, incidentally, Muttiah Muralitharan, appear to be such obvious 'chuckers' and published our findings first in a scientific publication and then in Bob's book. The suspect action occurs because both Johan and Muttiah have an abnormal alignment of their bowling arms, with a prominent bend below the elbow, called elbow valgus.

We then showed that if their bowling actions are viewed in two dimensions, for example on a television screen, it appears as if both are pronounced chuckers of the ball. However, if their bowling actions are studied in three dimensions, as we do in the laboratory, neither throws the delivery, since neither extends his elbow more than fifteen degrees immediately prior to ball release – the current definition of an illegal delivery.

We also established that it is impossible for an umpire standing either behind the stumps or at square leg to detect a thrown delivery. The rather complex reasons are described fully in Bob's book and in our scientific publication.

This was an absolutely novel discovery that has widespread implications. It means that it is impossible to detect an illegal delivery either on the field during a match or when viewing that delivery in two dimensions from television footage. The sole way in which a thrown delivery can be detected is by the use of three-dimensional motion analysis in a sophisticated biomechanics laboratory. In turn, this means that a bowler should never be labelled a 'chucker' until he has been fully investigated using this equipment.

We therefore proposed that bowlers with suspect actions be treated with care; that it must not be disclosed to the media that they are under investigation until they have undergone biomechanical investigation, after which the result can be disclosed. For our work shows that the labelling of a specific bowler as a 'chucker' solely on the basis of an umpire's call or on analysis of television footage is wrong, as it is scientifically indefensible. Hopefully the international cricket authorities will acknowledge this new insight and adopt it for the future management of bowlers with suspect actions.

In working with Johan Botha, our team, led by Dr Kerith Aginsky, was able to rehabilitate Botha's career to the point where he was appointed captain of the Proteas' one-day team in 2010.

The proof of our success in introducing science into South African cricket between 1995 and 1997 was that the team was indeed fitter and healthier than ever before, our players had fewer injuries, and they became for a short time the best in the world.

The first indication of trouble occurred when I was with my wife in Monaco as a member of the panel responsible for selecting the winner of the International Olympic Committee (IOC) Prize in Sports Science. I was awakened in the middle of the night in my hotel room by the sound of a fax sliding under my door. A fax in the middle of the night seldom brings good news.

It was from Bob, and it began very simply: 'We have a problem.' He then explained the nature of the problem. It was the beginning of the end of my involvement with South African cricket and also of the use of science to enhance our ability to dominate world cricket. Within a year I was out; by January 1999, Bob's contract was under review and he was left in no doubt that his time with South African cricket was up.

I believe that I understand why Bob and I were jettisoned by South African cricket after October 1997. In writing this book I had the opportunity to explain what I think were the reasons for this and what led up to it. I consulted widely, and the advice I received was always the same – leave it alone; the less you write, the better.

I was also influenced by the recent publication of Herschelle Gibbs's autobiography. When the book hit the media, the early press reports focused on the scandals that make up a small portion of the book and, indeed, are a small part of the larger personality revealed in it. I was not prepared to have my book, and therefore some key events in my life, presented in the media as if it were only a bitter explanation of why I think South African cricket chose to ditch Bob and me, and the nature of the events and the personalities that were behind our expulsion. Either I explained everything or I explained nothing. Bob's untimely and tragic death further convinced me that nothing was to be gained by writing about our expulsion and the reasons and people behind it. Potentially, there was too much to lose.

Now I am past being angry about what happened. I am simply saddened by the fact that a great cricketing mind like Bob Woolmer was never fully appreciated in this country, and perhaps even globally. When Bob most needed the support of people of real substance, none was to be found.

So Bob died young and left much undone. But he paid me a wonderful compliment when he was quoted as saying, 'I was especially fortunate to be able to enlist the help of Professor Tim Noakes in helping the South African team into a new era in the mid-1990s. To me it was no surprise that Australia's rise to

FIGURE 23

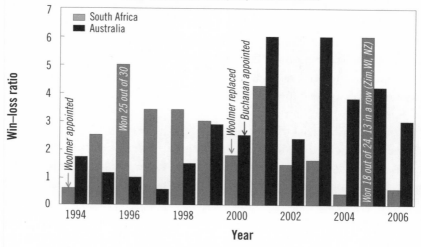

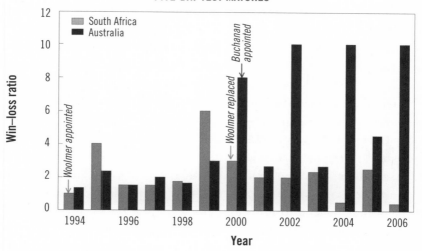

The win–loss record of the Proteas cricket team in one- (top) and five-day (bottom) Test matches during and after they were coached by Bob Woolmer. From 1995 to 1999, the performance of the Proteas was superior to that of the Australians in ODI cricket matches. In five-day Test matches, the Proteas equalled or outperformed the Australians in 1995, 1996, 1998 and 1999. Australian dominance returned immediately after Bob Woolmer was removed from South African cricket and John Buchanan was appointed as the Australian coach.

dominance in all sports coincided with their public embrace of scientific methods, while South Africa's decline over the last five years – especially in one-day cricket – started after that country's administrators decided to abandon Noakes as an advisor and assistant.'

So I complete this chapter with the tribute I paid to Bob at the memorial service held at Wynberg Boys' High School on Wednesday 4 April 2007, to celebrate the life and achievements of this special man whom I was privileged to know and to call a very special friend and mentor.

A tribute to a special friend

The problem with the tears is that they give no warning when they are about to reappear. Nor, in this part of the world, are tears considered particularly manly. But as I prepared this talk the tears soaked the pages of my notebook, reducing my words to an inky smudge. I cannot predict when the tears will return. So I ask for your understanding and indulgence.

For, by proxy, these are the tears of us all. They are the tears of all those individuals across the globe who treasured the time they shared with this remarkable man. Of his family, his sons Dale and Russell, and especially of his rock and soul mate, Gill, who understood him best and who allowed him the unshackled freedom to pursue his special destiny, a fate set by his father, Clarence, opening bat for the Uttar Pradesh Cricket Club in India, and who had placed a cricket bat and ball in the cot of his first son, Robert Andrew, with the words: 'Son, I hope this will be your life.'

Gill granted her husband the licence to pursue his father's calling; to develop his potential and to perfect that which he did best. Her selflessness is her eternal gift to her husband and so to us all. The loss to the Woolmer family dwarfs that which collectively we all feel. Yet they have, and will, shoulder their loss with a quiet dignity and resilience of which their husband and father will be so deeply, deeply proud.

The tears are also of the nation he adopted as his home and for which his passion ran deep; a country he described in his 1984 autobiography as 'God's Own Country'; a country which has now lost the coach and the captain of the team that restored the pride to its cricket in the 1990s and beyond. That he was the creative source of that renaissance is not disputed – perhaps, in retrospect, that was his greatest cricketing achievement.

They are also the tears of the global community of cricketers and

all who love the game. For they must now confront the possibility that
the sport they have treasured in their childlike innocence may have lost
its moral compass – a special morality that cricket has always claimed
as its own. And they worry lest theirs are the tears of an innocence lost;
a morality dishonoured.

Bob's favorite maxim for those confronting a cricketing failure was:
'Gentlemen, always remember that it is only a game. No one has died.'

So we fear for what may yet emerge. And we pray that perhaps our
fears are groundless and that there is, after all, a simple explanation.
For Bob's life was about that which is most pure; it offered no refuge
for that which is base.

Besides his transparency, the essence of Bob was his modesty,
a natural humility which informed everything he did. Perhaps he subscribed to the American coaching axiom, which holds that a truly great
coach must be clever enough to be successful. But stupid enough to
think that it matters! In fact, his life proved that coaches of his standard
really do matter. That they truly do make a difference that extends
far beyond the apparent modesty of their daily chores. His life was a
celebration of achievements for which there was no need for reticence.

His personal modesty explains why he could be so self-contained
– how he could live for prolonged periods away from the tranquillity
of his home and his family, in the company of his team, set about by
the relentless tensions of international cricket. For his needs were
simple – for his happiness he required just four ingredients: his
wife, Gill, who was the key without whom his work could not have
happened, and his boys, Dale and Russell. His family was the steadfast
foundation on which he built his life. In his home he had his special
space – among his library of cricket books and his cricket videos –
where he could read and write. And watch. And plan.

Next he required a team of cricketers willing to be coached.
It mattered not how good they were. For he had begun his coaching
career in 1968 as a twenty-year-old, coaching those who had the least
– and therefore the most – to gain from his embryonic wisdom: in
Johannesburg there were the young men of four Afrikaans primary
schools and in Tunbridge Wells, England, the Holmewood House
Preparatory School. To these young men he devoted three hours of
coaching a day, five days a week during their summer terms. Later,
in Cape Town, he helped to grow the promise of the Avendale Cricket

Club, graciously represented today by Reverend Jerome Francis and Bert Erickson; and in the Langa community he coached both cricket and the other sport he had learnt in India, field hockey. His players from Langa remember him as 'stern, punctual and disciplined – but lots of fun'.

So it mattered only that those he coached should share his passion for improvement; his total commitment in the quest for an unattainable perfection.

Next he needed his technologies – his computer, which became his special trademark and which acquired its own affectionate name in the world's media: Bob's laptop. Into his laptop he entered the details of every match his teams played. With it he shared his secrets as he wrote his daily diary. It was also the portal through which he communicated with this worldwide group of friends. His laptop was his second brain, for it also stored the videos of his players and the scoring patterns and the bowling channels of his players and their opponents.

And, finally, he needed his circle of friends on the five continents on which he played his life.

Besides friendship, knowledge and wisdom, he sought little else, because he considered it superfluous and unnecessary. He had no appetite whatsoever for money or for the material trappings of life; that money he had, he spent on his passions – his family; his team; his friends and on anything that would help him to become a better coach. His dream was to win the South African Lotto and so build a cricket academy more glorious in its design than any yet conceived. It was a dream that never faded.

His humility was so genuine that he would have been overwhelmed by the global outpouring of sentiment at his death. He would have struggled to understand it – after all, cricket is only a game, even if someone has died. Only after his death has the true extent of his global influence become obvious. But we should have known it.

Ten weeks ago, as Pakistan was playing South Africa in Cape Town, I was checking into a hotel in a Canadian city in Western Ontario. The receptionist, seeing my passport, said: 'Ah, Mr Noakes – you are South African. Do you follow cricket?' Noting his name badge, I responded: 'Yes, Mr Malik. I follow Pakistan cricket quite closely. I know of your skilled bowlers and your stylish batsmen. In fact, I even know your present coach, Mr Bob Woolmer, quite well.' At this, Mr

Malik let out a gasp. He could not believe that in his life he would ever meet someone who actually knew Mr Woolmer. In the global cricketing community, there are many millions like Mr Malik.

For Bob had coached cricketers on four continents and had played against the world's best on the fifth. In North America he had helped to prepare the Canadian team for the 2003 Cricket World Cup. In Europe, he played for Kent and England, and had coached most notably Warwickshire to a success that remains unmatched in the history of English County Cricket. In Europe he also assisted with the coaching of Holland and Ireland. In Africa he coached Namibia, Kenya and, of course, South Africa, and, in Asia, Pakistan. He was truly a citizen of the world, perhaps because he had been born an Englishman in India, where he had lived for the first decade of his life. The hospital ward in Kanpur where he was born on 14 May 1948 is now known as the Bob Woolmer Maternity Ward.

On the fifth continent, Australasia, he represented his county in the Centenary Test in Melbourne in 1976 and played in what became known as the Packer World Series. And it was the Australians who brought out the best in him; yet they proved also to be his nemesis. In ten Test matches against Australia between 1975 and 1981, he scored three centuries, including a match-saving innings of 149 in eight hours and nineteen minutes at the Oval in 1975. It was only his second Test match. He scored slowly because he had been ordered to block every delivery by the normally pugnacious English captain, Tony Greig, formerly of Queenstown in the Border region, South Africa. Clearly, Bob was good at following instructions.

His Australian nemesis came in the shape of two of their greatest cricketers. Steve Waugh's batting at Headingly and Shane Warne's bowling at Edgbaston during the 1999 Cricket World Cup denied Bob one of the ultimate coaching achievements – a victory in the Cricket World Cup.

So Bob's influence circled the globe; from Vancouver and Jamaica in the West to Sydney and Christchurch in the East. Indeed, he was one of a handful of South Africans – for that is how I choose to remember him – who is recognised as a global leader. To followers of cricket, his name carries the same recognition as do Bobby Locke, Gary Player and Ernie Els to different generations of golfing enthusiasts.

Another consequence of Bob's humility and his natural modesty was that he did not fall for false flattery; nor did he hanker for celebrity status. Nor was he impressed by rank or position – he treated all he met equally. So, although he had shaken the hand of the Queen of England and had dined with presidents, he treated all he met presidentially. He was impressed only by the extent to which they committed themselves to an individual perfection.

I suspect that he would not wish me to draw attention to any special people present at his memorial; he would have said that all are equally important and must be acknowledged in the same way. But it would not be correct in my view if I failed to recognise one or two special people who have made an extra effort to be here today.

Mr Nasim Ashraf, president of the Pakistan Cricket Board, has travelled from Lahore to represent his nation's president and the cricketers and people of Pakistan. Two weeks ago his president, Pervez Musharraf, conferred on Bob the Star of Excellence, one of the highest civilian honours awarded to a citizen of Pakistan. The award recognises Bob's work of 'great distinction and commitment' for Pakistan cricket. Bob was fascinated by the Pakistan nation, its people, their religion and its cricketers, who have been especially hard hit by this tragedy. His belief was that the depth of talent in Pakistan cricket is unmatched.

It is easy to project Bob as he was – a modest and humble man who was not scared to express his opinion and who was universally admired for his warmth, his sincerity and his integrity. But the nature of his death, seemingly in circumstances that were the antithesis of these personal qualities, and the press reports that it has spawned, requires a response from those who knew him best.

It has, for example, been suggested, even on the front page of the *New York Times*, that Bob was about to expose a Machiavellian world of cricket match fixing. But his written and spoken record leaves nothing to support this theory. His major work – his book on cricket coaching, soon to be released – does not include the words 'match fixing'. I know this because I had helped him with that book for the past eight years and I have read the proofs. The sole exposé in that book is Bob's unique approach to cricket coaching. Nor, in the past five years, did he ever mention match fixing to me or to his family, except in relation to the case against one Kenyan player. His laptop diary also contains no such reference. Thus this theory is without substance.

Second, Bob was a cricket coach, not a policeman. He also understood the nature of proof, since that is what he had engaged me, a scientist, to teach him about. And to what absolute proof could he alone have been privy? The sole comfort in this speculation has been the universal assertion that Bob was himself totally and utterly incorruptible. Of him, former English cricket captain David Gower has written: 'There is nobody I can think of who better represented the high principles of sportsmanship and behaviour that have been traditionally associated with cricket.' Hopefully these will be the last words on this topic.

If a person is true, the future trajectory of his or her life can be predicted at any time in the past. In remembering Bob, I went back to the foreword I had written for his 2000 autobiography. I wrote then: 'One definition of a genius is someone who creates novel employment by doing precisely what he or she wishes. By that definition, Bob Woolmer does not qualify in this category. His profession, cricket coaching, has a long and venerable tradition not just in England, the land of his sport, but in many other cricket-playing nations around the globe. Bob is just one of many who has plied this historic trade. But if a genius is someone who redefines his trade, then he has a strong claim to that label.'

My argument, seemingly supported by a recent article in *Wisden*, the cricketer's bible, is that Bob redefined the role of the coach in international cricket. He was perhaps the first to elevate the role of the coach to more than that of an underling to the captain at international level. He could do this because he understood cricket as well as anyone else alive. And this wisdom he had taught himself. He began by coaching schoolchildren, cautiously advancing to the next level as his expertise grew. He told me that if you cannot teach a concept to your wife or to a six-year-old, you cannot expect an international cricketer to understand. He tested all his explanations first on Gill; only when she had helped him to refine his story could it be tried out on his players.

He was not a 'how to' coach. Always he asked the question: Why? Why does doing it this way produce a better result than doing it some other way? He sought to produce thinking cricketers who understood that there were options. But he would explain why he thought that all the options were not equal. The player was then left to make his choice.

He understood, too, that cricket is too complex a game for one man to have a complete command of all its components. So he searched for those who had the expertise that he lacked but which he knew his players required. To do this, he could not have the common human failing of insecurity. The weakness of wondering: But what if they do it better? Or worse. What if they should draw the credit from me? His vision did not allow for such pettiness.

As a result, he was the first to introduce into international cricket the concept of a team of coaching experts and support staff, each with a specific area of responsibility.

His vulnerability occurred because he was so far ahead of the game and his peers, particularly in his understanding of the potential that science and technology could bring to cricket. So he was not really understood by those who employed him and who set the financial boundaries within which his vision had to be expressed. It was his Warwickshire captain, Dermot Reeve, who of all his captains best understood Bob, since together they shared the same zeal for change, innovation and calculated risk-taking. And so it was for a few brief summers at Warwickshire that Bob was able to express the full potential of his genius. And the results showed why he was so special. I know that he would like me to express a special thanks to Dermot and to Dennis Amiss, chairman of Warwickshire during that time and who is with us today, for the special support he received during that distinctive period of his coaching career.

Bob began the final chapter of his 1984 autobiography with the sentence: 'Cricket has always resisted change. If the game is to survive we must ensure that it moves with the times.' Of Bob the cricketer, his greatest mentor, Sir Colin Cowdrey, wrote: 'Bob Woolmer's strength was his determination to keep looking for ways in which he could adapt and improve his game both as a bowler and batsman. He understands more than most players I have played with that you cannot afford to stand still: the game soon overtakes you if you are not alert to change.'

It was through Bob's constant search for change and improvement that he changed lives. By his inspiration he dragged the rest of us along in his wake. He was one of the four most influential men in my life, and that is why I find this parting so hard. One of his most important memorials is those whose lives he changed and who remain to continue expressing his influence.

So his memorial is in the person of Allan Donald, whom Bob helped to become what some believe is the perfect international fast bowler. Allan's contribution to the success of the Proteas team in the mid-1990s is not always recognised. He was always the 'go to' man when the game was getting away from his team.

His memorial is in the person of Jacques Kallis, who learnt his cricket on the very grounds of this school and who was brought to maturity by Bob and Jacques' headmaster, Keith Richardson.

His memorial is in the person of Jonty Rhodes, whom Bob taught how to perform the cover drive without compromising his trademark pull shot. And so Jonty was good enough to play international cricket and become the iconic inspiration as a peerless fielder. I have said that Bob treated everyone equally, but I suspect just a little that he allowed himself just one indulgence. And that was Jonty. I think he cared for Jonty just a fraction more than he would ever have cared to admit.

His memorial is in the person of Shaun Pollock, surely one of the most complete, dedicated and professional cricketers yet produced by South Africa.

His memorial is also in the person of Gary Kirsten, whom Bob, together with Duncan Fletcher, helped to become the most capped South African cricketer of all time, who is the gentleman cricketer and who seems destined to accept the coaching mantle that has fallen vacant with Bob's death.

And his memorial was in the captaincy skills of the late South African captain who, with Bob's tutelage, became the best captain he could be.

It is not possible to understand cricket and cricketers without reading what is for me the greatest sporting book in the English language – *Beyond a Boundary* by C.L.R. James. That James was born near the Port of Spain in Trinidad is especially appropriate at the time of the World Cup in the West Indies.

James posed the compelling question: What do they know of cricket who only cricket know? His point was that cricket is just the point of entry to a larger reality, the reality that Bob made his life work.

James also wrote that 'Cricket is a game of high and difficult technique. If it were not, it could not carry the load of social response and implication which it carries.'

And what is that 'load of social response' and implication? James describes what he learnt through cricket: 'On the cricket field we [the schoolchildren with whom he played school cricket] did what ought to be done. The best and most-respected boys were precisely the ones who always kept them. Before long I acquired a discipline for which the only name is puritan. I never cheated, I never appealed for a decision unless I thought the batsman was out. I never argued with the umpire. I never jeered at a defeated opponent ... My defeats and disappointments I took as stoically as I could. If I caught myself complaining or making excuses, I pulled up ... For the eight years of school life this code became the moral framework of my existence. It has never left me. I learnt it as a boy, I have obeyed it as a man and now I can no longer laugh at it. I failed to live up to it at times but when I did I knew and that is what matters.' James, who like Bob was given a bat and a ball by his father, also wrote, 'We know nothing, nothing at all, of the results of what we do to children.'

James's puritan values are those that Bob upheld each day of his life. And so his death plunges cricket into the greatest crisis in its entire history. It is a crisis that cannot be ignored.

Bob and I were born one year apart. We grew up in the sixties listening to the poetry of protest, often in the words of the American folk singer, Bob Dylan. In one of his most profound poems, he writes:

And how many ears must one man have
Before he can hear people cry?
Yes, 'n' how many deaths will it take till he knows
That too many people have died?

The answer, according to Dylan, is blowin' in the wind. The answer is blowin' in the wind.

21 | A Friendship with Gary Kirsten

If there is one person who can fulfil Bob's legacy to South African cricket, it is Gary Kirsten. Apart from my friendship with Bob, the other exceptional reward I received from my time with South African cricket was to meet and befriend Gary. My good fortune was to be seated next to him on the flight with the Proteas to the 1996 Cricket World Cup. I had known his stepbrother, Peter, who had been a special hero of mine, especially as a result of his batting heroics at the 1992 Cricket World Cup, where his exceptional performances kept us in the competition. On the flight, Gary and I soon fell into conversation.

One of my first questions was to ask him about his goals in one-day cricket. When he replied that he had none, I suggested, 'How about ten one-day centuries in less than 100 deliveries?' By the end of his career, Gary had achieved this. He wrote to me every time he got one, saying, 'Prof, that's one more down.'

As our conversation on that flight deepened, his answers intrigued me even more. I wanted to compose his story and include it in a book I was planning to write about the 1996 Proteas World Cup team. Some of what appears in the following pages was gleaned from my ideas for the start of that book. Unfortunately, the book was never written, but Gary remains a source of inspiration for me.

My friendship with Gary really blossomed after he retired in 2004. For six months he took an office in the Sports Science Institute of South Africa, and we met regularly to discuss whatever was on our minds. At first we spoke about Bradman's batting technique. Gary, who had played more Tests than any other South African, who had faced some of the meanest and cleverest bowlers in the world, was prepared to listen patiently to an eccentric professor who had absolutely no credentials to talk about anything involving cricket. Yet not once did he state the obvious – that I really had no right to be saying what I was saying. Instead, he corrected my obvious errors and educated me as best he could. I suspect that in time he came to appreciate the Bradman technique, because some of the Indian batsmen he coached to the ultimate success in the 2011 Cricket World Cup came quite close to using Bradman's technique, a point that I am now never shy of mentioning to him.

Gary's strength lies in his ability to deal with people. Like all great coaches, his greatest virtue is his emotional intelligence. He truly understands how to bring the best out of all those with whom he interacts. So it was natural that when he first began to coach the Indian team, he initially did, well, nothing. He knew that the team was scarred as a result of an unfortunate relationship with their former coach, Greg Chappell. It seems that Chappell had come in with all guns blazing: he believed fervently that the only way to play cricket was the Australian way.

So to prove that he was not another Greg Chappell, for nine months Gary did little other than tell his cricketers: 'You are all skilled cricketers who know how to play this game. I am going to be here for you. When you need me, just ask.'

Nine months later, the Indian captain Mohendra Dhoni came up to Gary and said: 'Coach, we trust you.' Only then did his coaching begin, and even then he focused more on the players' mindsets than on their skills. Indeed, when we spoke at the Institute, Gary often commented that he had played 100 Tests for South Africa without really understanding how to play Test cricket. Then he had discovered the philosophy of Paddy Upton, the Proteas' fitness trainer under Bob Woolmer, who, after leaving the Proteas and completing an M.Sc. degree with me, had branched out into the study of the psychology of superior athletic performance. In particular, he has studied how an organisation develops a learning culture in which all of its members, cricket players included, develop as more complete humans. In the process the organisation becomes a more competitive unit. Among the books he suggested I read are those by Peter Seng, Paul Tournie and Ken Wilber.

Paddy Upton taught Gary that although it is appropriate for an opening batsman to be fearful, that fear must be managed. So Paddy developed a technique to help Gary cope with his fears. He told Gary to take Fear with him onto the field, but to consign Fear to square leg before each delivery by saying, 'Fear, you stay right here while I face this delivery.' Then he would return to the batting crease, thus separating himself from his fear. If the ball was delivered and he suddenly felt Fear coming on, he would say, 'Fear, I can't talk to you just now. My focus is solely on this delivery. Go back to square leg. We can chat after this delivery.'

Like Bob, Gary questions continuously. As a player he was an intellectual cricketer who wanted to be the best he could be in whatever he did. It came as no surprise to me when India invited Gary to become their coach in 2007. Nor was I shocked when, under his coaching, India rose to the number-one Test-cricket nation in the world. I was not surprised when the world's greatest batsman after Sir Donald Bradman, Sachin Tendulkar, declared that as long as Gary Kirsten is the Indian cricket coach, he would be prepared to continue playing for India. Sometimes it takes a unique individual like Sachin Tendulkar to recognise a fellow traveller like Gary Kirsten.

Fortunately, on the very day that I finalised the corrections to the page proofs of this book, it was announced that Gary Kirsten would be the next coach of the Proteas cricket team.

BATTING IS ONE OF THE HARDEST TRADES EVER

Gary Kirsten's life has been shaped by two major forces. The first is the legacy of his surname. South African sport is enriched by the great sporting families of brothers and sons – the Pollocks, the Du Plessis family and others. Yet the combined successes of the Kirsten brothers – Peter, Andrew, Gary and Paul – is unusual in any company. All of the brothers have achieved sporting success in at least two sports at provincial level, and two of them have become international cricketers. Peter Kirsten, the eldest son, would certainly have been a double international, but a freak knee injury during his first representative rugby game when he was nineteen convinced him to devote all of his considerable sporting talents to just one sport, cricket.

Peter was born in 1955 and became South Africa's most prolific batsman during the country's period of isolation from international cricket between 1970 and 1991. His first-class career began in 1973. Perhaps the best measure of his genius was that, in his only real chance on the world stage, in the 1992 World Cup in Australasia, Kirsten, then aged thirty-six, was the second most successful batsman and was largely responsible for keeping South Africa in the competition. Given the opportunity, the elder Kirsten might well have emerged as the most successful South African batsman of all time.

In the shadow of his brother's success, Gary had to develop his own sporting life, first at school and then at the highest level of cricket. As Gary grew up in the fiercely competitive and parochial atmosphere of school sport in the southern suburbs of Cape Town, he discovered that the Kirsten name was initially helpful, as it stimulated inquisitiveness and attracted attention and opportunity. Later, it brought the pressure of expectation when the public recognised the name and began to make comparisons. The time came when Gary had to prove his own worth.

By the time he left school, Gary had represented Western Province Schools at both rugby and cricket and had captained the South African Schools cricket team. Within two years of leaving school he had played provincial rugby for Western Province at scrumhalf.

Gary made his debut for the Western Province cricket team in the 1988/89 season and for South Africa in December 1993, when he joined the team touring Australia, replacing the injured Brian McMillan. His first international match was the famous second Test, played at Sydney, where he scored 67 and 41, launching his international career. The key event in his transition from schoolboy to international cricketer was the influence of coach Duncan Fletcher. Fletcher saw Gary's potential when he was batting at number nine for the University of Cape Town's first cricket team, and informed a disbelieving Gary that if he could develop self-belief, he had the ability to become an international cricketer.

Gary considers Peter to have been the most talented Kirsten brother, with the strongest belief in his own ability. He feels that his own range of cricket shots was more limited than that of his brother and that, perhaps, as a result, his self-belief was not as strong. But his perception that Peter had the stronger self-belief and the greater talent did, if anything, act as a catalyst for his own ambitions. He managed to distance his own performances from those of his older brother and did not allow his brother's success to intimidate him.

Gary spoke of the ongoing fight to prove his ability and to refute the self-doubt arising from his perception that he lacked the skill and talent of some of the other South African batsmen. He conceded that other members of the South African team probably believed that he had more talent than he credited himself with. He maintained that self-doubt surfaced when he had a succession of low scores, and his solution to feeling down after making low scores was to apply himself more diligently, to practise harder and to continue to churn out the runs.

He describes cricket as a game of extremes in terms of the emotions, and says that he would like to close the gap between the mania induced by success and the depression that follows failure, as he believes that a more balanced response, especially to failure, would have improved his own overall performances.

Gary appreciates that to play cricket one must accept that it is impossible to be successful all the time, and that the greatest batsmen in the world succeed by scoring fifty or more runs on only every third or fourth visit to the wicket.

Indeed, there have been some consistent batsmen in world cricket, but they have sacrificed flair for a dogged defence and have often been characterised by their selfishness.

To compensate for his perceived shortcomings, the younger Gary Kirsten had only one recourse – in an epic determination to succeed, he posed two questions to himself every day: 1. How badly do I want to succeed? and 2. How much work am I prepared to put in to achieve that success?

Apart from his personal goals, Gary identified strongly with his team and was inspired by the goals that his team set. In his own favourite saying, he 'shocked' himself when he achieved his first one-day century, against England at Centurion Park in January 1996. Less than eight weeks later, his innings of 188 not out against the United Arab Emirates in Rawalpindi during the 1996 Cricket World Cup was a World Cup record. His goal in the 1995/96 series against England was to score three centuries; he achieved two.

In reality, Gary had a real talent, but at that time he was still in the process of coming to terms with the magnitude of his ability. He had set himself the highest possible standards and had made a great deal of progress. The nature of his personality was that he would not rest until he was the best possible Gary Kirsten that he could be.

But Kirsten's assessment of his ability may also have been a defence against the failure he feared more than anything – a loss of personal humility. He values humility enormously and to this day is adamant that if arrogance is needed to succeed in cricket, then he is not prepared to make the change. Success in cricket, he says, requires that one remains humble and adheres to the same rules that determine success in life generally. Generosity and personal humility, to the extent of being self-effacing, were values he learnt growing up in the Kirsten family, and these values have remained important to him.

The influence of his father on Gary Kirsten's cricketing career was twofold. The positive influence was that he had a great interest in all his sons' achievements; he encouraged all the brothers to try hard and he wanted them all to be successful. Gary's father taught him to work hard and to do the extra training in order to achieve success, but there was another side to his influence.

In retrospect, Gary believes that his father erred in his approach to his failures on the cricket field. He was very critical of Gary when he failed and was committed to the belief that the sole measure of a batsman's success is the number of runs that he scores in each innings. This induced a fear of failure in Gary. The effect on him was to inhibit any natural game that he might have developed as a schoolboy. His goal became one of accumulating runs, and to this end he learnt to avoid playing risky shots lest he get himself out. He now considers this to be the wrong goal for a young player, as it prevents him from developing a full range of strokes at the very time that the acquisition of such skills is the easiest. In his case, the paternal emphasis on scoring runs limited his full development as a young cricketer. Now he will advise against placing any emphasis whatsoever on the need to score runs in schoolboy cricket.

Pressure to succeed in school sport is counter-productive, Gary says, as success at that level is of little consequence. He learnt this lesson when, the year after captaining the South African Schools team in 1985, he found himself batting at number nine for the University of Cape Town. He was particularly incensed by his father's refusal to allow him to go on an overseas rugby tour in December, as this would have meant missing the school's cricket tournament, which would be played at the same time.

The second force that shaped Gary's life was of his own making – his choice of profession.

Gary was an opening batsman in an era of cricket when hostile fast bowling had become an acceptable, indeed crucial, offensive weapon for any world-class team. To succeed as an opening batsman, a cricketer had first to overcome fear – a very real fear of injury inflicted by a ball released less than twenty metres away and travelling at up to 150 kilometres per hour. At that speed a blow to the chest or neck can produce fatal results. The electrical impulse generated as the ball strikes the chest can induce a fatal heart-rhythm disturbance, ventricular fibrillation. Each year a few cricketers around the world die as a result of this injury. More common, however, are painful blows to the thigh or abdomen, or to the head.

According to Gary, defending your person would be easy if it were not necessary also to defend your wicket. The opening batsman thus has a simple choice: to give priority either to his personal safety or to his wicket. The international cricketer chooses the latter, and with each delivery he has less than 400 milliseconds after the ball leaves the bowler's hand to gather his courage and enact his choice.

The opening batsman must also score runs. In the one-day competition, the opening batsman needs to score his runs at a rate that is fast enough to give the innings the necessary momentum. This is an especially crucial component of the game plan for one-day cricket, adopted by the South African team under coach Bob Woolmer. In essence, the goal is to average a scoring rate of a run per ball from the first ball so that a competitive score can be reached fast. This approach spares the tail-end batsmen – who are in the team for their bowling ability and not their batting prowess – the responsibility of scoring more than six runs an over at the end of the innings.

The opening batsman must also contend with the opposition's best bowlers, bowling with all the conditions in their favour, including a hard, shiny ball that will swing, bounce and seam, often on a pitch that will favour these movements early in the innings, at the very time when his own reactions are not yet finely tuned to the light and the pace and movement of the pitch. Thus the challenge for the opening batsman is to ignore his own safety, to protect his wicket and, if he plays in a team aspiring to be the best one-day unit in the world, to score a run off each ball that he faces. It is an unusual person who would choose such a calling and have first the courage and then the motivation to stay in the game at the highest level for a sufficient length of time to master this intricate art.

Gary began the 1996 World Cup tour to the Asian subcontinent just two days after suffering a severe blow to the head while batting in the follow-on innings for Western Province against Natal. The delivery had been bowled by the late Malcolm Marshall, the great West Indian fast bowler who took 376 wickets in eighty-one Test matches between 1984 and 1991.

Knocked momentarily unconscious, Gary, 1 not out at the time, retired to the dressing room to recover his senses and for ice treatment to reduce the swelling on the side of his head, where the ball had struck. As soon as the swelling had subsided sufficiently to allow him to replace his helmet, he returned to the crease, batting for a further three hours, scoring 76 not out and helping to save the game for his province.

The only external evidence of the satisfaction that Gary must have felt was a hint of the generous smile that is the true window to his soul. When the grin breaks into a resounding laugh, as it does when he is on top of his game, it speaks of the joy experienced by someone who has met daunting challenges and may, just perhaps, have succeeded beyond his dreams.

The public reward Gary received for this disregard of his personal safety in the match against Natal was a column in the local press decrying the effect that one-day cricket was having on the ability of the 'current generation' of players, whose judgement and technique were, as a result, 'not always up to scratch'. The writer's argument was that batsmen in one-day matches are protected from the 'genuine lifting delivery'. The helmet and the restriction on short-pitched deliveries were said to further corrupt the technique of the modern opening batsman. The truth might be somewhat different, especially when one considers the infamous 'Bodyline' series between Australia and England.

The first time that fast bowling was aimed specifically at the batsman's body was in this series, played in Australia in 1932/33. As Jack Fingleton related in his book on the topic, the English captain, Douglas Jardine, was determined to beat the Australians on their home ground. In order to do this, they had to contain the greatest batsman of all time, Sir Donald Bradman. In the previous Ashes series, in England, Bradman had been unstoppable. If he continued to bat with such dominance, England would not be able to win the Ashes back in the Australian series. However, the idea had arisen that Bradman's sole weakness was a tentativeness when playing short-pitched fast bowling. To exploit this weakness, Jardine devised the bodyline theory using his fast bowler Harold Larwood, still considered to be the fastest bowler of all time. Using the bodyline theory, the ball is bowled from around the wicket and aimed at the stomach and chest of the batsman. Against this type of delivery, the batsman has no choice but to defend his body. Jardine positioned six or more fielders close to the bat on the leg side to catch any balls that the batsman was lucky enough to fend off.

The bodyline tactic was effective: Bradman was restricted to an average of 'only' 56.6 runs per innings (compared to his lifetime Test average of 99.94) and England won the series. The effect on relations between England and Australia, however, was catastrophic, and gave rise to the famous phrase: 'It's just not cricket.' It produced such disharmony in world cricket that none dared try it again. Rules were also changed specifically to prevent this tactic from ever being used in the future. As a result, Douglas Jardine's idea that fast bowling could be used as an offensive weapon was shelved for forty years.

But by the early 1970s, sport was becoming more professional and, therefore, more competitive. It was only natural that any change that would give a temporary advantage would be sought by sport's progressive thinkers. The Australians had waited long enough for revenge, and it was their bowlers who initiated the next era of intimidatory fast bowling.

In the opinion of Bob Woolmer, it was during the 1974/75 Ashes series in Australia that the Australian opening fast bowlers Dennis Lillee and Jeff Thomson began to use intimidatory short-pitched fast bowling aimed at the throat and head. At the time there were no restrictions on the number of such balls that could be bowled during each over, and batsmen wore no head protection.

During the 1975/76 tour to the West Indies, the same two bowlers introduced the West Indians to their aggressive fast bowling. For all opening batsmen who would ever have to face a future West Indian pace attack, that was an error of the highest order, as aggressive fast bowling perfectly suited the psyche and the natural physical abilities of the tall, powerfully built West Indians of that era.

When the West Indies toured England in 1976, captain Clive Lloyd relied on an attack that comprised four fast bowlers – Andy Roberts, Michael Holding, Wayne Daniel and Vanburn Holder. Since then, the West Indians have produced a string of the greatest fast bowlers of all time, including Joel Garner, Malcolm Marshall, Colin Croft, Courtney Walsh, Curtly Ambrose, Ian Bishop and many others.

The fast bowler succeeds because there is a finite limit, defined by the courage of the batsman, to the amount of physical punishment that the batsman will accept during any innings. A few milliseconds of doubt and the slightest hesitation in getting into line with the ball's trajectory risks another painful blow to the body and leaves the batsman sparring the ball into the air in the direction of the closest fielder. Laws controlling intimidatory bowling were first introduced in 1981, but these limit only the number of bouncers that the bowler may deliver each over.

The opening batsman has three options when playing short-pitched, intimidatory bowling – in cricketing lingo, the throat ball. He may choose to duck, but if the ball does not rise, he will be struck on the head, as Gary Kirsten was in 1996; if he uses his bat, he risks losing his wicket if the ball carries to a fielder after contacting either his bat or his glove. The only attacking option is to pull or hook the ball to the square-leg area. But this requires that the player must detect the length of the ball early and be prepared to place his head directly in the path of the onrushing ball. His face is not fully protected, and a ball coming off the top edge of the bat may enter the gap between the visor and the peak of the helmet, striking him on the nose, eye or cheekbone. Even a blow to the helmet can cause concussion, as the modern helmet is not designed sufficiently well to absorb all of the force imparted by the sudden deceleration of a cricket ball travelling at 150 kilometres per hour.

Gary's response to the article claiming that his technique was inadequate was to suggest that the batsmen of the 'Bodyline' era had to have been unusually gifted to succeed before the introduction of adequate helmets in 1977 and their widespread use by most batsmen by 1981. The introduction of the helmet has allowed greater numbers of the less gifted players to continue playing cricket at all levels of the game. Without the helmet, only the most talented players in the world, with a wide range of shots, would be able to survive and retain their health and sanity. The helmet has therefore extended the talent pool of people who can play the game and has allowed the less gifted players, prepared to make the most of their talent, the opportunity to continue in the game.

This in itself is a recurring theme in Gary's personal ethos, which is that the less talented, less artistic cricketers deserve the same support and praise for their perseverance as those with great talents, for whom the game is somewhat easier. Gary has also pointed out that the nature of the game is determined by the rules – if there were no restriction on short-pitched deliveries, batsmen would adapt and practise to become better hookers of the ball. The current rules encourage the bowler to pitch the ball up and to seek ways of dismissing the batsman with a fuller-length delivery. Thus modern batsmen must be able to play most of their shots off the front foot. Those who also master the hook shots will be the more complete batsmen.

GARY KIRSTEN AND COACHING

Coaching has played a major role in Gary Kirsten's life, and he has expressed very strong opinions on the attitude of sports coaches in the schools in which he grew up. The determination of schools with a long tradition of sporting excellence to produce batsmen who will score runs to win matches for the school is detrimental to the development of the cricketer. Morné du Plessis and I have written extensively on the less-than-ideal psychological effect that this approach also has on rugby players required to win games for their schools. It wreaks the worst possible psychological damage – the fear-of-failure syndrome. But, until I spoke to Gary, I was completely unaware of the effect that this approach has on the development of the skills of the young cricketer.

Gary argues that the 'hyped' approach to schools rugby, in which he was also highly successful, is less damaging, because that sport requires much less skill than cricket does. So motivation, not skill, becomes the crucial factor on which the rugby coach must work. Bravado and commitment can substitute for a lack of skill on the school rugby field, Gary believes.

Cricket, however, is different, as it places such a high demand on skill. Gary contends that young players must be taught to play and master all the cricketing shots. Those are the skills that are needed to succeed at the higher levels of the game. Unfortunately the measure of a batsman's ability at school is still the number of runs he scores and not the range of shots he can play. The measure of success of the school's cricket team is how many matches it wins, not how many players in the team have been taught the skills to enable them to succeed at the highest levels of the game.

In Gary's opinion, the school approach is successful only in the short term, because most school cricket is played on flat pitches on which the ball seldom rises above knee height. The result is that bowlers are taught to bowl with little aggression and to pitch the ball on a full length, to bowl 'line and length' and to 'get the ball in the right area'.

The result is that the high-school batsman soon learns to attack only on the front foot, while on the back foot he plays defensively only. However, one of the keys to success in international cricket is to be able to attack short-pitched bowling off the back foot, since on responsive pitches the really fast bowlers attack the batsman by bowling just short of a length. Therefore most young batsmen with ability have to learn the techniques they will need for success in senior cricket only *after* leaving school. A central tenet of skill acquisition is that it is easier to acquire skills at a younger age.

To teach players the correct technique requires, of course, that the coach knows the details of those techniques and has the ability to convey the information. Being a great player does not necessarily mean that one will be a good coach. In fact, it is often those for whom an activity does not come easily who become the best analysts and teachers in any aspect of human endeavour. Perhaps Bob Woolmer would never have been challenged to achieve greatness as a cricketing coach had he been as naturally talented a cricketer as was, for example, his compatriot Ian Botham.

Gary's experience at school was that some professional English coaches, who make up the majority of coaches at the elite South African cricketing schools, still did not have the ability to teach cricketing technique. Why should they? A career as a professional cricketer in the United Kingdom does not include formal training in teaching techniques. Nor is there an established curriculum that aspirant coaches must complete. The coach is, above all, a teacher, yet he requires no formal training in the basic educational techniques that will allow him to convey his on-field skills to those who, because of either their youth or their physical limitations, will have difficulty acquiring those skills. If the professional coaches are failing in their task, what is the probability that the average school cricket coach in South Africa will be successful? Gary also questioned the commitment of some of these coaches to the South African children and their approach to the game.

The general feeling was also that county cricket lacks the aggression and commitment of the South African equivalent, mainly because the players are forced to play too much cricket. Within a month of the start of the season the players in those teams that are not in contention reduce the level of their commitment. Gary felt that this lack of total commitment bred coaches who are not sufficiently aggressive for the South Africans. They are reluctant to teach the aggressive aspects of the game – the hook, the cut and the short-pitched delivery. He still believes that there are sufficient young South African players who can fill the role of these overseas coaches, and he argues that past players should be involved. He feels that there should be communication between the schools and former players, especially those who were former students at the school. Successful former South African players, properly trained and properly remunerated, should coach the young South African players.

In addition, Gary is concerned about the format of high-school cricket. He would prefer to see a limited-overs competition in schools to teach players the skills of that type of game, and he would like to see the top teams forming a super league and competing in matches over two days. One-day cricket, says Gary, allows for a draw, which contributes to negative cricket.

All of this explains why cricket, and especially batting, is so hard to master. But when I first showed him some of the material I had written in 1996 after being seated next to him on the aeroplane trip to the World Cup, Gary asked if he could add his own thoughts on why cricket, especially batting, is 'the most difficult profession in the world'. He wrote:

> To me, cricket is a way of life. It teaches you humbleness, but at the same time you must be super confident almost to the point of being cocky.
>
> First, you need to be humble because no matter how successful you have been over a period of time, every time you walk to the crease, you have to start again from nought regardless of what you did in your last innings. You must respect the bowler no matter who he is. What will the wicket do? Is the ball swinging or seaming today? Basically as an opening batter, it's a matter of survival for the first hour. The first hour, as [legendary former Indian opening batsman Sunil] Gavaskar said, belongs to the bowler. But as the batter's innings progresses, the equilibrium shifts to the batter. Tell me the sport in the world that you need merely to survive to be successful. Tell me [another] sport in the world in which there are such extremes between success and failure and in which the gap between the two is so small. This game teaches you to be humble because on Monday the ball can look like a pumpkin and on Friday it can look like a squash ball. Then all it takes as well are the outside forces such as bad umpiring decisions.
>
> Second, confidence is essential as, in any walk of life, it's probably a matter of self-belief and preparation that determines success in cricket. In most walks of life, though, good preparation will ensure that one has a high percentage success rate. But in cricket, success every fourth time you go to the crease makes you a top cricketer.

I feel that part of your preparation must be to focus on the innings that you are going to play, as every innings requires an enormous amount of concentration. One needs to be organised when batting, especially as an opener, as a solid technique is vital for success. To maintain this concentration over a period of three to five hours is very tiring, as one misjudgement could be the end of your innings. I feel that every innings I play is mentally draining purely because I would love to succeed each time I go to the wicket, but just one bad score and the pressure is immediately on to perform next time, regardless of the team's performance. Two or three bad performances and the pressure really starts to mount, again, regardless of how the team is performing. This to me makes it a unique game, as one can feel really disappointed over a period of time despite playing in a winning team. The mental stress experienced can be high, as no one likes not to contribute to a winning team.

I find what can snap you out of that situation is desire and determination to succeed. I just wish it could be more consistent.

So, today, following his coaching of India to victory in the 2011 Cricket World Cup, and especially because of the impeccable manner in which he achieved that success, Gary Kirsten is perhaps the most sought-after coach in the world.

I would guess that his success is based as much on his personality as on his cricket knowledge; on his personal humility, his intellectualism and his high degree of emotional intelligence. His progress from club to international cricketer taught him that success is founded on self-belief, the discipline to work as hard as one is able, and to take personal responsibility for the outcome. But, ultimately, Gary has the intelligence to understand that that which determines success at the very top levels of international cricket is the players' collective mental skill. That is the winning edge that he taught the World Cup–winning Indian team in 2011.

Did Bob Woolmer put Gary on the road to becoming one of the greatest cricket coaches of all time? I certainly hope so.

part six

THE CENTRAL GOVERNOR

'Ex Africa semper aliquid novi'

22 | It's All in the Mind: It's Not about Your Body

OPENING THE MIND

My strength as a scientist lies more in formulating important research questions and designing experiments than in collecting the data to test ideas and theories. This, I think, is because I lack patience when evaluating a new idea. The problem with a well-designed experiment is that the answer may become apparent after the very first test has been completed. However, the results of a single experiment do not constitute proof, at least in the biological sciences. So one has to repeat the identical experiment ten or twenty times before enough data have been collected to evaluate the theory in question. My problem is that if the first experiment provides the likely ultimate answer, my mind moves on to the implications of the result and begins to focus on the next set of experiments that needs to be designed. It becomes very difficult to focus on the job at hand if one's attention has already moved on to the next stage.

I also have many other weaknesses as a scientist, in part because I trained as a medical doctor and not primarily as a scientist. I have a frail grasp of mathematics and know less than I should about statistics. A number of new scientific disciplines, like molecular biology and genetics, have advanced in leaps and bounds since I was trained and I know very little about those fields. So, bearing my own shortcomings in mind, I have focused on attracting and supporting people who have the skills necessary to produce a winning scientific team. When the skills of all the team members are combined, there is very little that the team as a collective cannot and will not achieve. My contact with great coaches like

Jake White and Bob Woolmer has taught me that the team is always greater than the individual.

But the true art of delegation is to understand that, as the team leader, one must take full responsibility for the outcomes, especially when they are bad. That is the only way to build a team that is cohesive, trusting and ultimately prepared to take intellectual risks without forever trying to find scapegoats when things go wrong, as they inevitably will. A sporting example of this again comes from the role of the coach – when a team wins, it is due to the team's work; when it fails, it is the coach who has failed.

Frequently, scientists fail because they lack the skills necessary to assemble a cohesive and trusting team that focuses on science and not on who will get the credit for any findings emanating from that laboratory. Attitude, character, emotional intelligence and an absence of narcissism are as important in directing the success of a scientific research team as they are in producing a winning sports team. A successful scientific team – like a successful sports team – requires that each member of the team fulfils his or her responsibilities to ensure that the entire team produces a winning outcome.

The second key to successful science is to ask the correct question: the world's greatest scientists are those who ask the right question at the right time. My medical training taught me the importance of the ability to ask the correct question, in that the patient always knows the answer but cannot give it to you unless you ask the appropriate question. Less successful scientists fail either because they are unable to build a successful scientific team or because they are unable to ask the right question.

Albert Einstein once said that, if he had just one hour of life left to solve a problem, he would allocate the first fifty-five minutes of that hour to considering the right question to ask. Once he had decided on the question, he would spend the final five minutes of his life answering it. In this way, with one second of life left, he would have solved the problem. So it was that Einstein could ask the question: What would it be like to travel on the front of a light beam speeding through deep space? The answer to that question unlocked the theory of general relativity, which, alongside Darwin's theory of evolution on the basis of natural selection, is the most remarkable theory that I have ever encountered (or have pretended to understand). Einstein knew that when humans fall freely in space, they do not feel the effects of gravity. That knowledge and his question were enough to revolutionise human understanding.

To answer complex questions, however, scientists need at least the basic tools. When I began teaching sports science as a B.Sc. honours course at UCT in 1981 with Dr Johan Koeslag and Professor Wieland Gevers, we had almost no equipment. We had a bicycle, which we still have, and a home-made treadmill that quickly became tired and began to wheeze if required to run faster than about ten kilometres an hour. Fortunately, assistance from two friends, James Murray and Dr Matt Haus, and the help of the then Cape Heart Foundation in the early 1980s, allowed us to purchase a decent treadmill (which we still have and which is still 100 per cent functional) and systems to analyse oxygen consumption during exercise.

The fact that this was the equipment we bought first is significant, since in the 1980s – and even today – an exercise scientist has to be able to measure oxygen consumption during exercise. I have always viewed equipment simply as tools that allow the scientist to answer important questions; in other words, the sole value of equipment is the nature of the questions it allows the scientist to answer. I am always frustrated when I visit other laboratories and am taken on the grand tour to admire their 'assets' – their scientific 'bling'.

A visit to our laboratories at the Sports Science Institute in Newlands will show you that now, thirty years after we began, we do indeed have lots of 'bling'. But it is not the equipment that ought to be focused on; instead, it is the rows of framed scientific papers, each considered a scientific 'classic', as each has been cited by colleagues more than fifty times in the scientific literature. It is the published research outputs, not the 'bling', that is the true measure of the scientist's value. Indeed, one of the most daunting realisations is that one's impact as a scientist is utterly quantifiable on the basis of how frequently one's work is cited – favourably or unfavourably – by one's colleagues. At the end of a career, a scientist knows with exquisite – and sometimes painful – precision exactly what his or her impact on the scientific world has been. The scientist truly runs the race every moment of his or her career, and at any moment knows exactly where he or she lies in that race.

In the 1980s, when enough equipment had been acquired to be able to measure oxygen consumption in human athletes during exercise, we began to ask the question: Are there physiological variables that can be measured in the laboratory that will tell us who the best athlete is, and why? We began by studying runners, since we had a treadmill. (The growth of recreational cycling in South Africa had yet to happen.) Interestingly, as a medical student in 1972, I had asked Professor G. Williams, then at Stellenbosch University, if we could arrange to measure the exercise response of a group of UCT runners competing in the 1972 Comrades Marathon to see if we could predict their performance. Our results showed that the maximum amount of oxygen that these athletes could consume when they were running at maximum effort – the so-called maximal oxygen consumption (VO_2 max) – was not of any great value in predicting the order in which the athletes would finish the race. This was perhaps my very first scientific study, and its negative outcome might perhaps have influenced my subsequent lack of enthusiasm for the value of this particular form of exercise test in predicting athletic potential.

In the early 1980s, however, when we began to take our first tentative steps into exercise science research, the Holy Grail of exercise physiology was quite simple. The maximum rate at which the athlete could consume oxygen when running at the top speed he or she could sustain for about five minutes – VO_2 max – was all that one needed to measure accurately and predict the athlete's performance in any sport requiring endurance, such as distance running, swimming or triathlon.

So, according to the wisdom of the day, we were expected to show that in the initial phases of the test the oxygen consumption would rise as a function of the increasing work rate, in this case caused by the increasing speed of the treadmill, as shown in **Figure 24 opposite**. However, a point would be reached at which oxygen consumption reached its maximum value and could increase no further, regardless of how much faster the athlete was able to run. This failure of oxygen consumption to increase any further became known as the 'plateau phenomenon'.

The graph comes from an article published in 1971 by J.H. Mitchell and G. Blomqvist, two of the world's most respected cardiovascular physiologists. It was also published in the world's premier medical journal, the *New England Journal of Medicine*. So how could it be anything other than the 'truth'?

This 'plateau phenomenon', so beautifully depicted in the graph, was first described in the English scientific literature by the British scientist and Nobel Prize winner Professor Archibald Vivian Hill in a classic paper published in 1923. He argued that this failure of oxygen consumption to rise further once the VO_2 max had been achieved was because of a limiting capacity of the heart to pump any more blood to the exercising muscles. As a consequence, the muscles become 'anaerobic' – that is, they are forced to continue working without an adequate oxygen supply. This anaerobiosis causes the exercising muscles to produce lactic acid, which, according to Hill's theory, acted as a muscle poison, ultimately causing fatigue and a failure of muscle function. (This process is explained in more detail below.) Since Hill was a Nobel Prize winner, any theory he developed would naturally enjoy a very high degree of acceptance. This was especially true in a young discipline like sports science, which needed the input of high-profile scientists like A.V. Hill if it was ever to be taken seriously.

FIGURE 24

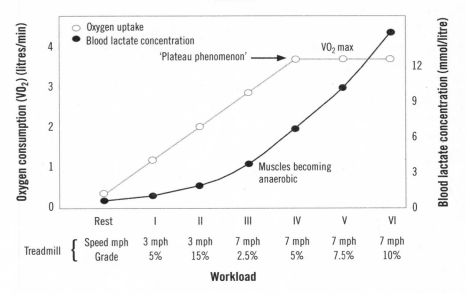

According to this diagram published in the New England Journal of Medicine in 1971 and based on the theory first developed by Professor A.V. Hill and H. Lupton in 1923, the oxygen use by an athlete increases as a linear function of the increasing workloads I to IV. But ultimately two consecutive workloads (V and VI) are achieved that require an oxygen consumption that exceeds the subject's maximum ability to transport oxygen to her muscles. This point is detected by the presence of a 'plateau' in oxygen consumption. This phenomenon, as explained above, is called the maximal oxygen consumption – VO_2 max. I have spent much of the last twenty-five years questioning whether this phenomenon really exists.

But our immediate problem in our early experiments was that we could not find this 'plateau phenomenon' in the majority of the athletes we tested. So the question arose: If the majority of the athletes that we test terminate this maximal exercise bout without showing the 'plateau phenomenon', then why do they stop? According to the logic of **Figure 24 above**, this cannot be because their muscles have run out of oxygen. If there is no 'plateau phenomenon', then there cannot be a limited oxygen supply to the muscles in those particular athletes. So I began to wonder how this strange idea had arisen.

At the time, my two intellectual heroes in the sports sciences were Dr George Sheehan and Dr David Costill. Dr Sheehan, who was mentioned earlier, had become the philosophical guru of the new marathon-running movement that had begun after 1976 and had written the definitive books of that era. Dr Costill was the global guru of applied exercise science. Indeed, were you to ask me whom I modelled myself on when I had completed my work in Lionel Opie's laboratory and moved into the exercise sciences, I would respond that it would be these two gentlemen. Sheehan was unique; there will never be another like him. Costill was a pioneer who established the modern applied exercise sciences in the United States and elsewhere. He simply wanted to answer one question: How does the athletic body function and how can that information be used to help athletes perform better? I was fortunate to have these two professors and Professor Opie as my mentors, and I was also lucky to be starting out in the exercise sciences in the early 1980s, when everything in our discipline was new and anything seemed possible.

So it was perhaps natural that I should turn to the writings of Costill to see how he understood this problem. In the first edition of his popular book, on which I modelled some aspects of *Lore of Running*, I discovered the following statement: 'Since the early work of Hill and Lupton (1923), exercise physiologists have associated the limits of human endurance with the ability to consume larger volumes of oxygen during exhaustive exercise.' Clearly, to understand the problem, I needed to track down the writings of Professor A.V. Hill.

So I went to my favourite haunt on the UCT medical campus, the library, and began to search for all I could find on Hill. It was in that library that I discovered the information that directed the most important aspects of my scientific work.

I need to make the point that I, characteristically, want to know *everything* about any topic that interests me. The result is that I have a massive collection of scientific articles and books that overwhelms the storage capacity I have at work and at home. When two rooms at home and my office at work could no longer house the material that I had collected, I moved into the garage. The internet has not helped, for it makes it possible to track down almost everything that has ever been published. So I am, I suspect, one of few who has all of Hill's books – all in pristine condition, even though some were printed nearly eighty years ago.

Thanks to David Costill's book, I was directed to work undertaken by Hill between 1923 and 1925 at the University College London. In turn, his interpretation of what he believed was happening – we term this his 'model of exercise physiology' – was critically influenced by the 1907 publication of another Nobel Laureate, Frederick Grover Hopkins, who was then at Cambridge University.

So Hill and his colleague Hartley Lupton were perhaps the first English-speaking scientists to measure oxygen consumption during exercise, and to speculate on the role that oxygen supply plays in determining athletic ability. Because they wrote in English rather than in French or German, it is their work that is most often remembered as pioneering in the scientific literature, since it is the most easily accessible to English-speaking scientists.

Hill and Lupton popularised the belief that, during exercise, human muscle can use either or both of two different energy sources. For low-intensity exercise, they suggested that the energy comes from aerobic (oxygen-requiring) sources. However, as the exercise intensity increases, these aerobic sources ultimately reach a maximum capacity and are unable to supply the muscles with all of the energy they require to continue exercising at very high intensities. So if humans wanted to run at their very fastest, Hill and Lupton suggested, they had to access a second energy source, that provided by anaerobic (in the absence of oxygen) sources.

Their most famous set of experiments used Hill himself as the principal research subject. Hill's oxygen consumption was measured as he ran for three minutes at different speeds on a circular grass track of eighty-five metres in circumference. On the basis of these experiments, Hill and Lupton concluded: 'There is clearly some critical speed for each individual above which the maximum oxygen intake is inadequate, lactic acid accumulating, a continuously increasing oxygen debt being incurred, fatigue and exhaustion setting in.'

Their hypothesis therefore proposed that during exercise there is a work rate or exercise intensity that requires that the muscles need more oxygen than can be provided through the blood stream by the heart and circulation. As a result, the rate of oxygen consumption measured by sampling the athlete's exhaled breaths reaches the 'plateau' shown in **Figure 24**. To provide the extra energy that cannot be supplied by the metabolism of oxygen – the aerobic energy supply – the muscle must turn on its anaerobic energy production with the production of lactic acid. Rising muscle and blood lactic acid concentrations then act to terminate the exercise. So, basically, the theory of Hill and Lupton requires that these 'chemical' processes poison the muscles, causing the activity to terminate. This is the theory that has dominated the exercise sciences for nearly ninety years.

Hill and his colleagues also argued that there was an absolute and universal VO_2 max value of four litres per minute (L/min) that occurred at a running speed of about thirteen kilometres per hour in all human athletes. Indeed, if you look carefully at **Figure 24 on page 299**, you will see that they also indicated that the VO_2 max occurred at a rate of oxygen consumption of four L/min. But surely they could not have accepted *all* of Hill's beliefs so completely in 1971?

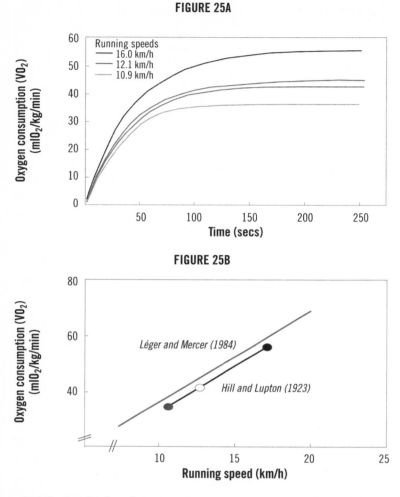

FIGURE 25A

FIGURE 25B

Figure 25A depicts the data from an experiment conducted by A.V. Hill on himself in 1923. It shows that his oxygen consumption, measured at regular intervals as he ran at three different speeds, increased rapidly before reaching steady-state values after about 100 seconds. Since he felt tired when he ran at sixteen kilometres per hour (top line), he concluded that he was running anaerobically at that speed – that is, that he had exceeded his VO_2 max. But Figure 25B shows that his average oxygen consumption at the three different running speeds rose as a linear function and was essentially the same as modern values reported by Léger and Mercer in 1984. This establishes that Hill's oxygen consumption, when running at sixteen kilometres per hour, was sufficient to cover all of his energy requirements. Hence he was not running 'anaerobically'. This disproves his conclusion that he had reached his VO_2 max.

Reviewing the original data that Hill used to develop his theory, I discovered, to my complete surprise, that Hill had not analysed his data objectively. Instead, he had allowed his subjective opinions of what *should* happen to influence how he interpreted exactly what *did* happen.

I discovered that, in the experiments he performed on himself, Hill had not shown that his oxygen consumption reached a maximum 'beyond which no effort can drive it'. Instead, his oxygen consumption rose as a linear function of his running speed, indicating that his muscles were receiving all the oxygen they required, even at the point at which he had stopped running, believing that his muscles were starved of oxygen.

I made this discovery in 1987 while preparing a lecture for the annual American College of Sports Medicine conference that was held that year in Las Vegas. The paper was published the following year under the title 'Implications of Exercise Testing for Prediction of Athletic Performance: A Contemporary Perspective'. From this discovery I learnt that, as so often happens in science, an unproven opinion becomes the accepted dogma for the following generations. No one takes the trouble to go back to the original work to check exactly how the original ideas were conceived. This is known as scientific gullibility.

I established in 1987 that Hill had never shown that an oxygen deficiency caused him to stop running. Therefore the interpretations of those who had advanced his theory over the next ninety years, believing Hill to be absolutely correct, including Mitchell and Blomqvist, were not likely to be right. Interestingly, my 1987 paper did not cause a major outcry in the exercise sciences, although it remains the second most frequently cited paper that I have ever written. Most of those who have cited it have been in agreement with this idea. The paper certainly didn't evoke the same emotional response as my suggestion a decade later did, that the brain, rather than the heart, is the organ that truly regulates human exercise performance.

After 1987, the main direction of my research interest became, for obvious reasons, EAH, as I described in Part II of this book. Then, in about July 1995, shortly before I became involved with Bob Woolmer and South African cricket, I was invited by my friend Dr Stephen Blair, then of the Dallas Aerobics Center, to present the J.B. Wolffe Memorial Lecture at the annual American College of Sports Medicine meeting to be held in Cincinnati in June 1996. This lecture is the opening event of the conference, and an invitation to deliver it is considered to be one of the greatest honours bestowed on an exercise scientist, especially a non-American. I think I was about the sixth non-American to present this lecture in its history and I was mindful of the fact that, among those who had done so before me, were the intellectual giants of our discipline – the legends who had inspired me and many others to greater effort. I had not expected to share the platform with such illustrious names, partly because it is unusual for a non-American to be invited to deliver this lecture and also because I was keenly aware that with such an honour comes an important responsibility: to fashion a message that is relevant and an inspiration to the broader scientific community.

As the speaker usually lectures on a singular specialist topic, I decided to talk about my speciality – challenging dogmas. So the title of my lecture was 'Challenging Beliefs: *Ex Africa semper aliquid novi*'. The Latin '*ex Africa semper aliquid novi*' means, 'from Africa always something new' and is attributed to the Roman philosopher Pliny. I spoke about five accepted beliefs that I consider to be questionable dogmas. The first was the concept that exercise performance is limited by the development of an oxygen deficiency – the original Hill theory.

And so it was that, with a warning to the audience that I have been called a 'gentle iconoclast' as well as a 'loose cannon', I presented the original explanation of what has since become – with additional research – the 'central governor theory'. I began by pointing out that, as Pliny had correctly observed, Africa has indeed always provided something new.

One of the oldest known medical texts, the Papyrus Ebers, dated 1550 BCE, comes from Egypt and contains arguably the first correct description of the pulmonary circulation, made by the Egyptian physician Ibn al-Nafis. That is more than three thousand years before the Englishman William Harvey provided what is accepted as the definitive description of how blood circulates in the body. Harvey is recognised as the first great biological scientist, but it may be that that accolade belongs instead to a long-forgotten Egyptian scientist. Similarly, the African origins of man was actually discovered by Professor Raymond Dart, former dean of the Medical School of the University of the Witwatersrand, Johannesburg.

And so I began my address: 'The Viennese philosopher, Sir Karl Popper, wrote, "It may become necessary to attack beliefs which, whether or not they are consciously held, are taken so much for granted that any criticism of them is felt to be perverse or insincere."'

Then followed my 'attack': 'An unusual feature of the exercise sciences is that certain core beliefs are based on an historical physiological model that, it will be argued, has somehow escaped modern, disinterested intellectual scrutiny ... The challenge for future generations of exercise physiologists is to identify how the body anticipates the possibility of organ damage and evokes the appropriate control mechanisms at the appropriate instant. We will best serve our science if we continuously question all our beliefs, regardless of their origin or how hallowed they have become.'

At the end of my lecture, I challenged the audience to embrace new ideas from Africa by citing a quote from columnist Jeff Wise: 'If the West means anything at all, it is not a specific set of values, but a meta-value, an idea about ideas. It is about throwing open the gates to the richness of world culture and daring to embrace the best of what you find.' Perhaps I should have remembered that science is a conservative profession and that a majority of scientists prefer ideas not to change – at least in their lifetimes!

More recently, I witnessed another example of this narrow-minded thinking in the life of Mark Richard Shuttleworth, and in the extremely competitive field of commerce.

On Thursday 12 December 2002, it was my honour to deliver the address to the vice-chancellor of the University of Cape Town (UCT) marking the awarding of a Doctor of Philosophy – *honoris causa* – to Mark. The award of an Honorary Doctorate to a twenty-nine-year-old was unprecedented in the eighty-four-year history of the university.

I was struck by Mark's miraculous story and what was truly a stupendous achievement. Born in Welkom on 18 September 1973, Mark is the eldest of three sons born to Ronell and Richard Shuttleworth. His father, a specialist surgeon, is a UCT alumnus who graduated in the medical class of 1969.

Mark was educated in Claremont at Hill Pre-primary School and Western Province Preparatory School, and in Rondebosch at Diocesan College (Bishops). The fact that in Bishops we shared the same school, and that he was in the same class as my son Travis Miles, made his story resonate even more with me.

Mark was an extraordinary all-round talent. He represented his high school at the national Olympiads in science, maths, English and Latin, and was selected to represent South Africa at the World Science Week in London. He was head prefect, yet found time to both direct and act the lead role in the annual school play. On the sporting front, he achieved provincial school colours in judo. And then, just for good measure, he ranked eighth in the 1991 Western Cape matriculation examinations.

But, as in my own career, which began when I was first exposed to the news of Chris Barnard's successful heart transplant and so discovered my passion, it was at Western Province Preparatory School that Mark first discovered his defining medium – the computer – and was exposed to computer games. Yet his young mind was intrigued not by games but by the greater mystery – how such games were constructed, and what they revealed of the minds of their creators.

The theme of his final speech as matriculating head prefect at Bishops was of thinking, dreaming and the future. In a prophetic moment, he urged his fellow scholars to 'wake up each day with an idea, no matter how small, and do [y]our utmost to put it into practice'. He concluded by urging his audience to dream big: 'As South Africa, and indeed the world, warms to a new age of communication, there is no reason why we should not be at the forefront of the movement.'

Here was a new light from Darkest Africa, and it came from a computer screen. Mark's universal intellect meant that he could register in any faculty for any degree at UCT. He chose commerce, registering for the degree of Business Science in Economics in 1992. His campus education allowed him the freedom to engage his insatiable intellectual curiosity. With parental money set aside for his tertiary education, he purchased a personal computer and had a telephone line installed in his room in Smuts Hall. And one day, he connected to the Internet. Perhaps he was the first student and one of the first members of staff at UCT to do this; for the Internet was still a toddler in 1992. So he pursued his computer interests and explored the Internet while learning the business of commerce. Of course, he was informed by those who knew better that the Internet was not a suitable medium for commercial transactions. It was the South African equivalent of telling Henry Ford that there is no future in the motor car.

Following graduation, and by now absolutely certain that the Internet provided the commercial gateway to the future, Mark's vision was fixed. He alone knew where to aim. He re-registered as a double Honours Major in Finance and Information Technology at UCT, but was exposed to an inconvenient reality: he ran out of money. If he was to unlock the commercial promise of the global Internet, he first had to discover a way to pay his rent.

Mark's first venture into the job market was not auspicious. His vision of the Internet as a slumbering commercial giant, awaiting the ignition of his creative genius, was not shared by his first Cape Town employers. They fired him for being 'useless'. So he tried again and designed websites for two other companies, Independent Newspapers and Hirt & Carter. Today, the Independent Online website is one of the largest news portals in southern Africa. To ensure that his money stretched further, he acquired office space in his parents' garage in Durbanville.

Now Mark began to focus on the four crucial challenges to be overcome if e-commerce was to be launched. First was the capacity to process business transactions on the Internet. Second was the need to ensure that such trans-actions were absolutely secure, especially when they involved the transfer of sensitive credit-card details. How do you ensure that the rest of the universe does not share this information? The third challenge was a consequence of the natural anonymity of the Internet. How can you ever be certain who it is you are talking to? Indeed, how do you know that they sell the product or service that you desire? And, finally, for a complete unknown working from the southern-most tip of the Dark Continent, there was the fourth challenge: how to be noticed in a business that is dominated by a publicly listed North American giant that controls a global monopoly.

Mark was determined to develop a better product – a faultless, world-beating system that provided e-commerce producers and consumers with secure websites that could be absolutely trusted because they were digitally verified and certified by a trusted third party, his company.

In 1996 he wrote the software program named Sioux. It was the world's first 'webserver software modified to allow secure business transactions' over the Internet. He reinvested all the money that he earned from the product, and later from the sale of that technology, to fund his own start-up company, THAWTE Consulting. He began the search for solutions to the three remaining problems: those of secure credit-card encryption and transfer, the digital certification of secure websites, and of challenging a global monopoly.

But how does a twenty-four-year-old South African with no access to capital, and a business run on three battle-scarred computers in his parents' garage, compete in the global economy? It is the classic case of a poorly resourced Third World David against the corpulent Goliath. But, as in the Biblical story, Goliath is not without his weakness, not least because he inhabits the First World.

As a medical doctor, born light years before the first personal computer was even an Apple in the eye of Steve Jobs, please forgive me if my explanation of how Mark finally outwitted Goliath sounds simple to today's more sophis-ticated and highly trained minds.

The basis for trust on the anonymous Internet was provided by an individual code or password, equivalent to the bank PIN number of which we are all aware. Banks use only a five-digit PIN, not because absent-minded professors are unable to memorise more than five digits, but because the mathematics of encoding five-digit PINs is relatively simple. The systems used by the United States e-commerce community to encode the sixteen or more digits of the credit-card number are so sophisticated and top secret that they enjoy the same level of protection as the United States nuclear arsenal. However, Goliath's weakness was that such programs could only be used by American companies under licence. Mark's target was therefore obvious, but would require more than a slingshot for its solution.

Mark took just three months to develop the necessary software required to produce his slingshot – the 128-bit encryption code, the equal of any other system available in the world. He now had the world's best product for safe information transfer and website verification. But he lacked the final crucial ingredient – global presence.

To achieve that, he had to build an international distribution network and acquire the confidence of those who controlled access to the Internet through their Internet browsers, including Netscape and Microsoft. He concluded that any approach to those who ran these companies was likely to be rebuffed. So he engaged those whom they employed – the computer geeks who wrote their programs but who understood his language. He was successful, and THAWTE was appointed the trusted third party for the provision of secure website certificates by both Netscape and Microsoft. Since his product cost about one third of the North American version, his business grew rapidly.

By the end of 1999, 41 per cent of the global secure-website-certificate market was controlled by THAWTE. Realising that David had grown into a formidable opponent and would eventually dominate the global market, Goliath capitulated and agreed to accept Mark's asking price. On 20 December 1999, Mark signed the contract, barefoot in white shorts and crumpled shirt, in the garden outside his offices in 12 Plein Street, Durbanville. He donated some of that money to form the Shuttleworth Foundation, the goal of which is to assist in the development of education in South Africa.

To fulfil his childhood dream, in late 2001 he travelled to Star City near Moscow to begin his training as a fare-paying cosmonaut for an eight-day trip to the International Space Station. He learnt Russian in less than eight months.

He also personally funded and undertook three medical research projects in space on behalf of South African scientists, including Karen Sharwood, Lara Keytel and Professor Wayne Derman of UCT. His space flight is one of the greatest modern achievements by a South African and received coverage in the international news magazines *Time* and *Newsweek*, and on all the major global television networks. Less well known is that his participation and that of the American, Dennis Tito, helped to ensure the continued viability of the joint Russian and American space programmes.

The space flight represented the exposed, visible tip of what is now the Shuttleworth pyramid of influence. Immediately underneath that exposed tip are the two layers that benefited directly from the flight – his personally funded medical research programme in space, and the layer of warm national pride and reflected prestige that South Africa and the African continent enjoyed during those eight memorable days, when it felt so good to be a South African.

When I think of Mark, I think of the words of Sir Winston Churchill in 1942, when he said of the British victory over the German Afrika Korps at the Second Battle of El Alamein in Egypt: 'Now this is not the end, it is not even the beginning of the end. But it is perhaps the end of the beginning.'

Mark's influence is unique, global and for all time. He stands alone on the threshold, *the* scientific pathfinder for the African Renaissance. He has challenged beliefs in a way I understand and have always respected. Standing before those scientific luminaries at the annual American College of Sports Medicine in Cincinnati in 1996, I was on a similar crusade.

Since the lecture, delivered to 5000 attendees, had been well received, I decided to write it up as a full manuscript. In former times this was the standard practice, but for some reason it no longer is. The article was published a year later in the ACSM journal *Medicine & Science in Sports & Exercise*. Unbeknown to me, the article had been forwarded by the editor to two US exercise scientists, Drs David Bassett and Edward T. Howley, who had been invited to write a rebuttal, which was published alongside my original article. I was surprised, as I had not been informed of this. The editor-in-chief of *Medicine & Science in Sports & Exercise*, Peter Raven, became involved when he wrote, 'In my opinion, the challenge by Noakes is one that we as members of the scientific community, which accepts the concept of maximum oxygen consumption and its measurement as a parameter of physiological function, must address and one that may lead us to accept a revised definition.'

I first learnt about the publication of this article two minutes before I was to give a speech at the 100th-anniversary celebrations of the iconic Finnish runner Paavo Nurmi. I had been invited to Finland to participate in the celebrations and to speak on Nurmi and his importance to the history of running. As I was invited onto the stage to begin my talk, my mischievous Finnish host whispered in my ear: 'Tim, I really liked your article in *Medicine & Science in Sports & Exercise*, but did you read the rebuttal from Bassett and Howley?' With that he thrust the journal into my hands, open at the correct page to reveal the article by Bassett and Howley. I had just enough time to glance at the opening paragraph before

I was up on stage. Fortunately, years of marathon running have taught me how to switch off, focus on the task at hand and not be distracted.

Later, I was able to digest the nature of the challenge posed by Bassett and Howley. Their concluding statements were particularly direct: 'When we weigh the scientific evidence on both sides of the issue, it appears that Hill's views were amazingly accurate. Scientific investigation in the 70 years since Hill have served mainly to reinforce his paradigm and confirm that his scientific "hunches" were correct. Only relatively minor refinements to his theories have been needed. In contrast, Noakes' views are not supported by strong scientific evidence, and they raise numerous paradoxes and unresolved dilemmas.' They were also not above pointing out that Hill was a Nobel Laureate, whereas I come from 'Darkest Africa'.

Fortunately, their rebuttal forced me to go back and reread what Hill had written in 1923, and for this I am forever in their debt. For there, in Hill's own words, I discovered the key to the understanding of exactly how human exercise performance is regulated.

If my doctoral training had not been with Professor Lionel Opie and had not focused on how the function of the heart is controlled and how this differs from skeletal muscle function control, I doubt that I would ever have made the critical connections. It is said that fortune favours the prepared mind. In this case, my mind had been prepared by that sequence of chance events.

THE HEART OF THE MATTER

In Hill's writings I discovered the single paragraph that explained what he really believed. It was subsequently forgotten, because it was so inconvenient. Hill wrote:

> Certain it is that the capacity of the body for muscular exercise
> depends, largely, if not mainly, on the capacity and output of the heart.
> It would obviously be very dangerous for that organ to be able as the
> skeletal muscle is able, to exhaust itself very completely and rapidly, to
> take exercise far in excess of its capacity for recovery ... the enormous
> output of the heart of an able-bodied man, maintained for considerable
> periods during vigorous exercise, requires a large contemporary supply
> of oxygen to meet the demand for energy ... When the oxygen supply
> becomes inadequate, it is probable that the heart rapidly begins to
> diminish its output, so avoiding exhaustion; the evidence for this,
> however, is indirect and an important field of research lies open in the

study of the recovery process in heart muscle, on the lines of which it has been developed in skeletal muscle ... It would seem possible that a deciding factor in the capacity of a man for severe prolonged exercise might often be the efficiency of the coronary circulation.

Hill knew that, if there was indeed this 'plateau' in oxygen delivery to the exercising muscles, then this could only be because the heart had reached its limit. Indeed, the single most important question that must be answered by advocates of the model that Hill proposed in 1923 is: If the heart limits the blood supply to the muscles, then what limits the function of the heart?

Their most common argument is that it has to do with the ability of the heart to stretch and so to fill optimally before it contracts, expelling the blood it contains in its pumping chamber. This, however, is a silly explanation that can easily be disproved, for there is clear evidence that when humans exercise maximally in the upright position, the heart reaches a smaller maximum filling volume than it does when exercising in the supine or lying position. Hence, the heart does not reach its largest filling volume when exercising in the upright position, for example when running or cycling. The 'stretchability' of the heart does not therefore limit either its maximum performance or the VO_2 max.

Hill realised that if the blood supply to the muscles reaches a limiting value, then so too must the blood supply to the heart, since the heart itself is also dependent on its own pumping capacity to provide it with an adequate blood supply. Thus Hill realised that, in his model, the first organ to feel the effects of a limited blood supply would be the heart itself. The immediate result would be a drastic impairment in the heart's ability to pump, which could obviously be catastrophic, since it would lead to a sudden drop in blood supply to the other critical organ, the brain. Without an adequate blood supply to the brain, the athlete exercising maximally would, according to the original model, develop in rapid sequence a reduced blood supply to the heart, muscles and brain, causing three catastrophic outcomes: the onset of chest pain, leading to a heart attack; failure of the exercising muscles to relax, causing them to go into muscle rigor; and unconsciousness. Since maximal exercise does not usually end this way, the model does not explain what actually happens when humans exercise to their limit.

I have often wondered: If this is so obviously true, why has nobody stopped to ask why? As mentioned earlier, the answer, I learnt, is because of a collective gullibility that is the acceptance of a result for which there is not sufficient evidence. The opposite, reverse gullibility, is the refusal to accept as true a result that is supported by adequate evidence.

As I reread Hill's work, I discovered what he had actually written. He believed that there had to be a mechanism in the body (either in the heart muscle or in the nervous system) that caused a 'slowing of the circulation' as soon as the oxygen supply to the heart (and exercising muscles) reached the maximum that he had described. He called this mechanism a 'governor' – not in the sense of a politician, but as a regulator that controls or governs the maximal output of a mechanical device. The key function of a governor is that it prevents a system from ever going full-out. Instead, a governor always ensures that the system has reserves so that it reaches a false 'maximum'. In this way, a governed biological system cannot fail catastrophically as the original Hill model predicts.

Hill and his colleagues therefore correctly realised that, even if the ultimate limits of exercise are set by the cardiovascular system, there must be a mechanism, other than a lack of oxygen supply to the muscles, that will terminate exercise before the heart is damaged and the athlete collapses.

So perhaps Hill's greatest insight was the following:

It would seem probable … that the heart is able to regulate its output, to some extent, in accordance with the degree of saturation of the arterial blood, either of that which reaches it through the coronary vessels or by some reflex in other organs produced by a deficient oxygen supply … We suggest that in the body (either in the heart muscle itself or in the nervous system), there is some mechanism which causes a slowing of the circulation as soon as a serious degree of unsaturation occurs, and vice versa. This mechanism would tend to act as a 'governor', maintaining a high degree of saturation of blood.

Hill should therefore be remembered for this crucial insight but, erroneously, scientists developed the belief that it is the functioning of the heart that determines our maximum exercise performance.

So, for the past eighty-eight years, physiologists have been promoting the theory that oxygen transport and its use alone determines the maximum exercise capacity in humans. This, despite the fact that Hill and his colleagues never conclusively proved this, or even provided substantive evidence that it might be so. For example, there is only one laboratory in the world that consistently finds that the output of the heart reaches a 'plateau' or maximum value immediately before the athlete chooses to terminate the exercise. Everyone else finds the opposite: that the output of the heart rises linearly with increasing work rate and continues to rise to the point where the athlete chooses to terminate the exercise.

So, the true biological meaning of the 'plateau phenomenon', central to the Hill theory that has been vigorously defended for so long, is still unknown. Our work suggests that it is little more than an artefact of exercise that is as likely to be present during submaximal exercise as it is at the moment the exercise terminates. These uncertainties of exactly what the plateau means convinced me that it would be an unproductive use of our time to focus on that particular issue.

My moment of inspiration came when I finally discovered Hill's description of the governor. I instantly realised that the governor would not 'slow the circulation' by acting directly on the heart. Instead, my training in Opie's cardiology laboratory had taught me that the way to protect the stressed heart is by reducing the work of the whole body – the best way to do that during exercise is to reduce the work of the skeletal muscles. For as my other hero, Professor Christiaan Barnard, famously wrote: 'The heart is just a pump.' So during exercise the demand on the heart is set by the work of the exercising muscles. Thus, the way to protect the heart from overexertion is to control the amount of work that the exercising muscles are allowed to do.

The moment I read Hill's explanation of the governor, I also 'knew' that the only effective governor would be one that exists in the brain and that regulates the exercise performance by controlling how much muscle can be active during exercise. We call this phenomenon 'muscle recruitment'.

Thus the central governor theory, which was conceptualised at that moment, predicts that the amount of skeletal muscle that the brain chooses to recruit or activate at any time will always be regulated to ensure that the welfare of all the organs of the body are protected during exercise. So we realised that exercise is a brain-regulated behaviour, the primary goal of which is always survival and never an absolutely maximal effort. This is very different from the Hill model, which predicts that the body will allow a truly maximal effort, and that such an effort can exceed the capacity of one or more of the body's organs, causing the catastrophic failure that we recognise as 'fatigue' and 'exhaustion'.

Together with my colleagues, at first Professors Alan St Clair Gibson, Frank Marino and Vicki Lambert and, more recently, a growing list of South Africans, including Drs Ross Tucker, Elske Schabort, Laurie Rauch and Jeroen Swart, as well as Professor Dan Stein and foreign visiting scientists Eduardo Fontes, Dom Micklewright, Tim Lindsay, Fernando Beltrami, Fabian Bassett and Rodrigo Hohl, we have developed an exercise model that proposes that subconscious processes in the brain are responsible for the regulation of exercise performance.

So it was that during my time with the Proteas cricket team in Pakistan for the 1996 Cricket World Cup, when I began to plan my J.B. Wolffe Memorial Lecture, I first formulated the beginning concepts of what would ultimately evolve into the central governor model. It seemed obvious to me then that exercise had to be a *regulated* process that terminated *before* the body reached any limits. In the J.B. Wolffe lecture, I said the following:

> … an alternate physiological model is proposed in which skeletal muscle contractile activity is regulated by a series of central, predominantly neural, and peripheral, predominantly chemical regulators that act to prevent the development of organ failure or even death in both health and disease and under demanding environmental conditions … Regulation of skeletal muscle contractile function by central mechanisms would prevent the development of hypotension and myocardial ischemia during exercise in persons with heart failure, or hypothermia during exercise in the heat, and of cerebral hypoxia during exercise in extreme altitude. The challenge for future generations of exercise physiologists is to identify how the body anticipates the possibility of organ damage and evokes the appropriate control mechanism(s) at the appropriate instant.

The next key event was the realisation, thanks to the rebuttal of my J.B. Wolffe lecture by Bassett and Howley, that the system of regulation would be through a 'governor' in the brain.

In retrospect it is often difficult to be certain of the exact origin and sequence of these ideas. I do know that the first time I properly presented the idea of the central governor was at the Fourth International Olympic Committee Congress on Sports Sciences held in Monaco on 22 to 26 October 1997. I was invited to give a keynote lecture titled 'Training and Care of Athletes – Current Concepts and Technologies'. This was the perfect title, as it allowed me to speak on just about anything.

The talk I gave there had its origins, in turn, in another talk I'd delivered in Nairobi in September 1997. The title of that presentation was 'Why do Africans run so swiftly: A challenge for African scientists'. The focus of the talk was my attempt to explain why the Kenyans are such exceptional runners. As I finalised the talk on the veranda of my hotel in Nairobi, I realised that many scientists have offered different explanations for the success of the Kenyans. Each has focused on a single organ or part of the body – always the part that fell within the discipline in which the particular scientist was an expert. So biomechanists, for instance, were keen to claim that Kenyans run faster than all others (except perhaps the Ethiopians) simply because they have long, thin legs that act like springs, propelling them faster and more efficiently than, especially, Caucasians, who, according to the Kenyans, have legs that are as thick as the trunks of oak trees. Cardiologists 'know' that Kenyans run so fast because they have large, 'stretchable' hearts able to pump more blood faster than any other group of runners, while psychologists tell us that Kenyans outlast all others because of the tough culture in which they are reared and in which they must not flinch or show any trace of discomfort when they are publicly circumcised. Muscle physiologists, by contrast, ascribe the Kenyans' success to their muscle-fibre composition – Kenyans, we are told, can run faster because they have a different muscle-fibre composition from all other runners. The geneticists argue that it is all due to the natural selection of an isolated population that became great runners because of their predilection for cattle raiding: according to this theory, those who could not run fast were unable to accumulate enough cattle to marry and so preserve their genes, or else they were unable to escape the spears of those whose cattle they had recently acquired. And so on.

I realised then that it is improbable that the success of the Kenyans can be attributed to any one single factor, and that the ultimate explanation would be that all are important collectively. A better explanation might be that all of these factors are contributory, but all are under the control of a single regulatory mechanism – the brain.

At the IOC meeting in Monaco in 1997, after my talk in Nairobi, I presented this theory for the first time: that human exercise performance could not be explained by looking at each individual component separately, but that all worked together under the ultimate control of the brain.

As a result of that talk, I was invited to speak on the same topic in Finland in November 1998. There I presented a lecture titled 'Limits of human endurance performance: what and where are they?' The paper was subsequently published in the *Scandinavian Journal of Medicine & Science in Sports* under the title 'Physiological models to understand exercise fatigue and the adaptations that predict or enhance athletic performance'. This has become one of the most frequently cited articles that I have written. Its core conclusion is that exercise physiologists have used many different models to explain the factors determining exercise performance under different exercise conditions. The article shows, however, 'that many findings are incompatible with the predictions of one or more of these models. Rather than simply continuing to accept these inconsistencies uncritically, the modern generation of exercise physiologists should challenge old dogmas and so approach more closely the unattainable truth.'

Emboldened by these successes, our team realised that it was time to go back to the beast – the American College of Sports Medicine – to present a more complete explanation of the central governor model.

Thus, at the 2001 ACSM annual meeting in Baltimore, Maryland, together with my colleagues Alan St Clair Gibson and Vicki Lambert, we presented a series of lectures that described exactly how we perceived the central governor to work. The presentations were extraordinarily well received and many people hung around for almost an hour after the talk. Perhaps they realised that they had witnessed a watershed moment in the understanding of human exercise performance.

Our next task was to write up and publish all this novel material. In 2004 and 2005 we published a series of five articles in the *British Journal of Sports Medicine*. All, which have become instant classics, describe in a more complete way exactly what the central governor model entails.

In its simplest form, our theory proposes that (i) physical activity is controlled by a central governor in the brain; (ii) the multiple organ systems in the human body function as a complex system during exercise; (iii) no single physiological system is ever used to its maximal capacity; and (iv) the goal of the brain is to ensure that the exercise terminates while all bodily systems remain in homeostasis so that none is pushed beyond its normal functional range.

To achieve this, the brain uses feedback from multiple physiological systems in order to control the extent of muscle recruitment during exercise. This leads to a continuously altering pacing system in which athletes regularly change the intensity at which they exercise – indeed, we now know that this happens on a stride-to-stride basis in running or with each pedal stroke in cycling. In essence, with each new stride in running the brain must make one of four choices: continue at the same pace, slow down, speed up or stop altogether. The outcome of each decision is the pacing strategy that the athlete chooses.

Finally, my colleague Professor St Clair Gibson added the remarkable insight that the sensation of fatigue is simply the conscious expression of these regulatory control mechanisms in the brain. Thus, we now believe that fatigue is purely an emotion that the brain uses to ensure that the exercise is performed within the constraints of the body's ability without threatening its homeostasis.

Our central governor theory reopened this debate and shed new light on a belief that had been misinterpreted in the exercise sciences since 1923.

BRAINLESS PHYSIOLOGY

There are, I believe, two reasons why our ideas of a central governor, while appearing eminently logical at least to me, have not been embraced by more scientists as rapidly as I might have expected. The first is that many scientists have received considerable research funding based on the belief that the Hill model is correct. Some of these scientists act on the editorial boards of important scientific journals, so they can exert significant influence on what is published in them. They and others also influence the way in which research funding is distributed. So if they don't think much of the central-governor theory, they can make it difficult for studies that support the concept to be published or to be properly funded. Science is not necessarily as transparent and honest as it might be. As is so often the case, human narcissism and the need to be right frequently get in the way.

The second reason for resistance is that many exercise physiologists do not like the idea of subconscious physiological processes that function 'in anticipation' of what is going to happen in the future, not simply in response to what has already happened. They do not want to believe that perhaps not all aspects of our exercise performance are under the exclusive control of our conscious thoughts. Prediction of future biological events in our bodies cannot be decided in the conscious part of our brain that resides in the higher brain centres. Instead, these decisions must be made in the archaic parts of our brains that are not under our conscious control and that have evolved over hundreds of millions of years as we developed from less complex organisms. In these parts of the brain, all biological controls act subconsciously (or so we currently believe).

Yet we are proposing a theory in which a central brain governor can anticipate what is going to happen and, as a result, can produce the appropriate behaviour to ensure that the exercise can be completed safely. Our earliest evidence for this anticipatory response was the established human response to exercise at increasing altitude, in which the oxygen content of the air is reduced.

According to the traditional theory, a lack of oxygen in the inhaled air at altitude causes the exercising muscles to become anaerobic at a lower exercise intensity than it does at sea level. As a result, the higher-than-expected blood lactic acid concentrations cause the muscles to stop working at a lower exercise intensity at altitude than at sea level – an easy explanation that does not need further debate. The only problem is that the data collected on climbers at very high altitudes does not fit this explanation.

Instead, blood lactic acid concentrations in climbers approaching the summit of Mount Everest are no higher than they are at sea level, yet their fatigue is extreme. Nor do their hearts make any attempt to pump more of this oxygen-starved blood to their muscles. In fact, climbers reach the summit of Mount Everest with heart rates of less than 120 beats per minute. Simply by jogging up a steep incline at sea level, the heart rate can be elevated to a similar extent; this would not leave a person close to death, as is the case with climbers on the summit of Mount Everest.

FIGURE 26

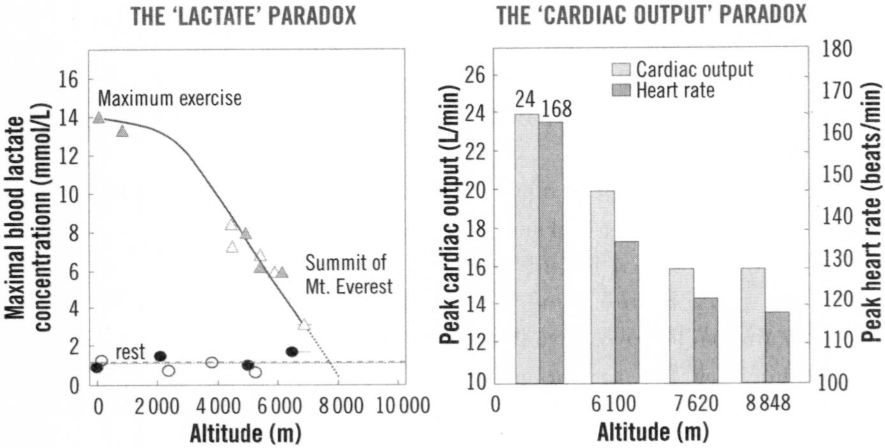

Blood lactate (lactic acid) concentrations at the end of maximal exercise (left panel) and maximal heart (cardiac) output and heart rate become progressively lower when tested at progressively higher altitudes. Neither can be explained by the Hill model, which requires that fatigue occurs only after muscle lactate concentrations have risen sufficiently to 'poison' skeletal muscle function. The heart should also always reach a maximal output regardless of environmental conditions if its function is always simply to supply the muscles with all the oxygen they can get.

Surely this is paradoxical? I have called this the 'lactic acid and cardiac output paradox of high altitude'. It is a paradox that many exercise scientists wish would simply disappear, so they tend either to ignore it or to offer an explanation that is known to be wrong.

The traditional Hill explanation is that the heart's sole function is to do whatever it can to ensure that the needs of the muscles are properly looked after. So in a hypoxic (oxygen-deprived) environment, the oxygen demands of the muscles must become the overriding responsibility of the heart. Thus, the heart must do all in its power to provide the oxygen-starved muscles with all the oxygen it can muster. This means that during maximal exercise at extreme altitude, the heart's output must reach at least the same maximal value that it can at sea level.

However, the finding that the heart's output during maximal exercise actually falls with increasing altitude conclusively establishes, at least in the minds of those whose understanding is not dictated by a historical dogma, that some mechanism must actively 'constrain' muscle activity at altitude, thereby ensuring that the exercise intensity is never so great that it threatens the body's delicate oxygen homeostasis.

All the evidence therefore is that maximal exercise at altitude is terminated before anaerobiosis develops in the heart, the muscles and probably also the brain. It is the central governor in the brain that ensures that this outcome is produced.

The difference between our theory and what has long been accepted in the exercise sciences is as follows. Our theory sees the functioning of the body during exercise as a regulated process, the aim of which is to prevent the development of bodily damage under all circumstances. So the governor does not, as Hill suggested, reduce the pumping capacity of the heart during exercise, but rather the work output of the muscles. Any reduction in the work output of the muscles would naturally also reduce the work of the heart, thereby protecting the heart from damage. But it is not solely the heart that must be protected.

Perhaps of greater importance, we now realise, is the oxygenation of the brain. There is a growing body of evidence to show that the brain is acutely sensitive to any fall in its own oxygenation, or even the threat of a possible fall. In response to any threat to its own oxygenation, the brain reduces the rate at which oxygen is being used by the body, particularly by the exercising muscles, by reducing the amount of skeletal muscle that it allows to be active. Of course, the immediate effect of reducing the extent of skeletal muscle recruitment is that the exercise intensity will fall, since there is less muscle actively producing power. Conversely, under conditions in which homeostasis is not threatened, it may be possible to increase the level of muscle recruitment and so increase the exercise intensity.

In contrast, the traditional model is based on the belief that exercise terminates only after one or more bodily limitations have been exceeded; in other words, after the system has already failed. These 'failure' models assert that the failure of oxygen delivery to the exercising muscles causes lactic acid to accumulate in the muscles, leading to a progressive impairment of muscle contraction. This leads to another misconception, namely that high lactic acid levels occur in muscles whenever the muscles' demand for oxygen exceeds the heart's ability to supply them with sufficient oxygen. As a result, generations of runners have been led to believe that the fatigue they encounter near the end of a race is due to high levels of lactic acid.

The reality is that the oxygen requirement for running is determined by the running speed. To run faster, more oxygen is needed, in direct proportion to the speed at which the athlete runs. No amount of training will change this relationship. It is also true that the faster one runs, the higher the blood lactic acid concentrations. We now know that this is not because the muscles are becoming 'anaerobic', but merely because they are contracting rapidly, as rapid muscular contractions require that most of the energy comes from the breakdown of carbohydrate sources in the muscles. And the immediate result of rapid carbohydrate combustion by the exercising muscles is the production of large amounts of lactic acid (for reasons that are still not fully understood).

So it turns out that while blood lactic acid concentrations may indeed be quite elevated in vigorous sporting events that last for up to fifteen or so minutes, longer events like the marathon do not produce high blood lactic acid concentrations. So the fatigue experienced by marathon runners has nothing to do with elevated blood lactic acid concentrations.

As explained in **Figure 26 on page 318**, every person has an individual limit to the amount of oxygen he or she can absorb in one minute – think of it as an individual performance fingerprint, unique to each person.

We know that world-class athletes belong to a physiologically select group whose maximum oxygen-uptake values are as much as 60 per cent greater than the values in average athletes. We accept that this difference is largely genetically determined. Great athletes start with high VO_2 max values, and, when they train, their VO_2 max values increase faster than those of average athletes. In other words, as the eminent Swedish physiologist Per-Olof Astrand said, 'To be an Olympic champion, I am convinced one must choose one's parents carefully.'

Another important discovery that advanced our understanding of the factors regulating exercise performance occurred in 1962, when a group of Scandinavian physiologists discovered that exhaustion in marathon runners could be linked to the depletion of almost all the glycogen (the primary fuel of muscles) stores in the muscles, and that the rate at which the muscles burn their glycogen stores depends on the intensity of the exercise and the fitness of the athlete.

This means that the central governor must also ensure that the exercise is never either so prolonged or so intense that complete muscle-glycogen depletion develops. The stores of muscle glycogen are limited, but can be increased by exercise and dietary manipulation.

The body has two major muscle fibre types – slow twitch (ST) and fast twitch (FT). This classification is based on the speed at which the different muscle fibres can contract. ST muscles are perfectly designed for prolonged exercise, like marathon running, while FT muscles burn up energy more quickly and therefore lend themselves to the shorter distances, such as sprinting. In fact, my colleague Dr Tertius Kohn has recently shown that the speed at which athletic mammals like lions, antelope and cheetahs can run is a function of the proportion of FT fibres that their limb muscles contain. According to this analysis, humans, including even Usain Bolt, are really quite pedestrian sprinters (compared to these athletic mammals), because our muscles contain too many ST muscle fibres. These ST fibres also burn fats more readily than they do glycogen, and fats are available from the bloodstream in unlimited quantities. This makes ST fibres especially well adapted for endurance running, an activity in which humans are without match in the animal kingdom.

So, to sum up, the make-up of an elite marathon runner is based on the genetic endowment of large maximum-oxygen consumption and a particular muscle fibre composition, among many other important factors. The rate of muscle-glycogen depletion depends on the intensity of the exercise, but training increases the capacity of the body to use fats even in high-intensity exercise, thus slowing the rate at which the limited muscle-glycogen stores are used. But all runners are not born equal, and poor genetics cannot be trained to world-class performance. You either have it or you don't; or, as they say, 'You can't put in what God left out.'

However, what we all do have is a capacity for metabolic adaptation that we call fitness. The degree to which training will allow us to increase our performance, however, is set by the extent to which those adaptations allow us to exercise harder while staying within metabolic equilibrium or homeostasis. Since the brain 'knows' the exercise intensity that will exceed the metabolic capacity of our bodies, it will not allow that exercise intensity to be achieved. For an elite marathon runner, this will be a running speed in excess of twenty kilometres per hour that can be sustained for a period of two hours; for the rest of us, the running speed at which a threatened metabolic failure occurs will be much slower – and so our brains will ensure that we are not ever allowed to run anywhere near as fast for such a prolonged period.

So, in my opinion, the real failure of the 'failure' models is that they leave the brain out of this entire process.

Since 1923, an exercise physiology has been taught that excludes any contribution by the brain. It's all been what I call a brainless physiology in which the body is driven to exhaustion and failure without any attempt of the brain to ensure that this does not happen. This is the catastrophe model of exercise physiology. I believe that the debate has to move from this concept of catastrophe to one of complexity – the complex regulation of exercise performance specifically to ensure that no such catastrophe can occur.

For nearly 100 years people have been told that they get tired because their muscles get tired. That's in all the textbooks on exercise physiology and athletic coaching everywhere. I always ask my students, 'Okay, what causes fatigue? Is it lactic acid?' And they all say, 'Yes, Professor Noakes.' Students everywhere around the world are still being taught this. But it's just not true. If this were in fact the case, surely humans would continue to exercise until their exercising muscles finally ran out of *all* energy and reached the point of muscle rigor – the perpetual state of muscular contraction that occurs in all muscles shortly after we die?

The reason that this does not happen is that the final control of exercise performance resides in the brain.

HOW THE CENTRAL GOVERNOR WORKS

You exercise, you get tired and eventually you stop because you are fatigued. It seems simple enough. But how does this happen?

The central governor in the brain monitors the state of metabolic balance in all the critical organs of the body – the brain, the heart, the liver, the skeletal muscles and the blood, among many others. At the onset of exercise, the brain decides on intensity of exercise (or pace) that the body, in its current physiological state, will be able to sustain for the duration of the planned activity. Thus, if the exercise is to be for only ten kilometres, the brain will allow a much faster initial pace than if the distance to be covered is 100 kilometres. It does this by allowing a large mass of muscle to be activated, or recruited, from the start. This larger muscle mass can then produce more force with each muscular contraction, and hence a faster running speed. Indeed, it is one of the great failings of the Hill model that it has promoted the idea that we run faster only because our hearts pump more blood to the muscles. In fact, we run faster because we recruit more muscle fibres in our active muscles. So recruitment always comes before, not after, any increase in blood flow to the active muscles.

Then if the brain detects the presence of anything that will impair the exercise performance, it will modify the pace by reducing the amount of muscle that it recruits to ensure that a slower pace is chosen right from the start of the exercise.

Alternatively, if the athlete's conscious control tries to override this to allow the athlete to run faster, the brain will ensure that it causes the symptoms of discomfort and fatigue to rise at an accelerated rate. As a result, the athlete will ultimately slow down as the discomfort rises to a level that is no longer acceptable.

Once the athlete begins the exercise, symptoms of fatigue and discomfort rise as a direct function of the duration of the expected exercise bout. I discovered this unexpected truth in 2003, when reading a paper written by J. Baldwin, R.J. Snow and others from Australia. I had pondered for a while the timing of the increase in the sensations of fatigue that develop during prolonged exercise. From personal experience in marathon and ultramarathon running, I believed that the sensations of fatigue rise as an exponential function of the duration of exercise – that is, they rise much more rapidly near the end of the exercise than they do at the start. Surprisingly, no one had ever addressed this question.

After reading this paper, I realised that the authors had provided the data to answer this question but had *not asked the question*, so they had missed the truth contained in those specific data. In that study, the authors measured the ratings of perceived exertion (RPE) – a measure of the fatigue that the subjects experienced – in a group of trained cyclists exercising for as long as they could, having started out with muscles that were either full of glycogen or depleted of glycogen. Remarkably, this was one of the first studies to report RPE values measured every few minutes during exercise lasting more than sixty minutes. Usually the RPE is measured during exercise of short duration, since it is traditionally believed that the RPE is simply a measure of the *intensity* of exercise. I was able to show that this historic interpretation is wrong, as the RPE is actually a measure of the duration of exercise that still remains, or the duration of exercise that has already been completed.

Plotting the Australian data on a sheet of scrap paper, I became increasingly excited as each new data point that I added fell on a straight line. Thus my analysis showed that their RPE values rose as a linear function of the duration of exercise, but that the rate of rise was slower when subjects exercised for longer, which occurred when they began exercise with muscles filled with glycogen. However, when both exercise bouts were expressed in terms of 100 per cent of the exercise duration, the rate of rise in RPE was identical.

Thus I was able to establish a fundamental biological truth that had not been recognised previously – that the RPE is a measure of the duration of the exercise bout and not its intensity, as originally described by Dr Gunnar Borg, who developed the RPE scale. The higher the exercise intensity, however, the

FIGURE 27

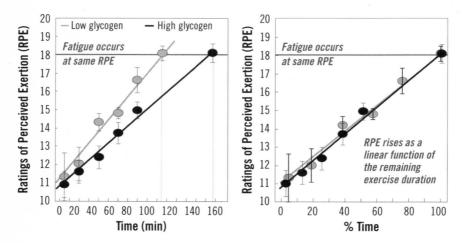

A plot of the data from the study of Baldwin et al., published in 2003, showed that, regardless of whether subjects began exercise with low or high muscle-glycogen concentrations, there was a linear increase in their ratings of perceived exertion (RPE) with exercise duration (left panel). However, the rate of rise was higher during exercise that began with lower muscle-glycogen concentrations. When the RPEs for the two exercise conditions were plotted against percentage of total exercise time, the data fall along the same line. These data therefore suggest (i) that the maximum RPE that can be sustained determines the point at which the athlete will choose to terminate the exercise and (ii) that the rate at which the RPE increases during exercise may determine the duration of exercise. Furthermore, this interpretation suggests that the duration of prolonged exercise may be set (by the subconscious brain) and hence is known at or shortly after the onset of exercise.

shorter the exercise duration. As a result, the RPE is higher and increases more rapidly during exercise at a higher intensity.

There were two important intellectual consequences of this finding. First, it established that the brain uses the RPE as the ultimate regulator of the exercise performance, as once the RPE value exceeds about eighteen units, most athletes will stop exercising. This confirmed that Professor Alan St Clair Gibson had been correct when he proposed that fatigue is simply an emotion generated in the brain to ensure that the exercise will always terminate before there is a catastrophic biological failure. Second, the fact that the RPE rises as a linear function of the exercise duration proves that, either before the exercise begins or shortly after it starts, the brain already knows when the exercise is going to terminate, for before the exercise bout begins, each individual's brain knows the maximum RPE that it will tolerate. By determining the rate at which the RPE rises to reach that maximum, the individual's brain shows that it 'knows' how long each exhaustive exercise bout will last.

As a result, we now know that the following takes place during each exercise bout that ends in exhaustion:

- The body experiences progressively more fatigue as a linear function of the duration of exercise that has been completed or that still remains. Like pain, this sensation of fatigue is generated exclusively by the brain.

- The sensations of discomfort that are experienced are unrelated to the real state of the body at the time that the fatigue is sensed. We know this, as the degree of fatigue that is experienced is independent of the actual distance covered. Thus the sensation of fatigue experienced at, say, nine kilometres is quite different in races of ten, twenty-one, forty-two and 100 kilometres, even though the muscles have done the same amount of work in covering the distance. (This is because the energy cost of running a set distance is independent of the speed of running. Running faster simply gets you to the finish quicker – but the total amount of energy expended is the same and is independent of how fast you reach the finish.)

- The amount of work that the brain will allow the body to do is regulated to ensure that exercise always terminates before there is a catastrophic failure of any of the bodily organs. This regulation is provided by the progressive rise in the RPE and other sensations during exercise. When the RPE reaches the maximum value that the athlete is prepared to sustain, the athlete has reached the finish line and the exercise will terminate.

Exercise capacity is therefore a process, coordinated subconsciously by the brain and limited by the maximum capacity of each athlete's body to maintain homeostasis in all bodily systems during exercise at different intensities and for different durations.

The central governor predicts that all exercise will end before damage occurs. For this to happen, the brain needs to know before the exercise begins when that exercise bout will end. With this information, the brain can set the appropriate exercise intensity that will use up the available fuel reserves and generate heat at the correct rate so that the exercise ends before the body's energy reserves run out or it overheats.

The brain does this by establishing the correct pacing strategy early on in the exercise session. This pacing strategy is established on the basis of the athlete's physiological potential, the expected duration of the activity, the environmental conditions, and the athlete's previous experience of that particular type of exercise.

When looked at this way, the explanation of the exercising potential of humans enters an entirely new dimension. This leads to the obvious question: What causes fatigue?

THE CAUSE OF FATIGUE

Anyone who has ever exercised has experienced it. You get to the point where your lungs are gasping for air, your muscles are in pain and your whole body is screaming at you to stop. Physically, you are uncertain how you are going to be able to continue.

But what if I told you that all of this is taking place in your mind and is pretty much unrelated to what is going on in your muscles and heart?

For centuries, physiologists have believed that fatigue is a physical process in which the muscles in the body simply hit a physical limit, run out of their fuel – be it oxygen or glycogen – and then flood themselves with toxins like lactic acid, and this forces an end to the torture.

We now believe that fatigue is purely an emotion affected by factors such as motivation and drive, memory of prior activity, and other emotions, such as anger and fear.

The problem we face when we study fatigue is that it is defined in many different ways by different experts. For example, doctors might say that fatigue is a debilitating consequence of a number of different systemic diseases or nutritional deficits. Neurophysiologists might say that fatigue is caused by a reduction in motor commands to the active muscles from the brain, resulting in a decline in the amount of force that the muscles can produce. As a result, the exercise performance is impaired – that is, fatigue has developed.

Exercise physiologists might say that fatigue is an acute impairment of exercise performance, which leads to an eventual inability to produce maximum muscular-force output as a consequence of either the accumulation of 'poisonous' chemicals – the products of increased metabolism in the muscles during exercise – or because the muscles simply run out of fuel – substrate depletion.

All are very impressive definitions of fatigue, but none explains clearly to the suffering marathon athlete why he becomes progressively tired during a marathon race and why, on occasion, he is suddenly so tired that he hits what has been called 'the wall'.

We *do* know that we don't know how this conscious feeling of fatigue is created, or in which parts of the brain it originates. We are finding that many areas of the brain are involved, but we haven't yet found any specific areas that might qualify as a central governor. Part of our evidence that a central regulator is involved in this process comes from an early study in which we measured the electromyographic (EMG) activity in the *vastus lateralis* (the largest part of the quadriceps or front thigh muscle) of cyclists during a 100-kilometre time trial in which subjects were also asked to complete sprints of one and four kilometres at quite regular intervals. The EMG activity is a measure of the extent to which the brain is activating or recruiting the muscles in the legs.

We found that EMG activity fell progressively during the sprint sections of the time trial. This proved a clear difference between fatigue in the muscles – so-called peripheral fatigue; the kind that Hill believed caused the termination of maximal exercise – and a centrally regulated fatigue that originates in the brain and in which the brain simply reduces the amount of muscle that it is prepared to activate as the exercise progresses.

For if the muscles become fatigued according to the peripheral mechanisms favoured by the catastrophists, the brain should simply go on recruiting more and more fresh muscle fibres to assist the fatiguing ones. This would maintain a constant output without any evidence of failure and fatigue. When this happens, there must be a progressive increase in EMG activity in the exercising muscles. But the opposite occurred – EMG activity in the leg muscles fell progressively, indicating that the brain had chosen to reduce the overall number of muscle fibres that were activated, not to increase their recruitment. To me, this was clear evidence that the traditional theory of peripheral fatigue was wrong. Instead, it seemed obvious that the brain was regulating the performance, presumably to ensure that a catastrophe did not occur. Even muscle biopsies have disproved the theory that the muscles run out of any sort of fuel, causing fatigue.

In other studies, we and others have shown that the levels of glycogen and adenosine triphosphate (ATP) – the immediate source of energy for muscle contraction – do indeed decline with exercise, but they never completely run out. Even at the end of a marathon, muscle glycogen levels do approach zero but never actually get there, and ATP levels are never lower than 60 to 80 per cent of the resting values. While the glycogen levels may be low, muscles still have a large reserve of other fuels to draw on, particularly fat, at the end of a marathon.

Add to this the fact that during exercise the brain never recruits 100 per cent of its available muscle fibres, and probably closer to 30 to 50 per cent during marathon and ultramarathon races, and the conclusion seems quite obvious that athletes still have plenty left in the tank by the time they start feeling fatigued.

The presence of this substantial reserve also explains why the world's leading athletes can produce the legendary end spurt to win a race, and often run their fastest in the last kilometre of a marathon.

How would this be possible if fatigued muscles were 'poisoning' themselves with lactic acid and other noxious chemicals to force the body to quit? If this were the case, runners would slow down to the point where they would find it impossible to walk to the finish line, never mind sprint for it.

Our theory is that when athletes slow their pace near the end of a race, they do so because the brain chooses to reduce the amount of muscle that it is prepared to activate in the exercising muscles. As a result, the exercise continues, but at a lower work rate, as a smaller muscle mass is active. This explains why exercise can continue at a lower intensity when the athlete is unable to sustain a higher intensity.

We propose that fatigue is a combination of the brain reading various physiological, subconscious and conscious signals and using these to pace the muscles in order to ensure that the body does not burn out before the finish line is reached. I am not saying that what takes place physiologically in the muscles is irrelevant. What I am saying is that what takes place physiologically in the muscles is not what causes fatigue. Instead, metabolic and other changes in the muscles provide part of the information that the brain needs to be able to calculate the appropriate pace for events of different distances and in different environmental conditions.

For reasons that I still do not understand, the brain (or, at least, my brain) always wanted me to quit when I had covered about 66 per cent of the race distance. I gather that this is not an uncommon response. I still do not know why my brain developed this almost overwhelming desire to give up (as described in the first chapter), since it does not seem to make biological sense, as once I had overcome these negative thoughts I would be able to continue to the finish without suffering a catastrophic failure. So what was the purpose of these symptoms?

What I do know is that since understanding the nature of these regulatory processes in the central governor, I no longer suffer from this specific symptom of wanting to quit either in training or racing. Others report the same. Thus, the desire to quit is purely a mental construct and has no biological reason. (Except when the sensations are caused by a disease process, as sometimes happens when athletes develop heart attacks during exercise, for example. But the nature of the symptoms caused by such diseases are quite different from the sensations of fatigue.)

Because the central governor works according to its knowledge of when exercise will begin and end, its pacing strategy becomes very important. With the brain knowing the end is near, the central governor allows the body to tap into its reserves, giving the athlete that ability to 'dig deep' and produce that classic end spurt.

Sir Roger Bannister could well have been speaking about the central governor when he wrote of the sensations he experienced at the end of his epic run to break the four-minute-mile barrier. 'My body had long since exhausted all its energy,' he said, 'but it went on running just the same. The physical overdraft came only from greater will power.'

The really exciting new developments on the central governor concern the pacing strategy of the body. The ability of the mind to set itself an exercise target and produce symptoms of fatigue accordingly, and the possible manipulation of this, fascinates me. Pacing is a really interesting athletic phenomenon. Despite increased sensations of fatigue, we can always continue, but at a slower pace. So our new definition of fatigue is:

> ... a (central brain) perception that is based on the sum of the sensory feedback from a variety of organs to the central governor, and which is expressed physically as an alteration in pacing strategy (running speed) caused by a reduction in the muscle mass activated by the motor cortex in the brain.

Fatigue is merely the emotional expression of the subjective symptoms that develop as these subconscious controls wage a fierce battle with the conscious mind to ensure that the conscious ultimately submits to the superior will of the subconscious – and the athlete reaches the finish line tired but still alive.

Ultimately, this is a battle in the mind for the soul of the body.

23 | The Power of the Mind

Polly Shorts. It doesn't *sound* terrifying, but to a runner in the 'up' run of the Comrades Marathon, this 2.5-kilometre hill on the outskirts of Pietermaritz-burg is the most difficult part of the epic race. It is to the Comrades runner what the Hillary Step on Mount Everest is to the mountaineer. As Bruce Fordyce explains, 'It is very steep and has a number of deceptive bends, each beguilingly promising the summit and then crushing the hopes of the broken runner.'

Fordyce will tell you that Polly Shorts is by no means the toughest hill in the Comrades. 'Fields Hill is the monster, and Botha's Hill, Ashburton and Inchanga are the monster's offspring,' he says. 'All of these hills are longer, steeper and far worse than Polly Shorts. It is, however, the sadistic positioning of Polly Shorts that makes it so tough ... Polly Shorts is positioned at eighty kilometres, or fifty miles, and the running spirit is very low when arriving at the hill ... For lesser runners, the sight of the hill can break them ... Everyone suffers on Polly Shorts.'

Despite these comments, in the 1983 Comrades I watched Bruce Fordyce run Polly Shorts as if it were flat, and I wrote at the time:

> The television broadcast bore witness to one of those supreme
> moments in sport: a vision of athletic perfection that is unlikely to be
> equalled. I am happy to admit that watching Bruce running up Polly
> Shorts, with the strains of Vangelis's famous music in the background,
> moved me to tears of joy. Never before had the Comrades seen such
> poetic running, nor had such fast running ever been achieved so
> effortlessly in the last third of the race. Bruce's running expressed an
> intangible beauty: the now great runner, oblivious of the camera,

content with his own most private thoughts, proving that man is beautifully made and indeed the wonder of the universe.

I am constantly amazed at the dominant role played by the brain in determining exercise performance. As mentioned, Plato was definitely on to something when he instructed, 'Avoid exercising either the mind or body without the other, and so preserve an equal and healthy balance between the two.'

I believe that the mind remains the most important frontier for exercise science and, indeed, for medicine, in this new millennium – specifically, an understanding of the way in which the central governor works and the nature of the psychological tricks it plays in order to control us during exercise.

Every single sporting competition, be it a cricket, soccer, rugby or tennis match, or an endurance event like the Comrades Marathon, is influenced by the actions of the brain and the annoying doubts that it expresses, always at the wrong time. The great athletes are those who do not allow doubt to enter their minds; or, if doubt does enter, are able to control their thoughts and not allow them to interfere with performance.

One who understands the importance of the mental component of sport is South Africa's greatest sportsman of the twentieth century, golfer Gary Player. He has written:

> The mental aspect of sport is very important and in many cases the most critical factor in winning. I may not have been the most talented player of my generation, but I was the best prepared both mentally and physically. I loved pressure. I fed off it. I revelled in it. I knew that when the time came for me to hit the shot or sink the putt I needed to, to win, I could do it. The thought of failure was never in my mind – I wouldn't let myself think that way. If the conditions were horrible I would tell myself that I would love playing in the rain and the wind and I would have a great round. When I heard my competitors complaining about how hard it was to play in those conditions, I knew that I had an advantage. They had already set themselves up for failure.

Before I took up endurance sports, I was never any good at controlling my mind. Only when I started rowing did I begin to learn this control. It probably took four years before I was able to row 2 000 metres without fearing that I might not last the distance. In my last competition, the South African University Championships in July 1972, I rowed in four races in one afternoon for a total of 7 000 metres of racing. We won each event. I had learnt to control my mind. It was the ideal preparation for the more difficult challenge that lay ahead: learning to control my mind for much longer periods – those hours required to complete marathon and ultramarathon races like the Comrades Marathon.

The paradox is that the only way to learn how to control thoughts and emotions once they enter the conscious mind is to evoke opposing conscious thoughts, the nature of which can only be discovered by actually being in the situation. Practice does indeed make perfect.

So I discovered that marathon and ultramarathon running, and in fact all endurance events lasting more than a few hours, lay the athlete bare by pushing him or her to perceived bounds of human endurance. It's usually at this point that the endurance athlete hits 'the wall'.

Until fairly recently, 'the wall' has not been properly understood. This is because scientists looked for a physiological explanation in the muscles to explain why athletes suddenly slow down so dramatically and feel so awful within a few kilometres. If the brain is the source of these sensations, then the explanations become easier and seem to make better sense.

Mark Allen, the six-time Hawaiian Ironman Triathlon world champion, best summed up the ability of the world's leading athletes to 'reprogramme' their central governor when he said that it is easy to be motivated at the 7 a.m. start of the Ironman but, as the race progresses, 'It's like you're tested to the core of your intent.'

The value of setting a goal may be simply that it programmes the central governor to accept a greater maximum effort before it senses danger.

In being the first to break the four-minute-mile barrier, Roger Bannister was able to convince his central governor that it was achievable, while the Australian athlete John Landy was not able to do so. Landy could only achieve this once someone else had provided the clear evidence that this 'impossible' performance was indeed achievable. So after he had run the mile in four minutes and one second seven times in competition, eventually in January 1954 Landy wrote: 'Frankly, I think the four-minute mile is beyond my capabilities. Two seconds may not sound much, but to me it's like trying to break through a brick wall. Someone may achieve the four-minute mile the world is wanting so desperately, but I don't think I can.'

Yet forty-six days after Bannister had run the mile in 3 minutes 59.4 seconds, Landy ran three seconds faster than he had ever run when he reduced Bannister's mile record to 3 minutes 58 seconds.

The top athletes have different ways of accomplishing this mental control, especially before a race. Bruce Fordyce locked himself away in his hotel room before a big race, and Paula Newby-Fraser, voted the Triathlete of the Millennium, would read a long and engrossing novel for the last two to three days before a big event. The end result, I think, is that the really exceptional athletes don't place the same subconscious limits on their performance as the rest of us do. Their belief in their capacity to achieve is extraordinary. This 'manipulation' of the central governor opens up an entirely new field of study in the exercise sciences. All sorts of possibilities in the psychology of exercise and of competing become conceivable.

It explains how, as genetically superior as Bruce Fordyce is for long-distance running, other psychological elements also played a role in how he programmed his central governor. Bruce recalls how a good friend, Gordon Howie, gave him the best advice he has ever received: 'He told me, "Get used to winning. Become accustomed to the fear, pressure and loneliness of leading. Run time trials, fun runs, anything, but get used to being in front." He was right. Winning is another country – far away and very foreign. It isn't fun, except for the bit when you break the tape. Winning hurts a lot, and a potential Comrades winner has to become familiar with the feeling and embrace it.'

There is also the potential of top athletes to use their understanding of the central governor to 'psych out' their opponents. For example, the central governor needs to know the duration and expected difficulty of the exercise for it to programme the body for the task ahead. So what happens when something unexpected is thrown into the mix? A hill that you did not know was part of the race that suddenly appears before you when you were expecting a flat stretch?

The great Comrades runner Alan Robb used this to good effect in the 1982 Comrades. Fordyce recalls how, as the lead pack of runners passed the fifty-six-kilometres-to-go mark, Robb shouted out, 'Okay boys, only the Two Oceans marathon to go.' Just the thought of what still lay ahead was enough to 'psych out' the majority of the competition that day. The central governors of most of those athletes couldn't process this new information, and they fell by the wayside as their minds allowed them to become intimidated by what Robb had pointed out – except, of course, for the indomitable Fordyce. Fordyce and Robb produced one of the epic battles in Comrades Marathon history, which Fordyce eventually won.

Fordyce was himself expert at manipulating the mental state of his opponents. In the 1984 Comrades, he eventually caught up to a strong-running Bob de la Motte. Bruce admitted that he had underestimated De la Motte's potential. As he passed De la Motte with less than ten kilometres to go, he said, 'Bob, you are running like a star.' Bruce will most likely tell you that he was showing genuine admiration for the performance of De la Motte, but any sports psychologist will tell you that in De la Motte's mind would have been: 'If I'm doing so well, how come you've just passed me?'

So when it comes to athletic performance, the body is controlled by the mind. The mind itself has a central governor doing all of this controlling, and the central governor can be programmed according to the will of the athlete. In this last statement lies the great beyond in exercise sciences – self-belief.

In my work with great sportsmen and women, and some great teams, I have seen how important a role self-belief plays in performance. Yes, like us, they all have that stop button in their brains. The difference is that they never get to the point where they push it.

THE POWER OF SELF-BELIEF
Lewis Gordon Pugh – freezing out the negative

It is 15 July 2007, and I am cold. But I am nowhere near as cold as Lewis Gordon Pugh. Or, rather, as cold as Pugh is about to get.

We are standing on the edge of sea ice at the North Pole. I am wrapped up in the latest cold-weather clothing. Pugh is wearing a Speedo and a pair of swimming goggles. Even the polar bears think he's mad. The water temperature is −1.7 °C. Pugh has set himself the goal of swimming one kilometre in the coldest ocean on earth. My role is to make sure that he doesn't die in the process.

Pugh and I first met in my office at the Sports Science Institute in Cape Town several years earlier. As part of his dream of becoming a pioneer swimmer, he had developed the idea of swimming around the Cape Peninsula, from the Victoria & Alfred Waterfront to Muizenberg. It would be a gruelling 100-kilometre journey – broken down into thirteen swims on consecutive days – in some of the roughest seas on the planet, not to mention the possibility of predators. And, of course, there was the cold water.

By the time he stepped into my office, Pugh had already been told by a number of local swimmers that it was not humanly possible – worse, he would probably die in the process. He later wrote in his book *Achieving the Impossible*:

> One person whose view interested me greatly was Professor Tim Noakes's, a world-famous exercise physiologist … Although we had once shared a walk on Table Mountain with a mutual friend, Alan Danker, I didn't really know Professor Noakes.
>
> After making an appointment, I showed up at his office … fearing

he might be about to end my Cape Peninsula project. My feeling was that Professor Noakes knew what was and wasn't possible physiologically; if he said it wasn't possible, I doubt I would have tried it.

I remember our first meeting quite clearly. Pugh stepped into my office and said, 'Professor Noakes, I want to swim around the Cape Peninsula. Nobody has done it before. The water temperature, as you know, will be cold, and on some days it may get to nine or ten degrees; on other days the wind will make the sea rough and progress will be slow. So, can my body handle it?' He looked at me, and I do believe that I saw in his eyes trepidation that I was going to join his list of doomsayers and tell him that he was mad and that it was impossible; indeed, too dangerous even to consider. But throughout my career I have seen what the challenge of the impossible does to some athletes' minds – once their minds accept that the impossible is achievable, their bodies soon follow.

So I gave him my answer in just one word: 'Yes.'

According to Pugh, 'That was good enough for me.'

Then I told him how he was going to do it. I told him to train with us at the Sports Science Institute, where I could guarantee him access to great physical trainers who would make sure that he was where he needed to be physically. I also planned to monitor his progress. Because of the mental fortitude I recognised in Pugh, I had no doubt that he would be successful. And he was.

While he was doing the swim, Pugh did not tell me how he was going. But when he reached the beach at Muizenberg, he phoned me. I was surprised that he had already finished the swim. He said simply: 'I could not have done it without you.' I did not understand what he meant, so I asked him. His answer was simple: 'You believed in me.' So it was that I began to understand the important role that the 'coach' plays in sport. If the athlete is to succeed, the athlete must believe absolutely in his or her coach. This is perhaps even more important than the training programme provided by the coach.

A few months later, Lewis Pugh visited me again, proposing a new challenge. He planned to swim in the sea of Spitsbergen, an island that forms part of the Norwegian archipelago called Svalbard. He explained to me that at its northern tip, Spitsbergen is 80 degrees North. The Arctic Circle begins at 66 degrees North. There was no doubt that the water there would be unbelievably cold – anywhere between 4 °C and −1.7 °C. He wished to improve on the 'furthest north' swim record that he had established in 2003, when he swam off the North Cape, the most northern coast of Norway.

Again, he provided me with all of this information as we sat in my office. 'Can I do it?' he then asked.

I paused and asked him what the water temperatures were likely to be. After he had told me that the temperatures would be between 0 °C and 4 °C, I said, 'I am sure *you* can do it. But I am not so sure that you will live!' My view was similar to that of his close friend and swimming partner Dr Otto Thaning, a heart surgeon who took Pugh aside and told him that he was convinced that a one-kilometre swim in 0 °C water would be life-threatening. He began to have serious doubts. So he went away and thought about it before visiting me again.

'Look,' I said, 'it so happens that at the time you are planning to do this, I am giving a lecture in Norway that ends the day before you plan to go to Spitsbergen. Why don't my wife and I extend our trip by a little and go with you to Spitsbergen?'

Pugh was thrilled with the idea of our joining him, as I would act as both his doctor and his scientist. I do remember giving him one proviso. I told him that I would only do it if he could convince my wife, Marilyn, to join me. My work had taken me to many overseas destinations, and I had discovered that I hated being away from her for an extended period. This I learnt during the 1996 Cricket World Cup in Pakistan – I had returned and told Marilyn I would never again travel out of the country for a prolonged period without her.

So while Pugh gave me the task of ensuring that he didn't die while trying to become the first human to swim a long distance so far north, I presented him with what I believed was the far more daunting challenge of convincing my wife that it would be fun to join us on this trip!

Pugh knew that Marilyn loves to paint flowers, so he researched the Arctic's flora and found out that it is rich in flowers that would be in bloom while we were there. So Marilyn was easily convinced to come along. As for me, I was looking forward to studying the physiological effects of swimming in extremely cold water. I had already challenged the conventional thinking around exercising in the heat, and I sensed something equally worthwhile for science in this project.

There was essentially no research on the effects of swimming at such low temperatures. There was certainly a great deal on English Channel swimmers, but that was in water temperatures of between 12 °C and 18 °C, very much warmer than the water in which Lewis would be swimming.

There was other research, but unfortunately it was tainted with the horrors of Nazi Germany. German scientists in the concentration camp of Dachau used their Jewish prisoners as a means to study the effects on humans of immersion in cold water. Of course, many of their subjects died. This was a horrifying atrocity against the Jewish people and, as such, it forever contaminated any similar studies.

But I knew that there was something important here for science, so I applied to the Ethics Committee at the University of Cape Town for permission to study Lewis Pugh in this project. They granted it.

I had the privilege of working with an elite athlete in supreme conditions. He would be perfectly prepared for such an undertaking, offering our scientific team the best possible chance to study the physiological effects of immersion in such cold water. Pugh was a firm believer in science benefiting the athlete, and embraced the idea that we could contribute to the advancement of knowledge in this field. In fact, he went even further. He realised that there was no water in Cape Town that would be as cold as that off Spitsbergen. So he developed his own cold-water training centre at the Waterfront in Cape Town. He knew that the fish trawlers leaving the Irvin & Johnson Ltd (I&J) facility at the Waterfront use massive amounts of ice to keep their catches cold. So he asked I&J to supply him with enough ice to cool the water in a Portapool to the temperatures of the Arctic Ocean. They agreed, and Pugh suggested that he be studied as he immersed himself in the water for progressively longer periods of time at progressively lower temperatures, until he reached the temperatures he was likely to face in the Arctic. I asked three of my students, Lara and Jonathan Dugas, and Ross Tucker, if they would like to be involved. They readily agreed, and our scientific adventure began.

Owing to the limited time left before the first swim in the Arctic, we were able to complete only two test swims in ice-cold water. The results were exciting – during a twenty-minute exposure to a water temperature of 6 °C, Pugh's core body temperature fell by only 1 °C while he was in the water. (His temperature continued to fall a further 2 °C after he exited the water, but this did not concern us, since by then he was safely out of the water.) Since we were pretty certain that Pugh would be able to swim one kilometre in about twenty minutes, we were encouraged to believe that he would not die in his attempt to swim so far north in water temperatures of between 0 °C and 5 °C.

Travelling to the most north-westerly point of the Norwegian archipelago, we eventually found ourselves in a small bay in the Magdalene Fjord. I decided that this would be the perfect place for Pugh to attempt his one-kilometre swim, and suggested that he swim it in two 500-metre legs. The water temperature was 4 °C, but Pugh completed the swim successfully, covering the one-kilometre distance in 21 minutes 30 seconds to become the first human being to do the most northerly long-distance swim.

As serious as our endeavour was, we also shared some wonderful laughs. Before leaving Cape Town, Pugh begged me to remember to bring K-Y Jelly with me. You see, to ensure his safety during the swim, I had to monitor Pugh's core body temperature. I did this by using a specially designed thermometer, which was inserted into Pugh's rectum and then connected to a radio sender and antennae that fed the data to my laptop.

As Pugh said, without the K-Y Jelly, that thermometer probe is not your friend. When I arrived on the island of Spitsbergen, Pugh was horrified to learn that I had forgotten the K-Y Jelly. I thought it was quite funny, and the rest of our team had a good laugh about it as well. But, as Pugh commented, 'Everyone saw the funny side except the poor guy who would have to have the plastic thermometer inserted where the sun doesn't often shine.' The result was that he took the responsibility to find some K-Y Jelly when we arrived on the island of Spitsbergen. The problem was that no one in our team knew the Norwegian name for K-Y Jelly or its equivalent. Later we discovered that the Norwegians call this product 'gliding cream'. I am still wondering about the meaning of the look on the face of the Spitsbergen chemist when he sold the tube of 'gliding cream' to Pugh and me.

But Pugh's ultimate goal was a swim in the sub-zero temperatures of the North Pole, which he attempted in July 2007. Three days before he was to do the swim, he was given permission to do a practice swim. The captain stopped the Russian ice-breaker and our team was flown onto the ice in a helicopter. Pugh completed a test swim of five minutes, during which his fingers became so cold that they swelled considerably, causing him substantial pain.

He admitted that that test swim shattered his self-belief. 'In attempting to swim at $-1.7\,°C$, had I pushed myself beyond the limit of human endurance? It was less difficult to climb Mount Everest after Edmund Hillary had done it; it was easier to run the mile in under four minutes after Roger Bannister. No one had done a long-distance swim at $-1.7\,°C$.'

And, again, as was the case that first time I told him I believed he could survive a swim around the Cape Peninsula, Pugh said to me, 'Prof, I have the courage to do this swim because you have the courage to believe in me.'

Pugh was exceptional throughout that swim. I watched every second of it and was astounded by what he achieved. To keep out the negative thoughts and the doubt that had crept into his mind, he imagined a Rottweiler standing at a gate and barking viciously every time a negative thought popped into his head.

It reminded me of the tactic employed by Gary Kirsten when he went out to bat and left Fear at square leg.

Afterwards, I saw a visible transformation in Pugh, and was reminded again of the power of a single event to change a sportsperson's life radically. I have witnessed this twice in my career – once when Joel Stransky kicked the winning drop goal in the 1995 Rugby World Cup final, and now with Pugh's North Pole swim. Both became more complete and confident people after achieving such sporting milestones.

Pugh, like so many great athletes, knew that his would be a battle that would be won in the mind and not by the body. As he wrote in his book, 'If my body fails me, I will almost certainly die. But this is not simply about my body but also about my mind – if it takes me to the right place, I will survive … Without doubt, the best motivation comes from within yourself and the desire to be as good as you can be … Over time, I learnt to rely more on and put greater trust in the motivation that came from within.'

The University of Cape Town Ikey Tigers rugby team wins the 2011 Varsity Cup

While I take great pride in having helped Lewis Pugh to achieve his goals, I take even greater satisfaction in having helped to raise the standard of rugby at my university. To achieve this, we had to overcome significant hurdles, including a history of chronic underfunding of sporting activities at UCT, based on the belief that the sole purpose of real universities is to educate the mind. The irony was that only by engaging totally and absolutely the minds of these most physical athletes were we able to reverse a historic attitude that accepted second-best as good enough.

It all began in October 2007, when my future son-in-law, John Dobson, came to see me. At the time I was barely aware that he was dating my daughter or that he had serious intent. The challenge he posed was simple. 'Prof, a new competition for university rugby has been started, called the Varsity Cup,' the rugby coach said. 'It involves a two-month-long competition that will be shown on national television every Monday evening. Eight universities will take part. We have been included, but we are seeded last. We have been warned that there will be promotion/relegation play-offs at the end of the first season of competition and that we should not expect to be in the competition after the end of the 2008 season.' He continued, saying, 'There is a real risk that we will be beaten by at least forty points by the traditional rugby-playing universities of Stellenbosch, Pretoria, Free State, Potchefstroom, Port Elizabeth and Johannesburg. If we are relegated, it could mean the end of competitive rugby at UCT. We have no resources and no money to pay coaches, players or support staff. Our facilities are the worst of any team in the competition. Nor do we recruit players to come to UCT. Worse, our entrance requirements are the toughest of any university.' He then asked me, 'What can we do?'

I took a deep breath and considered my response. 'Coach,' I said, 'we have to teach your players to believe in themselves.' Under my breath, I added that we would also have to teach them to believe in miracles. 'If they believe that they are going to lose by forty points a game to the other teams, then that is exactly what is going to happen. We have to teach them to believe that they can beat all the other teams in the competition.' He responded instantly, 'Prof, when can we start?'

We began with a talk at the Sports Science Institute in November 2007, in which I introduced the concept of beginning with the end in mind. I told the players that the outcome of their first year in the Varsity Cup would be determined by what they wanted for themselves. If they wanted to be successful, they would need to train over the next two months as if their lives depended on it. They had to train as if it were their destiny to win the 2008 Varsity Cup. If they trained with any other goal in mind, then, I assured them, that is exactly what the outcome would be. So they had somehow to develop the training intensity of champions, based on the belief that that would be the only way they would ever become those champions.

By chance, in January 2008 I had been invited to give a talk at a conference organised by the Irish Association of Sports Medicine in Dublin, hosted at Croke Park Stadium. I chose as my title 'Beyond the VO_2 max – the role of self-belief in superior athletic performance'. I chose the title for two reasons: first, the Springboks had just won the 2007 Rugby World Cup, in part because of the self-belief that they had developed; and, second, I knew that in the audience would be another speaker who was particularly dismissive of the central governor theory. Indeed, in an article published that very month, Dr Ben Levine from Dallas, Texas, had written in praise of Hill's model of the VO_2 max concept. He saw no value in the 'vague actions' of a 'mystical central governor'. I knew that the best offence in this case would be to show the audience that anyone who argues that oxygen delivery alone can explain all forms of exercise performance will have great difficulty justifying how self-belief works.

After I had returned from Ireland, I suggested to John that I repeat this lecture for the team. So on a wet and cold Sunday morning in a cramped room at a youth hostel in Stellenbosch, where the team was on a training weekend – the team's budget did not allow the use of more luxurious facilities – I repeated the talk to a room full of young, enthusiastic and impressionable rugby players. After I had ended the talk, one of the senior players stood up and said, 'Where are the Maties [Stellenbosch University rugby team]? Can't we play them right now, because we are going to beat them.'

Subsequently, in the nine games of the 2008 Varsity Cup competition, the team had only two moments of disappointment. They lost the first game when they ran out of time against the team from the University of the North West (Potchefstroom). The game finished with the Potchefstroom team five points ahead but with the Ikey Tigers camped on their try line. It was from that moment that the team began to believe that they could become the equals of all the other teams in the competition.

Then, after winning their next seven games, in the eighty-first minute of their ninth game, the final against the Maties, after the hooter had sounded and the game was technically over, the team managed to lose control of the ball, allowing Stellenbosch to score a game-winning try and snatch victory. Afterwards, the team gave me a signed jersey with the words, 'Professor Noakes, you made us believe. You made us.'

This, of course, is only a small part of the truth, since without the expert coaching that they received, all the self-belief in the world would not have produced these victories. The point is that without self-belief, the best-coached team will not beat the less-skilled team that has self-belief.

It would require another three years of work before the team finally lifted the Varsity Cup for the first time after a dramatic 26-16 victory in the final against the University of Pretoria, played in Pretoria on Monday 11 April 2011. To win the 2011 Varsity Cup trophy, the Ikey Tigers did not have to play the team that has been UCT's nemesis for the past eighty years, the Maties. They had beaten the Ikeys in both the 2008 and 2010 finals, but after winning all three previous Varsity Cup competitions, the Maties failed to make the 2011 play-offs.

So when the two teams met later in the same year at the annual Cape intervarsity match at Stellenbosch, the question that had to be answered was: Had the Ikey Tigers developed the self-belief to beat the Maties and to prove that their victory in the Varsity Cup was fully deserved? Fortunately, the answer was a resounding yes, as the Tigers were comfortable 28-19 winners after trailing 6-19 early in the second half.

There is still much to be done, but by adding the proper mental approach to all the usual aspects of proper preparation, we have been able to add a dimension that has perhaps been missing from the club in the past.

Roger Bannister – the mind barrier

One of the premier examples of self-belief that we used to influence the thinking of our Ikey players was the story of how, on 6 May 1954, Sir Roger Bannister became the first human to run the mile in less than four minutes.

Roger Bannister was a great athlete who really understood the power of the mind. In my quest to understand why Bannister, and not other, possibly more gifted athletes at the time, was the first to run the mile in less than four minutes, I came to the conclusion that he understood better than anyone that this battle was fought in the mind, not in the body.

Gunder Haegg, the man who in 1945 came within 1.3 seconds of breaking the four-minute barrier for the mile, wrote before Bannister's attempt that he thought Bannister was the man to do it. His reason? 'He uses his brains as much as his legs. I've always thought the four-minute mile was more of a psychological problem than a test of physical endurance.' As Bannister himself observed, 'Racing has always been more of a mental than a physical problem to me ... The mental approach is all important, because the strength and power of the mind are without limit. All this energy can be harnessed by the correct attitude of the mind.'

When Bannister finally achieved his objective at Oxford's Iffley Road track on 6 May 1954, he wrote one of the most significant paragraphs in running literature: 'Though physiology may indicate respiratory and circulatory limits to muscular effort, psychological and other factors beyond the ken of physiology set the razor's edge of defeat or victory and determine how closely an athlete approaches the absolute limits of performance.'

Bannister also understood the power of inspiration. In John Bryant's book *3:59.4: The Quest to Break the 4 Minute Mile*, he writes of the relationship between the athlete and his coach, Franz Stampfl. 'Stampfl, like Bannister,' he says, 'refused to acknowledge any limits to human performance.' Bryant also quotes Bannister's training partner, Chris Chataway, on Stampfl: 'He didn't know a hell of a lot about running, but he had this fantastic ability to inspire ... what I know is that he could touch what we were doing with magic. By the time you'd listened to Franz, you would be in no doubt that breaking the world record would be as good as painting the *Mona Lisa* ... He made you certain that you could do it, and that it would be a disgrace if you didn't. If you missed the chance to break a record, how could you ever forgive yourself? All this made a huge impression on me, and it must, I think, have made an impression on Roger too.'

In 1989, when I performed one of the great academic rituals – the inaugural address by a newly appointed professor at the University of Cape Town – I dedicated the lecture to Sir Roger Bannister, so important did I believe his contribution to have been.

Bannister's genius was his ability to condition his mind so that it would 'release in four short minutes the energy I usually spend in half an hour's training'. But without the input of his coach at the critical moment on that fateful day, even Bannister's mental fortitude might not have been enough. Arriving at Oxford's Iffley Road track some hours before the race, Bannister became disheartened, for it was cold and rainy, the track was wet and the wind was blowing – all conditions that, in his mind, made it impossible for him to break the four-minute mile on that day. But in an interview fifty years later, Bannister explained what had happened to change his mind: 'The crucial thing that he [Stampfl] said was: "Well, I think you can run a 3:56 mile." If he believed that – I hope he did – it certainly was a helpful comment. And he said if you have the chance and you don't take it, you may regret it for the rest of your life.'

Chris Chataway, who paced both Bannister and Landy a few weeks later to sub-four-minute miles, also explained how discussions with Stampfl helped his own mental approach to racing: 'It was a sort of pre-race mental calisthenics. I would say I was tired, and he would explain why he was absolutely convinced that my finishing burst would be strong. In a way, I knew he didn't know any better than I did whether or not I would win, because it was a totally unknown quantity, but just hearing someone say the things … was useful.' Always Stampfl taught that the 'great hurdle was the mental barrier'.

So Bannister went out and ran the 3:59 mile that his coach had said he could do under those conditions. While his performance in breaking the four-minute mile showed immense mental fortitude, I believe it was Bannister's race against the Australian John Landy – the 'mile of the century' – that showed most impressively the extent to which Bannister had mastered the mental aspect of racing.

When Landy had built up a commanding lead towards the end of the second lap and showed no signs of tiring, Bannister made the important mental shift that he described in his book:

> I won back the first yard, then each succeeding yard, until his lead was halved by the time we reached the back straight of the third lap … I now connected myself to Landy again, though he was still five yards

ahead. I was almost hypnotised by his easy shuffling stride ... I tried to imagine myself attached to him by some invisible cord.

With each stride, I drew the cord tighter and reduced his lead ... As we entered the last bend, I tried to convince myself that he was tiring. With each stride now I attempted to husband a little strength for the moment at the end of the bend when I decided to pounce ... When the moment came, my mind would galvanize my body to the greatest effort it had ever known.

With seventy yards to go, Bannister passed Landy and went on to win.

That Bannister was ahead of his time in the mental approach to sport is therefore not in doubt. Yet there was precious little material on this topic at the time.

We used the experiences of Bannister, as well as two other runners, to teach the Ikey rugby players how important it is to believe in the outcome of the event, even though it makes no logical sense to believe that it is possible to predict the outcome.

The first example is that of Jim Ryun, the first schoolboy to run the mile in less than four minutes. In his book, Ryun explains how, at the age of fifteen, when he had been running for only two years, his coach had called him in to talk about his running goals. Ryun relates what happened next:

'Let's talk about goals,' he [his coach] began. 'What do you think you can do a mile in?'

'This year?' I said. 'Oh, I don't know, maybe—'

'Not this year,' interrupted the coach. 'I mean by the time you're a senior ... ultimately.'

I'd never really given it any thought. 'Maybe 4:10,' I said ...

'I'm talking about the four-minute mile, Jim. No high school boy has ever run one. I think you can be the first ... I'm convinced you can do it.'

'Coach, I think you're crazy!'

At the time, I had no idea what a four-minute mile signified ... I was only fifteen years old, basically still a child ... He was certain of my ability, even if I wasn't myself. He had already tutored several very successful milers and believed in his coaching system ... As difficult as it was to make the adjustment to consider myself a champion, a front runner, as a 'good' athlete, I did my best to trust in the coach's judgment and to believe his words.

Though I was initially dumbfounded by his prediction, it did in fact prove not only to be accurate but to set me on target for what would be the essence of my life for some time to come.

Two years after this discussion, Ryun duly became the first schoolboy in history to run the mile in less than four minutes. Without the belief of his coach, Ryun would never have achieved this remarkable performance.

The most successful South African distance runner of the recent past, Hendrick Ramaala, winner of the 2008 New York City Marathon, writes:

> What I realise is that once the mind accepts anything, the body will respond ... If you don't convince yourself that you are going to win, then you aren't going to win it. For New York, I have to tell myself thousands of times that I am going to win this thing. I have done it before and I must do it again – before the start, at the start, during the race and at the finish. I have to tell myself that I am going to win it and that I am better than the other guys. You have to talk to yourself otherwise you are not going to win ... You have to say: 'Whatever happens I am going to win.' In my opinion, the person who wins the race has already won it inside his head before the start of the race.

With these words, Ramaala demonstrates the remarkable power of the mind.

Terry Fox – running for life

A final story that I'd like to tell is that of Canadian Terry Fox, an athlete who used his mind to overcome a tragic disability to achieve immortality. I use this story to make the point that however bad any athlete might feel during sporting competition, according to the central governor theory, that discomfort is generated by the athlete's brain and not by his muscles. As a result, it can be overcome by mental processes – just as Terry Fox must have done when he ran across Canada on his one remaining leg.

In 1977, Fox's right knee became so unbearably painful that he was forced to seek medical attention. His physician would no doubt have hoped that the problem was simply a stress fracture and that, after six weeks of rest, Fox could return to his calling as one of the brightest lights of the Simon Fraser University basketball team.

But as his physician searched the X-rays, he saw everything he had dreaded.

It was a death sentence. Codman's triangle, the sunray sign and the moth-eaten edge indicated the presence of disorganised malignant bone-cancer cells.

On that day, this highly talented eighteen-year-old student discovered he had the most disabling form of cancer. Ironically, Fox was a student of kinesiology – the science of motion. Within three days of the diagnosis, he was told that his right leg would need to be amputated through the hip joint – this for the man who a year earlier had graduated from his high school as athlete of the year.

For Terry Fox, there would be no more sport. Yet Fox went on to achieve many awards. On the eve of his operation, his mind was already made up – he had decided that whatever he opened his eyes to and whatever the surgeons left him with he would use to run across Canada.

For the first sixteen months after surgery, Fox endured the most rigorous chemotherapy. After twenty-four months, he began training for his goal. Within eight months of starting, he was running thirteen-and-a-half miles a day, and on 12 April 1980 he began his Marathon of Hope.

For five months and 3 100 miles, a one-legged cancer patient shook Canada, providing the country with a daily example of rare inspiration and supreme courage. Fox was able to raise $1 million for cancer research before more tragedy struck him – a persistent cough and inordinate fatigue.

On 2 September 1980, Fox said, 'Take me to a hospital.' When he arrived, he had only one question: 'Is it cancer?' It was.

The X-ray revealed that the cancer had spread to both of his lungs. Fox vowed to fight on. Even when his fight ended in July 1982, he was still not ready to give up. He was named Canadian of the Year and Canadian Sportsman of the Year.

As cricket legend Peter Pollock once observed, 'You have not lived in the world of competitive sport until you have fought a battle that is not against an opponent, but against yourself.' The key, of course, is that we now know that 'yourself' is, in fact, your mind.

part seven

TIM NOAKES ON ...

24 | Coaching the Coaches

Countries such as Australia, America and England invest about as much in their coaches as they do in their athletes. Their coaches have a collective coaching knowledge that they are happy to share with each other. In short, they coach their coaches.

This culture of coaching is something we don't have in South African sport. It is evident every time our Springbok rugby team selects a new coach. We begin from scratch again, instead of building on the achievements of the previous coach.

The late cricketing genius Bob Woolmer was one of many who agreed with me that South Africa lags behind the rest of the world in its coaching methods. In as early as 1994, I was quoted in *South African Cricket Action* as saying, 'Most [South African] coaches can only sift for existing talent rather than try to develop new talent.' I pointed to the wealth of sporting talent coming out of our school cricket system that fails to find its way to provincial or international level, writing:

> Something is wrong. Schools turn out good schoolboy players, but they fail later on. Talent gets you into a Nuffield cricket team, but it's coaching that gets you beyond that. That's where the problem lies. Our coaches have never been taught to approach coaching scientifically, using measurement rather than just observation.
>
> South African coaches expect the player to do the job. Coaches should intervene when something goes wrong, but they don't have the training or ability to do so. Take [Darryl] Cullinan for example: his return to form followed a single net practice with a scientifically

trained expert who had been working with him for seven years and understood his problems. That's all it took – so why wasn't it done sooner?

As a scientist, I have always wanted to understand the components that can be changed in a player's game to produce a better performance. However, very few coaches seem keen to learn about the contribution that science can make. The most obvious example of our unwillingness to use science was in cricket, when Shane Warne first toured South Africa. Here was a player who quite clearly was unique and could make the difference between winning and losing. Yet in his time on South African pitches, he was never once filmed. Nobody even thought to record, dissect or research his action and thus understand more about what makes him so successful.

We talk a great deal about sports development in South Africa, but it doesn't help to develop players if they're not being coached correctly. Coaches should continually be asking new questions and looking for ways to improve. Unfortunately, this concept is still foreign to many of our administrators. They don't have the vision to take new directions. Until they do, we will have mediocre or inconsistent performances, we will waste talent and we will blame our players for their poor performances. Coaches should always believe that half of what they are doing is wrong and should consistently look for ways to change for the better, rather than perpetuate errors.

We need to develop a new generation of coaches who are not scared to admit that they're wrong and to try something else. We must get rid of the dead wood and put in young people who have been properly trained. We need coaches who do not have fixed ideas, who are prepared to listen to everyone, from any sporting or professional background. We have to develop a culture of coaching.

Imagine Jake White and Peter de Villiers having dinner together and sharing ideas about coaching the Springbok team. In the leading sports countries of the world, this is exactly what happens. In America, coaching is a profession and the coaches act professionally towards each other. They understand that the responsibility of all coaches is to improve their knowledge constantly and to keep learning and sharing information and ideas so that they always raise standards in their sport.

That is why, if twelve years ago the swimmer Michael Phelps had been cloned and sent to six different countries, I believe that only one country would have been able to secure eight gold medals at a single Olympics from him. That country is America, because they have developed a culture of swimming coaching that is the best in the world.

The value of investing in coaches can be seen at Olympic level. At the 1976 Olympics in Montreal, Australia won five medals, but not a single gold medal. It was a national crisis for them. Then, at the Sydney Olympics in 2000, they won fifty-eight medals, sixteen of them gold.

What made the difference? After 1976, they established the famed Australian Institute of Sport in Canberra, and they paid good salaries to bring the world's top coaches into contact with their top athletes. The more money they spent on their coaches, the better their athletes performed. Eventually, they no longer had any dumb coaches.

Another example is England. In 1996, England took home only one gold medal from the Olympics in Atlanta. At the 2008 Olympics in Beijing, that number increased to nineteen gold medals. The reason is that they followed the Australian model of investing in coaching – they now pay their coaches more than even the Australians can afford.

Our sports federations plead for better funding of our athletes and teams, but we need to match that investment with equal investment in our coaching structures. If we don't start investing in our coaches more seriously, we're going to continue with the lack of leadership that currently exists in South African sport.

We have to uplift our coaches, starting in the schools. If we succeed at that level, our teams and athletes will begin to think like champions at an early age. That's exactly how Australians think. Somehow, South Africa needs to start finding ways to pay our coaches, perhaps according to a tier of coaching at amateur level, with remuneration based on the level of experience. We need to develop our collective intellectual capital as a nation of coaches and reward the coaches who have done well and proved themselves.

Coaches need to be taught how science and scientific findings can be used to their advantage. They need to be assured that scientists do not replace coaches; the role of the scientist is simply to help the coach become more effective. I maintain that coaching, training and genetic ability account for 98 per cent of a player's success. Science adds the last 2 per cent – and, at the elite level of sport, that 2 per cent will be the difference between success and failure.

James Counsilman, the former swimming coach at Indiana University and guide to more exceptional swimmers than almost all the other American coaches combined, believed that the essence of coaching is the application of classroom psychology to the sports field. He revolutionised coaching by introducing this previously ignored psychological element to the profession.

He spoke about the 'X-factor' – the ability of a coach to decide what is important and therefore needs attention, and what is unimportant and can safely be ignored. According to him, the coach who lacked the X-factor would spend so much time labouring to understand the nuances of physiology and different training techniques that he would ignore the really important issues of the correct psychological approach to his athletes. In understanding the psychological needs of the athletes and their coach, Counsilman described eight important points:

1. **Love and affection** – the coach must have a genuine affection for his athletes and he must convey that affection whenever he can.

2. **Security** – the world of the athlete can be a forbidding place. Yet when he arrives at the sports field, this changes. He must be met with a friendly greeting by the coach, whom he respects, whom he knows to be a mature individual with an enthusiastic and positive attitude and who has his best interests at heart. He is part of the team, in a familiar environment, and he knows what to expect. It is only in the security of this type of environment that the athlete will produce his best.

3. **Self-esteem** – an essential function of the coach is to build the self-esteem of the athlete. In a team environment, he does this by making sure that all the members of the team feel that they are contributing something to the team's success. He is genuinely interested in the whole team, not just its champions. He must do everything in his power to avoid belittling, humiliating or ridiculing his athletes. He must never prove any of his athletes wrong by saying, 'I told you so.' He must develop a high sensitivity about what he says and does.

4. **Status** – life is often a desperate struggle for status. The coach must provide his athletes with an excellent programme that will allow them to become successful and to enhance their status.

5. **Achievement** – the coach must provide his athletes with a sense of accomplishment. He must set realistic goals for each athlete and must assist them in evaluating what he or she has achieved.

6. **Recognition** – no one ever does anything for nothing. Recognition is one of the most important goals for any athlete. The coach must always recognise his athletes during their training – a slap on the back is a form of recognition and tells the athlete that he or she is being noticed. The coach must at all times

suppress his own ego, remembering the TATNAM rule – Talk About Them Not About Me.

7. **The role of the challenge** – people are attracted to sport because they enjoy a challenge. So the coach must plan his programme to be innovative, interesting and challenging.

8. **The group instinct** – the coach's job is to foster group orientation, or team spirit. He must set common goals and allow his athletes to have a say in the decision-making. Authoritarianism, the use of negative psychology (hate the opponent) and self-aggrandisement ('my' team) undermine the group instinct and fail to promote team spirit. The key is to promote 'our' team and the feeling of 'we'. Each individual should know that the interests of the team come first. The use of ritual, ceremony and tradition are also key in this process and are achieved through award dinners, special events and trips.

Self-confidence was another key element of success for Counsilman. The athlete often looks to the self-assured coach to give him the confidence he lacks. The coach needs to build the confidence of the athlete to the point where the athlete believes that he can achieve what his body is capable of.

Other elements in the Counsilman coaching philosophy include providing the correct environment for the athlete, good equipment, and good officials who are interested in the welfare of their athletes and not in their own power or publicity, as well as building a correct attitude to practice – practice must be enjoyable; the athlete must learn that only hard work will be accepted in training and to take pride in the toughness that this provides.

Ultimately, said Counsilman, the responsibility of the coach is to be positive, honest and to show integrity at all times. Every coach will at some time face criticism, and Counsilman suggested two responses to this: first, if it is unjustified, he can laugh it off and simply feel flattered that someone considers his ideas worthy of comment; and, second, he must find out why people don't like him and be prepared to change. Under no circumstances can he ever afford to sit back and be satisfied.

My opinion is that Counsilman achieved coaching greatness because of his understanding of human nature. His intuition told him that the key to success lay in understanding his athlete's psyche rather than in a detailed knowledge of physiology and training techniques. Coaching begins and ends in the head – of the athlete and the coach.

Coaching an athlete or a team remains the ultimate and most visible test of leadership.

JUST CALL ME 'COACH'

As a result of my experience with great coaches like Bob Woolmer and Jake White, I came to the conclusion that the ultimate goal in life is to be a great coach. So in early 2011, I wrote the following column for the Discovery Health magazine:

> The highest calling in life is to be a great coach. The most influential people in my life – my wife, my parents, those who taught me my sports and my profession – are my heroes and my role models. But, more importantly, they have coached me in the art of life.
>
> We tend to think that coaches work only in sports; that it is only athletes who require coaching. Next, we think that the sole job of the coach is to produce a winning team by whatever means necessary – all else is irrelevant. But the great coaches know better.
>
> American gridiron football is unquestionably the single sport that, like no other, has defined the art of coaching. It is the most competitive and arguably the most complex sport in the world. We know that because it pays its coaches more than Kings and Queens; more even than most of the stars of Hollywood. To succeed against such odds requires that a great coach must understand what motivates each individual and how to help each player to act in the pursuit of a greater good.
>
> So the first lesson those great coaches teach us is the need to behave ethically. To be a coach of others, all our actions must be beyond ethical reproach. Over a lifetime, coaches who behave without ethical constraint will not extract the full potential from those entrusted to their care. For unethical behaviours undermine respect and trust, without which the coach is powerless to direct her athletes towards the path of hardship – the only sure route to a lasting success. Great teams are built by outstanding humans who can be trusted always to act with impeccable honesty and integrity. Great coaches teach that the only actions worth doing are those that are right. Actions that do not improve the individual or the team are simply not worth doing.
>
> The second lesson is to be an exceptional teacher. The great teachers are those who comprehend the true complexity of their subject material and are able to present it simply; they care deeply for their students and expect those they teach to aspire only to the very highest standards – in ideal circumstances to aspire to an elusive perfection. The basis of great teaching is the ability to communicate motivation.

So the great teachers must inspire their students to achieve that which all others consider impossible. Great coaches understand that the impossible is just a state of mind; the impossible is only that which has yet to be achieved.

The third lesson is to develop a tireless (but balanced) work ethic, conducted with unconstrained passion, seven days a week, forty-nine weeks a year. The coach who lacks the passion to work as hard as anyone else in his profession cannot expect his athletes to understand the value and rewards of working harder than their opponents.

The fourth lesson is the need to be egoless, to learn that my life is not about 'me'. The great coaches do not care who receives the credit for success, provided that all are working in pursuit of perfection. The great coaches know that when their teams win it is because the players excelled. And when the team loses it is because the coach failed to do his job. Great coaches understand that leadership is not a position; leadership is the action of serving others. So that the greatest coaches, like the greatest leaders, are those who are the best servants.

And the final characteristic of the most winning coaches is to understand that great sport is not even about winning. It is not even about sport. It is so much more important. As Tony Dungy, a man of faith and the first African-American coach to win the gridiron Super Bowl has written: 'But winning the Super Bowl is not the ultimate victory. And once again, just to make sure we're on the same page, it's not all about football. It's about the journey – mine and yours – and the lives we can teach, the legacy we can leave, and the world we can change for the better.'

The greatest coaches are therefore not judged by their win–loss records, or even by how much they earn. The sole measure of their importance is how many lives they have changed for the better. Indeed, the greatest compliment on earth is to be called 'Coach' by those whose lives have been changed.

So, if you really want to make my day, don't call me 'Doc' or even 'Prof'. Just call me 'Coach'.

25 | Bruce Fordyce and Lessons on Overtraining

As we learn why the body breaks down when exposed for too long to one particular stress (exercise), we will learn more about its tolerance for other unavoidable everyday stresses, such as work pressures.

Bruce Fordyce always referred to overtraining as the 'dead legs' syndrome, or feeling 'the plod'. Once reduced to 'the plod', it's only a matter of time before injury, infection or a bad competition performance occurs. We've come to understand this as the protective response of an exhausted body, which, rather than suffer additional damage, aims to make training impossible.

For me, Bruce Fordyce embodied athletic perfection. In my view, the search for a personal perfection will always be life's most vital struggle, and I applaud him for this achievement. I remember this most clearly in the 1983 Comrades Marathon, when Bruce ran a new 'up' record of 5 hours, 30 minutes and 12 seconds.

Bruce's mastery that year was so complete that he made his victory by fifteen minutes, and the improvement of his previous 'up' record by seven minutes, seem effortless. I recall being mesmerised by what I can only term 'poetic running', described in Part V, and I began to consider how it is humanly possible for one man to possess such an abundance of athletic talent.

Bruce did indeed have genetic ability. But he also discovered the dangers of overtraining early on in his running career.

In an interview with *Fair Lady* magazine in June 1983, Fordyce declared, 'My advice is going to be different from a lot of advice you will be given. This is because I place my emphasis on rest and recovery. I do believe in hard training, but there is only so much hard training that the body can take, and the timing and duration of any hard training phase is very important. If in doubt, rest.'

Arthur Newton, the man who in 1935 was described as the most phenomenal distance runner the world had ever known, was another athlete who thought deeply about his sport. All modern training approaches are based on his writings, and I have collected all of his superb books on running. His contribution is fully described in *Lore of Running*.

During his competitive running years in the early 1930s, Newton won five of the six Comrades Marathons he ran, holding both the 'up' and 'down' records, the London to Brighton Marathon record, the world thirty-, thirty-five-, forty-, forty-five-, fifty-, sixty- and 100-mile records, and the world twenty-four-hour record.

Of training, Newton wrote, 'You ought never to get really breathless or pant uncomfortably. Train each day until you feel that you have had a decent dose. Go so far every day that the last mile or two become almost a desperate effort. So long as you are fit for another dose the following day, you are not overdoing it. But you must never permit yourself to approach real exhaustion. You must never become badly tired.'

Bruce Fordyce came to this realisation through pure chance. Prior to the 1978 Comrades Marathon, at a time when he was still learning a great deal about his ability as a long-distance runner, he was injured. Unable to train in both January and February, it was a devastating blow. However, with the training he was able to complete in the twelve weeks before the race, Bruce still managed to finish fourteenth.

He later told me that he realised then that the key to success in ultra-distance running was not simply training harder than anybody else. To understand the revolutionary nature of this insight you need to understand that, until Bruce came along, the way you trained for the Comrades was very simple: training began on 1 January for the race, which was held on 31 May. For five months you would simply train harder every day until race day, when you would supposedly be so tough that nothing could hold you back. The reality, however, was different – athletes who trained in this way usually peaked in April or early May. On race day, they were tired and past their peak.

Before the 1982 Comrades Marathon, Bruce experienced the pressure of being the defending champion. As such, he could easily have fallen into the trap of overtraining, but he was again injured, and he later admitted to being saved by that injury. This time it was the soleus muscle, between the calf and the shin-bone. This muscle assists with the flexing of the foot, and as Bruce was always an excessive pronator, he had suffered a series of chronic tears in the soleus muscle. Again, injury prevented him from training properly in January and February of that year. This was proving quite a challenge for the defending Comrades champion.

Bruce phoned me to ask my advice and I agreed to meet him at what is now O.R. Tambo International Airport on my next trip to Johannesburg that week. I told him about a new treatment called 'cross friction'. Cross-friction massage is much deeper than traditional massage. In addition, no lubrication is used, so the fingers applying the massage take the skin with them. The motion of the massage is small and across the muscle tissue rather than with it. It is a painful treatment, and I told Bruce that if he doesn't scream during the massage, it's not working. (Today we know that this is not the ideal treatment, but at that time it was the best we had.)

The treatment was successful and Bruce was back in training within a few days. In a memorable battle with Alan Robb, Fordyce triumphed in the Comrades Marathon that year. I ran the Comrades that year as well, finishing in a time of 7 hours, 17 minutes and 30 seconds for a silver medal. Bruce always referred to me as 'a gold-medal mind in a bronze-medal body', so I was particularly pleased with what my mind had encouraged my body to achieve!

Bruce made the Comrades Marathon his speciality and, as such, did not allow himself to be drawn into running many other races in the lead-up to the race. It was a philosophy that concurred with the statement made by Newton that racing too frequently drained the reserves in the build-up to a major race.

Bruce also kept detailed diaries of his training. He referred to them as his 'textbooks', saying, 'I always go back to them. If I didn't have them, I would be very worried.'

Bruce's wisdom had one other outcome that is not widely known. In January 1986, Paula Newby-Fraser phoned me from San Diego to ask for advice on her training. She had recently left South Africa so that she could train full time as a professional triathlete in the United States. Her problem, she said, was that she was utterly exhausted, so tired that she could barely get out of bed in the morning. I asked her how she was training. Her response was that the American triathletes loved to train. When she finished third in her first Hawaiian Ironman Triathlon on a minimum of training, they had said to her: 'Imagine what you will do if you train properly.' So she had started to train 'properly'. The result of all this 'proper' training was that she had become utterly exhausted.

My response was that she should adopt the Fordyce model. The only change should be that she increase the intensity of her hard training. I told her that simply increasing the volume of her training would not necessarily improve her performances.

In the end, she adopted this model and developed her own training methods, which were hugely successful. At the end of her career, in which she won twenty-four Ironman Triathlons, including eight Hawaiian Ironmans, Paula was described as the 'greatest all-around female athlete in the world'; one of the 'top 5 pro female athletes of the last 25 years' and the 'Triathlete of the Millennium'.

Chalk up another victory to the genius of Bruce Fordyce.

26 | The Springboks Are Overplayed

During the past decade of studying the Springbok rugby team, I have repeatedly made the call for rugby authorities to scale down the number of matches our top players are involved in during a season. Overplaying is the biggest danger to our desire to remain world champions.

I thought that this point had been proved by the work we did with Jake White and his winning World Cup team. Our science has advanced to the point where we are able to predict with a degree of certainty when a top player will succumb to injury. This prediction is based purely on game-time exposure in the previous year. Yet commercial interests and personal greed continue to override the need for our players to be given much-needed rest.

Our data suggest that the maximum game time for our Springbok players should range between 1 400 and 1 800 minutes per year, if they are to escape injury and loss of form. A sum of 1 800 minutes per year equates to thirty games of sixty minutes each, or twenty-three games of eighty minutes each.

Currently, most of our Springboks play about thirteen Super Rugby matches per season – more when our top teams reach the final, as has been the case over the past few years – and four to six Currie Cup matches. That leaves them with between five and ten matches for the Springboks, depending on their time on the field. I think a figure here of about eight matches is desirable. Of course, the Super 15 competition initiated in 2011 means that players will play even more games in the first six months of the season before the Tri Nations competition begins.

I originally worked out that a season should last only seven months, or twenty-eight weeks of match play. This allows for eight weeks of rest per year, three months of pre-season or in-season preparation, and seven months of matches. This is based on my belief that elite athletes need at least eight weeks a year away from the sport of their choice – downtime they need for rest and recovery and being with their families and loved ones.

I think that twenty-three to twenty-eight matches is the maximum that our players should play. If you look at our longest-serving Springbok players, that is exactly what they have done for the past decade. Once they do more than that, their careers are not likely to last much longer. Take a player such as former Springbok Marius Joubert, for example: in 2004 he played over thirty-five games, and this ended his international career.

Look at our Springbok performances on the 2009 end-of-year tour. The Springboks were not as dominant, because that year top players such as John Smit, Bismarck du Plessis and others had played more than the number of matches we now recommend.

In my opinion, the perfect Springbok player would:

- Play between 1 400 and 1 800 minutes of rugby a year.
- Play in twenty-three to twenty-eight matches per season.
- Compete in eight Test matches a year.
- Spend three months of the year on pre-season and in-season training.
- Spend seven months of the year in competitive matches.
- Take eight weeks off to rest.
- Have at least forty-eight to ninety-six hours to recover after a match.

27 | Doping

The idea of using illegal substances in order to gain an advantage over the competition is certainly not new to sport. As far back as the early Olympics in Ancient Greece, athletes consumed extracts of mushroom and plant seeds to improve performance.

In 1886, the first sporting death from substance overdose was recorded when cyclist Arthur Linton reportedly overdosed on either strychnine or trimethyl. However, others argue that Linton actually died of typhoid as a result of 'over-exertion'.

At the 1904 Olympics in St Louis, Thomas Hicks won the marathon by ingesting a mixture of raw egg white and brandy laced with strychnine, while in the 1930s, amphetamines were introduced into the arsenal of sports doping. In the fifties, steroids began to make their presence felt, especially among the power athletes at the Olympic Games.

Of course, the use of anabolic steroids is banned in all competitions that fall under the auspices of the International Olympic Committee and other related sporting federations. As a sports scientist and doctor, I never have and never will prescribe steroids or any other banned substances to a competitive athlete. I believe them to be a distasteful and nefarious element in sport.

Steroids are believed to enhance power by up to 20 per cent, and to improve speed, endurance, racing performance and rate of recovery from competition by as much as 10 per cent.

But the use of steroids by competitive athletes constitutes cheating, and its use on a grand scale in events such as the Tour de France has cast a gloomy pall of scepticism over any significant athletic achievement in those sports in which steroids might provide a significant advantage (and so explain an unexpectedly brilliant performance).

Increasing oxygen delivery to the brain, and perhaps also to the muscles, is a confirmed means of improving athletic performance, and the banned hormone erythropoietin (EPO), as well as the technique of blood doping, achieve this.

At the 1976 Olympics in Montreal, the great Finnish athlete Lasse Viren is alleged to have employed the blood-doping technique. This process involves artificially increasing an athlete's circulating red-blood-cell count by reinfusing red blood cells previously drawn from the athlete and stored under special conditions for a minimum of four to six weeks. Blood doping, or blood boosting, violates the IOC code.

Viren won gold in the 5 000-metre and 10 000-metre races in both the 1976 and 1980 Olympic Games, but there was never any evidence that his success was due to blood doping. To the contrary, he was one of the greatest peakers in the history of running.

By the 1980 Olympics, blood boosting had become quite popular. Scientific studies have revealed that blood boosting does indeed work. However, the need to police this form of cheating became less necessary purely because EPO does this job far more effectively (albeit illegally).

EPO is a hormone produced naturally by the kidneys to increase red blood cells. It can be manufactured and mass-produced, and competitive athletes soon began using it as an alternative to the more laborious process of blood boosting. By the late 1980s, EPO was firmly established in Europe in the professional cycling fraternity. By the 1990s, it was widespread in the sport, and it also became a firm favourite among other endurance athletes, such as cross-country skiers, swimmers, distance runners and triathletes.

Testing procedures have advanced rapidly over the past few years, but they are still farcical compared with the advances in illegal drug use and the techniques that the cheats have developed to avoid detection.

Few seem to understand that doping in sport is a massive industry, which some argue is under the control of an international mafia. Some even believe that the global income from sports doping exceeds that from recreational drugs, and that this income is used to finance some of the evils of modern times, including, perhaps, global terrorism.

Large industries expend a great deal of effort to ensure that their products are freely available and continue to sell well. I see no reason why this should not apply equally to those who direct the sports-doping industry. Important ways in which that industry works to secure its future are, first, to ensure that doping control is ineffectual (this requires that the illegal industry influences or, even better, controls, the efforts of those whose job it is to police sports doping); and, second, to develop drugs that are undetectable by current methods.

The major threat to sport is athletes having to decide whether they are going to compete honestly – and probably at a disadvantage – or if they are going to use banned substances. At present, the majority decision is to use any drugs that will provide an advantage, a decision usually made for commercial reasons. A doped athlete is more likely to be successful, to become more famous and to earn more money than an honest, undoped athlete.

There is not much that science can do to impose honesty in the face of such dishonesty and overriding commercial interest.

28 | Why the Kenyans Are such Good Runners

In Part V, I mentioned giving a talk in Nairobi in 1997 on Kenyan athletes, the focus of which was my attempt to explain why the Kenyans are such exceptional runners. I came to the conclusion then that it is improbable that the success of the Kenyans can be attributed to any single factor, but that a number of factors contribute to their running prowess. These factors are all under the control of a single regulatory mechanism – the brain. In this final chapter, I discuss some more facts about the Kenyan runners that I find interesting.

Most of the exceptional Kenyan runners come from a small number of tribes. Approximately 72 per cent of the most successful Kenyan runners originate from the Rift Valley, which contains only 20 per cent of the Kenyan population.

Interestingly, the Rift Valley, the area populated by the Pokot, Marakwet, Tugen, Keiyo, Kipsigis and Nandi groups, which form part of the Kalenjin tribe, produces the most successful runners. In fact, studies have shown that a runner from the Nandi clan has a twenty-threefold higher probability of achieving success in running than has his average Kenyan counterpart.

In 1992, a group of top Swedish runners travelled to Kenya, where they were unable to hold their own even against schoolboy Kenyan athletes. The Swedes themselves calculated that there must have been at least 500 Kenyan schoolboys who were faster than the very best Swedish distance runners.

In South Africa, black runners also dominate distance running.

In our studies over the years, we have concluded that the superior performance of black distance runners must be due to at least some genetic determinants. Specifically, these runners have a great capacity to resist fatigue during repeated muscle contractions. This is perhaps due to an ability to sustain higher levels of skeletal muscle recruitment before developing fatigue. Black distance runners also seem to have more Type II (white) muscle fibres than their white counterparts.

But there is no evidence that black runners have a superior cardiovascular function, or a greater capacity to transport oxygen to their muscles. Rather, it seems that the success of the Kenyans is due to a multitude of physiological factors that allow their central governors to drive them to higher levels of skeletal muscle recruitment while their bodily homeostasis is retained. No one has yet properly studied this question. We are planning to do this some time over the next few years.

We will also focus on the strength of the Kenyans' leg muscles. To run so fast, the Kenyans' muscles must be incredibly powerful – a point that has been fastidiously ignored. These muscles may not be quite as strong as those of Usain Bolt, but their (hidden) strength will amaze those who believe that it is the heart (and not the muscles) that determines exceptional running ability.

Perhaps the answer lies in a quote by Professor Bengt Saltin. After studying Kenyan runners for some time, he concluded, 'There are definitely some genes that are special here. But these genes will code for many different functions ... small advantages in each will produce the greatest runners the world has ever witnessed'.

When I look back on my career, I marvel at how far the professions of sports science and sports medicine have progressed from the days when exercise was considered dangerous to human health. The fact that I actually felt better the more I exercised was one of the first moments of personal realisation in my quest to challenge these, and other, beliefs.

I have been privileged to be able to pass this on in my career, and also in my personal life, where I have derived as much pleasure watching the wondrous world of exercise open up before my children.

As I had started thirty-seven years ago – by running around a cricket field, one lap at a time – so I began the process of passing on the baton to my daughter, Candice. We began by running a third of a lap and walking the rest. Our first goal was to complete ten such circuits. My daughter, ever the realist, had commented that when we were not walking, we weren't really running. Nor were we even jogging. Perhaps, she suggested, we were just 'slogging'.

But we persevered. When we were able to complete twenty laps without walking, we were ready for the next step – to run for the same time on the forest trails. And so began the consolidation phase leading to our first race, a five-kilometre run through the streets of Gugulethu. We progressed to a ten-kilometre race, and now my daughter's ambitions were extending. I began to wonder whether my ageing body would be able to stay the course.

Her goal became the 2005 twenty-one-kilometre Two Oceans half-marathon. In training we would have to run for up to 150 minutes. This we accomplished. But, still unsure of our joint abilities, we would run our Two Oceans on Good Friday in the company of those whose religious beliefs precluded their participation on a Saturday. As we ran that race, we planned the final challenge – the full forty-two-kilometre marathon. But it would not be possible in South Africa, since the concept of the slow marathon runner has yet to reach our shores and an obsession with early cut-off times here precludes running a marathon in this way.

Rather, we would run in the United States, where runners are allowed up to six or more hours to complete the historic distance. We chose the Chicago Marathon, as it also offered a scientific conference on marathon running.

On 22 October 2006, we found ourselves in the company of 40 000 equally excited runners at the start. Expecting snow, we wore three layers of clothing, including waterproof jackets and long pants appropriate for the wet and windy conditions and 6 °C air temperature. But, more importantly, we had our special secret – a fail-proof pacing strategy. In training we had learnt to cover the longer distances by running for thirty minutes, followed by fifteen minutes' walking. Three decades in the sports sciences had taught at least one valuable lesson.

Our plan was to run for three miles (4.8 kilometres) and to walk for one mile (1.6 kilometres). Repeated six times, we would cover twenty-four miles. We would walk the remaining two miles, but at the start, not at the finish. Provided we ran each mile in less than twelve minutes and walked each mile in less than seventeen minutes, we would reach the finish before the six-hour cut-off time.

From the start, our enthusiasm took control; by halfway we were twenty-five minutes ahead of schedule and in danger of breaking five hours. The only constraint to our progress was the knowledge burnt into my brain by seventy previous distance races, that unless you feel immortal at twenty-one kilometres, the last half of the race will be a long, slow and taxing affair. My daughter, feeling immortal but sensing my discomfort, agreed to my suggestion that perhaps we might just slow the pace a little and walk more often. By thirty kilometres she had taken charge; ordering me into a roadside café, where she plied me with food and fluid to treat the low blood glucose concentration that she had diagnosed. Next she told me that I was too hot and should take off my two outer layers of clothing. These she placed in my rucksack, which she offered to carry for the next hour. Only when certain at forty kilometres that I could be trusted to finish without her coercion did she unleash her final effort, covering the last two kilometres four minutes faster and 306 places ahead of me. As we embraced at the finish, she wondered why so much fuss is made about finishing a marathon. What real challenge comes next? she asked.

My joy was complete. Her question confirmed that she had grasped the greater challenge: that running and physical fitness are one basis for the fulfilled life.

It is my hope that in this process I have achieved what I consider to be the greatest tribute paid to me by my friend, the late George Sheehan. George once wrote of me: 'He has explored the areas of living beyond the physical. He has integrated the science and art of living ... We all have within us the drive towards excellence. Timothy Noakes writes of how he sought this excellence ... and in so doing blazes a path for us all.'

My experience in sport has taught me that the human body is a wondrous creation. But I have also discovered that in everything we do – be it work, physical activity or sport – it is our minds, and especially our perception of what can be, rather than our physical capabilities which ultimately determine the extent to which we succeed. It is as Franz Stampfl wrote more than fifty years ago: 'The great hurdle is the mental barrier.'

Bibliography

Adler, B. *Coaching Matters: Leadership and Tactics of the NFL's Ten Greatest Coaches.* Washington, DC: Brassey's Inc., 2003

Aginsky, K.D., and T.D. Noakes. 'Why it is difficult to detect an illegally bowled cricket delivery with either the naked eye or usual two-dimensional video analysis'. *Br. J. Sports Med.* 44, 2010, pp. 420–425

Almond, C.S., A.Y. Shin, E.B. Fortescue, et al. 'Hyponatremia among runners in the Boston Marathon'. *N. Engl. J. Med.* 352, 2005, pp. 1550–1556

Anderson, K.M., W.P. Castelli, and D. Levy. 'Cholesterol and mortality. 30 years of follow-up from the Framingham study'. *JAMA.* 257, 1987, pp. 2176–2180

Anonymous. 'Rugby injuries to the cervical cord'. *Br. Med. J.* 1, 1977, pp. 1556–1557

Arlott, J. (ed.). *Cricket: The Great Captains.* Newton Abbot: The Sportsman's Book Club, 1972

Armstrong, L.E., D.J. Casa, M. Millard-Stafford, et al. American College of Sports Medicine position stand. 'Exertional heat illness during training and competition'. *Med. Sci. Sports Exerc.* 9, 2007, pp. 556–572

Armstrong, L.E., Y. Epstein, J.E. Greenleaf, et al. American College of Sports Medicine position stand. 'Heat and cold illnesses during distance running'. *Med. Sci. Sports Exerc.* 28, 1996, pp. i–x

Atkins, R.C. *Dr Atkins' Diet Revolution.* New York: Bantam Books, 1972

Australian Rugby Football Union. *Australian Rugby Football Union Handbook.* New South Wales: Kingsford, 1993

Baldwin, J., R.J. Snow, M.J. Gibala, et al. 'Glycogen availability does not affect the TCA cycle or TAN pools during prolonged, fatiguing exercise'. *J. Appl. Physiol.* 94, 2003, pp. 2181–2187

Bannister, R.G. *The Four-Minute Mile.* New York: Dodd, Mead and Co., 1981

Banting, W. *Letter on Corpulence, addressed to the Public by William Banting* (4th Ed.). London: Harrison, Pall Mall, 1869

Barron, J.L., T.D. Noakes, W. Levy, et al. 'Hypothalamic dysfunction in overtrained athletes'. *J. Clin. Endocrinol. Metab.* 60, 1985, pp. 803–806

Barrow, Graeme. *All Blacks versus Springboks.* Auckland: Heinemann Publishers, 1981

Bassett, D.R. Jr, and E.T. Howley. 'Maximal oxygen uptake: "classical" versus "contemporary" viewpoints'. *Med. Sci. Sports Exerc.* 29, 1997, pp. 591–603

Beilock, S. *Choke: What the Secrets of the Brain Reveal about Getting It Right when You Have to.* New York: Free Press, 2010

Borg, G. *Borg's Perceived Exertion and Pain Scales.* Champaign, IL: Human Kinetics, 1998

Bradman, D. *The Art of Cricket.* London: Robson Books, 1998

Bramble, D.M., and D.E. Lieberman. 'Endurance running and the evolution of Homo'. *Nature* 432, 2004, pp. 345–352

Broom, R. *Finding the Missing Link.* London: Watts & Co., 1951, pp. 1–111

Bryant, John. *3:59.4 – The Quest to Break the 4 Minute Mile.* London: Arrow Books, 2005

Burry, H.C., and C.J. Calcinai. 'The need to make rugby safer'. *Br. Med. J. (Clin. Res. Ed.)* 296, 1988, pp. 149–150

Burry, H.C., and H. Gowland. 'Cervical injury in rugby football – a New Zealand survey'. *Br. J. Sports Med.* 15, 1981, pp. 56–59

Cade, J.R., H.J. Free, A.M. de Quesada, et al. 'Changes in body fluid composition and volume during vigorous exercise by athletes'. *J. Sports Med. Phys. Fitness* 11, 1971, pp. 172–178

Cade, R., G. Spooner, E. Schlein, et al. 'Effect of fluid, electrolyte, and glucose replacement during exercise on performance, body temperature, rate of sweat loss, and compositional changes of extracellular fluid'. *J. Sports Med. Phys. Fitness* 12, 1972, pp. 150–156

Calcinai, C. 'Cervical spine injuries'. *New Zeal. J. Sports Med.* 20, 1992, pp. 14–15

Cameron-Dow, John. *Bruce Fordyce – Comrades King.* Johannesburg: Guide Book Publications, 2001

Campbell, G.D. 'Diabetes in Asians and Africans in and around Durban'. *S. Afr. Med. J.* 37, 1963, pp. 1195–1208

Castelli, W.P. 'Concerning the possibility of a nut...' *Arch. Intern. Med.* 153, 1992, pp. 1371–1372

Cherry-Garrard, A. *The Worst Journey in the World.* New York: Carroll and Graf, 1989

Chorley, J., J. Cianca, and J. Divine. 'Risk factors for exercise-associated hyponatremia in non-elite marathon runners'. *Clin. J. Sport Med.* 17, 2007, pp. 471–477

Christie, C.J., L. Todd, and G.A. King. 'Energy cost of batting during a simulated cricket work bout', in R.A. Stretch, T.D. Noakes and C.L. Vaughan, *Science and Medicine in Cricket.* (eds.), Port Elizabeth: Second World Congress of Science and Medicine in Cricket, 2003, pp. 288–299

Cleave, T.L. *The Saccharine Disease. Conditions caused by the taking of refined carbohydrates, such as sugar and white flour.* Bristol: John Wright and Sons, 1974

Cleave, T.L., and G.D. Campbell. *Diabetes, Coronary Thrombosis and the Saccharine Disease.* Bristol: John Wright and Sons, 1966

Convertino, V.A., L.E. Armstrong, E.F. Coyle, et al. American College of Sports Medicine position stand. 'Exercise and fluid replacement'. *Med. Sci. Sports Exerc.* 28, 1996, pp. i–vii

Coon, G.P. 'Echoes of the Marathon'. *N. Eng. J. Med.* 257, 1957, pp. 1168–1169

Cooper, D. *Chris Barnard by Those Who Know Him.* Cape Town: Vlaeberg Publishers, 1992

Cordain, L. *The Paleo Diet.* New Jersey: John Wiley and Sons, 2011

Costill, D.L. *A Scientific Approach to Distance Running.* Los Altos, California: Track and Field News, 1979

Coyle, D. *The Talent Code: Greatness Isn't Born. It's Grown. Here's How.* New York: Bantam Dell, 2009

Currens, J.H., and P.D. White. 'Half a century of running. Clinical, physiologic and autopsy findings in the case of Clarence DeMar ("Mr. Marathon")'. *N. Engl. J. Med.* 265, 1961, pp. 988–993

Curtis, E.N. *The Cholesterol Delusion.* Indianapolis: Dog Ear Publishing, 2010

Dart, R.A. *Adventures with the Missing Link.* London: Hamish Hamilton, 1959

Davis, D.P., J.S. Videen, A. Marino, et al. 'Exercise-associated hyponatremia in marathon runners: a two-year experience'. *J. Emerg. Med.* 21, 2001, pp. 47–57

De Lange, Pieter. *The Games Cities Play.* South Africa: C.P. de Lange Inc., 1998

Dent, J. *The Junction Boys.* New York: Thomas Dunne Books, 1999

Doherty, J.K. *Modern Training for Running.* Englewood Cliffs, New Jersey: Prentice-Hall, 1964

Duffield, R., and E.J. Drinkwater. 'Time-motion analysis of Test and One-Day international cricket centuries'. *J. Sports Sci.* 26, 2008, pp. 457–464

Duffy, W. *Sugar Blues.* New York: Grand Central Publishing, 1975

Dukan, P. *The Dukan Diet: 2 Steps to Lose the Weight, 2 Steps to Keep It Off Forever.* New York: Crown Archetype, 2011

Dungy, T. *Quiet Strength: The Principles, Practices and Priorities of a Winning Life.* Carol Stream, Illinois: Tyndale House Publishers, 2007

Dwyer, B. *The Winning Way.* Auckland, New Zealand: Rugby Press, 1992

Eichner, E.R. 'Genetic and other determinants of sweat sodium'. *Curr. Sports Med. Rep.* 7, 2008, S36–S40

Eichner, E.R, D. Laird, D.B. Hiller, et al. 'Hyponatremia in sport: symptoms and prevention'. Sports Science Exchange. Roundtable. *Gatorade Sports Science Institute 1993*, 4, pp. 1–4

Fingleton, J.H. *Cricket Crisis.* Melbourne: Cassell and Company, 1946

Fletcher, J.G. 'Calories and cricket'. *Lancet* 268, 1955, pp. 1165–1166

Fletcher, W.M., and W.G. Hopkins. 'Lactic acid in amphibian muscle'. *J. Physiol.* 35, 1907, pp. 247–309

Francis, T. *The Zen of Cricket: Learning from Positive Thought.* London: Hutchinson, 1992

Frieden, T.R., and D.M. Berwick. 'The "Million Hearts" Initiative – Preventing heart attacks and strokes'. *N. Engl. J. Med.* 29, 2011, p. 365

Frizzell, R.T., G.H. Lang, D.C. Lowance, et al. 'Hyponatremia and ultramarathon running'. *JAMA* 255, 1986, pp. 772–774

Gardner, J.W. 'Death by water intoxication'. *Mil. Med.* 167, 2002, pp. 432–434

Gladwell, M. *Outliers: The Story of Success.* London: Allen Lane, 2008

Goldacre, B. *Bad Science.* London: Fourth Estate, 2008

Goulet, E.D. 'Effect of exercise-induced dehydration on time-trial exercise performance: A meta-analysis'. *Br. J. Sports Med.* (in press), 2010

Greyvenstein, Chris. *20 Great Springboks – Morné du Plessis.* Cape Town: Don Nelson, 1987

Harris, D. *The Genius: How Bill Walsh Reinvented Football and Created an NFL Dynasty.* New York: Random House, 2008

Harrison, D.H., L. Walkden, R. Moffat, et al. 'Rugby injuries in schools'. *BJSM* 14, 1980, pp. 234–235

Hermanus, F.J., C.E. Draper, and T.D. Noakes. 'Spinal cord injuries in South African Rugby Union'. *S. Afr. Med. J.* 100, 2010, pp. 230–234

Hertzog, M. *Annapurna (8000m).* London: Jonathan Cape, 1952

Hew-Butler, T.D., C.S. Almond, J.C. Ayus, et al. 'Consensus Document of the 1st International Exercise-Associated Hyponatremia (EAH) Consensus Symposium, Cape Town, South Africa 2005'. *Clin. J. Sport Med.* 15, 2005, pp. 207–213

Hew-Butler, T.D., C. Anley, P. Schwartz, et al. 'The treatment of symptomatic hyponatremia with hypertonic saline in an Ironman triathlete'. *Clin. J. Sport Med.* 17, 2007, pp. 68–69

Hew-Butler, T.D., J.N. Chorley, J.C. Cianca, et al. 'The incidence, risk factors, and clinical manifestations of hyponatremia in marathon runners'. *Clin. J. Sport Med.* 13, 2003, pp. 41–47

Hill, A.V. *Muscular Activity.* London: Bailliere: Tindall and Cox, 1925

Hill, A.V., C.H.N. Long, and H. Lupton. 'Muscular exercise, lactic acid and the supply and utilisation of oxygen: parts VII–VIII'. *Proc. Royal Soc. Bri.* 97, 1924b, pp. 155–176

————. 'Muscular exercise, lactic acid, and the supply utilization of oxygen: Parts I–III'. *Proc. Royal Soc. Bri.* 96, 1924a, pp. 438–475

Hill, A.V., and H. Lupton. 'Muscular exercise, lactic acid, and the supply and utilization of oxygen'. *Quart. J. Med.* 16, 1923, pp. 135–171

Hite, A.H., R.D. Feinman, G.E. Guzman, et al. 'In the face of contradictory evidence: Report of the Dietary Guidelines for Americans Committee'. *Nutrition*. 26, 2010, pp. 915–924

Holtzhausen, L.M., and T.D. Noakes. 'The prevalence and significance of post-exercise (postural) hypotension in ultramarathon runners'. *Med. Sci. Sports Exerc.* 27, 1995, pp. 1595–1601

——————. 'Collapsed ultraendurance athlete: proposed mechanisms and an approach to management'. *Clin. J. Sport Med.* 7, 1997, pp. 292–301

Holtzhausen, L.M., T.D. Noakes, B. Kroning, et al. 'Clinical and biochemical characteristics of collapsed ultramarathon runners'. *Med. Sci. Sports Exerc.* 26, 1994, pp. 1095–1101

Hoskins, T. 'Rugby injuries to the cervical spine in English schoolboys'. *Practitioner* 223, 1979, pp. 365–366

Huntford, R. *The Last Place on Earth*. London: Pan Books, 1981

Irving, R.A., T.D. Noakes, R. Buck, et al. 'Evaluation of renal function and fluid homeostasis during recovery from exercise-induced hyponatremia'. *J. Appl. Physiol.* 70, 1991, pp. 342–348

James, C.L.R. *Beyond a Boundary*. London: Serpent's Tail, 1963

Johnson, R.J., S.E. Perez-Pozo, Y.Y. Sautin, et al. 'Hypothesis: Could excessive fructose intake and uric acid cause type-2 diabetes?' *Endocr. Rev.* 30, 2009, pp. 96–116

Kannell, W.B. 'Lipids, diabetes, and coronary heart disease: Insights from the Framingham study'. *Am. Heart J.* 110, 1985, pp. 1100–1107

Kendrick, M. *The Great Cholesterol Con*. London: John Blake, 2007

Kew T., T.D. Noakes, A.N. Kettles, et al. 'A retrospective study of spinal cord injuries in Cape Province rugby players, 1963–1989. Incidence, mechanisms and prevention'. *S. Afr. Med. J.* 80, 1991, pp. 127–133

Keys, A., and M. Keys. *Eat Well and Stay Well*. New York: Doubleday and Company

Khaw, K.T., N. Wareham, S. Bingham, et al. 'Association of hemoglobin A1c with cardiovascular disease and mortality in adults: The European prospective investigation into cancer in Norfolk'. *Ann. Intern. Med.* 141, 2004, pp. 413–420

Kohn, T.A., R. Burroughs, M.J. Hartman, et al. 'Fiber type and metabolic characteristics of lion (Panthera leo), caracal (Caracal caracal) and human skeletal muscle'. *Comp. Biochem. Physiol. A. Mol. Integr. Physiol.*, 2011

Lambert E.V., G.A. St Clair, and T.D. Noakes. 'Complex systems model of fatigue: integrative homoeostatic control of peripheral physiological systems during exercise in humans'. *Br. J. Sports Med.* 39, 2005, pp. 52–62

Land, M.F., and P. McLeod. 'From eye movements to actions: how batsmen hit the ball'. *Nat. Neurosci.* 3, 2000, pp. 1340–1345

Levine, B.D. 'VO_2 max: What do we know, and what do we still need to know?' *J. Physiol.* 586, 2008, pp. 25–34

Liebenberg, L. 'Persistence hunting by modern hunter-gatherers'. *Curr. Anthropology* 47, 2006, pp. 1017–1025

——————. *The Art of Tracking: The Origin of Science.* Claremont: David Philip Publishers, 1990

——————. 'The relevance of persistence hunting to human evolution'. *J. Hum. Evol.* 55, 2008, pp. 1156–1159

Mackarness, R. *Eat Fat and Grow Slim.* London: The Harvill Press, 1958

Mann, G.V. 'Coronary heart disease: The doctor's dilemma'. *Am. Heart J.* 96, 1978, pp. 569–571

Marais, E. *The Soul of the Ape.* Middlesex: Penguin Books, 1969

Marnewick, M. *Quest for Glory: Successes in South African Sport.* Cape Town: Zebra Press, 2010

Marshall, B. (ed.). *Helicobacter pioneers: Firsthand accounts from the scientists who discovered helicobacters, 1892–1982.* Victoria: Blackwell Publishing, 2002

Marshall, B.J., J.A. Armstrong, D.B. McGechie, et al. 'Attempt to fulfil Koch's postulates for pyloric Campylobacter'. *Med. J. Aust.* 142, 1985, pp. 436–439

McLeod, P. 'Visual reaction time and high-speed ball games'. *Perception* 16, 1987, pp. 49–59

Medical Officers of Schools Association. 'Rugby injuries to the cervical spine'. *Proc. Rep. Med. Off. Schools Assoc.* 26, 1979, p. 18

Mitchell, J.H., and G. Blomqvist. 'Maximal oxygen uptake'. *N. Engl. J. Med.* 284, 1971, pp. 1018–1022

Moran, L. *The Anatomy of Courage.* New York: Carroll and Graf Publishers, 2007

Morrow, L. 'United States – 1968', *Time* 131(2), 1988, pp. 4–15

Nathan, M., R. Goedeke, and T.D. Noakes. 'The incidence and nature of rugby injuries experienced at one school during the 1982 rugby season'. *S. Afr. Med. J.* 64, 1983, pp. 132–137

Newton, A.F.H. *Running.* London: H.F. & G. Witherby, 1935

Nichols, E.H., and F.L. Richardson. 'Football injuries of the Harvard squad for three years under the revised rules, 1909'. *Clin. Orthop. Relat. Res.,* 2003, pp. 3–10

Nichols, E.H., and H.B. Smith. 'The physical aspect of American football'. *Boston Med. Surg. J.* 54, 1906, pp. 1–8

Noakes T.D. 'Challenging beliefs: ex Africa semper aliquid novi: 1996 J.B. Wolffe Memorial Lecture'. *Med. Sci. Sports Exerc.* 29, 1997, pp. 571–590

——————. 'Changes in body mass alone explain almost all of the variance in the serum sodium concentrations during prolonged exercise. Has commercial influence impeded scientific endeavour?' *Br. J. Sports Med.,* 2010 [ePub ahead of print]

——————. 'Comrades makes medical history – again', *SA Runner,* 4 September 1981, pp. 8–10

——————. 'Fluid Replacement during Marathon Running'. *Clin. J. Sport Med.* 13, 2003b, pp. 309–318

——————. 'Hydration in the marathon: using thirst to gauge safe fluid replacement'. *Sports Med.* 37, 2007, pp. 463–466

——————. 'Implications of exercise testing for prediction of athletic performance: a contemporary perspective'. *Med. Sci. Sports Exerc.* 20, 1988, pp. 319–330

——————. 'In memory of Bob Woolmer (1948–2007)'. *Int. J. Sports Sci. & Coaching* 2, 2007, pp. 97–103

——————. 'Letter: Heatstroke during the 1981 National Cross-Country Running Championships'. *S. Afr. Med. J.* 61, 1982, p. 145

——————. 'Linear relationship between the perception of effort and the duration of constant load exercise that remains'. *J. Appl. Physiol.* 96, 2004, pp. 1571–1572

——————. 'Overconsumption of fluids by athletes'. *Br. Med. J.* 327, 2003a, pp. 113–114

——————. 'Physiological models to understand exercise fatigue and the adaptations that predict or enhance athletic performance'. *Scand. J. Med. Sci. Sports* 10, 2000, pp. 123–145

——————. 'The limits of endurance exercise'. *Basic Res. Cardiol.* 101, 2006, pp. 408–417

——————. 'Viewpoint: Evidence that reduced skeletal muscle recruitment explains the lactate paradox during exercise at high altitude'. *J. Appl. Physiol.* 106, 2009, pp. 737–738

——————. 'Why do Africans run so swiftly? A research challenge for African scientists'. *S. Afr. J. Sc.* 94, 1998, pp. 531–535

——————. 'Why marathon runners collapse'. *S. Afr. Med. J.* 73, 1988, pp. 569–571

Noakes, T.D., B.A. Adams, K.H. Myburgh, et al. 'The danger of an inadequate water intake during prolonged exercise. A novel concept revisited'. *Eur. J. Appl. Physiol. Occup. Physiol.* 57, 1988, pp. 210–219

Noakes, T.D., J. Borresen, T. Hew-Butler, et al. 'Semmelweis and the aetiology of puerperal sepsis 160 years on: an historical review'. *Epidemiol. Infect.* 136, 2008, pp. 1–9

Noakes, T.D., J.P. Dugas, L.R. Dugas, et al. 'Body temperatures during three long-distance polar swims in water of 0–3 degrees Celsius'. *J. Thermal. Biol.* 34, 2009, pp. 23–31

Noakes T.D., and M. du Plessis. *Rugby without Risk*. Pretoria: J.L. van Schaik Publishers, 1996

Noakes, T.D., N. Goodwin, B.L. Rayner, et al. 'Water intoxication: a possible complication during endurance exercise'. *Med. Sci. Sports Exerc.* 17, 1985, pp. 370–375

Noakes, T.D., I. Jakoet, and E. Baalbergen. 'An apparent reduction in the incidence and severity of spinal cord injuries in schoolboy rugby players in the western Cape since 1990'. *S. Afr. Med. J.* 89, 1999, pp. 540–545

Noakes, T.D., and D.E. Martin. 'IMMDA-Aims Advisory statement on guidelines for fluid replacement during marathon running'. *New Stud. Athlet.* 17, 2002, pp. 15–24

Noakes, T.D., M. Nathan, R.A. Irving, et al. 'Physiological and biochemical measurements during a 4-day surf-ski marathon'. *S. Afr. Med. J.* 67, 1985, pp. 212–216

Noakes, T.D., R.J. Norman, R.H. Buck, et al. 'The incidence of hyponatremia during prolonged ultraendurance exercise'. *Med. Sci. Sports Exerc.* 22, 1990, pp. 165–170

Noakes T.D., L. Opie, W. Beck, et al. 'Coronary heart disease in marathon runners'. *Ann. N.Y. Acad. Sci.* 301, 1977, pp. 593–619

Noakes, T.D., L.H. Opie, A.G. Rose, et al. 'Autopsy-proved coronary atherosclerosis in marathon runners'. *N. Engl. J. Med.* 301, 1979, pp. 86–89

Noakes, T.D., A.G. Rose, and L.H. Opie. 'Hypertrophic cardiomyopathy associated with sudden death during marathon racing'. *Br. Heart J.* 41, 1979, pp. 624–627

Noakes, T.D., and D.B. Speedy. 'Time for the American College of Sports Medicine to acknowledge that humans, like all other earthly creatures, do not need to be told how much to drink during exercise'. *Br. J. Sports Med.* 41, 2007, pp. 109–110

Noakes T.D., and A. St Clair Gibson. 'Logical limitations to the "catastrophe" models of fatigue during exercise in humans'. *Br. J. Sports Med.* 38, 2004, pp. 648–649

Noakes, T.D., A. St Clair Gibson, and E.V. Lambert. 'From catastrophe to complexity: a novel model of integrative central neural regulation of effort and fatigue during exercise in humans'. *Br. J. Sports Med.* 38, 2004, pp. 511–514

Noakes, Tim. *Lore of Running* (4th edition). Human Kinetics, 2003

Noakes, Tim, and Morné du Plessis. *Rugby without Risk*. Pretoria: JL van Schaik Publishers, 1996

Noakes, Timothy David. *DSc Thesis*, 2002

O'Connell, J. *Sugar Nation*. New York: Hyperion, 2011

O'Connell, T.C.J. 'Rugby football injuries and their prevention. A review of 600 cases'. *J. Irish Med. Assoc.* 34, 1954, pp. 20–26

Petersen, C., D.B. Pyne, M.R. Portus, et al. 'Variability in movement patterns during One Day Internationals by a cricket fast bowler'. *Int. J. Sports Physiol. Perform.* 4 2009a, pp. 278–281

—————. 'Quantifying positional movement patterns in Twenty20 cricket'. *Int. J. Perf. Analysis in Sport* 9, 2009b, pp. 165–170

—————. 'Comparison of player movement patterns between 1-day and test cricket'. *J. Strength. Cond. Res.* 25, 2011a, pp. 1368–1373

Petersen, C.J., D. Pyne, B. Dawson, et al. 'Movement patterns in cricket vary by both position and game format'. *J. Sports Sci.* 28, 2010, pp. 45–52

Petursson, H., J.A. Sigurdsson, C. Bengtsson, et al. 'Is the use of cholesterol in mortality risk algorithms in clinical guidelines valid? Ten years prospective data from the Norwegian HUNT 2 study'. *J. Eval. Clin. Pract.* Dec 12, 2011

Pickering, G.W. 'The purpose of medical education'. *Br. Med. J.* 2, 1956, pp. 113–116

Pienaar, François, and Edward Griffiths. *Rainbow Warrior*. Johannesburg: Jonathan Ball Publishers, 1999

Pollock, Peter. *God's Fast Bowler*. Vereeniging: Christian Art Publishers, 2001

Popper, K.R. (ed. W.W. Bertley). *Realism and the Aim of Science*. London: Hutchinson, 1988

Procter, Mike. *South Africa – The Years of Isolation and the Return to International Cricket*. United Kingdom: Queen Anne Press, 1994

Psaty, B.M., and F.P. Rivara. 'Universal screening and drug treatment of dyslipidemia in children and adolescents'. *JAMA*. Dec 15, 2011 [Epub ahead of print]

Pugh, Lewis Gordon. *Achieving the Impossible*. Johannesburg: Jonathan Ball Publishers, 2010

Rae, D.E., G.J. Knobel, T. Mann, et al. 'Heatstroke during endurance exercise: Is there evidence for excessive endothermy?' *Med. Sci. Sports Exerc.* 40, 2008, pp. 1193–1204

Ravnskov, U. *Ignore the Awkward*. Uffe Ravnskov, 2010

Reid, S.A., D.B. Speedy, J.M. Thompson, et al. 'Study of hematological and biochemical parameters in runners completing a standard marathon'. *Clin. J. Sport Med.* 14, 2004, pp. 344–353

Rennie, D., and N.K. Hollenberg. 'Cardiomythology and marathons'. *N. Engl. J. Med.* 301, 1979, pp. 103–104

Riffenburgh, R.H. 'Reverse gullibility and scientific evidence'. *Arch. Otolaryngol. Head Neck Surg.* 122, 1996, pp. 600–601

Robbins, S.E., and G.J. Gouw. 'Athletic footwear: unsafe due to perceptual illusions'. *Med. Sci. Sports Exerc.* 23, 1991, pp. 217–224

Rogers, I.R. 'Water intoxication: a possible complication during endurance exercise – a commentary'. *Wilderness & Environ. Med.* 16, 2005, pp. 219–220

Roux, C.E., R. Goedeke, G.R. Visser, et al. 'The epidemiology of schoolboy rugby injuries'. *S. Afr. Med. J.* 71, 1987, pp. 307–313

Rovell, D. *First in Thirst – How Gatorade Turned the Science of Sweat into a Cultural Phenomenon*. New York: Amacom, 2005

Ryun, J. *In Quest of Gold*. San Francisco: Harper & Row Publishers, 1984

Sawka, M.N., L.M. Burke, E.R. Eichner, et al. 'American College of Sports Medicine position stand. Exercise and fluid replacement'. *Med. Sci. Sports Exerc.* 39, 2007, pp. 377–390

Scher, A.T. 'Rugby injuries to the cervical spine and spinal cord: A 10-year review'. *Clin. Sports Med.* 17, 1998, pp. 195–206

——————. 'Rugby injuries to the cervical spinal cord'. *S. Afr. Med. J.*, 51, 1977, pp. 473–475

Schweitzer, G. 'Rugby injuries'. *S. Afr. Med. J.* 43, 1969, p. 972

Semmelweis, I. (trans. K. Codell Carter). *The Etiology, Concept and Prophylaxis of Childbed Fever*. Madison: The University of Wisconsin Press, 1983

Senge, P.M. *The Fifth Discipline: The Art and Practice of the Learning Organization*. New York: Doubleday, 1990

Sharwood, K.A., M. Collins, J.H. Goedecke, et al. 'Weight changes, medical complications, and performance during an Ironman triathlon'. *Br. J. Sports Med.* 38, 2004, pp. 718–724

Sheehan, G.A. *Dr Sheehan on Fitness.* New York: Simon & Schuster, 1983b

—————. *Dr Sheehan on Running.* Mountain View, California: World Publications, 1975

—————. *Going the Distance: One Man's Journey to the End of his Life.* New York: Villard Books, 1996

—————. *How to Feel Great 24 Hours a Day.* New York: Simon & Schuster, 1983

—————. *Personal Best: The Foremost Philosopher of Fitness Shares Techniques and Tactics for Success and Self-liberation.* Emmaus, Pennsylvania: Rodale Press, 1989

—————. *Running & Being: The Total Experience.* New York: Simon & Schuster, 1978

—————. *Running to Win: How to Achieve the Physical, Mental and Spiritual Victories of Running.* Emmaus, Pennsylvania: Rodale Press, 1992

—————. *This Running Life.* New York: Simon & Schuster, 1980

Sheldon, W.H. *The Varieties of Temperament: A Psychology of Constitutional Differences.* New York and London: Harper & Brothers Publishers, 1944

Shem, S. *The House of God.* New York: Bantam Dell, 2003

Shillinglaw, A.L. *Bradman Revisited: The Legacy of Sir Donald Bradman.* Manchester: The Parrs Wood Press, 2003

Silver, J.R. 'Injuries of the spine sustained in rugby'. *Br. Med. J. (Clin. Res. Ed.)* 228, 1984, pp. 37–43

Siri-Tarino, P.W., Q. Sun, F.B. Hu, and R.M Krauss. 'Meta-analysis of prospective cohort studies evaluating the association of saturated fat with cardiovascular disease'. *Am. J. Clin. Nutr.* 91, 2010b, pp. 535–546

—————. 'Saturated fat, carbohydrate and cardiovascular disease'. *Am. J. Clin. Nutr.* 91, 2010a, 502–509

Smit, John, and Mike Greenaway. *Captain in the Cauldron.* Cape Town: Highbury Safika Media, 2009

Smith, S. 'Marathon runner's death linked to excessive fluid intake'. *Boston Globe,* 13 August 2002, p. A1

Speedy, D.B., R. Campbell, G. Mulligan, et al. 'Weight changes and serum sodium concentrations after an ultradistance multisport triathlon'. *Clin. J. Sport Med.* 7, 1997, pp. 100–103

Speedy, D.B., J.G. Faris, M. Hamlin, et al. 'Hyponatremia and weight changes in an ultradistance triathlon'. *Clin. J. Sport Med.* 7, 1997, pp. 180–184

Stampfl, F. *Franz Stampfl on Running.* London: Herbert Jenkins, 1955

St Clair Gibson, A., D.A. Baden, M.I. Lambert, et al. 'The conscious perception of the sensation of fatigue'. *Sports Med.* 33, 2003, pp. 167–176

St Clair Gibson, A., and T.D. Noakes. 'Evidence for complex system integration and dynamic neural regulation of skeletal muscle recruitment during exercise in humans'. *Br. J. Sports Med.* 38, 2004, pp. 797–806

Syed, M. *Bounce: How Champions Are Made.* London: Fourth Estate, 2010

Taliep, M.S., A. St Clair Gibson, J. Gray, et al. 'Event-related potentials, reaction time, and response selection of skilled and lesser skilled cricket batsmen'. *Perception* 37, 2008, pp. 96–105

Taubes, G. *Good Calories, Bad Calories.* New York: Anchor Books, 2007

————. *Why We Get Fat and What To Do About It.* New York: Alfred A. Knopf, 2011

Taylor, T.K., and M.R. Coolican. 'Spinal cord injuries in Australian footballers, 1960–1985'. *Med. J. Aust.* 147, 1987, pp. 112–118

Tournier, P. *The Adventure of Living.* New York: Harper & Row Publishers, 1965

Van der Valk, R., and A. Colquhoun. *Nick & I: An Adventure in Rugby.* Cape Town: Don Nelson, 2002

Walkden, L. 'The medical hazards of rugby football'. *Practitioner* 215, 1975, pp. 201–207

Walsh, B. (eds. B. Billick and J. Peterson). *Finding the Winning Edge.* Champaign, IL: Sports Publishing, 1998

————. (eds. S. Jamison and C. Walsh). *The Score Takes Care of Itself: My Philosophy of Leadership.* London: Penguin Books, 2009

Westman, E.C., S.D. Phinney, and J.S. Volek. *The New Atkins for a New You.* New York: Simon & Schuster, 2010

Wharam, P.C., D.B. Speedy, T.D. Noakes, et al. 'NSAID use increases the risk of developing hyponatremia during an Ironman triathlon'. *Med. Sci. Sports Exerc.* 38, 2006, pp. 618–622

White, Jake, and Craig Ray. *In Black and White.* Cape Town: Zebra Press, 2007

Wigglesworth, E.C. 'Spinal injuries and football'. *Med. J. Aust.* 147, 1987, pp. 109–110

Wilber, K. *A Theory of Everything: An Integral Vision for Business, Politics, Science and Spirituality.* Boston: Shambhala Publications, 2000

Willett, W.C., and D.S. Ludwig. 'The 2010 Dietary Guidelines – the best recipe for health?' *N. Engl. J. Med.* 365, 2011, pp. 1563–1565

Willett, W.C., and P.J. Skerrett. *Eat, Drink and Be Healthy. The Harvard Medical School Guide to Healthy Eating.* New York: Free Press, 2001

Woolmer, B. *Bob Woolmer: Pirate and Rebel?* London: Arthur Barker, 1984

————. *Woolmer on Cricket: Cricket under Scrutiny from the Sharpest Brain in the Game.* London: Virgin Publishing, 2000

Woolmer, B., T.D. Noakes, and H. Moffett. *Bob Woolmer's Art and Science of Cricket.* Cape Town: New Holland Publishing, 2008

Williams, C. *Bradman: An Australian Hero.* London: Abacus, 1996

Williams, J.P., and B. McKibbin. 'Cervical spine injuries in Rugby Union football'. *Br. Med. J.* 2, 1978, p. 1747

Wyndham, C.H., and N.B. Strydom. 'The danger of an inadequate water intake during marathon running'. *S. Afr. Med. J.* 43, 1969, pp. 893–896

Yudkin, J. 'Diet and coronary thrombosis hypothesis and fact'. *Lancet.* 273, 1957, pp. 155–162

———. 'Dietary fat and dietary sugar in relation to ischaemic heart disease and diabetes'. *Lancet.* 2(7349), 1964, pp. 4–5

———. *Pure, White and Deadly.* London: Penguin Books, 1986

———. *Sweet and Dangerous.* New York: Bantam Books, 1972

Index

The abbreviation 'TN' is used for Prof. Tim Noakes.

Do you have any comments, suggestions or
feedback about this book or any other Zebra Press titles?
Contact us at **talkback@zebrapress.co.za**

*

Visit **www.randomstruik.co.za** and subscribe
to our newsletter for monthly updates and news